Masters of the House

TRANSFORMING AMERICAN POLITICS

Lawrence C. Dodd, Series Editor

Dramatic changes in political institutions and behavior over the past three decades have underscored the dynamic nature of American politics, confronting political scientists with a new and pressing intellectual agenda. The pioneering work of early postwar scholars, while laying a firm empirical foundation for contemporary scholarship, failed to consider how American politics might change or recognize the forces that would make fundamental change inevitable. In reassessing the static interpretations fostered by these classic studies, political scientists are now examining the underlying dynamics that generate transformational change.

Transforming American Politics brings together texts and monographs that address four closely related aspects of change. A first concern is documenting and explaining recent changes in American politics—in institutions, processes, behavior, and policymaking. A second is reinterpreting classic studies and theories to provide a more accurate perspective on postwar politics. The series looks at historical change to identify recurring patterns of political transformation within and across the distinctive eras of American politics. Last and perhaps most important, the series presents new theories and interpretations that explain the dynamic processes at work and thus clarify the direction of contemporary politics. All of the books focus on the central theme of transformation—transformation in both the conduct of American politics and in the way we study and understand its many aspects.

Masters of the House

CONGRESSIONAL LEADERSHIP
OVER TWO CENTURIES

edited by

Roger H. Davidson
The University of Maryland

Susan Webb Hammond
American University

Raymond W. Smock
former Historian of the
United States House of Representatives

WestviewPress
A Division of HarperCollinsPublishers

Transforming American Politics

Copyright © 1998 by Westview Press, A Division of HarperCollins Publishers, Inc.

Published in 1998 in the United States of America by Westview Press, 5500 Central Avenue, Boulder, Colorado 80301-2877, and in the United Kingdom by Westview Press, 12 Hid's Copse Road, Cumnor Hill, Oxford OX2 9JJ

Library of Congress Cataloging-in-Publication Data
Davidson, Roger H.
 Masters of the House : Congressional leadership over two centuries
/ Roger H. Davidson, Susan Webb Hammond, Raymond W. Smock.
     p.   cm. — (Transforming American politics)
 Includes bibliographical references and index.
 ISBN 0-8133-6894-4 (hardcover). — ISBN 0-8133-6895-2 (pbk.)
 1. United States. Congress. House—Speaker—History.   2. United
States. Congress. House—Leadership—History.   3. Political
leadership—United States.   4. United States—Politics and
government.   I. Hammond, Susan Webb.   II. Smock, Raymond.
III. Title.   IV. Series.
JK1319.D38   1998
328.73'0762—dc21   98-11326
                                                                                    CIP

The paper used in this publication meets the requirements of the American National Standard for Permanence of Paper for Printed Library Materials Z39.48-1984.

10   9   8   7   6   5   4   3   2   1

Contents

Tables

Foreword

Everett Dirksen was my mentor. I represented the same district in Illinois that he did before he moved over to the Senate. My hometown of Peoria is across the river from Ev's hometown of Pekin and in the same part of central Illinois that was once represented by Abraham Lincoln. When I came to Congress in 1957, I felt a certain kinship with Senator Dirksen, who by that time was already a leader in the Senate.

One had to be impressed with Dirksen, the resonance of his voice and the linearity of his thinking. As my good friend, Howard Baker, once said, sometimes the linearity could be overwhelmed by the resonance. But I learned a great deal about leadership from Dirksen and from people like Charlie Halleck in the House and later from Jerry Ford.

That gets us to our purpose: to learn more about congressional leadership by examining the careers and contributions of those who served as leaders.

Several years ago the Dirksen Congressional Center sponsored a conference in Washington that looked into the topic of leadership in the U.S. Senate. The papers presented at that time examined the contributions of many outstanding senators who left their imprint on the role of Senate leader—individuals like Bob Taft, Lyndon Johnson, Everett Dirksen, and Mike Mansfield. The conference led to a book, *First Among Equals*, that was the first attempt to look at Senate leadership from a historical perspective.

The interest generated by that project led to discussions of a companion study to focus on leadership in the House of Representatives. Early in 1994 a series of papers was commissioned by the Dirksen Center to examine the shape and impact of House leadership, detailing the resources and strategies employed in differing eras and especially in the twentieth century.

As a member of the board of directors of the Dirksen Center, I encouraged and supported these efforts. The House has historically produced leaders who have put their stamp not only on the chamber but on the times in which they work and live. Sometimes they are Speakers, other times floor leaders. The chapters presented here look at some of the real masters of the people's House.

As I have mentioned, I have had the honor and privilege of serving with some of them and observing their talents. As background, I would like to suggest twelve characteristics that we seem to look for in choosing leaders: (1) strength of character—the ability to command respect from one's peers, (2) principled views but tolerance of dissent, (3) a high degree of self-confidence, (4) persuasive speech and communication of ideas, (5) good listening skills and consideration of others, (6) patience, (7) thoughtfulness in initiating ideas, (8) decisiveness, (9) high degree of self-control, (10) skill as a strategist, (11) excellence as a negotiator, and (12) willingness to delegate authority and give credit to others.

Do all leaders possess all these attributes? Of course not. Golly, I sure didn't. But it seems to me that a good mixture of these skills, combined with historical circumstances, the institutional setting, and, of course, politics, has produced some unique leaders in the House over time. Our times are no exception.

Robert H. Michel
House Republican leader, 1981–1994

Credits

Figure 1: Henry Clay. Engraving courtesy of the Library of Congress.

Figure 2: Thomas Reed. Cartoon courtesy of the Center for Legislative Archives of the National Archives and Records Administration.

Figure 3: Joe Cannon. Cartoon courtesy of the Center for Legislative Archives of the National Archives and Records Administration.

Figure 4: Oscar Underwood. Photo courtesy of the Library of Congress.

Figure 5: Nicholas Longworth. Cartoon courtesy of the Center for Legislative Archives of the National Archives and Records Administration.

Figure 6: John Nance Garner. Cartoon courtesy of the Center for Legislative Archives of the National Archives and Records Administration.

Figure 7: Sam Rayburn. Photo courtesy of the Center for Legislative Archives of the National Archives and Records Administration.

Figure 8: Hale Boggs. Photo courtesy of the Honorable Lindy Boggs.

Figure 9: Gerald Ford. Photo courtesy of the Gerald R. Ford Library.

Figure 10: Tip O'Neill. Photo courtesy of the Library of Congress.

Introduction: Rediscovering the "Masters of the House"

Roger H. Davidson and
Susan Webb Hammond

Great legislative leaders, it would seem, are the undiscovered heroes of U.S. political history. To the extent that we think at all about historical figures in politics, we tend to focus our vision upon presidents and the symbolic leaders of massive popular movements. Presidents, of course, receive concerted attention not only from the scholarly community but also, to an extent, from the attentive public. Modern presidents are acclaimed, or scorned, on the basis of their achievements or failures in bringing peace and prosperity to the nation. Past presidents, too, are subject to intermittent scrutiny and reevaluation. The Hall of Presidents at Disney World includes statues of every last one of them—even William Henry Harrison, who caught cold at his inauguration and served only thirty days in office. Scholars and serious writers, too, find presidents irresistible. Each and every president has, without exception, been the subject of biographical and other studies; the outstanding ones are repeatedly being researched and reassessed.

Not so with legislative leaders. When confronted with references to the legislative giants, most citizens respond with blank stares. Henry Clay, a seminal Speaker of the House, is remembered (if at all) as the Great Compromiser who ran for president and was, with Daniel Webster and John C. Calhoun, one of the Great Triumvirate of pre–Civil War Senate orators. Ask about Thomas Brackett Reed or Nicholas Longworth or Joseph G. Cannon, and you will doubtless be greeted with looks of puzzlement. Among modern House leaders, Sam Rayburn and Thomas P. "Tip"

O'Neill were in their time famous and recognizable figures, but how vividly are they remembered today?

This situation would strike our ancestors as odd. For most of our history, congressional leaders were widely recognized as first-string players in the great game of politics. Many were touted as contenders for the presidency; others were famous in their own right. During the second half of the nineteenth century, Speakers of the House of Representatives often eclipsed the presidents who served at the same time. And in truth, the contributions of many of these congressional leaders deserve far more attention and evaluation than they are usually accorded.

Elements of Legislative Leadership

House leaders—whom we call "masters of the House"—play a critical role in the national policymaking process. In our own era of divided government, globalization, and increasingly complex and crosscutting issues, House leaders are faced with significant challenges as they strive to encourage policy development, build winning coalitions, and oversee the work of the House. Divided party control of the presidency and Congress only heightens the stakes in contests among leaders of both policymaking branches.

Leadership of the House is fundamentally different from that of the Senate. Historically, the House of Representatives is characterized by greater hierarchy, complexity, and institutionalization. Its network of standing committees and subcommittees is more rigid than that of the Senate; their prerogatives and jurisdictions are more difficult to breach. Control of the House floor agenda remains concentrated in the hands of elected majority-party leaders. Even in the wake of post-1970s reforms that have encouraged participation by the rank and file, a countertrend toward leadership prerogatives can be identified. These new leadership powers are circumscribed, as in the past, by discord within and between the parties, by the traditional prerogatives of committee chairs, and by tensions with the White House.

Today's legislative leaders are at once strengthened and constrained by the legacy of their predecessors. The rules of the House, rulings and precedents laid down by earlier leaders, and unwritten norms of behavior ("folkways")—all these are conditions that current and future leaders must take into account in responding to novel situations.

The chapters in this volume present a compelling story of the evolution of House leadership—from its rise and development during the nineteenth century, through the advent of "modern" leadership in the twentieth century, and to the powers and strategies of contemporary leaders. The authors of these chapters describe the history of House leadership from the First Congress (1789–1791) to the Republican resurgence in the post-1994 period. In each time period, they examine House leadership from institutional, historical, and biographical perspectives. And, as the various authors make clear, these legislative "masters" include not only Speakers of the House but also majority-party floor leaders and whips and their counterparts in the minority party. The book therefore offers important perspectives on several types of House leaders.

These studies examine the dimensions and potentialities of congressional leadership and analyze the resources and strategies of leaders in the House in various contexts. Continuities abound in the history of Congress (see, for example, Chapter 1 on the early speakership of Henry Clay and others and Chapter 10 on the contemporary speakership of Tip O'Neill and his successors, including Newt Gingrich). At the same time the House is buffeted by social, economic, and political forces that can bring about changes in leadership operation and style and even in the rules that govern the leaders' work.

As mediators within their parties, these leaders bridge regional and ideological wings of their parties. Speakers Sam Rayburn and Tip O'Neill, for example, both represented what came to be known as the Austin-Boston alliance—linking urban liberal Democrats with the "boll weevil" southerners. In so doing, both Rayburn and O'Neill were in important ways atypical of their regions: Rayburn was a New Deal progressive among southerners, O'Neill a post–Vietnam War liberal among urban ethnic politicians.

House leadership posts are intertwined with other leadership roles throughout the national government. Although not all Speakers, for example, have been national political figures, many have been—including all the individuals described in this volume. Henry Clay was a policy leader who ran for president and was a fixture on the national political landscape for several decades. So too was Oscar W. Underwood a century later (also a shaper of policy and a presidential contender). John Nance Garner served two terms as vice president under Franklin D. Roosevelt. Gerald R. Ford's tenure as Republican minority leader won the respect of majority Democrats, who eventually informed President Richard Nixon that Ford was the most acceptable person to be named as vice president; the next year Ford succeeded Nixon as president.

Plan of the Book

Each chapter in this book focuses on a distinctive era (for example, Chapters 1 and 2 on the development of the nineteenth-century speakership and Chapter 10 on the postreform period since the 1970s). Although the narratives revolve around given individuals—Speakers Henry Clay,

Thomas B. Reed, and Tip O'Neill, for instance—these figures are presented as important exemplars of leadership patterns within a given time period. The chapters address common themes: the effect of political and institutional contexts for leadership operations, the importance of leaders' personalities and styles, the interplay of formal and informal leadership resources, the size of the majority and minority parties and the relationship between them, and White House–congressional relations. The studies weigh the elements of continuity against the forces for change. Chapter authors address also the shifts in the locus of leadership within the majority party (for example, Chapter 4 describes Oscar W. Underwood, who was a leader in fact but not in title); the effect of intraparty factions on the leaders' work, especially in building coalitions; and the role of the minority party and its leaders.

In Chapter 1, Elaine Swift analyzes the early speakership, 1789 to 1869. An institution inherited from the British House of Commons as a neutral moderator of debate, the speakership shifted during Henry Clay's tenure to a partisan, nonneutral, "majoritarian" position that continued in the post-Clay years but was flexible as to the degree of partisanship. Swift argues that the existing context and the prior experience of the House converged (she terms this "experiential learning") to transform the speakership into the majoritarian, partisan position of the present.

In Chapter 2, Randall Strahan analyzes leadership in the post–Civil War nineteenth-century House, detailing the development of party government and strong centralized leadership embodied in the imposing physical presence of Speaker Thomas Reed. Strahan stresses the importance of party homogeneity in this development and the role of factions in delaying or defeating legislation in the immediate post–Civil War years. Shifts in control of the House, the tradition of the Speaker as neutral moderator, and continuing attention to the rights of the minority—all these affected the speed and degree of change.

Scott Rager focuses in Chapter 3 on Speaker Joseph Cannon as "brakeman" of the House, increasingly out of touch with the changing context of the times and able only to delay but not stop change. A personally forceful Speaker, Cannon was unable to understand or stop the insurgents' revolt against strong, centralized leadership. A coalition of progressive Republicans and Democrats eventually revolted and removed Cannon from the powerful Rules Committee—a deceptively modest procedural change that nonetheless ranks as one of the landmark events in the history of U.S. political institutions. Thus Cannon is remembered as a barrier in a transitional era, seeking to halt momentum as the House moved into the twentieth century.

James Fleming picks up the story in Chapter 4 with his analysis of Oscar W. Underwood as the first modern House leader (1911–1915). Underwood exemplified the shift in the locus of power within a party and the new flexibility of House leaders. Typifying the rise of the committee barons in the post-Cannon House, Underwood vaulted into the Democratic party leadership through his membership on the Ways and Means Committee (whose Democrats served also as their party's Committee on Committees). As Fleming points out, although Underwood was simultaneously chair of Ways and Means and majority leader, his influence depended not only on his formal positions of authority, which he "skillfully integrated into a unified leadership of the House," but also on his own personal traits, "which were more in keeping with the emerging democratic norms of the House in the post-Cannon era."

Underwood presided over a newly decentralized party and House structure; his recognition of minority-party rights—the minority leader submitted that party's choices of committee assignments for its members—has been a continuing theme in congressional operations and persists today. During Underwood's tenure, intraparty changes affected House operations and structure. As in the contemporary era—when Speaker Gingrich and House Republicans, newly in control, gradually moved toward using the more restrictive rules for floor debate that they had previously derided—Underwood, having served so long in the minority, was sensitive to that position as he presided over majority-party processes.

Nicholas Longworth restored the speakership to a position of authority and prestige, as Donald C. Bacon details in Chapter 5. Bacon argues that Longworth's personality and style were his primary assets. His coalition-building skills and ability to work with members of the minority party enabled him to achieve legislative success as well as recognition as the premier leader of both his party and the House of Representatives.

In Chapter 6, Anthony Champagne focuses on John Nance Garner— party whip, Ways and Means Committee leader, and Speaker of the House of Representatives from 1931 to 1933. Here, too, continuing leadership themes are evident: skill at building coalitions, ability to cooperate with presidents, and adaptation to the larger political context within which the leaders perform. Garner's political leadership was anchored in his district constituency and power base. As with another Speaker from Texas, Sam Rayburn, constituency was a major factor in his leadership style.

In Chapter 7, Lewis L. Gould and Nancy Beck Young analyze the leadership of Speaker Sam Rayburn, emphasizing especially a neglected aspect of that role: his detailed legislative work on specific issues. The authors offer fresh insights into this political role. Rayburn presided over the House during the tumultuous years of World War II, the postwar adjustments, and the advent of the 1960s. He worked with Democratic and Republican presidents. Within the House, it was the heyday of the committee "barons." Rayburn was involved in the details of lawmaking: He

managed the legislative work of the House through bargaining and compromise, exercise of his formal powers, and a network of close personal
relationships. As with Garner and a later majority leader, Hale Boggs,
Rayburn's constituency and state background shaped his political concerns and his personal style, and his speakership left in place changes in
the House that were bequeathed to later leaders.

Chapter 8 sets forth Patrick Maney's analysis of the role of a modern
majority leader, Hale Boggs of Louisiana. Boggs exemplifies the tension
between the parameters set by leaders' constituencies and their wider political platform and the balance leaders must achieve between these two
forces. As a politician whom the youthful Bill Clinton met and admired,
Boggs is a link to present-day politics and also a case study in the politician's dilemma of seeking to mesh national aspirations with changing
contexts of regional politics—in Boggs's case, the South's peculiar racial
heritage.

In Chapter 9, James M. Cannon writes of Gerald Ford, minority leader
of the House—his style, his position within his own party conference, his
relationships with the Democratic majority leaders and party, his dealings
with presidents of both parties, and his coalition-building skills. As the
minority leader charged with helping achieve President Richard Nixon's
agenda, Ford faced daunting challenges. As with other leaders, the interplay of context (split party control; Republican ranks in the House at
times depleted, at other times a larger minority) and personal style—a
network of friendships and an ability to seek a position acceptable to a
majority of House members—were the hallmarks of Ford's tenure. These
factors are significant in the work of leaders, whether of the House majority or minority party and whether Republican or Democratic.

In the final chapter of the book, Barbara Sinclair analyzes leadership
changes of the late twentieth century. She focuses on Speaker Thomas P.
"Tip" O'Neill and his successors, including Newt Gingrich. She con-
cludes that the changes that occurred under Democratic leaders—more
inclusive participation by the rank and file and by expanded leadership
groups as well as centralization of the control of floor debate through the
mechanism of restrictive rules—are not confined to a single party but are
institutional adaptations adopted at least to a degree by Republicans
when they took control of the House in 1995. The continuities in leadership are significant, and changes are rarely reversed but are rather incorporated and adapted by later leaders.

Some Enduring Themes

Several themes and conclusions emerge from these chapters. Leadership
in the House has become more complex and differentiated and more in-

clusive. Change is a common theme: Major change occurred with the shift from a Speaker who was an evenhanded, nonpartisan moderator to a majoritarian, often highly partisan leader. The post–Civil War shift to strong party leadership was buttressed by both new formal powers and informal norms. Shifts in the locus of floor generalship within the majority party—from Speaker to majority leader—occurred in the early twentieth century. Late-twentieth-century leaders developed a more inclusive leadership style as rank-and-file members demanded that leaders consult more widely and allow even the most junior members fuller participation in developing the strategies and content of legislation. The interaction of the Speaker and other party leaders, including leaders of the minority party, and the context within which they operated affected the pace and the substance of institutional change. The president's role and leaders' working relationships with him, party strength within Congress and internally within the electorate, and the extent of factional division within each congressional party also affect the leaders' role, institutional change, and public policy. Individual Speakers and other leaders have served as agents of change (Henry Clay, Thomas Reed), responded to shifts in the external environment or within Congress by seeking mechanisms to adapt the institution to a new working environment (Oscar Underwood, Tip O'Neill, and the late-twentieth-century leaders), or served as "brakemen" to hold back change as long as possible (Joseph Cannon).

The fundamental story is one of change and adaptation, building on the work of previous leaders, and yet adapting to the demands and the context of the period within which a given leader serves. Overall, the authors conclude that the context within which leaders work shapes the parameters of their jobs, presenting opportunities as well as constraints. But those who are truly masters of the House are those few talented and skilled individuals who are able to superintend specific changes, strategies, successes, and failures and who labor mightily to reshape the institution and the national policies it produces.

1

The Start of Something New: Clay, Stevenson, Polk, and the Development of the Speakership, 1789–1869

Elaine K. Swift

To those of us fascinated with the performance of Newt Gingrich as Speaker of the House, questions posed by the early origins and development of the office seem to be, at best, distant and irrelevant prologue. Why the Speaker was originally expected to serve as a moderator, presiding over the chamber as impartially as possible, seems at best a quaint curiosity. How Henry Clay was able to transform the office from moderator to one of leader of the House majority does not seem any more relevant, given that his feat took place nearly two centuries ago, when the nation was much smaller, its parties very different, and the Congress a much simpler institution. Why the post-Clay speakership remained so flexible, with some of his successors aggressive partisans and others relatively evenhanded, concerns us even less: In his first term as Speaker, Gingrich appears to have set a new and high standard of partisanship for all holders of that office.

In this chapter I will argue that, however hoary their context, each of the questions posed by the past—the origins of the office, Clay's transformation of the office, and the shifting behavior of his immediate successors—can shed much light on developments today, an assertion that today's history professor–cum–Speaker least of all would find far-fetched. As an added bonus, the questions also allow us to probe the strengths and limits of leading theories of the office and to assess if and how we could better explain its shifts over time.

The Origin of the Moderator Speakership

As Hubert Bruce Fuller (1909), Mary Parker Follett (1909), and Ronald M. Peters, Jr. (1990), have recounted so well, the Speaker started out as a moderator, conceiving his duty to be "that of any presiding officer—to apply the rules of the House so as to ensure the opportunity for unhampered debate and secure the freest expression of the legislative desire" (Fuller 1909, p. 25). Early Speakers strove to be impartial in several ways. First, although House rules permitted them to participate in every vote, they did not vote unless by ballot or to make or break a tie. Second, they did not engage in debate. The rules enjoined them from doing so when presiding over the whole House, but they also chose to refrain even when not presiding over a House quorum or Committee of the Whole House. Third, though they were given the power to appoint all committees, they studiously avoided favoring the majority. Fourth, they took no initiative on the establishment of standing committees.

True, there were some notable departures from this moderator model that hinted of the office's majoritarian future. By the Third Congress, for example, the election for Speaker had become a partisan affair, with the majority elevating its candidate. Though occupants of the office diligently continued to cultivate a reputation for fairness, Federalist Theodore Sedgwick in the Fifth Congress (1797–1799) apparently crossed the partisan line: Republicans refused for the first time to join in the customary resolution of thanks at the end of his term. Nonetheless, the Speaker as moderator remained the office's beau ideal, to which its earliest occupants bowed.

Why was the Speaker expected to be a moderator? The framers themselves have left few clues. Although they aired their views on a great many matters, they barely mentioned the office, according to the records of the Constitutional Convention, *The Federalist Papers*, and the ratification debates. Nonetheless, some have credited the framers with the genesis of the moderator model, suggesting that George Washington's evenhanded leadership of the Constitutional Convention served as the office's inspiration. Indeed, some early House members had themselves been framers, and many others undoubtedly were acquainted with the role that Washington played. However, Washington is an unlikely source. Those who had not attended the Convention remained unaware of the details of much of its deliberations; those would not become common knowledge until 1840, with the publication of Madison's notes on the proceedings, the first widely respected, contemporaneous account of the event. Moreover, few saw many parallels between the Convention and the Congress it created. Contemporaries regarded the former as an unusually august body, with Jefferson going so far as to characterize it as "an assembly of demigods" (Farrand [1937] 1966, 3:76). By the 1790s, its proceedings had already acquired a mystique that the far more mundane proceedings of the early House could scarcely rival.

Other sources for the moderator speakership seem equally doubtful. The British Parliament was clearly not the origin. The sixteenth- and seventeenth-century British Parliament, for example, was the crown's agent, with the monarch attempting "whenever possible, to place in the Chair a speaker favorable to his interests" (Fuller 1909, 13). Though by the eighteenth century the speaker had gained a measure of independence, it was not until "the beginning of the nineteenth century that the English speaker became in fact, as well as in theory, the moderator of the House of Commons, neither servant to the Crown nor dominant over the House" (Fuller 1909, 14).

At first glance, the Confederational Congress and colonial assemblies appear to be more promising sources. The leader or president of the Confederational Congress "began as little more than a position for a parliamentarian to monitor open debate on the floor. Subsequent actions by presidents and members did little to enhance the president's ability to lead" (Jillson and Wilson 1994, 89). Six out of seven colonial assemblies had also featured moderator Speakers, endowed with only enough power to enable them to keep order (Jillson and Wilson 1994). However, although the Confederational Congress and colonial and later state legislatures made the moderator Speaker a familiar role, they did not make it a desirable one. Indeed, the opposite was more apt to be true. The Confederational Congress was widely condemned as an ineffectual body (Jillson and Wilson 1994). Framer and future senator Gouverneur Morris found "in Congress changeableness. in every department excesses agst. personal liberty private property & personal safety" (Farrand [1937] 1966, 1:512). Delegates had "no will of their own," Edmund Randolph declared at the Constitutional Convention. "[T]hey are a mere diplomatic body, and are always obsequious to the views of the States, who are always encroaching on the authority of the U. States" (Farrand [1937] 1966, 1:256). The reputation of state legislatures was, if anything, worse. Many regarded them as undisciplined, short-sighted bodies, responsible for a stream of ill-considered measures (Wood 1969). In his biting essay, "Vices of the Political System of the United States," James Madison indicted them for, among other offenses, "Violations of the law of nations and of treaties"; "want of concert in matters where common interest requires it"; "Multiplicity of laws"; and "mutability of the laws" (Madison [1787] 1975, 349, 350, 353).

From where, then, did the neutral ideal arise? It is the argument here that even though the framers themselves may not have explicitly articulated the ideal of the Speaker-as-moderator, they promoted beliefs about legislatures and parties on which it rested. Regarding legislatures, they believed that the lower house was particularly apt to reflect the intrinsic instability of the masses that it represented. The people, or the "unreflecting multitude" as Madison called them, were passionate, short-sighted, and unstable (Farrand [1937] 1966, 1:215). "[L]ed into action by the impulse of the moment," they too often fell prey to their own "transient impressions" (Farrand [1937] 1966, 1:430, 1:421). Though, as republicans, the framers "considered the popular election of one branch of the national Legislature as essential to every plan of free Government," they also believed that if the chamber was too close to its constituents, it would reflect their nature and be "governed too much by the passions of the moment" (Farrand [1937] 1966, 1:49; 2:626). This had been the case in Massachusetts, Rufus King explained: "[O]ne assembly would have hung all the insurgents in that State; the next was equally disposed to pardon them all" (Farrand [1937] 1966, 2:626–627).

The framers also believed that parties or factions, if unchecked, destabilized and ultimately destroyed government. Madison sketched their dangers in "Vices of the Political System of the United States," at the Constitutional Convention, and later, and most famously, in Federalist No. 10. Faction, he contended, was "sown in the nature of man." In fact, "[s]o strong is this propensity of mankind to fall into mutual animosities that where no substantial occasion presents itself the most frivolous and fanciful distinctions have been sufficient to kindle their unfriendly passions and excite their most violent conflicts" (Rossiter 1961, 79).[1]

In light of these beliefs on legislative assemblies and parties, House members' embrace of the Speaker-as-moderator seems natural. If the House was potentially volatile and parties an ever-threatening menace, a moderator Speaker presented an ideal way to keep order and prevent divisions. And early officeholders followed suit. As Frederick Muhlenberg pledged in the Third Congress, "I shall endeavor to conduct myself with that impartiality, integrity, and assiduity, which become the conspicuous station in which you have been pleased to place me." At the outset of the Sixth Congress, even Theodore Sedgwick promised his "impartial integrity" in discharging the duties of his station. Nathaniel Macon in the Ninth vowed "fidelity, impartiality, and industry." In the Tenth, Joseph Varnum said that he would "discharge the duties faithfully and impartially, and in a manner which, in my opinion, shall be the best calculated to meet your wishes, and afford me the consolation of an approving conscience."[2]

The Origin of the Majoritarian Speakership

Henry Clay pioneered the role of the majoritarian Speaker, challenging the hallmarks of the moderator role.

1. Frequent floor votes. Compared to his predecessors, Clay voted far more frequently than his predecessors. According to Fuller, "He never failed to cast his ballot on any measure before Congress, refusing to deprive his State of her full representation" (Fuller 1909, 41).

2. Active participation in floor debate. Remini noted that Clay "was the first Speaker to insist on his full rights as a member to debate and vote upon any issue to come before the House" (Remini 1991, 81).

3. Support for standing committees. Clay presided over the growth of standing committees in the House, leaving office with sixteen more in existence than had been the case when he entered (de Boinville 1982, 106). Although no one has uncovered documentation that shows that Clay was personally involved in the growth of the committee system, the fact that the most important additions were in accord with his political positions and headed by his supporters suggests at least his active support.

4. Bill referral. Clay "presumed the right to refer all bills introduced into the House to an appropriate standing committee," a power that allowed him significantly to affect the fate of legislation by sending it to friendly or unfriendly panels (Remini 1991, 82).[3]

5. Committee appointments. Clay departed from the moderator's norm of making committee appointments that were relatively proportional to

TABLE 1.1   Proportion of Majority Party Assignments to Ways and Means, 1801–1809

Congress[a]	Speaker (Party)[b]	House Majority Party	% Majority Party	% Majority Party Seats on Ways and Means
7th	Nathaniel Macon (JR)	JR	64.2	60.0
8th	Nathaniel Macon (JR)	JR	72.5	62.5
9th	Nathaniel Macon (JR)	JR	80.3	77.8
10th	Joseph Varnum (JR)	JR	81.7	85.7
11th	Joseph Varnum (JR)	JR	64.8	71.4
12th	Henry Clay (JR)	JR	74.8	85.7
13th	Henry Clay (JR)	JR	62.6	85.7
14th	Henry Clay (JR)	JR	65.0	71.4

[a]Only committee assignments made in the first session of each Congress were analyzed.

[b]Party identifications are those determined by Kenneth C. Martis (1989). JR = Jeffersonian Republicans.

Source: Data derived from David T. Canon, Garrison Nelson, and Charles Stewart III, "Congressional Committee Membership," in Elaine K. Swift et al., "Relational Database of the United States Congress, 1788–1993" (Ann Arbor: Inter-University Consortium on Political and Social Research, forthcoming).

party ratios in the House as a whole. More than any previous Speaker, he sought to ensure that the majority party would control the House by ensuring that it controlled key committees with a larger proportion of seats than its party margins would otherwise suggest. Table 1.1 presents the assignments to the House's most important committee, Ways and Means, made by his Republican predecessors, Nathaniel Macon and Joseph Varnum, and the assignments made by Clay during those Congresses over which he presided that had discernible and relatively partisan divisions. As the data in the table indicate, Joseph Varnum was the first Speaker to establish greater majority control of the panel, on average awarding his party 5.3 percent more seats than its proportion of total House membership otherwise suggested it should have. Clay significantly upped the ante. In the Twelfth, Thirteenth, and Fourteenth Congresses, he awarded his party an average of 13 percent more seats than its proportion of total House membership would otherwise have suggested.

Why did the transition from moderator to majoritarian occur under Clay? Major theories of congressional leadership suggest different reasons, none of which appears to account for the case in point. Joseph Cooper and David Brady developed an explanation that we will call partisan context theory, offering substantial empirical confirmation for its application to twentieth-century Speakers. As they explained, "[i]nstitu-tional context rather than personal traits primarily determines leadership style in the House," and in turn "the impact of institutional context on leadership power and style is determined primarily by party strength." More specifically, "[t]he higher the degree of party unity or cohesion the more power in both the formal and party systems can be concentrated in the hands of party leaders and the more leadership style will be oriented to command and task or goal attainment" (Cooper and Brady 1981, 423, 424). As applied to the early nineteenth century, partisan context theory would therefore direct us to look at the relative degree of partisanship that prevailed in the House at that time. However, it was not a time of party voting according to the indicator Cooper and Brady use: the per-centage of party votes defined as 90 percent of one party opposing 90 per-cent of the other. In the Twelfth Congress, which first elected Clay as Speaker, only 41 out of 314 (13 percent) roll-call votes met that criterion. Compare this to the Seventh Congress, which elected a moderator Speaker, Nathaniel Macon. Of the 142 ballots cast, 55 or 39 percent were partisan votes, a threshold of party voting meeting the high standard of partisanship that, the authors maintain, helped to support late-nineteenth-century czarist Speakers.[4]

For others, context is also the single most important influence on lead-ership but is better understood as membership preferences, with parti-sanship as only one possibility. As Erwin Hargrove summarized this per-spective, which is often called transactional leadership theory, "[t]he political leader acts within a set of stable boundaries. The individual players know their preferences and act in predictable ways to maximize them. The role of the leader is to create coalitions for decision out of the range of preferences. Leaders most commonly do this by structuring in-stitutional rules, by offering incentives to cooperate, and by manipulating situational factors" (Hargrove 1989, 57). As such, transactional theory un-derscores the influence that the rank and file may have. Does it illuminate Clay's innovations? As applied to the case of Speaker Clay, it would di-rect us to investigate the high degree to which he must have satisfied the majority of members' strongly held and clearly expressed preferences. Although one can argue that this characterizes Clay, again this also ap-pears to apply to Nathaniel Macon, a highly popular *and* relatively im-partial Speaker, elected on the first ballot for the first two of his three terms in office.

Personality studies usually look to the characteristics of individual Speakers to discern patterns in their leadership of the House. Employed chiefly, though not exclusively, by biographers, to a large degree these studies credit Speakers' triumphs and failures in office to perceived char-acter strengths and weaknesses. In his account of Clay's innovations, for example, Robert Remini looked to the man's charisma (Remini 1991). Indeed, charisma to a large degree may have accounted for Clay's election to the speakership five times, and on the first ballot each time at that. However, there is nothing in the quality of charisma per se that leads its possessor to undertake institutional innovation. As scholars of the presidency have emphasized, charismatic officeholders are just as likely to be strict conformists as innovators.

In addition, there are synthetic theories, which rely on both context and personality. In *The American Speakership*, Ronald Peters offered one such synthesis: "The 'contexts' that drive the 'style' are themselves a part of a pattern of political and social evolution that must be studied in order to understand the speakership. At the same time, within the 'contexts,' individual actors and events that are not historically or contextually determined will influence the House" (Peters 1990, 4). However, in his account of Clay, Peters ended up emphasizing the influence of charisma.

To explain the transformation of the speakership, the following will focus on the pivotal role played by *experiential learning*, an inductive process by which *both* rank and file and leaders draw on experience evaluated through a common cognitive framework, which can lead them to try other institutional arrangements. As such, experiential learning is premised upon a speakership that is a two-way street, with members and the Speakers each playing important, if not always equal, parts in shaping the office. Experiential learning thus stands in contrast to approaches that emphasize the unilateral importance of one over the other. Many scholars have rightly criticized theories positing that individual Speakers who possess the right mix of skill, charisma, and other characteristics can achieve any objective. However, contextual determinist approaches, such as principal-agent theories, promote the other extreme, turning Speakers into functionalist automatons, carrying out whatever the membership demands (Fiorina and Shepsle 1989).

To explore how experiential learning can help explain the origins of the majoritarian speakership, let us first look at the House's experience with moderator Speakers and then the cognitive framework that led Henry Clay and the House rank and file to establish the majoritarian speakership.

House Experience with Moderator Speakers, 1789–1811

Although the moderator speakership was conceived as a way to thwart the development of parties in the House, once they developed, the office adapted, awkwardly accommodating partisanship while still retaining a large degree of impartiality. As John F. Hoadley described the growth of parties, "[t]here was a clear movement from 1789 to 1803 in the direction of polarized voting in Congress" such that "[b]y the Fourth Congress, one can delineate two clusters—which can best be identified as the Republican and Federalist parties." And "[i]n the six years that marked the end of the era of Federalist domination and the beginning of the Jeffersonian era (1797–1803), voting in Congress remained highly polarized" (Hoadley 1986, 84–85, 77; see also Poole and Rosenthal 1997, chap. 3). Partisanship and polarization persisted throughout Jefferson's administration (1801–1809) (Cunningham 1963, 1978).

Though the majority party's rank and file that elected the Speaker might reasonably have expected him to promote their interests, the moderator speakership endured until 1811 for two important reasons. First, each party developed beliefs that legitimated the continuance of the moderator speakership. Jeffersonian Republicans, who dominated the House after 1801, championed equality and opposed concentrations of power in the House and elsewhere in the national government, which further legitimated neutral House leadership (Cooper 1970). Federalists, although friendlier to political hierarchy and authority, demonstrated a greater antipathy to political parties and their organizational needs (Fischer 1965). Unsurprisingly, during the Federalists' domination of the House between 1797 and 1801, they were not inclined to make the Speaker their undisputed partisan leader.

Second, leadership arrangements were devised to accommodate the House's partisan divisions and still retain the moderator speakership many continued to believe intrinsic to the institution's order, stability, and legislative effectiveness. More specifically, the chamber early on looked favorably on the following position, which would last until Clay's reign: The Speaker would remain largely neutral, leaving the political majority to prosecute its factional or partisan positions through floor leaders or through the chair of the Ways and Means Committee. Floor leaders were a flexible entity, informally designated and deployed to carry out a number of tasks. For most of Washington's administration (1789–1797), the emerging Federalist Party mainly relied on Treasury Secretary Alexander Hamilton to manage its affairs. To a significant degree, Hamilton did so by functioning as his own floor leader. Ignoring the separation of powers and adopting the methods of British cabinet ministers, Hamilton wrote legislation, orchestrated committee deliberations, and plotted legislative strategy. When the separation of powers proved to be more than a passing inconvenience, he turned to such prominent House members as Fisher Ames, Theodore Sedgwick, and William L. Smith for assistance, particularly in debate. In this period, the proto-Republican party developed as a result of the teamwork of Secretary of State Thomas Jefferson and Representative James Madison of Virginia, who cultivated their own supporters "out-of-doors," in committee, and on the floor. By the time that Jefferson resigned in 1793, Madison had a reliable cadre of followers. During the Adams administration, floor leaders continued to be the mainstay of both parties in the House. Unfortunately for the Federalists, the party had two sets: one loyal to former Treasury Secretary Hamilton and the other to President John Adams. The Republican party in the House was managed by Vice President Thomas Jefferson. Following Madison's departure in 1797, Jefferson worked through such faithful lieutenants as Albert Gallatin, William Branch Giles, and Wilson Cary Nicholas.

The 1790s pattern of floor leaders who were chosen and directed by the executive was an expedient that undoubtedly served the emerging Federalists and Republicans well. With the Speaker constrained by expectations of neutrality and lacking a central organization to plan and coordinate, members of the executive nicely filled the bill, borrowing from the parliamentary practice of ministerial influence to launch the House's first factions effectively. However, as time went on, and temporary factions hardened into enduring political parties, the disadvantages of floor leaders became more and more apparent. Perhaps most important, House members grew increasingly restive over executive direction and domination. It was, many justifiably believed, a violation of the separation of powers and an extension of British-style "corruption." In addition, these leaders were neither selected by House Federalists or Republicans nor accountable to them. For Federalists during the Adams administration, these features spelled disaster. Caught betwixt and between the demands of Hamilton's and Adams's floor leaders, they lacked a central House leader to supply direction and unity. Moreover, because the executive's floor leaders did not hold formal House leadership positions, they did not have the carrots and sticks needed to be truly effective.

During the Jefferson administration (1801 to 1809), Republicans initially resolved some of those problems with a new kind of party leader: the chair of the Ways and Means Committee, a position in many ways ideally suited to the task. For those Republicans jealous of House autonomy and prerogatives, the chair was chosen by the Speaker. Neither President Jefferson nor his cabinet sought to influence the selection (Cunningham 1978, 188; Malone 1974, 67). In addition, the sweeping legislative power exercised by the chair of the Ways and Means Committee in many ways ideally suited him to plan and execute party strategy. The Ways and Means Committee was the chamber's preeminent panel, considering all legislation on revenue and appropriations as well as conducting fiscal oversight of the executive. If members wished to exercise any legislative influence in the chamber, they had to defer to the committee chair. If the executive wished to see its fiscal plans succeed in the House, it too had to defer to him.[5]

Despite this promise, the chair of Ways and Means would prove even more disastrous than executive-designated floor leaders, since he was responsive neither to members nor to the executive. John Randolph was a brilliant but exceedingly difficult man, insisting on an ideological course too rigid for Jeffersonians realistically to pursue. "We are strong in the cause of truth," he maintained, haranguing those who seemed seduced by "the spirit of Federalism" (Malone 1970, 450, 451). Complained one representative, "His speeches were too personal—his allusions to brothel-houses & pig stys too course & vulgar—his arraigning the motives of members charging them with peculation, bribery, & corruption, were insufferable—He lashed demo's & feds indiscriminately—He treated no man that was opposed to him with either respect or decency" (Malone 1970, 451). However, he so enjoyed Macon's confidence that the Speaker was willing to risk his office rather than to replace Randolph.

Initially, Jefferson attempted to work through Randolph, and the association was at times a fruitful one, with the chair using his powers and oratorical skills to administrative advantage (Malone 1970). However, Randolph was ever volatile, leading Jefferson to also designate floor leaders. Members such as William Branch Giles, Caesar Rodney, and Wilson Cary Nicholas provided Jefferson with the dependable support he needed, but they lacked an institutional base of authority and legitimacy and often found their influence undermined by the powerful and skillful Randolph.

Following Randolph's outright break with the administration in 1806 and the election of Joseph Varnum as Speaker in the Tenth (1807 to 1809) and Eleventh (1809 to 1811) Congresses, House Republicans returned to floor leadership with the same mixed results this arrangement had yielded in the past. From the executive's perspective, such floor leaders as George Washington Campbell and Barnabus Bidwell appeared successful, marshaling administration forces on such key issues as the embargo and other high-profile measures aimed at limiting British aggression. However, it is difficult to separate their contributions from the effects of other strategies the executive used. And from an analysis of Madison's first two years in office, it is clear that floor leaders were insufficient to save the program of a maladroit executive. From the perspective of the House majority, floor leaders still lacked the legitimacy conferred by rank-and-file selection and the authority derived from holding a formal institutional position.

*Experiential Learning, Cognitive Frameworks, and the
Development of the Majoritarian Speakership*

By the Twelfth Congress (1811 to 1813), the majority party was thus well acquainted with the record of past leadership arrangements: the moderator Speaker/partisan floor leaders of the earliest Congresses and the moderator Speaker/partisan Ways and Means chair of the early 1800s. If the House so wished, it could continue to rely on them. At least one candidate for the office of Speaker, Nathaniel Macon, appeared ready to resume the moderator role and once again to appoint John Randolph as Ways and Means chair and chief partisan.

Ultimately, of course, the Twelfth Congress broke with House tradition, electing the first majoritarian Speaker. Because the speakership is a two-way street between rank and file and the officeholder, it is necessary to examine the part that each of them played. The rank and file and Henry Clay, it will be argued, were similarly influenced by experiential learning, the process by which members of an institution evaluate how arrangements did or did not work in the past. Evaluation is thus inductive rather than deductive. The former better characterizes how members of Congress actually assimilate and act on information. Richard F. Fenno, Jr., observed that modern representatives "are inductive thinkers. That is to say, they start with specific instances . . . to get a handle on what is going on." What the member "does best in the process of scrutiny . . . is to grasp some detail and work out from there" (quoted in Malbin 1979, 247). The same appears to hold true for their nineteenth-century predecessors. In particular, the framers and the post-Revolutionary "second generation" of U.S. political leaders, which included Clay, Daniel Webster, and John Calhoun, were intensely practical politicians. Experimenting with old and new institutional forms, they discarded, refined, and retained them depending upon how they did or did not appear to perform (Silbey 1991; Swift 1996; Watts 1987).

How is experience assessed? As Albert Bandura explained, "The more rudimentary mode of learning, rooted in direct experience, results from the positive and negative effects that actions produce." However, such learning does not take the form of a simple and mechanistic stimulus-response pattern. Rather, "learning by response consequences is largely a cognitive process" in which cognitive factors help "determine which external events will be observed, how they will be perceived, whether they leave any lasting effects, what valence and efficacy they have, and how the information they convey will be organized for future use" (Bandura 1977, 17, 18, 160).

Although the cognitive factors that form the crucial intervening variables between experience and learning vary, belief systems are often central. In the case of the House's experience with moderator Speakers, Clay and the majority of the House's rank and file drew on a cognitive framework informed by the loose ideology and policy objectives of the War Hawks, a dynamic faction of the Republican party committed to seizing the nation's policy initiative. According to the War Hawks, if the Republic were to endure, it had to combat militarily British violations of U.S. sovereignty. As a leading historian of the era noted, "These young men . . . supported the particular interests of their regions and demanded war to protect those interests, but they also had a genuine feeling that American national honor had suffered as a result of the events of the previous four years" (Horsman 1962, 226). These disastrous experiences, the War Hawks believed, had been largely engineered by James Madison, when he was secretary of state and when he was president. In their campaign for the nation to adopt a more aggressive stand, they neither expected nor solicited presidential leadership. Rather, they were fully prepared to take the initiative themselves.

Given this framework of beliefs, it was not surprising that Clay and the other War Hawks did not support a return to a moderator Speaker. Applying their framework to House experience, they had learned the following. When a moderator Speaker left partisan tasks to the chair of the Ways and Means Committee, the House lacked a direct way to hold him accountable, since the Speaker—and not the rank and file—made the appointment. If the chair of the Ways and Means Committee displeased the majority, its main recourse was to protest to the Speaker and threaten not to reelect him unless he sanctioned the chair. When a moderator Speaker left partisan tasks to a floor leader designated by the executive, the House again lacked a direct way to hold him accountable. Here, however, they had more powerful recourses. They could protest to the president or, more effectively, simply ignore his floor leader.

If the War Hawk rank and file did not wish to support a moderator, they lacked an obvious model for the office that built on House experience and accorded with their values and policy objectives. Fortunately for them, Henry Clay supplied an acceptable alternative. He, too, was a War Hawk, anxious for the House firmly and decisively to take the nation's lead. As a senator from 1806 to 1807 and 1810 to 1811, he had strongly advocated a military response to British aggression. Arguing in one debate that he was "for resistance by the *sword*," he declared that "[n]o man in the nation desires peace more than I. But I prefer the troubled ocean of war . . . to the tranquil, putrescent pool of ignominious peace" (quoted in Remini 1991, 60; emphasis in original).

In what direction would Clay take the speakership? He looked not only to his House experience but also to his state legislative experience. As Speaker of the Kentucky House, he had already strayed far from the moderator model with noteworthy success. Engaging in some of the speakership strategies he would introduce to the U.S. House, he had used his office actively to lead his party, not merely to preside while delegating partisan leadership to others (Remini 1991, chap. 6).

Little wonder, then, that the War Hawks and other Republicans elected their first-term colleague as Speaker. Once in office, he did not disappoint. Over his five nonconsecutive terms in office that ran from 1811 to 1825, he pursued a number of different directions. Before and during the War of

1812, he advocated aggressive military policy and shifts in domestic policy, such as national aid for manufactures, that he believed necessary to sustain victory. After the war, he emerged as the foremost advocate for those domestic policies that he would come to label his American System: nationally sponsored internal improvements, national aid to manufactures, and a national bank. In addition, he backed certain foreign policy measures such as support for independence movements in South America and Greece.

Institutionally speaking, Clay reconfigured his office and the House as a whole to sustain his policy leadership. As Speaker, Clay refused to give up his right to vote on most issues, thus providing his followers with the direction—and sometimes the political cover—of such a public act. More important, he refused to give up one of his greatest assets in that age of oratory—his right to debate when the House was in the Committee of the Whole. If moderator Speakers felt the need to protect their status and dignity by remaining above the fray, Clay suffered no such compunction. On important bill after important bill, he took the floor, aggressively rallying his House troops and inspiring public confidence. He was "[b]old, aspiring, presumptuous, with a rough, overbearing eloquence," one opponent observed (quoted in Remini 1991, 84). He was "a flame of fire," an admirer insisted, who "brought congress to the verge of what he conceived to be a war for liberty and honour, and his voice, inspired by the occasion, rang through the capital, like a trumpet-tone sounding for the onset" (p. 91). The "Speaker of the Ho[use] of Representatives was the second man in the Nation," John Randolph asserted (quoted on p. 83). Just as important, Clay mastered the standing committee system. He stacked the most important standing committees of the House, such as Ways and Means, Foreign Relations, and Military Affairs, with his allies. In addition, he presided over the expansion of the standing committee system, including the establishment of panels explicitly charged with superintending policies that were explicitly his own (Strahan 1994, 19–30). Most flagrantly, in 1816, six new standing committees began to oversee an executive branch that Clay believed insufficiently receptive to his leadership.

Stevenson, Polk, and the Flexibility of the Speakership

Henry Clay did in fact succeed in transforming the speakership. Following his reign, the office would never be the same. Though there would be Speakers who reverted to the moderator model, far more often than not Clay's successors also chose to be majoritarians. From the 1820s through the present, Speakers routinely voted, debated on the floor, made partisan committee appointments, and otherwise actively involved themselves in the work and structure of the committee system.

However, majoritarian Speakers adopted a flexible approach to the role: Some were staunch and aggressive partisans; others were far more evenhanded, if not impartial. Clay himself managed to be both during the course of his five terms in office. After establishing the majoritarian speakership, he later took a much less partisan approach to the office. Although continuing to provide forthright policy leadership, he acted to mollify supporters and foes in committee assignments and floor action. As one leading national newspaper observed,

> The National Intelligencer, in announcing the various committees appointed by the Speaker, said—
> "In performing this duty, it must be allowed, he has shown, all things considered, a laudable impartiality."
> What "*things considered*?" Let the gentleman out with them. Now, on looking over the lists, I had really concluded that Mr. Clay had aimed so much at "impartiality," that he was partial against his friends: or, like the Indian's tree, he was "so straight that he leaned 'tother way.'" . . . as *speaker*, no one ever did, and it is hardly expected that any one ever will, more ably or "impartially" perform the arduous duties of that station.[6]

In the speeches Clay made to accept his elections to the speakership, he underscored his evenhanded approach, pledging at different times, "an agreeable manner," "an undeviating aim at impartiality," and his intention to provide "the best arrangement and distribution of the talent of the House, in its numerous subdivisions, for the despatch of the public business, and the fair exhibition of every subject presented for consideration."[7]

Some of Clay's majoritarian successors were highly partisan, others were more evenhanded, and still others were both. Standing committee assignments capture this pattern. As Speaker Schuyler Colfax (1863–1869) noted, "the appointment of committees, as is known to all members, is the most delicate, perplexing, and responsible of all the duties imposed upon the occupant of this chair."[8] The standing committee assignments of the various Speakers clearly signaled the degree of partisan control they wished to exert over the House's business and were interpreted that way. John Quincy Adams's diaries contain repeated references to executive readings of committee appointments. As secretary of state under James Monroe, for example, Adams complained that Clay appointed John Randolph to the Committee on Foreign Affairs "to prevent anything's being done congenial to the views of the Administration." As president-elect, Adams conferred with Speaker John Taylor on appointments, reporting with relief that "he was disposed to arrange the members so that justice may be done as far as was practicable to the Administration" (quoted in Currie 1988, 24, 28).[9]

TABLE 1.2   Proportion of Majority Party Assignments to Ways and Means, 1825–1869

Congress[a]	Speaker (Party)[b]	House Majority Party	% Majority Party	% Majority Party Seats on Ways and Means
19th	John Taylor (Ad)	Administration	51.2	42.9
20th	Andrew Stevenson (Jac)	Jacksonian	53.1	57.1
21st	Andrew Stevenson (Jac)	Jacksonian	63.8	85.7
22nd	Andrew Stevenson (Jac)	Jacksonian	62.7	85.7
23rd	Andrew Stevenson (Jac)	Jacksonian	59.6	77.8
24th	James Polk (Jac)	Jacksonian	59.1	75.0
25th	James Polk (D)	Democratic	52.9	66.7
26th	Robert M.T. Hunter (W)	Democratic	51.7	25.0
27th	John White (W)	Whig	58.7	66.7
28th	John Jones (D)	Democratic	65.9	75.0
29th	John Davis (D)	Democratic	62.6	66.7
30th	Robert Winthrop (W)	Whig	50.4	66.7
31st	Howell Cobb (D)	Democratic	48.7	46.2
32nd	Linn Boyd (D)	Democratic	54.5	77.8
33rd	Linn Boyd (D)	Democratic	67.1	66.7
34th	Nathaniel Banks (Am)	Opposition	42.7	45.4
35th	James Orr (D)	Democratic	55.7	75.0
36th	William Pennington (R)	Republican	48.2	55.6
37th	Galusha Grow (R)	Republican	56.2	55.6
38th	Schuyler Colfax (R)	Republican	45.3	55.6
39th	Schuyler Colfax (R)	Republican	68.3	77.8
40th	Schuyler Colfax (R)	Republican	76.1	77.8

[a]Only committee assignments made in the first session of each Congress were analyzed.
[b]Party identifications are those determined by Kenneth C. Martis (1989). Ad = Administration; Jac = Jacksonian; D = Democratic; W = Whig; Am = American; R = Republican.
Source: Data derived from David T. Canon, Garrison Nelson, and Charles Stewart III, "Congressional Committee Membership," in Elaine K. Swift et al., "Relational Database of the United States Congress, 1788–1993" (Ann Arbor: Inter-University Consortium on Political and Social Research, forthcoming).

Table 1.2 presents data on majority party or factional dominance of the preeminently powerful House Ways and Means Committee during the 1825–1869 period. The data show the proportion of majority party members on the panel compared to the proportion of majority party members in the House as a whole. As noted in the earlier discussion of the chair of the Ways and Means Committee, Ways and Means was by far the chamber's most important panel. Until 1865, when the House Appropriations Committee was created, Ways and Means considered all fiscal measures, central to any partisan program. Little wonder that many considered its chair the second most important leader in the House, at times even overshadowing the Speaker. Panel members were usually prominent and capable representatives, respected by their colleagues.

As the data in Table 1.2 show, some Speakers sought far more partisan control than others. Andrew Stevenson, James Polk, and Robert Winthrop particularly stacked the deck, loading Ways and Means with a proportion of their partisans that exceeded their share of House seats by 15 percent or more. Other Speakers were less bold but still saw that their partisans on Ways and Means enjoyed a comfortable margin of control. Linn Boyd did both. In his first term as Speaker, his party strongly dominated the panel; in his second term, it had a smaller percentage of seats than it had in the House as a whole. A very few—John Taylor, Robert M.T. Hunter, and Howell Cobb—abandoned majoritarian behavior, awarding control of the committee to parties or factions other than their own.

Why did those Speakers who chose to be majoritarians come to adopt such variable degrees of partisanship? Let us look again at personality, contextual, and learning theories. Regarding personality theories, it does not appear that any one group of Speakers had a particular kind of personality. Stevenson and Polk, the best known of the highly partisan Speakers, were disparate individuals. Stevenson was "cheerful and happy, full of good humor and playfulness" and usually "the centre of attraction, the cause of merriment in others."[10] Polk was Stevenson's polar opposite. According to his biographer, "he was not naturally warm or outgoing and would never have any really intimate friends," though "he had trained himself to be affable and cordial" (Sellers 1957, 74).

Party context theory posits that "[t]he higher the degree of party unity or cohesion the more power in both the formal and party systems can be concentrated in the hands of party leaders and the more leadership style will be oriented to command and task or goal attainment" (Cooper and Brady 1981, 423, 424.) The data in Table 1.3 present information on party unity and partisan or factional speakerships. Again adopting the standard employed by Cooper and Brady, party unity is measured as the proportion of those roll calls in which 90 percent or more of one party opposes 90 percent or more of the other major party. Highly partisan Speakers are defined as those who awarded their partisans a proportion of Ways and Means seats 15 or more percent greater than their proportion of total House seats. Moderately partisan Speakers are defined as those awarding their partisans a proportion of Ways and Means seats 1 to 14 percent greater. Nonpartisan Speakers did not favor their party.

As the data in Table 1.3 show, in the 1825–1869 period there is little relationship between party unity and majoritarian party speakerships. Of the three highly partisan Speakers—Stevenson, Polk, and Winthrop—

TABLE 1.3   Speakers and Proportion of Party Unity Votes in the House, 1825–1869

Congress	Year	% Party Unity Votes[a]	Speaker (Party)[b]	Speaker Partisanship[c]
19th	1825	0	John Taylor (Ad)	Non
20th	1827	0	Andrew Stevenson (Jac)	High
21st	1829	0	Andrew Stevenson (Jac)	High
22nd	1831	1	Andrew Stevenson (Jac)	High
23rd	1833	2	Andrew Stevenson (Jac)[d]/ John Bell (Anti-Jac)	High
24th	1835	8	James Polk (Jac)	High
25th	1837	11	James Polk (D)	High
26th	1839	24	Robert M.T. Hunter (W)	Non
27th	1841	16	John White (W)	Moderate
28th	1843	11	John Jones (D)	Moderate
29th	1845	11	John Davis (D)	Moderate
30th	1847	18	Robert Winthrop (W)	High
31st	1849	8	Howell Cobb (D)	Non
32nd	1851	1	Linn Boyd (D)	Moderate
33rd	1853	1	Linn Boyd (D)	Moderate
34th	1855	NA	Nathaniel Banks (Am)	Not available
35th	1857	11	James Orr (D)	Moderate
36th	1859	18	William Pennington (R)	Moderate
37th	1861	22	Galusha Grow (R)	Moderate
38th	1863	33	Schuyler Colfax (R)	Moderate
39th	1865	27	Schuyler Colfax (R)	Moderate
40th	1867	31	Schuyler Colfax (R)	Moderate

[a]Party votes are defined as those roll calls in which 90 percent or more of one major party opposed 90 percent or more of the other major party.

Representatives who identified with other than the two major parties that existed were not analyzed.

[b]Party identifications are those determined by Kenneth C. Martis (1989).

[c]Highly partisan Speakers are defined as those who awarded their partisans a proportion of Ways and Means seats 15 or more percent greater than their proportion of total House seats. Moderately partisan Speakers are defined as those awarding their partisans a proportion of Ways and Means seats 1 to 14 percent greater. Nonpartisan Speakers did not favor their party.

[d]Andrew Stevenson resigned near the end of the first term, replaced by John Bell.

Sources: Data derived from Keith Poole, Howard Rosenthal, and Kenneth C. Martis, "Roll Call Votes of the U.S. House of Representatives, 1789–1992," in Elaine K. Swift et al., "Relational Database of the U.S. Congress, 1788–1993" (forthcoming).

only Winthrop enjoyed even a moderate degree of party unity. Of the moderately partisan Speakers, none faced lower levels of party unity than those of Stevenson, and few contended with levels lower than those of Polk.

What of experiential learning? Might it be the case that the rank and file and the Speakers turned to different leadership models depending upon lessons recently learned? However helpful it may be in accounting for the origin of the majoritarian Speaker, learning theory is difficult to apply to this question. The reason lies in the sequential nature of the origin of the majoritarian model versus the nonsequential nature of its flexible use. In a sequential process such as the former, in which stage *a* clearly leads to stage *b*, it is usually possible to identify what experience occurred in stage *a* and how it was cognitively framed as the basis for action in *b*. In a nonsequential process, where institutional antecedents offer numerous kinds of experience to which members can apply many different cognitive frameworks, experiential learning as explanation is too indeterminate.

What then accounts for the flexibility of the majoritarian speakership? Looking more closely at Table 1.3, we can see that Speakers dealt with similar prevailing political conditions in surprising ways. In general, as Cooper and Brady imply, those who served during periods of elevated party unity pursued a course of moderate partisanship—choosing, for example, to give their parties slim margins of advantage even on the House's most important committee.

However, there are important exceptions, Speakers whose leadership importantly affected the institution and public policy. Specifically, Speakers Stevenson and Polk served during periods of nonexistent to low party unity, yet established themselves as two of the strongest partisan leaders in the early-nineteenth-century House. In addition to their committee appointments, each assiduously worked to convert members into the ideological partisans they themselves were. Stevenson staked out bold positions on such issues as internal improvements, tariffs, and the Bank of the United States, rallying his troops behind these key Jacksonian measures. Polk matched Stevenson's zeal, sticking closely to the Jacksonian "gospel of simplicity, economy, and localism," dismissing Whigs as Federalists in disguise, and persuading his fellow partisans to view matters in the same light (Sellers 1957, 122). At the end of his tenure as Speaker, Whigs lined up to denounce him. "A more perfectly party Speaker," one noted on the House floor, "one who would be more disposed to bend the rules of the House to meet the purposes of his own side in politics, never pressed the soft and ample cushions of that gorgeous chair" (quoted in Sellers 1957, 339).

The preceding suggests that any theory of the majoritarian speakership must take into account the ultimately discretionary nature of the office.

Functionalist treatments posit that given certain membership expectations or prevailing institutional conditions, Speakers follow through as if straitjacketed. In practice, however, different leaders make different choices that often cannot be anticipated—or predicted—from the parameters under which they operate. Indeed, Speakers Stevenson and Polk engaged in what James MacGregor Burns has labeled transforming leadership. The transforming leader "recognizes and exploits an existing need or demand of a potential follower. But, beyond that, the transforming leader looks for potential motives in followers, seeks to satisfy higher needs, and engages the full person of the follower" (Burns 1978, 4).

There is indeed an art of politics, and students of politics must recognize the undeniable dimensions of free agency, choice, and creativity in the study of politics. Nowhere is this more apparent than in the realm of political leadership. This does not mean that at any given point, any leadership action is possible. Nor does it mean that there are no discernible patterns or explanations possible in its study. However, as studies of the presidency underscore, although there are clear regularities at work, individuals can clearly, creatively, and unpredictably confound expectations (Bond and Fleisher 1990; Peterson 1990).

Conclusion:
Early House Speakers and Newt Gingrich

In this chapter I have explored three issues posed by early House history: the origin of the moderator speakership, the establishment of the majoritarian speakership, and the subsequent flexibility of the majoritarian model. Though rooted in the eighteenth and nineteenth centuries, the explanations proffered for each are highly pertinent to the late-twentieth-century House.

As argued above, the origin of the moderator speakership lay in political beliefs articulated most influentially by the framers. Specifically, their beliefs in the instability of lower chambers and the ruinous influence of factions supported the notion that the Speaker ought to be a moderator who could check the House's volatility and tendency toward faction. Similarly, political beliefs about legislatures and parties continue to shape the speakership today. Congress, Republicans in particular asserted in 1994, was far too distant from the people. As evidence, they pointed to, among other signs, entrenched incumbents and a Capitol Hill governed by different laws than the ones it passed.[11] In addition, House Republicans promoted more responsible political parties by displaying greater party unity and ideological fervor. These perspectives on Congress and party support a speakership that is both populist and ideological. In his first term as Speaker, Newt Gingrich as populist supported his party's favored means to bring the House closer to the people, including term limits for all members, limited tenure for committee chairs, limited tenure for the Speaker, and congressional adherence to federal laws. In addition, he continued to demonstrate his longtime interest in innovative and promising, if sometimes questionable, ways of communicating Republican ideology and of recruiting and promoting Republican candidates. Also, in his first term, Gingrich served as a highly ideological Speaker, seeking to fulfill the Contract with America, centralizing committee power in the hands of conservatives, and aggressively pursuing his party's political and economic agenda.

The majoritarian speakership originated in experiential learning, in which Henry Clay and his party's rank and file evaluated the House's recent experience under moderators through a cognitive framework of ideological beliefs, leading them to support the establishment of a very different sort of leadership. So, too, before the 1994 elections, Newt Gingrich and his party's rank and file evaluated the House's experience under relatively weak Democratic Speakers through their own ideological framework, concluding that such leadership lacked the centralization, power, and initiative needed to legislate their views. During Gingrich's second term as Speaker, when he displayed less forcefulness and adopted more moderate policy positions, Republicans rebelled, openly challenging his occupancy of the office. Gingrich survived for many reasons, including his reversion to a more ideological posture on high-profile issues and, not to be overlooked, his reassurance that he intended to leave the House in a few short years, thereby clearing the way for a more zealous successor.

Last, the flexibility of the majoritarian speakership in the early nineteenth century seemed in large part due to the discretion of the Speakers, which led them to engage in behavior that is surprising given the prevailing contexts. Even though some Speakers, for example, responded to low party unity by engaging in fairly nonpartisan behavior, others were very partisan. Still others fell into Burns's category of transforming leaders, actively attempting to reshape their followers' views. Newt Gingrich also appears to be a transforming leader. As a minority whip who was originally elevated to the post over a more senior and traditional Republican by the slimmest of margins, he came to convert the great majority of his party to the value of aggressive, ideological leadership. As Speaker, he enjoyed high party unity in his first term, particularly from the large entering class of Republicans. This high party unity was not just a product of electoral gains and attendant euphoria. Rather, it was also the fruit of Gingrich's efforts to wean longtime House incumbents away from the accommodationist mentality of the seemingly "permanent minority" and actively to elect Republicans in his own highly ideological image by recruiting conservatives and assisting their campaigns. That Speaker Gingrich in his second term would fall victim to his own creation is ironic testament to just how effective a transforming leader he was.

NOTES

Thanks to Joseph Cooper, Kenneth Finegold, Susan Webb Hammond, Calvin C. Jillson, and Joel H. Silbey for their comments. I gratefully acknowledge financial assistance from the Everett C. Dirksen Center and from NSF grants SBR-9596001 and SBR-9496324.

1. On antipartyism in this era, see also Hofstadter 1972.

2. *House Journal*, 3d Cong., 1st sess., p. 4; 6th Cong., 1st sess., p. 5; 10th Cong., 1st sess., p. 5.

3. I should note here that James Sterling Young argued that Clay's reputation as majoritarian leader is overblown: "Of the seven policy controversies in which he is said to have been a major protagonist, and which came before the House in the form of specific bills or resolutions, Speaker Clay won clear victories on only two . . ." (Young 1966, 131). In a reexamination of this issue, Randall Strahan identified "25 issues on which Clay took an active role during the six Congresses in which he served as Speaker. Of these 25, the House voted in support of Clay's position on 15" (Strahan 1994, 18).

4. Data compiled from Keith Poole, Howard Rosenthal, and Kenneth C. Martis, "Roll Call Votes in the U.S. House of Representatives, 1789–1993," in Swift et al. forthcoming.

5. On the importance of the early Ways and Means Committee, see Cunningham 1978, chap. 10, and Furlong 1968, pp. 587–604.

6. *Niles' Register*, Dec. 20, 1823, 245–246; emphasis in original.

7. *House Journal*, 12th Cong., 1st sess., p. 5; 15th Cong., 1st sess., p. 7; 18th Cong., 1st sess., pp. 7–8.

8. *Congressional Globe*, 40th Cong., 1st sess., p. 61.

9. On Speakers and partisan committee appointments, see also Silbey 1989; Wayland 1949, chap. 7; White 1951, chap. 4.

10. *Richmond Enquirer*, Feb. 3, 1857.

11. The House passed, but Senate Republicans blocked, a last-ditch effort in the 103d Congress to end congressional exemption from federal workplace laws. See "Inside Congress," *Congressional Quarterly Weekly*, Nov. 5, 1994, p. 3148.

REFERENCES

Bandura, Albert. 1977. *Social Learning Theory*. Englewood Cliffs, N.J.: Prentice-Hall.

Bensel, Richard F. 1984. "The Antebellum Political Economy and the Speaker's Contest of 1859." Paper presented at the annual meeting of the Social Science History Association.

Bond, Jon R., and Richard Fleisher. 1990. *The President in the Legislative Arena.* Chicago: University of Chicago Press.

Burns, James MacGregor. 1978. *Leadership.* New York: Harper and Row.

Cooper, Joseph. 1970. *The Origins of the Standing Committees and the Development of the Modern House.* Houston: Rice University Studies.

Cooper, Joseph, and David W. Brady. 1981. "Institutional Context and Leadership Style: The House from Cannon to Rayburn." *American Political Science Review* 75: 411–425.

Cunningham, Noble E., Jr. 1963. *The Jeffersonian Republicans in Power, 1801–1809.* Chapel Hill: Institute of Early American Culture and History, University of North Carolina Press.

_____. 1978. *The Process of Government Under Jefferson.* Princeton: Princeton University Press.

Currie, James T. 1988. *The United States House of Representatives.* Malabar, Fla.: Robert E. Krieger Publishing.

de Boinville, Barbara R., ed. 1982. *Origins and Development of Congress.* 2d ed. Washington, D.C.: Congressional Quarterly Press.

Farrand, Max. [1937] 1966. *The Records of the Federal Convention of 1787.* 3 vols. New Haven: Yale University Press.

Fiorina, Morris P., and Kenneth A. Shepsle. 1989. "Formal Theories of Leadership: Agents, Agenda Setters, and Entrepreneurs." In *Leadership and Politics,* edited by Bryan D. Jones. Lawrence: University Press of Kansas.

Fischer, David Hackett. 1965. *The Revolution of American Conservatism.* New York: Harper and Row.

Follett, Mary Parker. 1909. *The Speaker of the House of Representatives.* New York: Longmans, Green.

Fuller, Hubert Bruce. 1909. *The Speakers of the House.* Boston: Little, Brown.

Furlong, Patrick J. 1968. "The Origin of the House Committee of Ways and Means." *William and Mary Quarterly,* 3d Series, 25:587–604.

Hargrove, Erwin C. 1989. "Two Conceptions of Institutional Leadership." In *Leadership and Politics,* edited by Bryan D. Jones. Lawrence: University Press of Kansas.

Hoadley, John F. 1986. *Origins of American Political Parties, 1789–1803.* Lexington: University Press of Kentucky .

Hofstadter, Richard F. 1972. *The Idea of a Party System.* Berkeley: University of California Press.

Horsman, Reginald. 1962. *The Causes of the War of 1812.* New York: A. A. Barnes.

Jillson, Calvin, and Rick K. Wilson. 1994. *Congressional Dynamics: Structure, Coordination, & Choice in the First American Congress, 1774–1789.* Stanford: Stanford University Press.

Jones, Charles O. 1981. "House Leadership in an Age of Reform." In *Understanding Congressional Leadership,* edited by Frank H. Mackaman. Washington, D.C.: Congressional Quarterly Press.

Madison, James. [1787] 1975. "Vices of the Political System of the United States." In *The Papers of James Madison,* edited by Robert A. Rutland. Chicago: University of Chicago Press.

Malbin, Michael J. 1979. *Unelected Representatives*. New York: Basic Books.

Malone, Dumas. 1970. *Jefferson the President: First Term, 1801–1805*. Boston: Little, Brown.

_____. 1974. *Jefferson the President: Second Term, 1805–1809*. Boston: Little, Brown.

Martis, Kenneth C. 1989. *The Historical Atlas of Political Parties in the United States Congress, 1789–1989*. New York: Macmillan.

Peters, Ronald M., Jr. 1990. *The American Speakership: The Office in Historical Perspective*. Baltimore: Johns Hopkins University Press.

Peterson, Mark A. 1990. *Legislating Together*. Cambridge: Harvard University Press.

Poole, Keith T., and Howard Rosenthal. 1997. *Congress: A Political-Economic History of Roll Call Voting*. New York: Oxford University Press.

Remini, Robert V. 1991. *Henry Clay: Statesman for the Union*. New York: W.W. Norton.

Rossiter, Clinton, ed. 1961. James Madison, Alexander Hamilton, and John Jay, *The Federalist Papers*. New York: New American Library.

Sellers, Charles Grier, Jr. 1957. *James K. Polk, Jacksonian: 1795–1843*. Princeton: Princeton University Press.

Silbey, Joel H. 1989. "After 'The First Northern Victory': The Republican Party Comes to Congress." *Journal of Interdisciplinary History* 20:1–24.

_____. 1991. *The American Political Nation, 1838–1893*. Stanford: Stanford University Press.

Strahan, Randall. 1994. "Congressional Leadership in Institutional Time: The Case of Henry Clay." Paper prepared for delivery at the annual meeting of the American Political Science Association.

Swift, Elaine K. 1996. *The Making of an American Senate: Reconstitutive Change in Congress, 1787–1841*. Ann Arbor: University of Michigan Press.

Swift, Elaine K., Brookshire, Robert R., Canon, David T., Fink, Evelyn C., Hibbing, John, Malbin, Michael J., and Martis, Kenneth C. Forthcoming. *Relational Database of the U.S. Congress, 1788–1993*. Ann Arbor: Inter-University Consortium on Political and Social Research.

Watts, Steven. 1987. *The Republic Reborn*. Baltimore: Johns Hopkins University Press.

Wayland, Francis Fry. 1949. *Andrew Stevenson: Democrat and Diplomat, 1785–1857*. Philadelphia: University of Pennsylvania Press.

White, Leonard D. 1951. *The Jeffersonians*. New York: Free Press.

Wood, Gordon S. 1969. *The Creation of the American Republic, 1776–1787*. New York: W. W. Norton.

Young, James Sterling. 1966. *The Washington Community*. New York: Columbia University Press.

2

Thomas Brackett Reed and the Rise of Party Government

Randall Strahan

The second half of the nineteenth century was the heyday of political parties in the United States, with parties attracting strong support from voters, controlling the selection of officeholders, and structuring congressional voting to a degree not seen before or since. The development of leadership in the House of Representatives from the Civil War through the end of the century was therefore strongly influenced by party politics and ideas about party government. A number of leaders who served during that period contributed to the growing influence of the speakership and of the majority party in directing the business of the House of Representatives. Of these, the most important was undoubtedly Republican Thomas Brackett Reed of Maine, Speaker from 1889 to 1891 and from 1895 to 1899. Reed engineered a major revision of House rules during the Fifty-first Congress, ending minority obstructionism and placing control over the House firmly in the hands of the majority party leadership. Yet after successfully leading the House for three Congresses by means of the centralized leadership regime he helped to create, and with his party ascendant in the wake of the 1896 and 1898 elections, Reed resigned the Speaker's office in 1899 rather than continue to lead a Republican majority bent on annexation of the Philippines, a policy with which he strongly disagreed.

In this chapter I examine the role of leadership in the House from 1869 through 1899, focusing on the contributions of Thomas B. Reed to the emergence of a centralized party government regime in the 1890s. I first survey major political developments that influenced the politics of the House during those decades, describe important changes in House rules and organization, and note briefly the contributions of each of the five Speakers who served from 1869 to 1889. I then turn to the political career of Thomas B. Reed and his role in the establishment of party government in the House. Reed's strategic use of the speakership to restructure House rules in 1890, his leadership style and legislative efforts during the three Congresses he served as Speaker, and his decision to resign from the House in 1899 are considered in turn. Finally, I assess Reed's influence on the institutional development of the House and consider what lessons his speakership offers for understanding congressional leadership.

House Leadership, 1869–1889

"The House of Representatives," James Madison observed in *The Federalist* No. 57, "is so constituted as to support in the members an habitual recollection of their dependence on the people" (Rossiter 1961, 352). Whether in the late nineteenth century, or today, politics and opportunities for the exercise of leadership in the House are determined in large part by political developments and conditions outside the chamber.

This openness to, or dependence on, those outside the institution is characteristic to some extent of all legislatures but is by design a continuous influence in the politics of the U.S. House. When looking at the role of leadership and the development of party government in the House of the late nineteenth century, it is important first to look outside Congress at some of the broad contours of U.S. politics during the period.

One very useful framework for understanding the influence of external political developments on congressional politics has been proposed by political scientist Joseph Cooper (1981). In Cooper's framework, the politics and operation of the House are understood as the product of four situational factors—electoral politics, the governmental agenda, executive-legislative relations, and public opinion on questions of institutional legitimacy—that interact within limits defined by relatively fixed features of the U.S. political system. The stability found in many aspects of congressional politics, according to Cooper, is traceable to broadly shared ideas about democratic procedures embedded in U.S. political culture; constitutional forms, including those that structure relationships with the electorate and the executive; and the basic lawmaking and oversight functions Congress is expected to perform. These "fixed parameters" circumscribe the range of possibilities for the organization and operation of the House, including opportunities for exercising leadership. However, within these parameters, the politics of the House and the prospects for leadership are shaped by the interplay of the four political factors, which may vary considerably over time.

The Political Context

When considering the politics of the House during the second half of the nineteenth century, it is clear that electoral factors, particularly developments related to political parties, are of paramount importance. Few would question historian Morton Keller's observation that "the most distinctive feature of late nineteenth century American politics was its domination by highly organized parties and professional politicians" (Keller 1977, 522). Ronald M. Peters, Jr. (1990, 51), described the period from 1861 to 1910 as the "partisan speakership," an era "in which the speakership of the House became an artifact and architect of party government in the United States." Some, focusing on patterns in congressional voting, place the zenith of strong parties in the issues and electoral alignments of the 1890s (Cooper and Brady 1981; Brady 1988, 14–16, 65–81); others, focusing more on control exercised by party organizations over patronage, nominations, and campaigns, note the gathering force of reformist elements in the late nineteenth century and place the high point of party influence in the 1870s and 1880s (Keller 1977, 522; Silbey 1991b; Mayhew

1991). Whatever indicator is used to determine the precise point at which party strength peaked, the era was marked by strong partisan attachments, resilient patronage-based party organizations, and, especially in the later years, high levels of party voting in Congress.

Developments in party politics are considered by a number of students of the period as the key to understanding the emergence of centralized leadership in the House. Two possible linkages between party strength and House leadership have been identified. Peter Swenson emphasized the role of hierarchical party organizations in recruiting and socializing members: "[T]he emerging party 'machines' produced indirectly a 'machine Congress'—an autocratic, centralized, and therefore radically different institution that met the needs and expectations of a new breed of politician" (Swenson 1982, 11). In this view, politicians accustomed to receiving benefits for deferring to party machines over time created a similar system in the House. A second view holds that the critical factor in the rise of party government in the House was increased Republican party unity during the 1880s and 1890s. This increased party cohesion has been shown to have coincided with increased polarization of the two parties' electoral constituencies along agricultural and industrial lines (Cooper and Brady 1981; see also Rohde and Shepsle 1987). In this perspective party government arose in the House not simply as a reflection of party members' similar experiences in party organizations but as a consequence of increased party unity arising from the issues and electoral alignments that were present toward the end of the century.

Other electoral factors that influenced House politics during this period were size and turnover in membership. As the population grew and new states were admitted to the Union, the number of members elected to the House increased from 243 in 1868 to 357 in 1898.[1] That period also marked the transition from the high levels of turnover characteristic of the early House to the longer careers that became the norm in the twentieth century. The mean percentage of new House members elected to the Congresses between 1869 and 1879 was 50.3. The mean percentage of new members declined to around 40 percent for the Congresses in the 1880s and 1890s (39.9 and 41.3 percent, respectively). Mean terms of service likewise began a steady upward trend during those years, increasing from 2.04 in 1869 to 2.79 in 1899 (Polsby 1968, 146–147). Though a long-running—and as yet unresolved—scholarly debate has arisen regarding the causes and longer-term institutional consequences of the increased careerism that began to appear around the turn of the century, for present purposes it is sufficient to note that it was a period in which the size of the chamber continued to increase and in which relatively few experienced legislators were to be found among the membership of the House.[2] Party leaders had to contend with a growing legislative body but had considerable leeway when few members could claim influence on the basis of congressional experience or substantive expertise.

A final important feature of electoral politics affecting the House during the late 1800s was that both parties were highly competitive nationally. Of the fifteen Congresses between 1869 and 1899, Democrats controlled the House for eight (Forty-fourth–Forty-sixth, Forty-eighth–Fiftieth, Forty-second, Forty-third) and Republicans for seven (Forty-first–Forty-third, Forty-seventh, Fifty-first, Fifty-fourth, Fifty-fifth). Although Republicans were the principal proponents of majoritarian party government and Democrats of the rights of the minority, frequent changes in party control may well have tempered both parties' natural tendencies with regard to the rights of the majority and the minority. Because Democratic leaders were regularly required to take up the task of managing the business of the House, procedural innovations redounding to the authority of the leadership took on a more bipartisan cast than one might have expected from the partisan rhetoric of the period. Republicans had greater success in maintaining control of the Senate (thirteen of the fifteen Congresses) and the presidency (six of eight elections). Both houses of Congress and the White House were under Republican control from 1869 to 1875, but in a pattern that looks remarkably familiar a century later, divided party government (in which at least one institution was under the control of the opposition party) was present during fourteen of the twenty-two years from 1875 to 1899.

A second set of factors that influenced House politics consisted of those that related to the agenda and workload. In the broadest terms, the governmental agenda during this period focused initially on issues arising from the Civil War and Reconstruction, then shifted primarily to economic issues. Historians of the period have described a transition from a highly charged, ideological post–Civil War politics centered on an activist national government to a more organizational, localistic politics focused on patronage and management of the social and economic conflicts that arose from continued economic development (Keller 1977; Morgan 1969). Republican President Rutherford B. Hayes, writing in his personal diary, described the political situation in the late 1870s thus: "We are in a period when old questions are settled, and the new ones are not yet brought forward. Extreme party action, if continued in such a time would ruin the party. Moderation is its only chance" (quoted in Morgan 1969, 56). Economic issues were repeatedly pushed to the fore by conflicts among regional, sectoral, and class interests, conflicts heightened by downward movement in prices and increasingly severe economic downturns in 1873–1878, 1882–1885, and 1893–1897. After a long period in which domestic concerns dominated congressional politics, foreign policy issues related to the Spanish-American War and territorial expansion in the Caribbean and Pacific became prominent at the end of the century.

David Brady's work on congressional voting in the nineteenth century offers a more precise characterization of the agenda in the House of Representatives at the beginning and ending points of this period. Brady identified five major issue dimensions that structured House voting into the early 1870s and found seven voting dimensions present in the 1890s. Of greatest importance in the earlier period were civil rights, public works, railroad and telegraph construction, money and banking, and tariffs (Brady 1988, 41–46). Public works, tariffs, and currency issues remained important dimensions in House voting in the 1890s; to these were added issues of territorial expansion, business regulation, immigration, and taxation (Brady 1988, 73–81). Other issues occupied the House over the 1869–1899 period— Civil Service reform and pensions, for example—but the principal issues facing congressional parties and leaders were economic.

From a party government perspective, a fundamental problem posed by the persistence of tariff and currency issues was the divergent economic and regional interests represented in each party. Both parties had sectional bases of strength: Republicans in the North, upper Midwest, and West; Democrats in the South, lower Midwest, and Southwest. And both parties, at least until the mid-1890s, also experienced sharp factional splits over economic policy. House Democrats, though generally supportive of the inflationary currency policies and lower tariffs popular in their southern base, had also to contend with sizable protectionist and hard-money wings in building party majorities. Congressional Republicans were less factionalized on tariff questions but experienced divisions on currency issues as a result of differing interests of eastern and western constituencies (Morgan 1969, 43–51, 165–170; Brady 1988, 53–55, 77). Prior to the realigning elections of 1894 and 1896, both parties' coalitions were threatened by the rise of agrarian discontent, with Republicans standing to lose the most support in the Midwest and West and Democrats in the South. Worth noting as well from a party government perspective is that partisan attachments for many during this period were rooted as much in local conflicts and ethnic-cultural loyalties and resentments as in national issues (Kelley 1977, 544–548; Silbey 1991a, 162–165), further complicating the task of maintaining unity among partisans at the national level.

Finally, the House of the late nineteenth century was faced with a growing workload. As shown by the data in Table 2.1, the number of public bills introduced in the House increased only modestly, but private bills and petitions more than tripled from the 1870s through the 1890s. Private bills during this period dealt primarily with compensation for war damage and veterans' pensions, whereas petitions were received on a very

TABLE 2.1   Public Bills, Private Bills, and Petitions Introduced in the House of Representatives, 42nd, 47th, and 52nd Congresses

Congress	Public Bills	Private Bills	Petitions
42nd (1871–1873)	2,207	1,845	6,788
47th (1881–1883)	2,398	5,287	15,059
52nd (1891–1893)	2,812	7,811	26,348

Source: Adapted from Joseph Cooper and Cheryl D. Young, "Bill Introduction in the Nineteenth Century: A Study of Institutional Change," *Legislative Studies Quarterly* 14 (1989): 84–85.

broad range of issues from tariffs and taxation to temperance and education (Thompson 1985, 42–48; Silbey 1991a, 184; Kennon and Rogers 1989, 195–96, 238).

Congressional leaders neither received nor accepted much in the way of direction from the executive in acting on this agenda. In the aftermath of the impeachment and near removal from office of Andrew Johnson, the post–Civil War years marked a low ebb in the influence of the executive in congressional politics. Leonard D. White (1958, 17–18) observed that "the curve of presidential power was upward" during the administrations from Grant to McKinley but that two mutually reinforcing features of late-nineteenth-century politics in the United States limited the upper range of executive influence. First, the constitutional system was generally understood to proscribe active presidential leadership of Congress, particularly of the type that seeks to mobilize public opinion in support of executive policy initiatives. Although the last three nineteenth-century presidents— Grover Cleveland, Benjamin Harrison, and William McKinley—on occasion spoke out publicly on policy matters, sustained attempts to mobilize public pressure on Congress were still deemed to be of questionable legitimacy (Tulis 1987, 84–87). Second, Lincoln's extraordinary conduct of the presidency notwithstanding, Republican party doctrine reflected its Whig antecedents on the question of relations between president and Congress. As Ohio Senator John Sherman characterized this doctrine in a letter to newly elected President Benjamin Harrison in 1888, "[t]he President should have no policy distinct from that of his party and that is better represented in Congress than in the executive" (quoted in Binkley 1962, 222; see also White 1958, 20–28). Grover Cleveland, the one Democrat to occupy the White House during this period, faced divided government six of the eight years he held office. Though he actively confronted Congress over pension bills (in the process exercising a record 301 vetoes in his first term) and pushed Congress to act on tariff and currency measures, he declared early in his administration: "I did not come here to legislate" (Morgan 1969, 270).

The principal instruments of presidential influence during this period were appointments and the executive veto. However, the assertion of presidential prerogatives by post–Civil War executives was largely defensive in character. Presidents Rutherford Hayes, Chester Arthur, and James Garfield clashed with the Senate in reestablishing some degree of independence in making executive branch appointments, and Hayes was forced to wield the veto repeatedly to block congressional efforts to overturn existing civil rights statutes through the device of appropriations "riders" (White 1958, 31–44). Only with the return of unified party control after 1896 and the reemergence of foreign policy issues on the national agenda did the presidency under William McKinley regularly work cooperatively with Congress in passing legislation. For the most part, late-nineteenth-century presidents reacted to congressional leaders rather than vice versa.

A final factor that defines the possibilities for leadership in the House is public opinion on matters of institutional legitimacy. Reform ideas were voiced throughout the period in response to revelations of corruption in public life. By the 1870s both parties were attentive to public concerns over corruption in the patronage system, as is evidenced by the creation of a Civil Service Commission in 1871 and the enactment of the Pendleton Civil Service Reform Act in 1883. Then, as now, members of Congress, and politicians generally, were held in low esteem. Yet calls for restructuring of parties, elections, and the civil service were largely the province of disaffected intellectuals and other "genteel reformers" and developed little political force prior to the turn of the century (Keller 1977, 268–275, 290–297, 312–314; Morgan 1969, 28–31). This was an era of "participatory partisanship" in which political attachments were strong, voters mobilized, and ideas of party loyalty and discipline widely understood and accepted by those involved in politics (Silbey 1991a).

In contrast to the congressional politics of the late twentieth century, the late-nineteenth-century setting was distinguished by strong parties and weak presidents. Partisan competition for control of national institutions was intense after 1875, and neither party was able to maintain consistent control of the House until the mid-1890s. Both parties had to deal with sharp factional divisions on the economic policy issues that dominated the agenda for most of this period, although the 1894 and 1896 elections created greater homogeneity in congressional parties and signaled Republican hegemony in national politics. With a steadily increasing workload, House leaders were faced with the problem of managing a larger but still mostly inexperienced membership. Because partisanship was the principal organizing factor in political life, partisan views provided the principal ground for establishing and justifying new institutional arrangements and forms of leadership.

From the vantage point of 1896, Mary Parker Follett (1896, 307) wrote: "The history of the House of Representatives shows that consolidation of power has been an inevitable development. Individual men have only emphasized and perhaps hastened that development. . . . Irrespective of party tenets, there is an inevitable tendency towards the centralization of power." Whether the political conditions of the late nineteenth century made centralized leadership in the House *inevitable*, or simply *possible*, is the central question in assessing the importance of leadership in the late-nineteenth-century House and one that I will consider in more detail. But first I survey the organizational developments that contributed to increased centralization of power in the hands of the majority party and the Speaker and discuss briefly the Speakers who served from 1869 to 1889. I then turn to Thomas B. Reed and his influence on the House over the decade that followed.

Organizational Developments

The tendency toward centralized control by the Speaker over the business of the House reached its completion with the adoption of the so-called Reed Rules in the Republican Fifty-first Congress (1889–1891). Speaker Reed's success in consolidating power in 1890, however, built upon a number of earlier organizational developments and precedents. Committee assignments had been made by the Speaker since 1790, a practice that provided nineteenth-century Speakers with a means of advancing party legislation and a store of punishments and rewards for individual members. During the 1870s and 1880s two additional developments added to the Speaker's prerogatives: increased discretion over recognition of members on the floor and assumption of the chairmanship of a standing Rules Committee with authority to expedite consideration of individual bills.

House rules adopted for the First Congress gave the Speaker authority to decide who would be recognized to speak if more than one member sought the floor. Initially understood primarily as a simple parliamentary function of deciding who had risen first, this power took on greater political significance as the House grew larger and the press of business intensified. A number of precedents established in the post–Civil War decades clarified and extended the Speaker's power of recognition. During the speakership of Republican James G. Blaine (1869–1875), the practice of granting precedence in floor recognition to members speaking on behalf of a reporting committee was formalized, and the principle was established that the Speaker would award recognition based on his judgment of the relative importance of the motions being offered (Hinds 1907, 875, 918). An even broader interpretation of the power of recognition was established in 1881 when Democrat Samuel J. Randall (Speaker from 1876 to 1881) ruled: "There is no power in the House itself to appeal from the recognition of the chair. The right of recognition is just as absolute in the chair as the judgment of the Supreme Court is absolute in the interpretation of the law" (House 1935, 838–839). As one historian of the House has pointed out, the consolidation of the Speaker's power over recognition during the 1880s "put members desiring recognition for measures not privileged wholly at the mercy of the chair" (Alexander 1916, 60). Speakers before Reed could and did use the power of recognition to reward and punish individual members seeking to advance constituency measures as well as to block movement of legislation the Speakers opposed for both personal and party reasons (Alexander 1916, 58–61; Follett 1896, 253–266).

Prior to 1880, the Rules Committee had functioned primarily as a select committee convened at the beginning of each Congress to review and make recommendations on House rules. The Speaker was first named chair of the committee in 1858. The potential influence of the committee expanded greatly when standing committee status was established under new rules adopted in 1880. Rulings by Speaker Randall the same year established that all proposed rules changes would be referred to the committee and that it could report on matters related to the rules of the House at any time. Interestingly, given its future development as a major instrument of House governance, the change to standing committee status excited little interest or controversy in the debate over adoption of the 1880 rules revision (U.S. House of Representatives Committee on Rules 1983, 55–61; Alexander 1916, 194–196; House 1935, 839–841).

Initial efforts to use the committee's newly established authority as a means to expedite House business came during the Republican-controlled Forty-seventh Congress (1881–1883). Thomas Reed, a newly appointed member of the committee, brought to the floor reports proposing rules changes to limit dilatory motions during consideration of contested election cases and to allow the rules to be suspended with a simple majority (rather than the normal two-thirds) to send a stalled tariff bill to conference (Alexander 1916, 196–204; U.S. House of Representatives Committee on Rules 1983, 61–63; Robinson 1930, 85–95). After the latter procedure was adopted in 1883, the Rules Committee, according to Alexander (1916, 204), "began to fill the public eye. Like Pandora's box it seemed to conceal surprising possibilities." During the Forty-eighth Congress (1883–1885), Democratic Speaker John G. Carlisle further heightened the prestige and visibility of the Rules Committee by initiating the practice of appointing the chairs of the Ways and Means and Appropriations Committees. Carlisle also continued the practice of reporting special orders during the period he served as Speaker (1883–

1889), although by one account this use of the Rules Committee was "still regarded as a practice of doubtful validity" in the late 1880s (U.S. House of Representatives Committee on Rules 1983, 64–65; see also Alexander 1916, 204–206).

By the 1880s the right of recognition and the chairmanship of the Rules Committee, together with the committee assignment power, gave the Speaker the potential to exert great influence over individual members and the now unwieldy order of business. The Speakers who occupied the office in the early post–Civil War years contributed to this pattern of development but were not in a position to consolidate power over the House. From the perspective of institutional prerogatives, those who served after 1880 were in a much stronger position. How each responded to the opportunities presented by political and institutional conditions during those years is the subject to which I now turn.

Leaders

Three Democrats and two Republicans held the office of Speaker over the years from 1869 to 1889: James G. Blaine (R-Maine), Michael C. Kerr (D-Indiana), Samuel J. Randall (D-Pennsylvania), J. Warren Keifer (R-Ohio), and John G. Carlisle (D-Kentucky). Partly because of their longer service (see Table 2.2) and partly because of their political skill and more active exercise of the powers of the office, Blaine, Randall, and Carlisle stand out in this group as leaders who left an imprint on the office and the institution. Kerr served only a short time, and Keifer was judged ineffectual by his contemporaries and left little mark as Speaker.

Along with Henry Clay and James K. Polk, James G. Blaine of Maine was one of the most prominent nineteenth-century U.S. politicians to hold the office of Speaker of the House. First elected to the House in 1862, Blaine was part of the Republican majority through the war years, served on the Rules Committee, and participated in formulating Reconstruction policies (Stanwood 1905, 60–104; Williams 1995, 177). As Speaker from 1869 to 1875, Blaine actively used the powers of the office, particularly the right of recognition, to influence the politics of the House. He was known to have withheld recognition from members until legislative measures they wished to propose were altered to his satisfaction (Follett 1896, 103–104, 261–262), and he regularized the use of a "Speaker's list" of members to be recognized as a means of bringing order to floor proceedings (Peters 1990, 56). In one prominent instance Blaine used both the power of recognition and committee appointments to thwart enactment of Reconstruction legislation he opposed, even though it had considerable support within the party (Stanwood 1905, 112–120; Follett 1896, 105, 261).

TABLE 2.2   Speakers of the House and Party Control of the House, Senate, and Presidency, 1869–1889

Speaker	Congress	Party Division in House[a]	Party Control Senate	Party Control Presidency
James G. Blaine (R-ME)	41st (1869–1871)	170R/73D	R	R
	42nd (1871–1873)	139R/104D	R	R
	43rd (1873–1875)	203R/88D	R	R
Michael C. Kerr (D-IN)	44th (1875–1876) Died in office	181D/107R/3	R	R
Samuel G. Randall (D-PA)	44th (1876–1877)			
	45th (1877–1879)	156D/137R	R	R
	46th (1879–1881)	150D/128R/14	D	R
J. Warren Keifer (R-OH)	47th (1881–1883)	152R/130D/11	R	R
John G. Carlisle (D-KY)	48th (1883–1885)	200D/119R/6	R	R
	49th (1885–1887)	182D/140R/2	R	D
	50th (1887–1889)	170D/151R/4	R	D

[a]D = Democratic; R = Republican. Numbers with neither D nor R indicate members from other parties.
    Source: Adapted from Norman J. Ornstein, Thomas E. Mann, and Michael J. Malbin, *Vital Statistics on Congress, 1993–1994* (Washington, D.C.: CQ Press, 1994), p. 40, table 1-18.

Although Follett reported (1896, 103) that some thought Blaine "managed the minority rather too summarily," Blaine's speakership is notable both for its expansive exercise of the prerogatives of the chair and for its continued tolerance of minority obstructionism. During his final Congress as Speaker, Blaine refused requests to end the practice of the "disappearing quorum," when opponents of a "force" bill in 1875 brought the business of the House to a halt by refusing to vote. "There can be no record [of a quorum] like the call of the yeas and nays," Blaine responded, "and from that there is no appeal." Acknowledging the continued strength of notions of minority rights and the potential for abuse of such a power, he added: "The moment you clothe the Speaker with power to go behind your roll-call and assume there is a quorum in the hall, why, gentlemen, you stand on the very brink of a volcano."[3]

In 1874 Democrats took control of the House for the first time since the Civil War. Though Samuel J. Randall of Pennsylvania had been the principal leader of the Democratic minority during the previous Congresses, the Democrats' desire to select a more unifying figure to lead the newly resurgent party resulted in the election of Michael Kerr of Indiana as the first postwar Democratic Speaker. Kerr had little opportunity to establish a distinctive Democratic speakership, as he fell ill and died after less than a year in office. After Kerr's death in 1876, Randall was elected Speaker and held the office until Republicans regained control of the House in 1881. Randall, a unionist Democrat who represented a waterfront district in Philadelphia, had entered the House the same year as Blaine (1862) but had made a national reputation by leading opposition to Republican reconstruction policies. He was also known as a strong proponent of economy in government during his tenure on the House Appropriations Committee. Randall's initial failure to win the speakership occurred in part because of his active leadership of a northern, urban wing of the party that favored high protective tariffs and was thus at odds with Democrats from the South and predominantly agrarian regions (Morgan 1969, 81–82; Peters 1990, 59; Kehl 1995, 1666). In this respect Randall both led the Democratic party in the House and symbolized one of the major problems it faced in achieving unity when governing.

Randall's most important contribution as Speaker was a revision in House rules enacted under his direction in 1880. The total number of House rules was reduced from over 150 to 44, and changes were made to streamline voting procedures and bring greater regularity to the deliberations of the House when sitting as the Committee of the Whole. As noted earlier, the 1880 rules also conferred standing committee status on the Rules Committee and provided that the panel would have exclusive jurisdiction over matters pertaining to the rules of the House. In retrospect, this change in the status of the Rules Committee stands out as an important institutional innovation because it established one of the principal instruments of the system of majoritarian party governance that would emerge over the next decade (House 1935; Peters 1990, 58).

But it is not at all clear that Randall or the bipartisan group that unanimously reported the new rules package to the House in December 1879 intended to lay the foundations for a new type of party government. The committee's report to the House indicated that the objective of the revision was to "simplify, revise and codify" and stated that the revision "neither surrenders the right of a majority to control business for which it is held responsible, nor invades the powers of a minority to check temporarily, if not permanently, the action of a majority believed to be improper or unconstitutional" (quoted in Alexander 1916, 194). Randall did, as noted before, hand down important rulings from the chair that eliminated the right of appeal of the Speaker's decision on floor recognition and established the precedent for the authority of the Rules Committee to report at will. However, as Peters noted (1990, 58), he also remained "as firmly committed to the preservation of those rules favoring minority obstructionism as he had been as a minority leader." That Randall's speak-

ership is an important one in the institutional development of the House
is clear; whether his contribution should be understood as one intended
to advance possibilities for party governance or simply to restore some
degree of parliamentary order to the House is an open question.[4]

Republicans regained the majority during the Forty-seventh Congress
(1881–1883) but, with no leading figure present, required sixteen ballots
to elect J. Warren Keifer of Ohio Speaker. Keifer had been elected to the
House in 1876 and was distinguished primarily by his identification with
the Stalwart faction in the party and his geographical base in the
Midwest. As Speaker he made what were widely judged to be unsuitable
committee assignments, handed down ill-considered rulings that "won
him the contempt of Republicans as well as Democrats," and brought the
taint of nepotism to the speakership by appointing family members to
staff positions (Follett 1896, 113–114; see also Peters 1990, 59). The
Pendleton Civil Service Reform Act and a number of other major pieces of
legislation passed the House during Keifer's tenure, but he exercised little if any independent influence on the development of the House or of
the speakership.

Control of the House returned to the Democratic party in 1883, where it
remained for three Congresses (Forty-eighth, Forty-ninth, and Fiftieth).
Although Samuel G. Randall sought reelection to the speakership, a three-
way contest developed among Randall, Samuel S. Cox of New York, and
John G. Carlisle of Kentucky. Aided by former Ways and Means
Committee chairman William R. Morrison of Illinois and pledged to advance the cause of tariff reform, Carlisle won on the first ballot (Alexander
1916, 241; Barnes 1931, 67–71).[5] Carlisle had been elected to the House in
1876, had served on the Ways and Means Committee, and by 1883 was regarded as an effective parliamentarian and prominent spokesman for the
interests of the South and for the cause of tariff reduction (Barnes 1931,
28–63). According to biographer James A. Barnes, "Carlisle had come to
the speakership with two fundamental principles: to carry out the will of
his party as interpreted by himself in regard to tariff reform, and to protect
the constitutional rights of the minority" (1931, 151).

For each of the three Congresses in which Carlisle served as Speaker,
the issue of tariff reform dominated the agenda of the House. Carlisle had
appointed Randall to chair the Appropriations Committee, which served
as a significant power base because of its control over spending measures,
privileged access to the floor, and capacity to legislate under the Holman
rule.[6] In a striking demonstration of the lack of deference to leadership
exhibited by some nineteenth-century partisans, Randall used his committee position to organize opposition to the Speaker's goal of tariff reduction. Voting with the Republican minority, Randall and forty
Democratic colleagues (dubbed "Randall and the forty thieves" by tariff

reformers) were successful in blocking consideration of tariff legislation during the Forty-eighth Congress (Alexander 1916, 241; Barnes 1931, 78–81). At the outset of the Forty-ninth Congress, Speaker Carlisle rejected requests that he enforce party discipline by removing Randall as Appropriations chair but did use the Rules Committee to propose rules changes that redistributed jurisdiction over appropriations measures from Randall's appropriations panel to five House committees and repealed the Holman rule. Undaunted, Randall again organized bipartisan coalitions that blocked two more attempts by the Speaker to pass tariff legislation during the Forty-ninth Congress (Barnes 1931, 95–109).

With the support of Democratic President Grover Cleveland, Speaker Carlisle finally succeeded in winning House passage of tariff legislation in 1888 during the Fiftieth Congress.[7] Carlisle actively used committee assignments to advance his legislative objectives and exercised the chair's power of recognition to block spending legislation that would have reduced the accumulating Treasury surplus and thereby relieved much of the pressure for tariff reductions (Follett 1896, 115–116; Alexander 1916, 69; Barnes 1931, 109, 131, 137, 152–154). Despite the skillful efforts of the Speaker to use the prerogatives of his office to manage the House, divisions in the Democratic party and Carlisle's refusal on principle to check the proliferation of obstructionist tactics—especially the disappearing quorum—frequently rendered the chamber immobile, and in the view of some caused his speakership to "come perilously near to being a failure" (Alexander 1916, 205).

Actions by Speakers of both parties over the 1869–1889 period laid the foundations for party governance. The use of committee assignments to advance the party's (or at least the Speaker's) legislative goals, the use of the power of recognition to control the agenda, and the use of the Rules Committee to restructure rules and procedures to the advantage of the majority were important steps toward this end. Still, the history of the House up to 1889 shows that the emergence of party government was *not* an inevitable product of late-nineteenth-century party politics. Many members and leaders recruited by hierarchical party organizations took seriously ideas about minority rights in the House, and strong state-centered party organizations consistently produced legislative parties that were rent by factions on the major issues on the national agenda.

At the beginning of the Fifty-first Congress, two important factors changed to alter the possibilities for new forms of leadership: The 1888 elections produced a more unified majority party than had been present in the Congresses of the previous decades, and a capable individual who was strongly committed to the idea of responsible party government was chosen Speaker. In exploring how leadership of the House changed during Thomas Reed's speakership (Fifty-first, Fifty-fourth, and Fifty-fifth

Congresses, 1889–1891, 1895–1899), it will be helpful first to look briefly at Reed's rise through the Republican ranks and the development of his views on House governance.

The Reed Speakership

Thomas Brackett Reed was first elected to the House in 1876, representing a district that included his home city of Portland, Maine. Prior to entering Congress he had attended Bowdoin College, done a stint in the Union navy, practiced law, served in both houses of the Maine legislature, and held the position of attorney general of Maine.[8] Although he received his initial nomination because of a conflict between the incumbent and the Maine Republican organization run by James G. Blaine and Senator Hannibal Hamlin, Reed was never very closely allied with the Republican leadership in the state. During his first term, Reed made a favorable impression as an articulate partisan and ably defended Republican interests as a minority member of a special committee charged with investigating voting fraud in the Hayes-Tilden presidential contest. Because of a surge in support for "greenbackism" in Maine, Reed experienced close races with greenback candidates in 1878 and 1880, after which he won re-election comfortably for the remainder of his House career. By his second and third terms, he had become a frequent participant in floor debates on both substantive and procedural issues.

The Rise to Power

When Republicans gained control of the House for the Forty-seventh Congress (1881–1883), Reed was appointed to the Rules Committee. In the aftermath of J. Warren Keifer's unhappy tenure as Speaker, Reed became the leader of the House Republicans and served as a member of both the Rules and the Ways and Means Committees during the three Democratic-controlled Congresses (Forty-eighth through Fiftieth) that followed. Over the course of twelve years in the House he had proven to be a forceful proponent of the main tenets of Republican orthodoxy: a system of protective tariffs, federal funding of public works, and a gold-backed currency. Reed's views on House governance evolved over the course of his House career, but by the time of his election to the speakership in 1889 he was firmly committed to the goal of establishing a system of party government in the House and had conceived a specific program of institutional reform to bring it about.

During his second term in the House, Reed had observed: "The best system is to have one party govern and the other party watch, and on general principles I think it would be better for us to govern and the

Democrats to watch" (quoted in McCall 1914, 82–83). But in the early years of his legislative career he shared the prevalent view that the minority had a legitimate right to delay legislation that it strongly opposed. When the procedural reform on which Reed would later stake his speakership—elimination of the "disappearing quorum"—was proposed in the course of the debate on the rules revision in 1880, Reed defended the right of the minority to refuse to vote even if the result was to delay action for want of a quorum. "It is a valuable privilege for the country," Reed argued, "that the minority shall have the right by this extraordinary mode of proceeding to call the attention of the country to measures which a party in a moment of madness and of party feeling is endeavoring to enforce upon the citizens of this land. And it works equally well with regard to all parties, for all parties have their times when they need to be checked."[9] However, from his third term on, Reed engaged in a continuing effort to establish a system of rules by which the Speaker and the majority party could both control and be held responsible for the actions of the House.

Utilizing his position on the Rules Committee, Reed began to act on his views on party government during the Forty-seventh Congress (1881–1883). In March 1882 he brought to the House floor a report proposing to change House rules to allow any measure to be brought up by a majority vote, but there was insufficient support among Republicans even to muster a quorum to debate the proposal. The following month, after members of the Democratic minority had blocked action for seven days on a contested election case, Reed brought forth a report from the Rules Committee establishing strict limitations on dilatory motions during consideration of election cases. When former Democratic Speaker Samuel J. Randall continued to offer delaying motions, Reed raised a point of order against dilatory motions during consideration of rules changes. The point of order was sustained by the Republican majority on appeal of Speaker Keifer's favorable ruling, and the rules change was adopted (Robinson 1930, 85–90; Alexander 1916, 196–202). In the debate on the Speaker's ruling, Reed made clear the view of the speakership that motivated his efforts: "Whenever it is imposed upon Congress to accomplish a certain work, it is the duty of the Speaker, who represents the House . . . to carry out that rule of law or of the Constitution. It then becomes his duty to see that no factious opposition prevents the House from doing its duty. He must brush away all unlawful combinations to misuse the rules and must hold the House strictly to its work."[10]

In the second session of the Forty-seventh Congress, Reed introduced on behalf of the Rules Committee the report discussed previously that made it in order to suspend the rules and send a tariff bill to conference with a simple majority vote. The action was heatedly denounced by the

Democratic minority and also came very close to the limits of what the Republican majority was willing to accept in the way of procedural innovations. As Alexander (1916, 204) described the situation:

> [Reed] was too shrewd to stake his growing prestige on this latest adventure without due warrant, so he spent several days in overcoming scruples and obtaining pledges. His precaution, however, scarcely justified his final action, for the disappearance of thirty-two members of his own party left him without a quorum. Even the next morning when he appeared with a file of recruits, failure stared him in the face until several Nationalists [a third party], suddenly seized with a desire to go on record in opposition, swelled the vote to a quorum.[11]

Democratic majorities in the three Congresses that followed (Forty-eighth through Fiftieth) supported Speaker Carlisle's use of special orders, committee appointments, and recognition to advance his legislative objectives but repudiated the new rules restricting dilatory motions and took no action on further proposals (some initiated by Reed) to place greater control over House business in the hands of the majority. By the Fiftieth Congress the result was what even Democrats agreed was unprecedented congestion in the legislative business of the House. Again, to quote Alexander (1916, 62): "By the time Carlisle had reached his third term as Speaker it became so easy to muster a sufficient number of disgruntled members to delay or prevent legislation that the House, in the Fiftieth Congress, although in continuous session longer than any of its predecessors, passed only one [major] measure except such as received unanimous consent."

Reed had received the nomination for Speaker from the Republican minority in both the Forty-ninth (1885–1887) and Fiftieth (1887–1889) Congresses but still encountered a contest for the office when Republicans caucused after winning a narrow House majority in the elections of 1888. Reed refused to engage in the common practice of exchanging commitments on legislation or committee assignments for support. He nonetheless succeeded in winning election to the speakership on the second ballot, besting his chief rival, William McKinley of Ohio, by eighty-five votes to thirty-eight (Robinson 1930, 195–198).[12]

In 1889, before the Fifty-first House convened, Speaker-elect Reed penned two essays elaborating his views of party government. In both he criticized the existing state of affairs in the House and advocated rules changes to allow the majority to govern. The only way to deal with the problem of minority obstruction, Reed wrote, "is to return to the first principles of democracy and republicanism alike. . . . It is the old doctrine that the majority must govern. Indeed, you have no choice. If the majority do not govern, the minority will; and if tyranny of the majority is hard,

TABLE 2.3   Speakers of the House and Party Control of the House, Senate, and Presidency, 1889–1899

Speaker	Congress	Party Division in House[a]	Party Control Senate	Party Control Presidency
Thomas B. Reed (R-ME)	51st (1889–1891)	173R/156D/1	R	R
Charles F. Crisp (D-GA)	52nd (1891–1893)	231D/88R/14	R	R
	53rd (1893–1895)	220D/126R/10	D	D
Thomas B. Reed (R-ME)	54th (1895–1897)	246R/104D/7	D	D
	55th (1897–1899)	206R/134D/16	R	R

[a]D = Democratic; R = Republican. Numbers with neither D nor R indicate members from other parties.
Source: Adapted from Norman J. Ornstein, Thomas E. Mann, and Michael J. Malbin, *Vital Statistics on Congress, 1993–1994* (Washington, D.C.: CQ Press, 1994), p. 40, table 1-18.

the tyranny of the minority is simply unendurable. The rules, then, ought to be arranged to facilitate action of the majority" (1889a, 794–795).

"When a legislative body makes rules," Reed argued in the second essay, "it does not make them as the people make constitutions, to limit power and provide for rights. They are made to facilitate the orderly and safe conduct of business" (1889b, 425). He noted also that when the House reconvened with a Republican majority, an effort would be made "to establish rules that will facilitate the public business—unlike those of the present House, which only delay and frustrate action" (1889b, 425).

Reed's Leadership in the Fifty-first Congress: Establishing Party Governance

In contrast to the situation in previous Congresses of the period, two factors encouraged increased partisan unity among the House Republican majority elected to the Fifty-first Congress. With Benjamin Harrison's defeat of Grover Cleveland, Republicans controlled both houses of Congress and the presidency for the first time in fourteen years (see Tables 2.2 and 2.3), and the party would have an opportunity to enact and take credit for a party program. Second, as Cooper and Brady (1981, 415) have shown, the constituency bases of the two major parties in the House were polarized along agricultural and industrial lines to a degree that would not reappear until the realigning elections of 1894 and 1896. These conditions, together with the frustrations and criticism that had surrounded the performance of the House in the previous Congress, created a "critical moment" in which an unusual opportunity was present for large-scale institutional innovation (see Strahan 1992, 1994, 1996).

As the newly elected Speaker, Reed seized the opportunity early in the Fifty-first Congress to complete his project of restructuring House rules. However, rather than beginning the session with a debate on new rules, Reed chose to operate under general parliamentary law. On January 29, 1890, the question before the House was a vote to take up a contested election case from West Virginia, Charles Smith versus James Jackson. The vote was 162 yeas, 3 nays, 163 not voting; at that point two Democratic members withdrew their votes. Because a quorum at the time consisted of 165 members and only 161 Republicans could be assembled on the floor, a change of two members to nonvoting status would have brought business to a halt for lack of a quorum. Amid cries from Democrats of "No quorum!" Reed broke with precedents traceable back to the 1830s by directing the clerk to record the names of members who were present but not voting. Reed's ruling that a quorum was present provoked intense protests from the floor and was immediately appealed by Democrat Charles R. Crisp of Georgia. The question was then debated before the House for two days. On the second day (January 31) Reed refused to entertain an appeal when he again counted a quorum on a vote to approve the Journal and, in response to a motion to adjourn offered by Democrat William Springer of Illinois, ruled that the Speaker would no longer entertain motions made only for purposes of delay. Each of the Speaker's rulings was sustained by the Republican majority, clearing the way for the introduction and enactment of a major revision of House rules in February.

The Reed Rules, adopted in February 1890, consolidated the Speaker's ability to manage the business of the House with the support of a party majority by changing House procedures in four areas: dilatory motions would no longer be entertained; nonvoting members would be counted as present for purposes of establishing a quorum; procedures for debating and amending bills in the Committee of the Whole were restructured and the quorum reduced to 100 members; and changes were made in the order of business, including granting the Speaker power to refer measures to committee without debate and formal recognition of the practice of adopting special orders, reported by the Rules Committee, by a simple majority vote (see Alexander 1916, 206, 220–222; Robinson 1930, 223–231).[13]

Reed's determination to establish the conditions for party government in the House and his skillful use of the speakership to effect these changes must be taken into account along with contextual factors in explaining the institutional changes that occurred in the Fifty-first Congress. It was not accidental that Reed delayed introducing a package of rules until after the session began. By forcing the issue of the Speaker's authority to count a quorum and refuse dilatory motions in the intensely partisan atmosphere of a contested election case, Reed acted strategically to mobilize Republican support for procedural innovations under the most favorable possible conditions (Robinson 1930, 220). Only after the Speaker won support of his rulings from the chair did he attempt to bring to the floor the report containing the revised rules. Reed himself was uncertain of success and had quietly made plans beforehand to resign the House and join a New York law firm if the House failed to sustain his rulings (McCall 1914, 167). As he later recalled in an interview with the Lewiston, Maine, *Evening Journal:*

> I knew just what I was going to do if the House did not sustain me. . . . I should simply have left the chair, resigning the speakership and my seat in Congress. There were other things that could be done, you know, outside of political life, and for my own part I had made up my mind that if political life consisted of sitting helplessly in the chair and seeing the majority powerless to pass legislation, I had had enough of it and was ready to step down and out. (Quoted in Offenberg 1963, 95–96)

Although it seems unlikely that the more homogeneous Republican majorities of the 1890s would have continued indefinitely to tolerate minority obstructionism, a more cautious leader might have been hesitant to risk sweeping reform with such a narrow majority (173 to 156), and a less skilled parliamentary strategist might have botched the task of maintaining majority support for the succession of precedent-breaking rulings that were required to succeed.

Reed's Leadership Style

As Speaker, Reed employed all of the powers at his disposal to keep the House in order and advance the legislative objectives of the Republican majority. He used committee assignments (or in one important case the withholding of committee assignments[14]), the power of recognition, and control of the Rules Committee to maintain control of the flow of business. In an often-quoted quip that illustrates both Reed's sense of humor and his method of using special orders to manage debates in the House, the Speaker once told Benton McMillin, a member of the Democratic minority on the Rules Committee: "Well, Mac, Joe [Cannon], McKinley and I [the Republican members] have decided to perpetrate the following outrage, of which we all desire you to have due notice" (Robinson 1930, 238).

Ironically, in a House well stocked with machine politicians, Reed was a cerebral type who had a distaste for distributive logrolling and patronage politics. His attitude toward patronage was reflected in a letter to one Professor Henry L. Chapman of Bowdoin College, who had written to Reed seeking his assistance in the appointment of a local postmaster:

Between you and me I have such a dread of these post office fights that I feel every time I hear of one in the air that I ought to call on every good friend for his sympathy and good wishes that I may be happily and safely delivered thereof. The man who gets appointed knows that it is owing to his own virtues and the man who don't, and his friends, are sure to doubt me being a statesman even if they acquit me of corrupt motives. But then I suppose even Professors have their troubles. In the shoes of all mankind there is sand and also unboiled peas (Reed 1884).

During his tenure as Speaker, Reed became well known for his willingness to block bills for local projects, a practice that limited the breadth of his regional support when he sought the presidency in 1896 (Robinson 1930, 158–159, 250–251). By all accounts Reed also refused to promise committee positions in seeking the speakership and executive appointments in his campaign for the presidency. As Morton Keller observed (1977, 302), Reed's approach to leadership was something of a throwback to an earlier era before patronage matters came to dominate party politics.

Reed and Party Governance, 1889–1899

Because of Reed's success in restructuring the rules, the legislative productivity of the House increased dramatically during the Fifty-first Congress. A major tariff bill requested by President Harrison and drafted by Ways and Means Committee chairman William McKinley was enacted in May 1890. Seeking to fulfill long-standing Republican commitments to protect black voting rights in the South, the majority also imposed strict limits on debate and passed an election bill providing for federal boards to oversee voting where irregularities had occurred. As growing agrarian discontent increased demands for inflationary currency policies from southern and western representatives, Reed kept proposals for unrestricted coinage of silver off the House floor. The tariff and currency issues had become linked in the Senate, where western Republicans demanded pro-silver legislation as a condition of supporting the tariff bill. The resulting Sherman Silver Purchase Act, which Reed shepherded to House passage, cleared the way for Senate passage of the McKinley tariff. The Fifty-first Congress also saw passage of the Sherman Anti-Trust Act and the act creating the Federal Circuit Courts of Appeal.

Total federal spending approved during the Fifty-first Congress exceeded $988 million, causing it to become known as the "billion dollar Congress" (Robinson 1930, 235–251; Morgan 1969, 325–353). In contrast to the strong support Reed received from his fellow Republicans, Democrats continued to question the propriety of the new mode of operation; at the adjournment of the Congress the minority demanded a roll call on the customary resolution thanking the Speaker for his service to the House, and 118 of 156 Democrats voted in opposition (Alexander 1916, 75).

Republican activism was rewarded with a sweeping defeat in the 1890 House elections. Democrats regained control of the House for the Fifty-second and Fifty-third Congresses (1891–1895) and elected Charles R. Crisp of Georgia to the speakership. One of the most vocal critics of the Reed Rules, Crisp oversaw adoption of a slightly modified version of the rules of the Fiftieth Congress, repudiating the prohibitions on dilatory motions and the disappearing quorum. Crisp also broke with the practice of appointing the chairs of Ways and Means and Appropriations to the Rules Committee, although he preserved the committee's authority to report special orders and included a provision restricting the motions that would be in order while its reports were under consideration (U.S. House of Representatives Committee on Rules 1983, 75–76). Because of the large Democratic majority present during this Congress, procedural questions receded somewhat, and attention was focused primarily on currency issues.

Although after 1892, Democrats controlled the White House and Congress for the first time since the Civil War, the Democratic majority in the House was narrower in the Fifty-third Congress, and its members were deeply divided on the currency and tariff issues that continued to dominate the congressional agenda. After convening early at the request of newly elected Democratic President Grover Cleveland, the House voted in 1893 to repeal the Sherman Silver Purchase Act, an action intended to restore confidence in the economy and one supported by Reed and many members of the Republican minority. On other matters, Reed and the Republicans turned the tables on their Democratic colleagues and repeatedly brought the business of the House to a halt by refusing to vote and by making motions requiring endless roll calls. Reed's actions forced Speaker Crisp to choose between losing control of the floor or reintroducing rules to check minority obstructionism. Finally, in April 1894, the Democratic majority chose to enact its own quorum-counting rule, vindicating Reed's position in the earlier debates over House rules. The major legislative action of the Fifty-third House involved passing the Wilson tariff bill, but the bill was heavily amended in the Senate and was seen by many as contributing to the country's deteriorating economic situation.

With Democrats discredited by a deepening economic crisis, Republicans regained control of the House by comfortable margins after 1894. Reed was returned to the Speaker's chair, and the Reed Rules were readopted with little debate at the beginning of the Fifty-fourth Congress. Reed had now become a national figure and competed unsuccessfully with former House colleague William McKinley for the 1896 Republican presidential nomination. With divided party control of Congress, little major action occurred on economic policy questions during the Fifty-fourth Congress. Instead, foreign policy matters, especially the issue of Cuban independence from Spain, began to occupy the attention of the country. After McKinley's decisive defeat of William Jennings Bryan in the 1896 presidential election and Republican gains in the Senate, unified government under Republican control returned after 1897. During the Fifty-fifth Congress, Reed's final period of service as Speaker, he steered the Dingley tariff bill to quick passage in an early special session but spent the remainder of the Congress occupied primarily with foreign policy issues (Robinson 1930, 351–354).

After the Cuban insurrection against Spain broke out in 1895, sentiment built in Congress for recognition of Cuban independence. Reed had kept resolutions to this effect off the floor during the Fifty-fourth Congress and the first part of the Fifty-fifth and was opposed to adopting a belligerent posture toward Spain. The Speaker also opposed efforts to expand U.S. territorial holdings in the Caribbean and the Pacific and criticized those who saw war with Spain as a means of achieving that goal. After the *Maine* incident in 1898, Reed had little choice but to acquiesce to overwhelming Republican support for recognition and war with Spain. Reed also found himself out of step with his party on the issue of annexation of Hawaii. After Reed had blocked action on the matter in the Rules Committee, a petition requesting that a resolution providing for annexation be brought to a vote began to circulate among House Republicans. When the resolution was finally brought up, it passed easily, 209–91 (Robinson 1930, 364–365).

Reed's resignation occurred in response to support by President McKinley and House Republicans for annexation of the Philippines, which had been ceded to the United States as part of the 1899 treaty ending the war with Spain. Though Reed had been returned to office for a twelfth term in 1898 and was expected to continue as Speaker, he resigned in September 1899 before the new Congress convened. In a letter to an old Maine friend who was abroad at the time, Reed explained his decision to step down:

> You can see that I was in a doubly impossible place. If I was again chosen Speaker, and nobody could have prevented that, my position would have been a representative's one and would not represent me. If I went on the floor I knew all too well how few followers I could muster until the people changed their minds. Hence it seemed to me that the best good of the cause would be subserved by doing what no man had yet done, resign a great place and people would then ask why and find out not by my direct outpourings but by their inferences. When a man finds a thing out for himself he's prouder of it than if it were told him by Shakespeare. Had I stayed I must have been as Speaker always in a false position aiding and organizing things in which I did not believe or using power against those who gave it to me. (1899)

Reed's voluntary departure demonstrated that his ambition to hold the speakership ended when he would have had to act as an agent of a party caucus with which he disagreed on a matter of principle. His resignation under these conditions also suggests strongly that responsible party governance rather than personal power had been his principal motivation in seeking and exercising the powers of the speakership.

Conclusion:
Leadership and the Rise of Party Government

The rise of party government in the late-nineteenth-century House of Representatives poses a number of important questions regarding leadership and institutional change in Congress. Among these is the question of the contribution of the active leaders of this era—James G. Blaine, Samuel J. Randall, John G. Carlisle, and especially Thomas B. Reed—to the institutional changes that placed effective control over House proceedings in the hands of the Speaker and the majority party. Most of the recent scholarship on Congress emphasizes contextual factors in explaining how the institution and its leadership change over time. From this perspective, effective leadership *reflects* rather than causes institutional or political change. The historical evidence presented in this chapter gives reason to question whether this view is an adequate explanation of the role of leadership in this important period in the development of the House.

The strongest statement of the contextual view holds that the emergence of a centralized party leadership regime in the nineteenth-century House was an inevitable consequence of the recruitment of legislators who were accustomed to working within hierarchical party organizations (Swenson 1982). Most late-nineteenth-century politicians were indeed accustomed to working within organizational hierarchies, but these were hierarchies that peaked at the local or state level (White 1958, 10–11; Keller 1977, 239–258, 531–544; Silbey 1991a, 1991b; Mayhew 1991). Working cooperatively with party members from other factions, states, and regions would not have been a familiar enterprise (see Marcus 1971). In fact, when the localized character of the party organizations of the period is taken into account, the emergence of a national party government regime in the House looks less like a natural or inevitable outgrowth of partisan politics and more like a political outcome in need of some further explanation. A less deterministic contextual explanation associates the rise of party government with greater homogeneity of interests within congressional parties due to new electoral alignments in the late 1880s and 1890s (Cooper and Brady 1981; Rohde and Shepsle 1987). Part of the explanation for this change no doubt is to be found in the new electoral alignments that weakened resistance to stronger leadership from dissident factions in both parties, but part is also to be found in House leaders' efforts to establish a workable system of governance in the House.

Speakers Blaine, Randall, and Carlisle helped create the possibility for party government by actively exercising the Speaker's prerogatives over standing committee assignments and recognition of members on the floor. Randall and Carlisle also helped legitimize what became one of the principal tools of party government, the use of special orders from the Committee on Rules to structure floor deliberations. However, as late as the Fiftieth Congress (1887–1889), the House was still well short of party government as both the minority party and factions in the majority party availed themselves of ample opportunities to obstruct legislative business. Only during the Fifty-first Congress (1889–1891) did the previous decades' uneven pattern of development toward increased control over the House by the Speaker and the majority party reach its completion in the enactment of the Reed Rules, transforming the operation of the House and its capacity to legislate. Thomas B. Reed made an important contribution to this transformation because he possessed the motivation and skill to take full advantage of the new opportunities for leadership presented by political developments in the late 1880s.

In conclusion, a simple contextual approach positing that party government in the House was an inevitable outgrowth of strong party organizations in the electorate does not take us very far in understanding the institutional development of the late-nineteenth-century House. A more satisfactory explanation involves the interplay between contextual factors (including a growing workload and new electoral alignments) that created opportunities for establishing new institutional forms, on the one hand, and actions by individual leaders in response to those changed political conditions, on the other. Students of leadership and institutional change in Congress need to be attentive both to contextual factors that create expectations for stability or demands for change and how strategically placed individuals and groups respond.[15] In some cases, as occurred in the 1880s and 1890s with Speaker Thomas Brackett Reed, leaders may play an important role in defining new institutional forms that alter the capabilities of the institution and the future course of its development.

NOTES

I gratefully acknowledge research support from the Dirksen Congressional Center; comments on an earlier version of this chapter from Joel Silbey, Joseph Cooper, and Susan Webb Hammond; and research assistance provided by Vincent Moscardelli.

1. Eight states were added to the Union between the elections of 1868 and 1898: Colorado (1876), Idaho (1890), Montana (1889), North Dakota (1889), South Dakota (1889), Utah (1896), Washington (1889), and Wyoming (1890).

2. At issue is the relationship among the electoral realignment of the 1890s, increased careerism, and the emergence of the seniority system. See Price 1977; Budgor et al. 1981; Swenson 1982; Stewart 1992a.

3. *Congressional Record,* 43d Cong., 2d sess., p. 1734. The force bill would have provided for additional federal supervision of elections in the South. Blaine was unsympathetic to the bill in question and Republican radicals and conservatives were divided on the issue (see Stanwood 1905, 117–120; Peters 1990, 56–57), facts that may also have made this an inopportune issue on which to test the extent of the Speaker's powers.

4. Albert V. House, Jr., observed (in one of the few studies that exist of Randall's speakership) that Thomas Reed's use of a special order from the Rules Committee to move a tariff bill to conference in 1883 gave Randall a "grim lesson in the 'legitimate' manipulation of this blossoming instrument of majority oppression" (House 1935, 841).

5. The vote was Carlisle, 106; Randall, 52; and Cox, 30.

6. Enacted in 1876, the Holman rule explicitly allowed substantive legislative provisions ("riders") in appropriations bills on the condition that they were germane to the bill and reduced expenditures (see Stewart 1989, 84–89).

7. All of Speaker Carlisle's efforts ultimately came to nothing, as the Mills Tariff (so called after Ways and Means Committee chairman Roger Q. Mills [D-Texas]) passed by the House in 1888 failed to emerge from the Republican-controlled Senate.

8. Unless otherwise noted, biographical information about Reed is drawn from Robinson (1930) and McCall (1914).

9. *Congressional Record,* 46th Cong., 2d sess., pp. 578–579.

10. *Congressional Record,* 47th Cong., 1st sess., p. 4306.

11. It is not clear from Alexander's account whether the Republicans opposed the tariff bill or opposed further limits on the rights of the minority.

12. The complete breakdown of the vote was Reed, 85; McKinley, 38; Joseph G. Cannon of Illinois, 19; David B. Henderson of Iowa, 14; and Julius Caesar Burrows of Michigan, 10.

13. These special orders, today known commonly as rules, allow measures to be taken from House calendars and brought up for debate on the floor of the House by means of a simple majority vote.

14. In the early special session of the Fifty-fifth Congress, Reed withheld all committee assignments until action was completed on tariff legislation.

15. For examples of studies that consider both the contextual and individual contributions to important institutional developments in Congress, see Gamm and Shepsle (1989); Swift (1989, 1996).

REFERENCES

Alexander, De Alva Stanwood. 1916. *History and Procedure of the House of Representatives.* Boston: Houghton Mifflin.

Barnes, James A. 1931. *John G. Carlisle: Financial Statesman.* New York: Dodd, Mead.

Binkley, Wilfred E. 1962. *President and Congress,* 3d rev. ed. New York: Vintage Books.

Bogue, Allan G. 1991. "Legislative Government in the United States Congress, 1800–1900." In L. Sandy Maisel, ed., *Political Parties and Elections in the United States.* Vol. 1. New York: Garland.

Brady, David W. 1988. *Critical Elections and Congressional Policymaking.* Stanford, Calif.: Stanford University Press.

Budgor, Joel, Elizabeth A. Capell, David A. Flanders, Nelson W. Polsby, Mark C. Westlye, and John Zaller. 1981. "The 1896 Election and Congressional Modernization: An Appraisal of the Evidence." *Social Science History* 5: 53–90.

Cooper, Joseph. 1981. "Organization and Innovation in the House of Representatives." In Joseph Cooper and G. Calvin Mackenzie, eds., *The House at Work.* Austin: University of Texas Press.

Cooper, Joseph, and David W. Brady. 1981. "Institutional Context and Leadership Style: The House from Cannon to Rayburn." *American Political Science Review* 75: 411–425.

Cooper, Joseph, and Cheryl D. Young. 1989. "Bill Introduction in the Nineteenth Century: A Study of Institutional Change." *Legislative Studies Quarterly* 14: 67–105.

Follett, M. P. 1896. *The Speaker of the House of Representatives.* London: Longmans, Green.

Gamm, Gerald, and Kenneth Shepsle. 1989. "Emergence of Legislative Institutions: Standing Committees in the House and Senate: 1810–1825." *Legislative Studies Quarterly* 14: 39–66.

Hinds, Asher C. 1907. *Hind's Precedents of the House of Representatives of the United States.* Vol. 2. Washington, D.C.: Government Printing Office.

House, Albert V., Jr. 1935. "The Contributions of Samuel J. Randall to the Rules of the National House of Representatives." *American Political Science Review* 29: 837–841.

Kehl, James A. 1995. "Samuel J. Randall." In Donald C. Bacon, Roger H. Davidson, and Morton Keller, eds., *The Encyclopedia of the United States Congress.* Vol. 3. New York: Simon & Schuster.

Keller, Morton. 1977. *Affairs of State: Public Life in Late Nineteenth Century America.* Cambridge: Harvard University Press.

Kelley, Robert. 1977. "Ideology and Political Culture from Jefferson to Nixon." *American Historical Review* 82: 531–562.

Kennon, Donald R., and Rebecca M. Rogers. 1989. *The Committee on Ways and Means: A Bicentennial History, 1789–1989.* House Document 100–244. Washington, D.C.: Government Printing Office.

Marcus, Robert D. 1971. *Grand Old Party: Political Structure in the Gilded Age, 1880–1896.* New York: Oxford University Press.

Mayhew, David R. 1991. "Party Organization in Historical Perspective." In L. Sandy Maisel, ed., *Political Parties and Elections in the United States.* Vol. 1. New York: Garland.

McCall, Samuel W. 1914. *The Life of Thomas Brackett Reed.* Boston: Houghton, Mifflin.

Morgan, H. Wayne. 1969. *From Hayes to McKinley: National Party Politics, 1877–1896.* Syracuse, N.Y.: Syracuse University Press.

Offenberg, Richard Stanley. 1963. "The Political Career of Thomas Brackett Reed." Ph.D. diss., New York University.

Ornstein, Norman J., Thomas E. Mann, and Michael J. Malbin. 1994. *Vital Statistics on Congress, 1993–1994.* Washington, D.C.: CQ Press.

Peters, Ronald M., Jr. 1990. *The American Speakership: The Office in Historical Perspective.* Baltimore: Johns Hopkins University Press.

Polsby, Nelson W. 1968. "The Institutionalization of the House of Representatives." *American Political Science Review* 62: 144–168.

Price, Douglas. 1977. "Careers and Committees in the American Congress: The Problem of Structural Change." In William O. Aydelotte, ed., *The History of Parliamentary Behavior.* Princeton: Princeton University Press.

Reed, Thomas B. 1884. Thomas Brackett Reed to Prof. Henry L. Chapman, Bowdoin College, Feb. 8, 1884. Thomas Brackett Reed Papers. Special Collections, Bowdoin College Library.

_____. 1889a. "Rules of the House of Representatives." *Century Magazine* 37 (March): 792–795.

_____. 1889b. "Obstruction in the National House." *North American Review* 149 (October): 421–428.

_____. 1899. Thomas Brackett Reed to George Gifford, Oct. 18, 1899. Thomas Brackett Reed Papers. Special Collections, Bowdoin College Library.

Robinson, William A. 1930. *Thomas B. Reed, Parliamentarian.* New York: Dodd, Mead.

Rohde, David W., and Kenneth A. Shepsle. 1987. "Leaders and Followers in the House of Representatives: Reflections on Woodrow Wilson's *Congressional Government.*" *Congress & the Presidency* 14: 111–133.

Rossiter, Clinton, ed. 1961. James Madison, Alexander Hamilton, and John Jay, *The Federalist Papers.* New York: New American Library.

Silbey, Joel H. 1991a. *The American Political Nation, 1838–1893.* Stanford, Calif.: Stanford University Press.

_____. 1991b. "Party Organization in Nineteenth-Century America." In L. Sandy Maisel, ed., *Political Parties and Elections in the United States.* Vol. 1. New York: Garland.

Stanwood, Edward. 1905. *James Gillespie Blaine.* Boston: Houghton Mifflin.

Stewart, Charles, III. 1989. *Budget Reform Politics: The Design of the Appropriations Process in the House of Representatives, 1865–1921.* Cambridge: Cambridge University Press.

_____. 1992a. "Committee Hierarchies in the Modernizing House." *American Journal of Political Science* 36: 835–856.

_____. 1992b. "The Growth of the Committee System from Randall to Gillett." In Allen D. Hertzke and Ronald M. Peters, Jr., eds., *The Atomistic Congress.* Armonk, N.Y.: M. E. Sharpe.

Strahan, Randall. 1992. "Reed and Rostenkowski: Congressional Leadership in Institutional Time." In Allen D. Hertzke and Ronald M. Peters, Jr., eds., *The Atomistic Congress.* Armonk, N.Y.: M. E. Sharpe.

_____. 1994. "Congressional Leadership in Institutional Time: The Case of Henry Clay." Paper presented at the annual meeting of the American Political Science Association. New York.

_____. 1996. "Leadership in Institutional and Political Time: The Case of Newt Gingrich and the 104th Congress." Paper presented at the 1996 annual meeting of the American Political Science Association. San Francisco.

Swenson, Peter. 1982. "The Influence of Recruitment on the Structure of Power in the U.S. House, 1870–1949." *Legislative Studies Quarterly* 7: 7–36.

Swift, Elaine. 1989. "Reconstitutive Change in the U.S. Congress: The Early Senate, 1789–1841." *Legislative Studies Quarterly* 14: 175–203.

_____. 1996. *The Making of an American Senate, Reconstitutive Change in Congress, 1787–1841.* Ann Arbor: University of Michigan Press.

Thompson, Margaret Susan. 1985. *The "Spider Web": Congress and Lobbying in the Age of Grant.* Ithaca: Cornell University Press.

Tulis, Jeffrey K. 1987. *The Rhetorical Presidency.* Princeton: Princeton University Press.

U.S. House of Representatives Committee on Rules. 1983. *A History of the Committee on Rules.* 97th Cong., 2d sess. Washington, D.C.: Government Printing Office.

White, Leonard D. 1958. *The Republican Era, 1869–1901: A Study in Administrative History.* New York: Macmillan.

Williams, R. Hal. 1995. "James G. Blaine." In Donald C. Bacon, Roger H. Davidson, and Morton Keller, eds., *The Encyclopedia of the United States Congress.* Vol. 1. New York: Simon & Schuster.

3

Uncle Joe Cannon: The Brakeman of the House of Representatives, 1903–1911

Scott William Rager

No Speaker in the history of the modern House of Representatives has been more controversial than Joseph Gurney Cannon, known by friend and foe alike as Uncle Joe. For seven years, from 1903 until 1910, he wielded more power than any of his predecessors. Cannon was second to the president of the United States alone in influencing national affairs. Only a change in the rules of the House brought about by a coalition of Democrats and insurgent Republicans in March 1910 finally broke Joe Cannon's power.

Speaker Cannon has been commonly portrayed in popular and scholarly literature as a "czar" and a "tyrant," an unbending autocrat who ruled the House with an iron hand. This image is not substantially different from the one first created by the muckraking press in the 1900s; although not altogether inaccurate, it presents only a caricature of the man. In this chapter I place Cannon's life and career within the context of current scholarship on the progressive era and the institutional development of Congress and provide a more complete and balanced picture of the former Speaker.[1]

Although he is associated with the Midwest, Joe Cannon was actually a transplanted southerner born in Guilford County, North Carolina, on May 7, 1836. His parents, Horace and Gulielma (Hollingsworth), were Quakers. Dr. Horace Franklin Cannon, a physician and an educator, moved his family to Indiana in 1840. Joe attended the Quaker Boarding School in Richmond, Indiana, until the age of fourteen. His education was cut short by the death of his father, and for several years he worked at a country store to help support the family. At the age of twenty Cannon went to read law at the office of John P. Usher in Terre Haute. He later attended the Cincinnati Law School, where he received his degree in 1857.[2]

In 1858, Cannon established his first law practice in Shelbyville, Illinois. Discouraged by a lack of clients, however, he moved to Tuscola and there built up a small practice. Cannon's long career in public life began in 1861 when he was elected to the position of prosecuting attorney of the 27th Judicial District on the Republican ticket. Shortly after taking up the duties of his new office, he married Mary Reed.[3]

Throughout the Civil War Cannon remained a civilian because, as he later explained, Illinois governor Richard Yates requested that he remain in the state's service as a district attorney to assist with the prosecution of Copperheads. Although the lack of a military record did his career no ultimate harm, for several years immediately following the war he was occasionally harassed by detractors who claimed he had failed in his duty to the Union.[4]

National politics beckoned to Cannon in 1870. His first bid for a seat in the House was a failure, but another try in 1872 brought success. Despite a strong Liberal Republican movement in Illinois, he defeated James H.

Pickrell and, along with many other regular Republican office seekers, rode to victory on the coattails of President Grant.[5]

Three years after Cannon's election to Congress, he moved to Danville, where he and his brother, William, had relocated the bank they owned in Tuscola. William Cannon was an astute businessman; his investments made brother Joe a considerable sum of money. In addition to owning farmland in Illinois, Indiana, and Nebraska, the congressman eventually had interest in the Danville Electric Light Company, the Danville Street Railway, and the Danville Gas Company. These assets were crucial for a politician hoping to pursue a long-term public service career.[6]

Throughout the time he spent in Congress, Cannon rarely authored or proposed legislation. In fact, had it not been for a postal reform package he was assigned to introduce as junior member of the Committee of Post Offices and Post Roads, no legislation could be directly attributed to him. In 1874, however, Cannon did propose and see passed a bill that established the pound rate for paying postage on second-class mail. He remained proud of this accomplishment throughout his career and later referred to it as an example of his "reform" record in Congress.[7] His presentation of the bill won the attention of the House and the public. Almost immediately after Cannon finished, one of his colleagues, William Phelps, a New Jersey Democrat, ridiculed the new member, remarking that he must have oats in his pocket. Cannon proudly retorted that he not only had oats in his pocket but hayseeds in his hair. This "hayseed" image stuck. It enhanced Cannon's appeal with his constituents, most of whom were farmers, miners, and railroad workers, and no doubt was a factor contributing to his regular reelection thereafter.[8]

Although not a brilliant lawmaker, Representative Cannon gained a reputation for being a fiercely loyal partisan of the Republican party; he rarely strayed from the dictates of party orthodoxy. In 1888 Cannon made a bid for the speakership but lost the contest to Thomas B. Reed of Maine. Nevertheless, membership on the Rules Committee and an appointment to the chairmanship of the Appropriations Committee made Uncle Joe one of Reed's chief lieutenants and a powerful man in his own right.[9]

It was during Reed's first term as Speaker that the so-called Reed Rules were implemented. The most controversial of these dealt with the infamous "disappearing quorum." The election of 1888 had given the Republicans a slender majority of four, and the Democrats were expected to employ this well-used strategy to thwart the majority party. The solution, employed by Reed for the first time on January 20, 1890, involved counting those members who were present but not responding to the roll call vote. In the storm that followed, the Speaker became known throughout the country as Czar Reed. On February 10 Cannon made the committee report formally recommending the rule for quorum counting and another

that empowered the Speaker to reject dilatory motions. Citing as precedent procedures in the New York State legislature, city councils in Illinois
and Indiana, and even in Britain's House of Commons, Cannon made a
persuasive case for the Reed Rules. He strongly argued against the
charges that the Speaker was overreaching his powers:

> Gentlemen say this is "tyrannical." I deny it. But if it be tyrannical the
> "tyranny" is exercised by the Speaker sustained by the majority of the House
> and on the other hand the tyrannical minority that has controlled heretofore
> fails to control now. If I must choose between the "tyranny" of the constitu-
> tional majority, responsible people, or the "tyranny" of an irresponsible mi-
> nority of one, I will stand by the Constitution and our form of government,
> and so act as to let the majority rule.[10]

After a lengthy and charged debate, the report was accepted. But the issue was not truly settled. Abuse of the Speaker's power would again be a
topic and the source of even greater controversy almost twenty years later
when Cannon's turn came to lead the House.

In the elections of 1890 the Republicans, largely as a result of the unpopularity of the McKinley Tariff, suffered major losses. Among the casualties was Cannon.[11] While he was back in Danville waiting impatiently
for the next congressional elections, the Democratic majority in the House
went back to the old rules. The Republicans responded by filibustering
and using other tricks that the Reed Rules had prevented. Speaker
Charles R. Crisp and the Democrats had grudgingly to adopt the Reed
Rules themselves.[12]

After Uncle Joe's reelection in 1892, he did not immediately regain all
of his privileges and power. The Democrats still controlled the House
during the Fifty-third Congress, and David B. Henderson of Iowa, the
ranking minority member of the Appropriations Committee, was next in
line for chairman. When Reed became Speaker again during the Fifty-
fourth Congress, however, he made Henderson chairman of the Judiciary
Committee, a move that allowed Cannon to once again become chairman
of Appropriations.[13]

Cannon became known as "Cerberus of the Money-box" and "Watchdog of the Treasury" and surely deserved his reputation for tough-
minded, tight-fisted, fiscal conservatism. "You may think my business is
to make appropriations, but it is not. It is to prevent their being made," he
once remarked.[14] As Appropriations chairman, Cannon became one of
the most conspicuous members of Congress. During debates concerning
his committee's reports, he was truly in his element. According to C. W.
Thompson, a correspondent for the *New York Times*, Uncle Joe was "a
sight worth seeing when a debate was on. His delivery was slashing,
sledgehammery, full of fire and fury."[15]

One of Cannon's accomplishments as head of the Appropriations Committee involved seeing through a $50,000,000 emergency deficiency bill that enabled the country to prepare for war with Spain. President McKinley was indebted to Cannon, but Thomas B. Reed, an outspoken opponent of imperialism, was greatly displeased with his lieutenant and resigned as Speaker the following year.[16]

With Reed's resignation, Cannon was a step closer to the speakership, but Henderson stood in his way. Cannon and many of his colleagues were unhappy with Henderson because he seemed weak and allowed the House to take a subservient role to the Senate. By 1903, however, Henderson had decided that he was ready to retire from the House, allegedly out of dissatisfaction with the clamor Republicans in his native Iowa were making for tariff revision. The field was, at last, clear. Cannon was elected Speaker in March with the promise that he would reassert the legislative agenda of the House and battle the domineering Senate.[17]

At age sixty-seven, Joe Cannon was the oldest and longest-serving representative ever to be elected to the speakership. As Cannon biographer William Rea Gwinn aptly observed, Uncle Joe had reached this point in his career mainly "by long experience, close study, and persistent effort." He did not become Speaker "by reason of the discovery of any overwhelming genius." But whatever he may have lacked in terms of brilliance or imagination, Cannon made up for with political savvy and pure blarney. No one in the House could equal his personal popularity or experience. The slight man with white, thinning hair, chin whiskers, and a cigar planted between his lips was considered by many to be practically an institution of the House.[18]

The Illinois Hayseed did not intend soon to vacate the position he had finally won.[19] Cannon realized that the key to exercising and retaining power as Speaker lay in his ability to appoint the members of all the standing committees and their chairmen. Under this system every Republican holding a prominent place in the House owed his position directly to the Speaker. In return for his favor, the Speaker expected complete loyalty. The circle Cannon established around himself was instrumental in helping him to remain one of the most powerful men in the United States for seven years.[20]

Three men in the House became indispensable to Speaker Cannon. This triumvirate consisted of Soreno E. Payne of New York, retained by Cannon in his positions as chairman of the Ways and Means Committee and majority leader; John Dalzell of Pennsylvania, the number-two man on both the Rules and the Ways and Means Committees; and James A. Tawney of Minnesota, party whip until 1905, when he was promoted to chairman of the Appropriations Committee. Other key players in the Republican House leadership included General Charles Grosvenor of Ohio, a senior member of the Rules Committee until 1906; James E. Watson of Indiana, Tawney's replacement as party whip in 1905; and James R. Mann of Illinois, Uncle Joe's legislative watchdog and assistant with committee assignments.[21] Cannon's "court" was composed of a fairly diverse group of individuals with a wide range of talents, but they were all dedicated regular Republicans. None came from the western states where the insurgency had its origins. All were defenders of the status quo. Therefore, the Speaker's top men were as oblivious as Cannon himself was to the warning signs that a significant shift in the political attitudes of their colleagues in Congress and the public was occurring.

Joe Cannon clearly felt no affinity for the progressive reform spirit that was just beginning to gain headway on the national level when he became Speaker. He saw no need for change; the country was "a hell of a success," according to Uncle Joe, and he intended to keep it that way. The formidable powers at his disposal allowed Cannon to keep reform legislation to a minimum. The Speaker could stack committees with loyalists; he could route legislation to specific committees; he decided what members were recognized to speak on the floor. And finally, he was the chairman of the small but powerful Rules Committee that, through its authority to report special orders, set the floor agenda for the consideration of bills. In short, the Speaker's powers effectively enabled him either to expedite or block the passage of legislation. He usually chose to do the latter.[22]

Cannon's power and dedication to standpat principles posed a challenge to an activist chief executive with progressive inclinations. Theodore Roosevelt had already served as president for over two years when Cannon was elected Speaker. Roosevelt immediately realized that Cannon was not another David Henderson, who could be expected to automatically rubber-stamp decisions made without his input, and immediately began soliciting the Speaker's advice on a regular basis. That he considered Cannon formidable enough to be courted by the Republican leadership rather than dictated to by it indicated that a significant shift of power in the Republican party (the GOP) had occurred.[23] Cannon recalled that he and Roosevelt spoke "two or three times a week when Congress was in session, and sometimes daily." Usually the two men met in the evening and often talked in the President's study until midnight. Cannon was the first Speaker since 1861 to meet with the president regularly. Uncle Joe believed that when he and Roosevelt met, "they were equals sharing their party." In order to ingratiate himself further with Cannon, in 1905 Roosevelt began the custom of the annual Speaker's Dinner.[24]

In part as a result of such efforts to accommodate Cannon, relations between him and Roosevelt were initially cordial. At first, few aspects of Roosevelt's policy were objectionable to the Speaker because, by and large, the president seemed satisfied with following the blueprint left for him by the late President William McKinley, whose term he was completing. But circumstances changed when Roosevelt was elected in his own right in 1904, and his progressive inclinations came more clearly to the fore. Anticipating that this might occur, Cannon commented to George B. Cortelyou following Roosevelt's victory over Alton B. Parker, "The sweep was so clean that we will have to both pull the load and apply the brakes."[25]

Cooperation between the president and the Speaker first began to undergo some difficulty when Roosevelt announced to Congress in December 1905 that, since state action had proven inadequate to the task, the federal government would begin to take a much more active role in the regulation and supervision of the "great corporations." Cannon came to the conclusion that Roosevelt rather disliked businessmen and viewed them as being concerned only with their profits. As Cannon later recalled, Roosevelt simply "failed to understand that without commerce there would be no civilization."[26]

What Roosevelt most wanted from Congress in the new session was a law that would secure the right of the Interstate Commerce Commission (ICC) to supervise and regulate the rates charged by the railroads. This request came as no particular surprise; he had often advocated railroad rate reform. In May 1905 the president had expressed the view that the ICC should have full authority to fix railroad rates subject to judicial review rather than to merely supervise and regulate them. Although he had moderated his position somewhat since then, Roosevelt clearly intended to have the bill passed during the current session of Congress.[27]

President Roosevelt also advocated pure food legislation and a new enabling act that would provide for additional forest and soil conservation. Missing from the president's message, however, was any mention of tariff reform or revision. In December 1904 this issue had also been excluded from the president's annual speech. The interfering hand of Joe Cannon was suspected by many observers.[28]

Cannon firmly believed that to tamper with the tariff meant to tamper with the prosperity of the country. Before Roosevelt's 1904 campaign, Cannon had warned that tariff revision in an election year was inadvisable. As a result the president removed any mention of tariff reduction from his annual message. However, the issue was brought up anew in early 1905. When the newspapers suggested that the Speaker and the president were at odds over the tariff once again, Roosevelt sent a letter to the Speaker requesting a meeting to sort out their differences. "I do not want the people of the country to get the idea," he wrote, "that there will be any split or clash between you and me over the tariff or anything else." In February the president did meet with Cannon and several ranking Republican senators for the purpose of discussing tariff revision. Only the

Speaker and Senator Orville Platt voiced opposition, but their disapproval convinced Roosevelt to delay tariff revision at least until after the next election.[29]

Although it is difficult to prove from the written record, Roosevelt had quite likely been forced by the tariff standpatters in the Republican party to accept a compromise; his railroad bill would be allowed to pass only if the tariff were left alone. To the president this seemed reasonable. Cannon subsequently allowed the Hepburn Bill (1906) to pass.[30]

Joe Cannon also stood at odds with the president on pure food legislation. Although this issue had been before Congress for more than a decade, measures that addressed the issue of misbranded and adulterated food and drugs had failed. But in the fall of 1905, following the publication of Samuel Hopkins Adams's articles on the subject in *Collier's*, President Roosevelt received an increasing number of requests to put pure food and drug legislation on his agenda and subsequently did so.[31] In February 1906 the Senate finally passed a pure food bill authored by Weldon Reyburn of Idaho, and Senator Albert Beveridge of Indiana introduced an amendment to the agricultural appropriation bill that provided for government inspection of meatpacking facilities. But the House failed to take prompt action on either, and Uncle Joe was partially blamed by the press. As had been his custom, Cannon responded to his critics through his secretary, White Busbey, who maintained that the Speaker had "aided the advocates of pure-food legislation in every way possible, except for assuming full responsibility." Concerning the Meat Inspection bill, Busbey maintained that Cannon had "done more than any other individual to bring together the president and the House Committee on Agriculture," which had charge of the matter.[32] In reality, Cannon probably had difficulty summoning much enthusiasm for legislation that would empower the federal government with further authority to interfere in the private sector. Dr. Harvey W. Wiley, the crusading Department of Agriculture chemist who urged Roosevelt into action, doubted that Cannon was ever "entirely won over to the wisdom" of the measures, suggesting that without the persuasion of his friend James R. Mann and public pressure, it was quite possible that Cannon would have chosen to "sit" on both the Pure Food and Drug Bill and the Meat Inspection Bill. The Speaker was a political realist, however, and after being called to a special consultation with President Roosevelt, he personally saw to it that the pure food bill was brought to the floor of the House on June 23. It passed by a vote of 241 to 17.[33]

Through 1906, Speaker Cannon and President Roosevelt experienced a reasonably workable and cordial relationship. By means of regular conferences, agreements and deals had been made that more or less allowed Roosevelt to maintain a progressive agenda without offending

Uncle Joe's conservative instincts too severely. Prior to the 1906 congressional elections, Roosevelt had spoken highly of the Speaker and of the "phenomenal amount of good work" the House had accomplished under his leadership. Cannon in turn spoke of the harmonious relationship Congress had with the president and commended his programs, calling the railroad rate law and the pure food and the meat inspection acts "one of the best records of legislation for the benefit of the people that has ever been made."[34] A report even circulated that Cannon had been designated by Roosevelt as his successor to the presidency. But Roosevelt's alliance with Uncle Joe was not as sturdy as it appeared to be. Several incidents in the latter part of the president's second term led to this erosion.

Roosevelt had a sincere desire to improve the relationship between government and the working man, and his attitude toward unions was at least moderately progressive, certainly more so than that of his predecessors. Cannon was at best a halfhearted supporter of Roosevelt's labor policy; he agreed that unions were useful and necessary, but the Speaker had also been among those who advised the president against taking a more radical course. It was the antagonistic relationship between Samuel Gompers and Cannon that particularly worried Roosevelt. This situation seriously threatened the gains the Republicans had made with labor. Roosevelt urged Cannon not to make personal attacks against the American Federation of Labor leader. But for the next several years scrapes with Gompers, who ultimately tried personally to defeat Cannon in his own district, continually endangered the administration's fragile relations with labor.[35]

Joe Cannon had absolutely no interest in Theodore Roosevelt's favorite reform issue, conservation of natural resources. Cannon's opposition toward conservation measures was long-standing. He could not abide waste of the public's money, and conservation seemed just that to his way of thinking.[36] During his tenure as Speaker, Cannon's chief opposition to conservation involved the creation of reserves in the southern Appalachians and the White Mountains. Both the president and the House Agriculture Committee had recommended that the reserves be created. The Speaker, however, ignored them and referred the matter to his infamous Judiciary Committee with a request that an opinion on constitutionality be rendered. The members found that although the federal government had no power to acquire lands within a state solely for reserves, it would be within its authority to acquire lands for the purpose of improving navigability of rivers and streams. A bill was promptly drafted that met this criterion, but Speaker Cannon, still dissatisfied, sent the new proposal to the Rules Committee, where it was finally buried. The president told the Speaker that he had "had his heart set" upon this bill, but he finally had to acquiesce.[37]

Although Cannon and Roosevelt eventually were able to mend their personal relationship, their political differences remained. Both Cannon and Senator Nelson Aldrich, the two top men in Congress, were unquestionably out of step with the Roosevelt Republicans, but the speaker was the more objectionable of the two. Difficult though Aldrich was, Roosevelt respected the urbane senator; Cannon, on the other hand, was rather an embarrassment. Roosevelt believed Cannon was uncouth in behavior and held archaic, indefensible attitudes. There can be little doubt that both Roosevelt and his choice for a successor, William Howard Taft, would have preferred to have Cannon out of the way. But the Speaker was too powerful to replace. Industrialists approved of his positions regarding the tariff, labor unions, and governmental noninterference. The rural communities trusted him as one of their own. Colleagues appreciated the role he had played in returning the House to political power, and many of them were grateful for favors he had granted. Removing Cannon could not be accomplished without invoking the wrath of these groups and endangering party unity.[38]

In 1908 Cannon made a rather uninspired bid for the Republican nomination for the presidency but ultimately posed little threat to William Howard Taft at the Republican National Convention. Still, Cannon had gotten his way with much of the platform and had managed to foist fellow standpatter "Sunny Jim" Sherman on Taft as a running mate.[39] Criticisms leveled against the Speaker by progressive groups during the 1908 campaign troubled candidate Taft. In October it was whispered in the press that Taft hoped Theodore E. Burton would give up plans to run for the Senate and might be persuaded to challenge Cannon for the speakership. Roosevelt, however, advised Taft against making an open break with the Speaker. He felt that, although Cannon was indeed a burden, it would not be in the party's best interest to oppose Uncle Joe when four-fifths of the Republicans in the House favored him. This state of affairs presented a particular dilemma for Taft. By no means a radical progressive himself, he still found having to work with the arch-conservative Cannon more difficult than had Roosevelt.[40]

Knowing that Roosevelt's advice to iron out his differences with the Speaker was sound, Taft subsequently met with Cannon. The Speaker came away from their parley claiming to be in sympathy with the president-elect's desire to carry out the pledges of the Chicago platform and promising to assist him in every way possible. Upon Cannon's suggestion, Taft also met with the Ways and Means Committee, which pledged him its support as well. The official relationship between William Howard Taft and Joseph Gurney Cannon therefore seemed to begin in a spirit of cooperation. Despite outward appearances, however, the president's personal affection for the Speaker did not grow.[41] Even though Taft was resigned to having Cannon remain leader of the House, he thought that the rules that authorized the Speaker to appoint committees should be changed. He realized that to do such a thing would practically emasculate the speakership but feared that unless something was done to quell the growing opposition to Cannon, the Republicans would splinter. Still, to those who planned to amend the rules, he offered no encouragement.[42]

Almost immediately after Taft took office, it became clear that the opposition to Cannon was indeed becoming more serious on both sides of the aisle. On March 15, the House convened in special session for the purpose of considering revision of the tariff, a major Republican campaign pledge. Twelve Republicans refused to vote for Cannon for Speaker. Although he was reelected, the insurgents and Democrats led by Minority Leader James Beauchamp "Champ" Clark of Missouri did manage to defeat ratification of the rules. Clark proposed a resolution that eliminated the Speaker's power to appoint committees. Instead, an enlarged fifteen-man Committee on Rules composed of six Democrats, five Republicans, and four insurgent Republicans would make all committee assignments. When a vote was taken, however, twenty-three Democrats sided with the regular Republicans and therefore managed to defeat the resolution 203 to 180. John J. Fitzgerald of New York then offered an amendment to the rules that provided for a unanimous consent calendar for minor bills, which made the Speaker's personal consent unnecessary. Fitzgerald's measure passed 211 to 172.[43]

The Fitzgerald resolution was little more than another pacifier; it failed to affect the Speaker's power to appoint committees or to control the Rules Committee. Theoretically it could help a member to get a bill brought up for consideration, but Cannon might still check such action merely by drawing tighter rein on the committees to ensure that certain measures were not reported.[44]

Although this affair had had little impact on Cannon or his power, the Speaker began to realize that he was no longer "good old Uncle Joe" to all of his colleagues in the House. But he had not yet fully come to grips with the reason for it. Cannon was convinced that his unpopularity was largely the fault of a muckraking press that had been attacking him regularly for the better part of a year, possibly because he had refused to support special tariff concessions for paper pulp.[45] The Speaker's problems actually ran much deeper than he imagined. The opposition to Cannon was by now entrenched and continued to grow among both the Republicans and the Democrats.

For more than a year the Democratic leadership had been actively plotting against Cannon, who had virtually destroyed the Democrats' ability to function effectively in the House. The emergence of the insurgents gave them an opportunity to get the rules changed and possibly remove the Speaker. In early 1909 Champ Clark, who had replaced John Sharp Williams as minority leader, and Oscar Underwood, his assistant, made contact with several insurgent leaders about the possibility of forging an alliance. As punishment for his involvement in the subsequent failed coup attempt of March 15, Champ Clark lost the privilege of appointing Democratic members to standing committees.[46]

The dissident Republican group was chiefly led by George Norris of Nebraska and Victor Murdock of Kansas. Murdock, a former newspaper editor, was the more dynamic of the two and became the spokesman for the insurgents.[47] George Norris, although not a firebrand like Murdock, was every bit as much an idealist and felt little compulsion to follow the party line. "I would rather be right than regular," Norris was known to say. Prior to the opening of the Sixtieth Congress, his stance on the rules question was unknown. He seemed at times to be an admirer of Speaker Cannon, and he apparently valued the friendship of the elder statesman from Illinois. However, in September 1907, when Congressman E. A. Hayes of California directly asked Norris where he stood concerning the Speaker's power, Norris replied that he was firmly committed to insurgency, and soon thereafter he assumed a leadership role in the movement.[48]

Joining Norris and Murdock were several other noteworthy individuals: Edmond W. Madison of Kansas, called by Theodore Roosevelt one of the "best Insurgents"; John M. Nelson of Wisconsin, a true radical and an admirer of Robert M. La Follette; Miles Poindexter of Washington, a staunch conservation advocate; Charles A. Lindbergh of Minnesota, an independent thinker who rarely compromised his positions; and Charles G. Fowlers of New Jersey, a latecomer who joined the insurgents after having his currency reform bill rejected by the Republican regulars in 1908. Together these men and thirty-five or so others were united by a desire to enact a change in the rules of the House.[49] Their motivation to do so can be attributed to several causes.

Cannon's system of rule was exceptionally rigid and made no provision for the factionalism that had begun to plague the Republican party in the early years of the twentieth century. A changing electoral base contributed significantly to the disunity of the GOP. After 1896, the Republican candidates began to attract more far westerners. Within a decade, this new western constituency along with the Middle West elected insurgents who demanded reforms to relieve social and economic problems in their regions. A number of these Republican congressmen entered the House in 1906 and 1908, years in which the Republican procedural majority was declining overall.[50]

But rather than attempt to accommodate the interests of these new members, Speaker Cannon responded by enforcing party regularity through the use of the caucus and committee assignments. Regarding the former, Cannon deliberately confused the distinction between a party conference, an informal meeting, and a caucus, which had binding power over the members. Putting this tactic into practice, the Speaker might call a conference meeting, only later to declare that it was in fact a caucus.[51] Cannon's use of committee assignments as a means to maintain party regularity caused even greater distress among the insurgents because the Speaker often showed little or no regard for the seniority system, an institution whose importance increased as more members sought extended careers in the House.[52]

During the first session of the Sixtieth Congress, the insurgents had done little to openly oppose Cannon. The Panic of 1907 and the coming presidential election made open strife within the party largely unthinkable. Still, on May 16 George Norris introduced a resolution proposing that all committees be appointed by the Committee on Rules, whose members in turn were to be chosen by the entire House from candidates representing different geographical areas. Although Cannon and the Rules Committee promptly disposed of the measure, they were forced to consider the sort of trouble that might arise if such a plan were ever allowed to reach the floor.[53]

After William Howard Taft was safely elected president, the insurgents were in a much better position to take action against Speaker Cannon. On February 9, 1909, a resolution was sent to the Rules Committee that provided for the establishment of a so-called Calendar Tuesday during which committees would be called in alphabetical order for the presentation of legislation. The resolution also reiterated Norris's earlier plan to deprive the Speaker of his power to appoint the Rules Committee. Twenty-nine congressmen signed the resolution. Several of the more moderate insurgents balked at putting their names to anything that would tamper with the Speaker's committee appointment power and favored only the Calendar Tuesday measure. Seizing upon an opportunity to split the insurgent ranks, Cannon's supporters countered with a resolution that would set aside Wednesday instead of Tuesday for hearing committee proposals for new legislation. Other than the specific day set aside, this plan differed from the insurgents' plan only in that a majority vote rather than a two-thirds vote could set aside the Calendar Day. The insurgents' proposal was never reported to the House, but on March 1 an amendment calling for the Calendar Wednesday plan was adopted by a narrow margin.[54] If Cannon had been willing to make more compromises, the revolt against him might have been effectively subverted.

Calendar Wednesday, however, did not significantly affect the Speaker's power. Although a few of the less committed insurgents were placated by it, most were not. George Norris observed that the measure was "a homeopathic dose of nothingness." Enraged by what they considered to be a dirty trick, the insurgents' resolve increased to break the Speaker's stranglehold on the House. Although temporarily set back by Cannon's maneuvering, they remained confident that the Speaker could yet be beaten with help from the Democrats. The insurgents' hopes were further buoyed by the fact that Theodore Roosevelt had given them reason to believe that he would persuade President-elect Taft to assist them in dealing with Cannon. No help came, however, and Roosevelt, instead of interceding on the insurgents' behalf with Taft, advised the president-elect to seek the Speaker's cooperation rather than to risk having him block the administration's policies. Frustrated and disillusioned by Taft's "defection," the insurgents began to have doubts concerning his commitment to the progressive cause. It seemed clear at any rate that the new president could not be expected to provide a challenge to Cannon's power. The insurgents therefore decided early that they would likely have to fight their battle without Taft's aid.[55]

After the first serious attempt to "unhorse" Speaker Cannon failed at the opening of the special session of the Sixty-first Congress on March 15, 1909, Cannon took no immediate action to discipline the insurgents who had rebelled against him but instead waited to see how they behaved concerning the tariff.[56]

Taft had made it clear to the Congress that he expected a thorough revision of the rates and schedules. The Republican platform of 1908 had made an unequivocal declaration for revision, but owing to the influence of standpat protectionists like Cannon, it had not specified what form revision would actually take. If the so-called maximum-minimum policy that Uncle Joe and Nelson Aldrich favored were followed, some of the schedules might be lowered, but others would be raised to penalize countries that discriminated against U.S. goods.[57] Soreno Payne's Ways and Means Committee was given the duty of drafting the House bill, which was read on the floor on April 8. Speaker Cannon, who was on record as saying that the old Dingley Tariff was "the best protective tariff law ever written on the statute books," favored the immediate passage of the bill to prevent alterations. Using tried-and-true tactics—restricting the offering of amendments, limiting floor debate, and binding the Republican members to support legislation through a caucus vote—Cannon made sure that the Payne Bill was passed without too many changes.

Uncle Joe had been unable to prevent some duties from being lowered, but his compatriot in the Senate, Nelson Aldrich, took care of that. The Senate made some 847 changes to the Payne Bill; most were increases in the customs rates.[58] The tariff bill then went to a conference committee, where the differences between the Senate and House were reconciled. Cannon saw to it that six protectionists from the Ways and Means Committee represented the House. Several members with seniority who were known to favor downward revision were bypassed.[59] After the Payne-Aldrich Tariff emerged from the conference committee, it was adopted by the House on July 31 and the Senate on August 5. It hardly deserved to be called a reform measure. Still, Taft believed that some revision was better than no revision at all and endorsed the tariff. Later, during a speech at Winona, Minnesota, on September 6, he severely criticized the insurgents for not supporting it.[60] Any hopes the insurgents had before the Winona speech that Taft might yet be brought over to their side were completely dashed.

Cannon managed to retain most of his power throughout 1909 and went so far as to shift the committee assignments of various insurgents in order to keep them from further mischief. Victor Murdock and George Norris were among those receiving committee demotions.[61] But opposition continued to mount against the Speaker within Congress and from the outside as well.

Extensive and sometimes biased press coverage of the rules controversy had alerted the public to the fact that Speaker Cannon might not be quite the benevolent character they had once believed him to be. The *Baltimore Sun* cited Cannon as being "the very embodiment of all the sinister interests and malign influences that have brooded over this land and exacted toil from every hearthstone." Both *Collier's* and *Success* magazines had been running articles in regular installments that not only detailed the Speaker's wrongdoings but also praised the insurgents. When a large segment of the public responded by turning against Cannon, some moderate Republicans realized that their own political futures would soon be in jeopardy if they continued to support him. The press, therefore, did the insurgents an absolutely invaluable service. The Speaker was angered by the press assault and the public response to it but refused to make changes in the way he ran the House.[62]

In January 1910, the House insurgents won a minor skirmish with Speaker Cannon that foreshadowed their much greater victory two months later. The Ballinger-Pinchot affair had put even greater strain on the already strained relationship existing between President Taft and the insurgents. Taft proposed that Cannon and Nelson Aldrich select a "congenial" investigating committee to look into the matter,[63] but a coalition of insurgents and Democrats voted instead to have the whole House make the selection. This action might have been prevented if the Speaker had been alert to what was happening. But neither he nor more than thirty of his loyal supporters were present when George Norris arose to propose the amendment. Walter I. Smith of Iowa, who was Speaker pro tempore, recognized Norris. The proposal was made and passed by a narrow margin, 149 to 146.[64]

Norris's success, although limited, encouraged the House insurgents. And as the magazine *Current Literature* noted, it was the first time on record when the Speaker had been given such a rebuke. Cannon had at last received a "jolt," according to John M. Nelson of Wisconsin, a leading insurgent. The insurgents could not be put off now; victory seemed at last imminent. Norris had kept in his pocket for some time a well-worn copy of his resolution to amend the rules governing the Speaker's committee appointment power; he now watched more intently than ever for a chance to use it.[65]

That opportunity came in March 1910. On March 16, Speaker Cannon ruled that a resolution concerning the census proposed by Edgar Crumpacker of Indiana could be voted upon even though it did not qualify for consideration according to the usual terms of Calendar Wednesday. Cannon justified his ruling on the basis that the census was provided for by the Constitution and therefore was constitutionally "privileged." George Norris saw this as an opportunity to get his own resolution before the House and stated on the following day, March 17, that because the Constitution provided that "[e]ach House may determine the rules of its proceedings," the House should consider his amendment to the rules. Surprisingly, Cannon allowed Norris to read his resolution, despite the fact that it had not been approved by a committee. The Speaker had unwittingly recognized the man who would bring his reign as "czar" to an end.[66]

One of the most hotly emotional debates ever to be recorded in the annals of the House then began. It was St. Patrick's Day, and as Cannon later was to recall, "[t]he insurgents were bent on driving the snakes out of America as well as Ireland." When Norris had read his resolution, John Dalzell, the Rules chairman, raised a point of order against the Nebraska troublemaker. The Republicans started to filibuster in order to gain time to round up regulars who had left Washington to attend festivities and parades in their districts. A contest began to determine which side could outlast the other. The Republicans were ready to give in first, but the insurgents and Democrats would not allow a recess. Hoping to force Speaker Cannon to rule on Dalzell's point of order, the coalition managed to keep the House in session until 2:00 P.M. on the 18th before agreeing to a two-hour break.

During this time the sides met to work out a compromise. The regular Republicans offered to accept the Norris resolution providing the Speaker would be allowed to remain on the Rules Committee. The insurgents rejected the idea.[67]

The House reconvened at 4:00 P.M. Speaker Cannon finally announced that he was ready to rule on the point of order Dalzell had raised against the Norris resolution, but a motion for postponement until 12:05 P.M. the next day carried, and the proceedings were delayed once again. On the morning of March 19 representatives of the opposing groups met for a second time to work out a compromise. But Cannon's instructions not to yield his membership on the Rules Committee prevented an agreement from being worked out. "If I agreed to get off the committee I would lose no less than I would if I should be berated in a fight . . . on the floor," Cannon told the press.[68]

During the various backroom deliberations that had gone on since the debate on the floor began, the Norris resolution had been changed. It now said that ten men, not fifteen as originally proposed, would be chosen by the entire House to serve on the Rules Committee. The Speaker would not be the chairman or allowed membership. This was the resolution read before the House on the afternoon of the 19th.[69]

The first order of business when the House reconvened was for Speaker Cannon to deliver his ruling on Dalzell's point of order. As expected, he ruled for his lieutenant. The membership of the House then overruled him, 182 to 163. Accordingly, the Norris Resolution was put to a vote; it passed 191 to 156. Rather than give up and leave the chamber, however, the indomitable Uncle Joe Cannon proceeded to make a speech that very nearly snatched victory from the jaws of defeat.[70]

Acknowledging that no coherent Republican majority existed in the House, Cannon stated that it was now the prerogative of the new majority—the insurgents and Democrats—to elect a new Speaker who was in harmony with their "acts and purposes." He would not step down, however, unless a motion to vacate the office of the speakership was formally introduced. To resign at once, Cannon said, would place in jeopardy the Republicans' ability to carry out their legislative program and would be "a confession of weakness or mistake or an apology for past actions." His remarks were met with applause.[71]

Cannon's speech was a carefully planned piece of political strategy. It had been prepared in advance by himself and James Watson at the Speaker's Vermont Avenue residence. If someone accepted his challenge to declare the Speaker's chair vacant—as someone almost surely would—the insurgents would be divided among the Murdock radicals who wanted Cannon deposed and the Norris moderates who only wanted a change of the rules.[72]

Cannon's "dare" was accepted by Albert S. Burleson, a Texas Democrat, on March 20. Several of Burleson's colleagues had tried to convince him not to present his resolution, fearing that it would be playing into the regulars' hands. Finis Garrett of Tennessee warned Burleson that if the Democrats succeeded in electing a new Speaker, he would have to control a minority House. Burleson chose to go ahead anyway. Satisfied with the accomplishments of the day and thinking it best to consider further action at a time when cooler heads might prevail, George Norris called for an adjournment. Cannon refused; a motion was already on the floor. Pandemonium broke out. The regulars made no effort to contain their pleasure. Amid their taunts of "Come on! Show your true colors!" Victor Murdock and George Norris split ranks and scrambled to collect votes. Just as Cannon and Watson had wagered, Norris proved to be the more successful. Owing to a genuine reluctance to break completely with their Republican brethren, a majority of the insurgents voted against the Burleson resolution, which consequently went down in defeat, 192 to 155. Victor Murdock had only been joined by eight other radicals in voting for Cannon's removal.[73]

"I'll just keep on speaking and praying" was Cannon's only comment concerning his retention of the speakership. Surely his emotions ran much deeper than he was willing to reveal. Despite the fact that they had just taken away his power to appoint the members or sit as chairman of the Rules Committee, most of his colleagues could not bring themselves to remove him from his office. Minority leader Champ Clark was openly disappointed. If the insurgents had not lost their nerve over the Burleson resolution, he would almost certainly have been elected the new Speaker. But more important, by failing to depose Cannon, the insurgents, according to Clark, had only "scotched" Cannonism and not killed it. Later, at a dinner of the Republican Association on March 20, Cannon accused all of the insurgents who had voted against the Burleson resolution of cowardice.[74]

With the rules fight settled, there seemed a chance that the Republican camp would no longer be so divided. Taft speculated hopefully that his party would fare well in the 1910 congressional elections. Cannon, however, was not finished with his battle against the insurgents; he would not end his career quietly. He went to Kansas in July to stump for several Republican congressmen seeking renomination in the primaries. The old warrior lashed out at the insurgents, saying that "hyphenated Republicans" did not exist, and claimed that he would "leave the Republican party and climb a tree or join the Democrats" if ever it became necessary to use an adjective to describe Republicans. He also talked of being available for reelection as speaker. "[A]s long as God lets me live the muckraking periodicals and the so-called independent or progressive Republicans shall not make me say that I will not be a candidate for speaker," Cannon announced. This was not the news Taft and many other Republicans had hoped to hear. Of the six congressmen for whom Cannon campaigned, four failed to win the primaries in their districts.[75]

Matters only worsened as the election drew closer. More regular Republican congressmen lost to insurgents in the primaries; James Tawney, Cannon's Appropriations chairman, was among them. Cannon's announcement had made Cannonism the most important issue of the off-year election. A real electoral upset for the regulars seemed possible. Taft, putting the best face on the matter, suggested that there might be a "slump." The results were far worse than he anticipated. The Republicans lost fifty-four seats in the House, which was subsequently taken over by the Democrats for the first time in sixteen years. The GOP retained control of the Senate but lost ten seats there. It should be noted that many of the Republicans who did win were of what Cannon called the "hyphenated" or progressive variety. Although reelected by the 18th District for another term, Joe Cannon would not be the Speaker of the next House.[76]

With the Republican party seriously divided, the standpatters in a much weakened state, and the House rules changed, Cannon had very little power during his last months as Speaker. Although Cannon was a lame duck, he was able to win one final round against the insurgents in the House. With the aid of James R. Mann, he demonstrated the ill wisdom of the committee discharge rule, which he had predicted would only encumber the House machinery. The discharge rule provided that on the first and third Monday of each month, committees were to be discharged from the consideration of bills they had buried and to bring the bills to the floor of the House for action. On December 19, Mann asked that the Post Office Committee be discharged from considering the postal reorganization act. The bill was extremely lengthy and would probably have required close to a week to read in its entirety. The insurgents made plans to amend the rule so that only the title of the bill to be discharged need be read. When Representative Charles Fuller of Illinois made the motion on January 10, Mann objected that other business was on the calendar already and that Fuller's amendment, not being privileged, could not be heard. This was a situation similar to the one George Norris had taken advantage of in March of the previous year. Cannon, asserting the same logic used on March 19, 1910, ruled that Mann's objection was in order, thereby daring the House to overrule him again. The result was as he expected: Recognizing the expediency of having the rules respected when they took over the Sixty-second Congress, the Democrats rushed to support Cannon. Only twenty-six of their number voted with the insurgents to overrule the Speaker. In a sense, Cannon felt vindicated, believing he had proof that the Democrats had supported Norris only in the interest of gaining a political advantage.[77]

Speaker Cannon continued to be a burden to President Taft, whom he fought on the issue of Canadian trade reciprocity right up until the day of the vote, which coincided with the day of the annual Speaker's Dinner. Taft nearly canceled the affair, cursing Cannon for his stubbornness over the tariff. The bill passed, however, and the dinner was held.[78]

On March 5, 1911, the former "czar," Uncle Joe Cannon, turned over the Speaker's gavel to Champ Clark.[79] The Democratic House, with Clark's blessing, further reduced the Speaker's powers when it adopted new rules in April 1911, taking away the power to appoint standing commit- tees. The Democrats determined that the Ways and Means Committee, which would be chosen by the party caucus, should make committee se- lections. Those selections would then be brought before the whole House for approval. Cannon was critical of the new process but did not see how it had changed anything significantly; most of the old-line regular Re- publicans remained on the same committees they had been on in the past Congress. He chose to overlook the fact that several insurgents had been given important committee appointments.[80]

Republican floor leadership of the new Congress was given to James R. Mann, whom Cannon himself nominated at the party caucus. The one- time Iron Duke was apparently now content to once again be just "one of the boys" and no doubt felt happy to be installed once more on the Ap- propriations Committee as its ranking member.[81]

Out of the political spotlight, Uncle Joe rarely caught anyone's atten- tion by his actions in the House in 1911 and 1912. He demonstrated, how- ever, that he had not entirely lost his old flair for debate when the House considered repeal of the Canadian Reciprocity Law. Despite his assertive speech against this "vicious" agreement, which in Cannon's opinion could only hurt the U.S. farmer, the repeal attempt failed.[82]

The election of 1912 was an extremely difficult one for Republicans. Theodore Roosevelt's decision to run as a third party candidate against Taft threatened to destroy party unity. Cannon, however, tried no new strategy. As always, he emphasized the good works of the Republican ad- ministration and disparaged change. But this time his old formula for success failed. Although the margin by which he was defeated was scant, Cannon lost to Frank T. O'Hair, a forty-two-year-old Democrat with pro- gressive aspirations. Cannon polled 18,707 votes to O'Hair's 19,485.[83] This was only the second time in his thirty-eight-year congressional ca- reer that Cannon had lost an election. It was symbolic, perhaps, that both Cannon and the Republicans had suffered their worst reversal since 1890.

Cannon, however, was not yet down for the count. To him, retirement from politics seemed, oddly enough, somewhat premature. Two years later, in 1914, the old campaigner was once again elected to the House, this time defeating Frank O'Hair by a vote of 29,485 to 22,035.[84] Cannon now assumed the position of the honored, senior statesman. His col- leagues were genuinely pleased to see him back in their midst. He posed no real threat, and most of the deeds committed while he was Speaker could now be forgiven, even if they were not entirely forgotten.

No longer a household word during the final phase of his career, Can- non served four relatively placid terms. He was, however, unchanged in his attitudes and beliefs and remained as intensely partisan as ever. Uncle

Joe was critical of the Wilson administration's domestic policy and took a particularly dim view of the president's having smashed the "Republican precedent of prosperity." Cannon also was caustic toward Wilson's foreign policy, asserting in 1915 during the second year of World War I that the United States should "stand as a great neutral nation, preserving neutrality to the end." Of course, once Wilson finally committed the country to war, Cannon was no less than "100% American" and stood with the president. He had, however, few kind words for either the League of Nations or the Fourteen Points.[85]

At the age of eighty-six in 1923, Cannon decided, at last, that it was time to leave public life. Before finally retiring from the House, he had seen the Republicans become the majority party once again and put Warren G. Harding in the White House. The progressive era had all but come to an end, and conservatism, under the guise of "normalcy," was once again the ruling dictum. Three years later on November 12, 1926, back in Danville, Illinois, Joseph Gurney Cannon died quietly in his sleep at the age of ninety.

Obituaries for Cannon tended to remember him with a certain fondness rather than with malice. In his last years he was more often referred to as the Sage of Danville than as the former Czar of the House. Cannon was the last of his kind; his death symbolized the passing of the rough-hewn, uncompromising frontier politician. As Cannon's former colleague in the House, James E. Watson, aptly observed, "the coming generations will never see his like."[86]

The speakership of Joseph Gurney Cannon will be remembered chiefly for the rules revolution of 1910. Was the rules fight inevitable? Although the argument could be made that Cannon might have prevented it by behaving in a less autocratic fashion, it is still likely that in time the rules would have been changed and the Speaker's power reduced. The House revolt of March 1910 was a rejection of the legacy left by the nineteenth-century House—a set of rules that placed the majority firmly in control and centralized power in the Speaker, who was the agent of the majority. The revolt subsequently paved the way for an institutionalized seniority system and the rise of autonomous standing committees.[87]

Joe Cannon had the misfortune to become the Speaker as this transitional phase was beginning. If he had been elected a decade earlier, he might have retired as one of the more popular leaders of the House. This is not to say that Cannon was simply a victim of circumstances beyond his control; he was certainly guilty of abusing his power and surely hastened along the decentralization process.

In the final analysis, Cannon may have been too far out of step with the times to be Speaker. The *Outlook* magazine appropriately and insightfully commented that "[o]n the political railway, Mr. Cannon was not an engineer but a brakeman."[88] The brakeman image is a useful metaphor to describe Cannon's congressional leadership. He was not inclined or prepared to lead the House into the twentieth century but attempted instead to suspend it in time. Cannon was a regular Republican, a politician of the nineteenth century, who had no understanding of progressivism and failed to see any relationship between it and the Republican insurgency. To him the insurgents were merely a group of self-interested politicians, deviants from party regularity just as the Liberal Republicans and Mugwumps before them had been. Moreover, Cannon considered the reform demands of the insurgents and those of the Democratic progressives to be of no great value and possibly detrimental to the country's welfare. Finding accommodation for this element was therefore unthinkable. So the Speaker applied the brakes forcefully and with the able assistance of his standpat colleagues was able for a time to slow the momentum of the House progressives. But in the end the brakes failed; the reformers passed Cannon by and in so doing steered Congress into a new era.

Notes

1. Speaker Cannon's life and career have been the subject of three books: L. White Busbey, *Uncle Joe Cannon: The Story of a Pioneer American* (New York: Henry Holt, 1927); Blair Bolles, *Tyrant from Illinois: Uncle Joe Cannon's Experiment with Personal Power* (New York: W. W. Norton, 1951); and William Rea Gwinn, *Uncle Joe Cannon: Archfoe of Insurgency* (New York: Brookman and Associates, 1957). Busbey's book is essentially Cannon's autobiography, since Cannon practically dictated the book to his longtime personal secretary. Although in no sense an objective source, it does provide the former Speaker's unique perspective on the events surrounding him and indicates how he preferred to have himself remembered. Bolles's book was the first actual biography written about Cannon. As the title suggests, the author's portrayal varies little from that of the muckrakers. Inadequate documentation compromises the study's complete reliability. The most objective and scholarly of the three authors is Gwinn. His book, although factually sound, is dated and therefore does not integrate any of the more recent scholarship on the progressive movement and the institutionalization of Congress.

2. Opal Thornberg, *Earlham: The Story of the College* (Richmond, Ind.: The Earlham College Press, 1963), p. 51; James B. Morrow, "Speaker Cannon; Original and Wise," *Ledger* (Philadelphia), July 7, 1906; Busbey, *Uncle Joe Cannon*, pp. 63–76; and Gwinn, *Archfoe of Insurgency*, p. 12.

3. Gwinn, *Archfoe of Insurgency*, pp. 12–13; Busbey, *Uncle Joe Cannon*, pp. 77–82. Mary Reed died in 1897; Joe Cannon never remarried.

4. Gwinn, *Archfoe of Insurgency*, p. 14; Busbey, *Uncle Joe Cannon*, pp. 88–89.

5. Busbey, *Uncle Joe Cannon*, pp. 120–121. Cannon won the Republican nomination away from incumbent congressman Jesse Moore.

6. Henry Boutwell, "The Claims of the Candidates," *The North American Review* (May 1908): 644; Gwinn, *Archfoe of Insurgency*, pp. 16–17; Will Payne, "A Plutocrat in Homespun," *The Saturday Evening Post* (July 28, 1906): 11.

7. Jay Monaghan, "North Carolinians," *North Carolina Historical Review* 22 (October 1945): 454; and Busbey, *Uncle Joe Cannon*, pp. 133–134.

8. Gwinn, *Archfoe of Insurgency*, pp. 21, 23. The area represented by Cannon underwent redistricting three times during his long career. When he was first elected in 1872 it was the 14th District. In 1882 it became the 15th, in 1894 the 12th, and finally in 1901, the 18th.

9. Ibid., p. 4; Sam Levin, "Joseph Cannon," *Heritage of Vermillion County* (Autumn 1965): 5.

10. Marion Mills Miller, *Great Debates in American History*, 14 vols. (New York: Current Literature Publishing, 1913), 9: 347; Gwinn, *Archfoe of Insurgency*, pp. 53–54.

11. Gwinn, *Archfoe of Insurgency*, p. 51; Bolles, *Tyrant from Illinois*, p. 33.

12. Busbey, *Uncle Joe Cannon*, pp. 184–185; Gwinn, *Archfoe of Insurgency*, pp. 58–59.

13. "The Passing of 'Uncle Joe' Cannon," *The Sun* (New York), November 17, 1912.

14. Gwinn, *Archfoe of Insurgency*, p. 63; "Groping for a National Budget," *Nation* (July 13, 1913): 4.

15. "Persons in the Foreground," *Current Literature* (June 1906): 599.

16. Gwinn, *Archfoe of Insurgency*, pp. 67–69; U.S. Congress, House, debate and vote on H.R. 8927, *Congressional Record*, 55th Cong., 2d sess., March 8, 1898, 31: 2603, 2621; and Busbey, *Uncle Joe Cannon*, pp. 186–189.

17. Horace S. Merrill and Marion G. Merrill, *The Republican Command, 1897–1913* (Lexington: University of Kentucky Press, 1971), p. 118.

18. Gwinn, *Archfoe of Insurgency*, p. 73; Robert W. Diamond, ed., *Origins and Developments of Congress* (Washington, D.C.: Congressional Quarterly, 1976), pp. 110–111.

19. Cannon had been an unsuccessful candidate for Speaker in 1881, 1889, and 1899 before finally being elected in 1903. See Diamond, *Origins and Developments of Congress*, p. 110.

20. Initially Cannon allowed Minority Leader John Sharp Williams to assign Democrats to committees, hoping that this might cause disunity, but the reverse occurred. The Speaker later took away the privilege from James Beauchamp Clark, who replaced Williams as minority leader. See Randall P. Ripley, *Party Leaders in the House of Representatives* (Washington, D.C.: The Brookings Institution, 1967), note pp. 90–91.

21. "Speaker Cannon's Lieutenants," *Public Ledger*, February 20, 1910; Bolles, *Tyrant from Illinois*, pp. 55–59; Charles O. Jones, "Joseph G. Cannon and Howard W. Smith," *Journal of Politics* 30 (August 1968): 620.

22. Steven S. Smith and Christopher J. Deering, *Committees in Congress*, 2d ed. (Washington, D.C.: Congressional Quarterly, 1990), p. 34; Jones, "Joseph G. Cannon and Howard W. Smith," p. 619.

23. Gwinn, *Archfoe of Insurgency*, p. 72.

24. Ibid., p. 79; Busbey, *Uncle Joe Cannon*, p. 216; and Ripley, *Party Leaders*, pp. 17, 77.

25. Cannon to George B. Cortelyou, November 13, 1904, cited in Merrill and Merrill, *The Republican Command*, p. 194; Theodore Roosevelt, *An Autobiography* (New York: Charles Scribner's Sons, 1929), p. 350.

26. Busbey, *Uncle Joe*, p. 210.

27. Gwinn, *Archfoe of Insurgency*, p. 100.

28. "President Has House," *Washington Post*, November 29, 1905; Gwinn, *Archfoe of Insurgency*, p. 101.

29. Theodore Roosevelt to Cannon, January 13, 1905, Joseph Gurney Cannon Papers, Cannon Manuscript Collection, Illinois State Historical Library, Springfield, Illinois; Busbey, *Uncle Joe Cannon*, pp. 207–208, 212–213; Theodore Roosevelt to Cannon, November 30, 1904, Theodore Roosevelt Papers, Library of Congress, Washington, D.C.; Henry Pringle, *Theodore Roosevelt* (New York: Harcourt, Brace & World, 1931), p. 291.

30. John M. Blum, *The Republican Roosevelt* (Cambridge: The Harvard University Press, 1954), pp. 80–81.

31. Lewis Gould, *The Presidency of Theodore Roosevelt* (Lawrence: The University Press of Kansas, 1991), pp. 165–166.

32. "Roosevelt Stirs House to Action," *Chicago Tribune*, June 5, 1906; "Speaker Cannon's Reply to His Critics," *Literary Digest* (June 30, 1906); "Speaker Cannon's Contentment with the Present Foods," *Literary Digest* (June 16, 1906); Gwinn, *Archfoe of Insurgency*, pp. 108–109.

33. Harvey W. Wiley, *An Autobiography* (Brooklyn, N.Y.: Bobbs-Merrill, 1930), p. 228; Gwinn, *Archfoe of Insurgency*, pp. 112–113. The Meat Inspection Bill passed the House on June 20, three days before the Pure Food and Drug Act.

34. Cannon's speech at Danville, Illinois, November 1906, Cannon Papers.

35. Theodore Roosevelt to Cannon, September 14, 1906, Cannon Papers; and Matthew Josephson, *The President Makers* (New York: Frederick Unger, 1964), p. 124.

36. Gifford Pinchot, *Breaking New Ground* (Seattle: University of Washington Press, 1972), pp. 240, 197–198; Gwinn, *Archfoe of Insurgency*, p. 36; Bolles, *Tyrant from Illinois*, p. 121.

37. Theodore Roosevelt to Cannon, March 2, 1907, Theodore Roosevelt Papers; "The Appalachian–White Mountain Bill," *Outlook* (May 16, 1908): 92; Gwinn, *Archfoe of Insurgency*, pp. 134–135; Bolles, *Tyrant from Illinois*, pp. 121–122.

38. Merrill and Merrill, *The Republican Command*, pp. 223–224.

39. Bolles, *Tyrant from Illinois*, pp. 137–138; Henry F. Pringle, *The Life and Times of William Howard Taft* (New York: Farrar & Rinehart, 1939), 1: 354. In the balloting for the presidential nomination, Cannon came in fourth with 58 votes, slightly behind both Charles Evans Hughes and Philander Knox, who received 67 and 68 votes respectively. See "Cannon to Take Stump for Taft," *St. Louis Globe-Democrat*, June 19, 1908.

40. Josephson, *The President Makers*, pp. 270–271; Pringle, *Theodore Roosevelt*, pp. 240–241; "Boycott of Joe Cannon a Feature in the West," *Daily Eagle* (Brooklyn, N.Y.), October 17, 1908.

41. Pringle, *The Life and Times of William Howard Taft*, p. 406.

42. Gwinn, *Archfoe of Insurgency*, pp. 162–163; George Mowry, *Theodore Roosevelt and the Progressive Movement* (Madison: The University of Wisconsin Press, 1947), p. 42.

43. Kenneth W. Hechler, *Insurgency: Personalities and Politics of the Taft Era* (New York: Russell and Russell, 1964), pp. 54–55; Jerome Clubb, "Congressional Opponents of Reform, 1901–1913" (Ph.D. diss., University of Washington, 1964), p. 132; Gwinn, *Archfoe of Insurgency*, p. 174; U.S. Congress, House, *Congressional Record*, 61st Cong., 1st sess., March 15, 1909, 44: 18–33. Prior to the Fitzgerald resolution there was a unanimous consent procedure in place by which any member of the House could move for consideration of a bill. Technically, the Speaker had no more power to object to this than did any other member. However, before he would recognize a motion for unanimous consent, the Speaker required advance notice; Cannon cleared or refused to clear such requests according to personal judgment. See Jones, "Joseph G. Cannon and Howard W. Smith," p. 625.

44. "'We Will Win,' says Mr. Murdock," *Chicago Record-Herald*, undated clipping from 1909, Cannon Papers.

45. Cannon to James A. Tawney, July 27, 1908, James A. Tawney Papers, Tawney Manuscript Collection, Minnesota Historical Society, St. Paul, Minnesota.

46. Geoffrey Morrison, "Champ Clark and the Rules Revolution of 1910," *Capitol Studies* 43 (1974): 50–51; Richard Bolling, *Power in the House* (New York: E. P. Dutton, 1968), pp. 75–76.

47. Hechler, *Insurgency*, p. 38.

48. Ibid., p. 33; Richard Lowitt, *George W. Norris: The Making of a Progressive, 1861–1912* (New York: Syracuse Press, 1963), p. 126.

49. Hechler, *Insurgency*, pp. 34–42.

50. Ripley, *Party Leaders*, note, p. 91; Joseph Cooper and David Brady, "Institutional Context and Leadership Style in the House from Cannon to Rayburn," *American Political Science Review* 75 (1981): 415; Jones, "Joseph G. Cannon and Howard W. Smith," p. 626.

51. Ripley, *Party Leaders*, pp. 44, 90.

52. Ibid., pp. 51–52; Nelson Polsby, "The Institutionalization of the House of Representatives," *American Political Science Review* 2 (March 1968): 155; Smith and Deering, *Committees in Congress*, p. 35.

53. Hechler, *Insurgency*, p. 33; Lowitt, *George W. Norris*, p. 127; U.S. Congress, House, debate and vote on Resolution 607, *Congressional Record*, 60th Cong., 2d sess., March 15, 1909, 43: 3567–3572.

54. Hechler, *Insurgency*, pp. 46–48; Lowitt, *George W. Norris*, p. 127.

55. Pringle, *The Life and Times of William Howard Taft*, vol. 1, p. 406; Hechler, *Insurgency*, pp. 47–49.

56. Alvin M. Josephy, Jr., *On the Hill: A History of the American Congress* (New York: Simon & Schuster, 1975), p. 286.

57. Stanley D. Solvick, "William Howard Taft and the Payne-Aldrich Tariff," *The Mississippi Valley Historical Review* (December 1963): 426.

58. Gwinn, *Archfoe of Insurgency*, pp. 179–180; Bolles, *Tyrant from Illinois*, pp. 190–191; Josephy, *On the Hill*, p. 286.

59. Bolles, *Tyrant from Illinois*, p. 192.

60. "Taft's Speech Knock-out for the Insurgents," *InterOcean* (Chicago), September 19, 1909; Gwinn, *Archfoe of Insurgency*, p. 186; Lowitt, *George W. Norris*, p. 149.

61. Jones, "Joseph G. Cannon and Howard W. Smith," p. 621.

62. "The Insurgents' First Taste of Blood," *Current Literature* (February 1910): 127.

63. One of the major controversies of the Taft administration, the Ballinger-Pinchot affair involved the sale of government coal fields in Alaska by Secretary of the Interior Richard Ballinger to a syndicate headed by J. P. Morgan and David Guggenheim. Against President Taft's wishes, Gifford Pinchot, head of the National Forest Service, leaked the information to the press and called for a congressional investigation. Subsequently fired for his insubordination, Pinchot's dismissal raised the ire of his insurgent supporters and widened the breach within the Republican ranks.

64. Bolles, *Tyrant from Illinois*, p. 213; Mowry, *Theodore Roosevelt*, p. 90.

65. Hechler, *Insurgency*, p. 65; *Current Literature* (February 1910): 127.

66. Hechler, *Insurgency*, pp. 66–69; U.S. Congress, House, debate concerning House Resolution 502, *Congressional Record*, 61st Cong., 2d sess., March 17, 1910, 45: 3292.

67. Hechler, *Insurgency*, pp. 70–71; Busbey, *Uncle Joe Cannon*, p. 244; Gwinn, *Archfoe of Insurgency*, p. 208.

68. Gwinn, *Archfoe of Insurgency*, pp. 211–212; Hechler, *Insurgency*, p. 71.

69. Gwinn, *Archfoe of Insurgency*, p. 213.

70. Hechler, *Insurgency*, p. 72; U.S. Congress, House, debate concerning House Resolution 502, *Congressional Record*, 61st Cong., 2d sess., March 17, 1910, 45: 3425.

71. Gwinn, *Archfoe of Insurgency*, p. 215; "Dares Them to Expell," *Baltimore Sun*, March 20, 1920; U.S. Congress, House, debate concerning House Resolution 502, *Congressional Record*, 61st Cong., 2d sess., March 17, 1910, 45: 3426.

72. Hechler, *Insurgency*, p. 75.

73. Lowitt, *George W. Norris*, p. 179; U.S. Congress, House, debate concerning House Resolution 502, *Congressional Record*, 61st Cong., 2d sess., March 17, 1910, 45: 3437–3439; Bolles, *Tyrant from Illinois*, p. 224.

74. Hechler, *Insurgency*, p. 78; "Champ Clark Jubilant," *Baltimore Sun*, March 20, 1910.

75. "Cannon's Hot Shot," *Kankakee Republican* (Kankakee, Ill.), July 19, 1910; Gwinn, *Archfoe of Insurgency*, pp. 224, 227.

76. Gwinn, *Archfoe of Insurgency*, p. 219.

77. Ibid., pp. 241–243; "The Speaker Wins," *Washington Post*, January, 10, 1911; "End of the Insurgent League," *The Globe* (St. Louis, Mo.), January 10, 1911.

78. Archibald Butt, *Taft and Roosevelt: The Intimate Letters of Archie Butt* (New York: Doran and Company, 1930), p. 596.

79. *Illinois Bluebook* (Danville: Illinois State Printer, 1911), p. 367; Gwinn, *Archfoe of Insurgency*, p. 237.

80. Gwinn, *Archfoe of Insurgency*, pp. 245–257. Another of the rules adopted by the Democrats amended the committee discharge rule so that only the title of the bill to be discharged could be read on the floor, thereby preventing the type of fil-

ibustering Cannon had permitted Mann to do during the previous session. See "Democrats Doom House Sinecures," *Chicago Tribune,* April 1, 1911.

81. "Mann Is Chosen Minority Leader in House Caucus," *Chicago Tribune,* April 4, 1911; Gwinn, *Archfoe of Insurgency,* p. 253.

82. Gwinn, *Archfoe of Insurgency,* p. 253.

83. *Illinois Bluebook* (Danville: Illinois State Printer, 1912), p. 592; "Cannon's Brush with O'Hair," *Literary Digest* (January 4, 1913): 42

84. The Justice Department investigated the possibility that there had been irregularities in the election that returned Cannon to his old seat but could find no evidence of anything to warrant prosecution. See "Uncle Joe," *The Item* (New Orleans, La.), November 6, 1914.

85. "Cannon Selects Text and Talks About War," clipping from unidentified source, July 12, 1915, Cannon Papers; "Cannon Caustic on Administration," *Evening Star* (Washington, D.C.), February 13, 1914; Gwinn, *Archfoe of Insurgency,* p. 262.

86. James E. Watson, *As I Knew Them: Memoirs of James E. Watson* (Indianapolis: Bobbs-Merrill, 1936), p. 128.

87. Cooper and Brady, "Institutional Context," p. 411; Jerome Clubb, William Flanagan, and Nancy Zingale, *Partisan Realignment: Voters, Parties, and Government in American History* (Beverly Hills, Calif.: Sage Publications, 1980), p. 285.

88. "'Uncle Joe Cannon,'" *Outlook* (November 1926): 393.

4

Oscar W. Underwood:
The First Modern
House Leader, 1911–1915

James S. Fleming

In a vivid description of the House revolt against Speaker Joseph G. Cannon in March 1910, George Rothwell Brown, who had observed the revolt from the House press gallery, wrote: "As Mr. Cannon's gavel fell, an epoch in the long and brilliant history of the American House of Representatives came to an end. A new era had begun."[1] Indeed, a new era did begin in the House of Representatives after the revolt against Speaker Cannon. But it was not immediately apparent, not even to the leaders of the revolt themselves, what the post-Cannon era would look like.

Oscar W. Underwood, a sixteen-year House veteran from Alabama and one of the Democratic leaders in the bipartisan revolt against Speaker Cannon, believed that the new leader of the House would be the chairman of the Committee on Rules. "If this resolution goes through, ultimately, if not today," Underwood said, moments before the House vote against Speaker Cannon, "the speaker of the House of Representatives will cease to be its leader and the chairman of the Committee on Rules elected by the majority party in the House will become leader."[2]

Contrary to Underwood's expectation, the chairman of the Committee on Rules did not become the new leader of the House of Representatives after the revolt against Speaker Cannon. Indeed, the Rules Committee chairman did in time become one of the principal leaders of the House, but the leadership of the post-Cannon House fell in 1911 to Oscar W. Underwood himself, as the newly elected chairman of the Committee on Ways and Means.

In one of the most dramatic shifts of power in congressional history, Underwood became not only chairman of the powerful Committee on Ways and Means (the most important legislative committee of the day with jurisdiction over the tariff) but also the first elected majority floor leader in congressional history and chairman of the newly created and newly powerful Democratic Committee on Committees. "For the first time in congressional history," Brown noted, "the leader of the House was not at the rostrum, but on the floor."[3]

As the first modern House leader in the post-Cannon era, Underwood had to work within a more decentralized and democratic House. Underwood's major contribution to the leadership of the House was that he showed how a new, more democratic House structure could be established and maintained in the post-Cannon Congress.[4] The more democratic structure the Democrats put in place in 1911, which focused on distributing influence more widely throughout the House through the caucus and committee system, became increasingly fragmented and difficult to manage after Underwood left the House for the Senate in 1915. But the leadership the "suave, diplomatic, and commanding" Underwood showed in making the new House structure work from 1911 to 1915 established him as one of the "giants" in whose footsteps future House leaders would have to walk.[5]

Underwood did not foresee his own leadership—certainly not the extent and configuration of power he would have in the new Congress. Nevertheless he was well suited, by intellect and disposition, for the fortuitous circumstances that would cast him into the major House leadership role from 1911 to 1915 and make him, in the opinion of Richard Bolling, arguably "the best Democratic legislative leader in this century."[6]

Born in Louisville, Kentucky, on May 6, 1862, in the midst of the Civil War, Oscar Wilder Underwood was forty-nine years old when he assumed the leadership of the House of Representatives in 1911. His father, Eugene Underwood, was a distinguished lawyer in Louisville, and his grandfather, Joseph R. Underwood, a popular Whig politician and colleague of Henry Clay, represented Kentucky in both the House of Representatives (1835–1845) and the U.S. Senate (1847–1853).

When young Oscar was three, his pro-Union family moved to St. Paul, Minnesota, where Underwood lost much of his southern accent and learned the ways of the frontier West. Ten years later he returned with his family to Louisville, where he attended an elite English-style preparatory school for boys. In 1881 he enrolled in the University of Virginia to study law. At Virginia he became a devoted follower of Thomas Jefferson and president of the Jefferson Society, a prestigious debating club on campus.

He returned briefly to St. Paul in 1884 to begin a legal practice, but he was soon drawn by his brother to the booming iron and steel center of the New South in Birmingham, Alabama (which at the time had a population of about six thousand people). There he prospered as a lawyer and quickly became involved in local Democratic politics. At thirty he was head of his party's executive committee in his congressional district. Three years later, in 1894, he was elected to Congress, defeating the incumbent Democratic congressman in the party nominating convention and then narrowly defeating his Republican opponent in the general election. Three days before his first congressional term expired on June 9, 1896, Underwood was unseated by the Republican-controlled Fifty-fourth Congress in an election dispute involving alleged disenfranchisement of several hundred black voters in his district. He was, however, reelected to a second term in Congress in November 1896 and won easy reelection in subsequent years.[7]

Though Underwood had spent his entire sixteen-year congressional career in the minority, he had established a reputation as a skillful and hardworking legislator. During his freshman year he impressed the Republican Speaker, Thomas Brackett Reed, who was "personally fond" of the young Democratic member[8] and whom Underwood regarded as "the greatest intellect I have known in public life."[9] Even more important to his career, Underwood also impressed his own Democratic colleagues. He became the first Democratic whip in the House in 1900–1901.[10] He served intermittently on several of the House's most prestigious committees: Judiciary, Appropriations, Rules, and Ways and Means. By the time of the revolt against Speaker Cannon in 1910, Underwood had risen to the second-ranking Democratic position on the Ways and Means Committee—just behind James B. "Champ" Clark of Missouri, the Democratic minority leader—where he was regarded as his party's leading expert on the tariff.

Arthur S. Link described Underwood's "commanding presence":

> Underwood was strong-framed and sturdily built. His round, clean-shaven face was serene and his blue eyes had a friendly twinkle in them. . . . There was little about him that suggested the old-fashioned southern politician. So conventional was his dress that he might have been mistaken for a banker, manufacturer, or prosperous merchant. His consummate tact, modesty, even temperament, and perfect self-control made him an ideal party leader. His years of assiduous study of tariff legislation and his clarity and conciseness in expressing his tariff opinion marked him as the outstanding Democratic authority on the important question. His associates in Congress knew him as a sound thinker, a student of the intricate facts and figures of tariff legislation, and a friendly compromiser and conciliator.[11]

In many respects Underwood was an old-fashioned Democrat. He strongly supported the fundamentals of traditional Jeffersonian Democracy. He favored tariff legislation "for revenue only." He opposed concentration of governmental power in the national government and supported state sovereignty with strong local government. He was not a progressive in the conventional sense of the word. He opposed, for example, the initiative, referendum, and recall—three of the most popular progressive reforms. But he did favor several other progressive reforms, particularly the reduction of the Republican protective tariff, despite the fact that he came from a protected iron and steel district in Birmingham, Alabama, where his second wife's father was a prominent iron producer. He was, in short, as Link observed, "honest and courageous" and the type of Democrat progressives respected, even though they disagreed with him on some of the important issues of the day.[12]

The immediate circumstances surrounding Underwood's rise to leadership came after the midterm congressional elections in November 1910, when the Democrats won control of the House of Representatives for the first time in sixteen years. The Democrats gained an impressive 56 seats in the House to win a 228 to 162 majority in the new Sixty-second Congress. They also picked up 10 seats in the Senate. But the Republicans, who were generally considered to be the majority party in the country at that time, retained control of the Senate with a 51 to 41 majority. The Republicans also maintained control of the presidency; the incumbent Republican president, William Howard Taft, remained in the White House.

The Democrats won control of the House of Representatives, most observers believed, because of the role they had played in overthrowing Speaker Cannon and because of their renewed campaign pledge (from their 1908 platform) to reform the rules of the House of Representatives so as to "enable a majority of its members to dictate its deliberation and control legislation." They had also promised, if elected to power, to lower the protective Republican tariff, which for years had been a symbol to the Democrats of economic privilege and elitism.[13]

Now that the Democrats were finally in charge of the House, there was widespread interest throughout the country in what they would do. "During their years in the minority," one observer noted, the Democrats "had lost a good deal of their reputation for cohesion and efficiency. Effective leadership was almost impossible with them. . . . On their return to power, there was unconcealed anxiety among prominent members of the party all through the country as to the result, while the Republicans openly predicted a continuance of the old disorganization and disregard for leadership."[14]

Much was at stake, therefore, for the victorious Democrats as they met together in their caucus in January 1911 to reorganize the House and prove to themselves and to the rest of the country that they could govern. In the process of reorganizing the House, the Democrats adopted a series of party and institutional reforms that went a long way toward reshaping House politics for years to come and making Oscar W. Underwood the first modern House leader of the twentieth century.

The Democrats made seven basic organizational decisions that shaped the institutional framework within which Underwood had to operate as the new House leader. They nominated Champ Clark as the new Speaker of the House, elected Underwood to be chairman of the Ways and Means Committee, selected the other thirteen Democratic members of the Ways and Means Committee, and instructed the Democratic members of the Ways and Means Committee to serve also as a Committee on Committees in the new Congress. In addition, the Democrats elected Underwood as their new majority floor leader, decided to use the party caucus to maintain party unity on the floor of the House, and adopted a number of rules changes to give individual members more influence in the House.

These decisions had the cumulative effect of distributing influence more widely throughout the House while at the same time giving Oscar Underwood the authority he needed to hold his party together and make the House work as an institution. Taken together, they marked one of the watershed changes in the internal organization of the House of Representatives.

The first decision the Democrats made when they met in their organizing caucus on January 19, 1911, was to nominate Champ Clark unanimously as their new Speaker—a position to which Clark was formally elected when the Sixty-second Congress convened three months later. A personable and beloved figure within his party, Clark had been the Democratic minority leader and ranking Democrat on the Ways and Means Committee in the previous Congress. It was only natural, therefore, for Clark to be chosen by the Democrats to be the new Speaker of the House. But Clark would become only the titular leader of the new House, without the powers of former Speakers to chair the Rules Committee or appoint standing committees.[15]

The Democratic caucus also unanimously chose Oscar W. Underwood to be the chairman of the Committee on Ways and Means, with responsibility for steering the important tariff legislation through the new Congress. The chairman of the Committee on Ways and Means had always been an important figure in the House, with three presidents (James Polk, Millard Fillmore, and William McKinley), for example, serving as Ways and Means chairman before becoming president. But with the diminution of the Speaker, Underwood would become one of the most powerful Ways and Means chairmen in congressional history and the real leader of the new House.[16]

"Perhaps no one ever came into greater power with less individual assertiveness," one of Underwood's former Republican colleagues observed, noting the ironic set of circumstances that now placed the quiet and unassuming Oscar Underwood at the head of the House leadership. "The choice of Champ Clark as Speaker, who had headed the minority on Ways and Means in the preceding House, left Underwood the ranking member and without a rival of sufficient strength to contest with him for the majority leadership."[17]

The Democratic caucus also chose the other thirteen Democratic members of the Ways and Means Committee, restricted them from membership on other committees, and instructed them to begin the immediate revision of the tariff. It would have been "both unwise and unfair," the new Speaker explained, "to lay upon the members of the Ways and Means Committee the onerous and delicate duty of preparing a tariff bill or bills and deny them sufficient time to accomplish that task carefully, intelligently, with credit to themselves and with satisfaction to us and to the country."[18]

In addition, the Democratic caucus decided after a long debate—and with the approval of the Speaker-to-be Champ Clark—that the fourteen

Democratic members of the Ways and Means Committee, not the Speaker, would choose the committees and the committee chairmen in the new Congress.[19] Prior to the January caucus, there had been some speculation that the Committee on Rules might be given the responsibility to make committee assignments in the new Congress, an action that would have been consistent with Underwood's prediction that the chairman of the Rules Committee would become the leader of the House after the revolt against Speaker Cannon. But this alternative was "quickly abandoned as conferring too much power on a committee that had been so severely criticized in the past." Instead, the Democrats decided that "a regular legislative committee of the House should prepare the list of committees to be presented to the caucus. It was only natural," one observer explained, that since the "Ways and Means Committee [had to] be selected early so as to work on the tariff, it should also be designated to nominate the committees."[20] The Democratic caucus therefore decided, almost unanimously by a vote of 166 to 7, to empower the Democratic members of the Ways and Means Committee to serve as a Committee on Committees in the new Congress.[21]

But not all of the Democrats were happy with the caucus's decision to deprive the new Speaker of his power to appoint committees. John J. Fitzgerald, a Tammany Hall politician from Brooklyn, New York, and the leader of the Tory Democrats (a group of Democrats who had supported Cannon in the past and favored a system of strong speakers[22]), moved in the Democratic caucus that the new Democratic Speaker should continue to make committee appointments "in accordance with the unbroken policy of the Democratic Party and the uniform practice of the House." The Democratic caucus, however, rejected the Fitzgerald resolution by a decisive vote of 166 to 29, indicating the overwhelming determination of the new Democratic majority to revolutionize the method of committee selection in the new Congress.[23]

The Democratic caucus also unanimously elected Oscar Underwood to be their new majority floor leader.[24] It was customary for the chairman of the Ways and Means Committee to be named majority floor leader during the first decade of the twentieth century, mainly because the most important business of most Congresses (the tariff) came before his committee. But Underwood's selection as majority leader in 1911 marked the first time in congressional history that the caucus, not the Speaker, had chosen the majority leader, a practice that continues to this day.[25]

The Democrats further decided that they would use their party caucus not only to elect their leaders and confirm committee assignments but also to bind members to party unity on the floor of the House. According to the caucus rules (first adopted by the Democrats in 1909), all Democrats were bound to support a policy decision made by a two-thirds vote of the Democratic caucus, unless they found the measure to be unconstitutional or had made contrary pledges to their constituents. This binding caucus, where individual policy decisions were shaped by the larger collective will of the party, played a major role in Underwood's leadership of the new Congress.[26]

Last, the Democrats incorporated three important rules changes that had been adopted during the previous Congress to give individual members of the House more influence in the legislative process. They retained and strengthened the Calendar Wednesday rule, first adopted in 1909, under which the standing committees of the House had an opportunity to call up bills without obtaining permission from the Rules Committee. They also preserved the Unanimous Consent Calendar, another 1909 progressive innovation, whereby two days a month were designated for the consideration of minor bills, important to individual members, without requiring the recognition of the Speaker. And they maintained the Discharge Calendar, which had been added to the House rules after the revolt against Speaker Cannon in 1910, to give a majority of the House an opportunity to discharge bills from reluctant committees.[27]

"On the surface," congressional scholar George B. Galloway noted,

> the 1911 rules had apparently succeeded in transferring control of the legislative process in the House of Representatives from the speaker to the House itself. To many students of these tremendous events it appeared, not that the House had rejected the principle of leadership, but rather that the House had rebelled against the dictatorial manner in which Speaker Cannon exercised his powers and had determined to shift the leadership of the House from the chair to the floor, leaving the speaker on the rostrum as merely a moderator of the legislative machine.[28]

Under the new system, another scholar observed in the same vein, "there was a wider diffusion of responsibilities." As a result, "effective leadership was made more difficult" and "the general public," accustomed to a Speaker-led House, was "frequently at a loss to determine where real responsibility for action taken, or not taken, lies."[29]

But beneath the surface, beneath the "diffusion of responsibilities" made necessary by a more democratic age, there was a plan for leadership. Though he would have to work within a more decentralized and democratic House, Oscar Underwood would have considerable authority to carry out his new leadership responsibilities. Those who saw beneath the surface saw clearly that "the power of the House of Representatives had been transferred from the speaker to the chairman of the Ways and Means Committee," who also, of course, served as majority floor leader and chairman of the Committee on Committees.[30] These three positions, when combined, made Underwood a formidable power in the new House.

Underwood would have to be careful, though, not to exceed the limits of his leadership of the new House. The 1910 revolt against a dictatorial Speaker, Charles O. Jones has observed, set some fairly clear limits beyond which no future leader of the House could go.[31] Henceforth, House leaders, acting in a more democratic institution, would have to be more responsive to the changing expectations of their followers. As one progressive journalist, attuned to the changing conditions of House leadership, reminded Underwood:

> The fact is that, although Uncle Joseph Cannon is politically dead, yet the power which made Uncle Joseph the Czar of the House still lives on after him. The famous rules fight of Murdock, Norris and company [in the 1910 revolt against Speaker Cannon] did not break or destroy that power. It merely transferred it to new hands. The precious sovereignty of the House today belongs wholly to the Floor Leader; it has descended to Underwood of Alabama. Should he misuse it, the American dictionary of politics will contain a fresh word to replace "Cannonism." This word will be "Underwoodism."
>
> Here's hoping the Democrats will run their machine well, not recklessly over the rights of the people, and here's giving Oscar Underwood a kindly word of warning not to joy-ride in his powerful car the way J.G. Cannon used to do.[32]

The fact that the dictionary of politics in the United States today does not contain the word *Underwoodism* is, in the final analysis, a quiet but fitting tribute to the success Oscar Underwood had in leading the House away from the one-man dictatorial rule of Joe Cannon into the more democratic, modern institution it is today. In leading the House into this modern age, Underwood had to work with several independent or emerging centers of power in the House: the president; the Speaker; the caucus; the standing committees, particularly the Rules Committee; and the minority party to a lesser extent. Underwood's effectiveness as a leader can most easily be seen by briefly examining the success he had in working with each of these power centers in the new Congress.

Underwood's relations with the president greatly depended on who was president: the Republican William Howard Taft during the Sixty-second Congress in 1911–1912 or the Democratic Woodrow Wilson in the Sixty-third Congress in 1913–1914. Under Taft, with the Republicans also in control of the Senate, Underwood became the focal point of Democratic opposition in Congress; under Wilson, with the Democrats in control of the House and Senate, Underwood became the new Democratic president's chief lieutenant for steering his domestic reforms through the House.

Taft had a rather narrow constitutional view of the presidency, which limited his involvement in the legislative process.[33] Taft did seek and receive Underwood's cooperation in early 1911 on the enactment of the

Canadian Reciprocity Act, an international agreement to lower trade barriers between the United States and Canada (which, ironically, Canada rejected). But other than this one incident, there was virtually no legislative cooperation between the Republican president and the Democratic House majority leader.[34]

The major policy difference between Underwood and President Taft, with significant political implications for both men, centered on the important question of the tariff. Taft, and the Republican Party generally, favored high tariff rates to protect U.S. industry. Underwood and the House Democrats, on the other hand, advocated a "tariff for revenue only." As Underwood, the leading Democratic expert on the tariff, explained the differences between the Republican and Democratic positions:

> I believe in a tariff for revenue only. That is, we should have the lowest rates that will raise the revenues which the exigencies of the Government require. The differential between domestic and foreign costs of production is the dividing line between the Democratic and the Republican theories of the tariff. It is the maximum of Democratic rates and the minimum of Republican rates.
>
> Just as soon as you come below the difference between domestic and foreign costs you make a competitive tariff. Just as soon as you go above it you make a protective tariff. A protective tariff is never a revenue tariff, because as soon as you make it protective you begin to dam back imports and competition.[35]

Underwood skillfully used his newfound positions as majority leader and chairman of the Ways and Means Committee to unite the House Democrats in the Sixty-second Congress behind a revision of the nation's tariff laws.[36] Acting to carry out their 1910 campaign promises to lower the tariff, Underwood got the Democratic House to enact seven separate tariff reduction bills in the Sixty-second Congress, five of which also passed the Republican Senate, with a bipartisan Democratic-Republican majority, only to be vetoed by the protectionist Republican president.[37]

Underwood's success in organizing the House Democrats against the Republican president quickly gained the attention of the nation's press and propelled him into the public spotlight. "A Democratic majority in the lower branch of Congress has become, for the first time in a generation, an effective, harmonious, smoothly working legislative machine," one journalist noted:

> Instead of spending all its time in internal dissensions, this Democratic majority has devoted itself intelligently and conscientiously to the consideration of pressing national problems. It has abolished certain rules of legislative procedure which had prevailed for more than a century, and given Congress

a new representative and deliberative character. And, as a result of its legislative program, the lower House, probably for the first time since the Civil War, has ceased to be the unassailable headquarters of special privilege.

The dominating force in this new Congress, and the man chiefly responsible for its changed character, is a round-faced, tall, broad-chested, boyish figure from Alabama—a gentleman who, a year ago, was scarcely known outside of legislative circles in Washington.[38]

Underwood's leadership of the House also propelled him into contention for the Democratic presidential nomination in 1912, along with Speaker Champ Clark and Woodrow Wilson, the progressive governor of New Jersey. The Underwood presidential movement was never able to generate significant support outside the South. But Underwood played a crucial role in determining the outcome of the convention, by eventually swinging the 117 delegates he captured at the convention to Woodrow Wilson, who won the Democratic nomination on the forty-sixth ballot in the summer of 1912.[39]

Wilson went on to win the presidency in a four-way contest with William Howard Taft, the Republican incumbent president; Theodore Roosevelt, the Bull Moose challenger and former Republican president; and Eugene Debs, the Socialist nominee. Though Wilson received only 42 percent of the popular vote, the combined votes for Wilson and the two other reform candidates, Roosevelt and Debs, amounted to over 70 percent of the total vote, indicating widespread public support for political change throughout the country.[40]

Even more important to Underwood, the new Democratic president carried with him a Democratic majority in both houses of Congress for the first time since 1892. The Democrats won 62 additional seats in the House of Representatives (which was expanded in 1912 from 391 seats to its current size of 435) to command a staggering 290 to 127 majority (with 18 Progressives) in the new House. The Democrats also gained 10 seats in the Senate, where they had a 51 to 44 majority (with one Progressive).

"When the 63rd Congress met" in April 1913, Underwood later wrote,

> there was a large and thoroughly organized Democratic majority prepared to do business for the nation. They were not raw recruits in legislative matters; they were veterans organized and trained in legislative work and procedure. They had not been in power long enough to become divided into cliques, or to be swayed by outside influences. They were primarily loyal to their party and its principles, and desirous of passing legislation that would be responsive to the needs of the country.[41]

The new Democratic president wasted no time in presenting an ambitious reform agenda to the new Democratic Congress. Unlike President Taft, Wilson believed in a strong executive with the president fully involved in the legislative process. The president "must be prime minister," Wilson believed, "as much concerned with the guidance of legislation as with the just and orderly execution of law."[42]

Underwood moved quickly to assist Wilson in carrying out his legislative agenda. Acting with impressive speed and efficiency, in 1913 Underwood got the House to pass both the Underwood-Simmons Tariff Act (the first comprehensive downward revision of the tariff since the Civil War, which also included the first income tax levied under the newly ratified Sixteenth Amendment) and the Federal Reserve Act (which fundamentally restructured the nation's monetary system). And the accelerated pace continued in 1914 with the enactment of the Federal Trade Commission Act and the Clayton Anti-Trust Act—two equally significant laws in the area of trusts and monopolies.[43]

The legislative pace of enacting such major policy changes in such a brief period of time was so hectic as "almost to destroy [Underwood's] health," one observer noted.[44] Indeed, "physically exhausted" on at least one occasion (during the caucus debate on the tariff in April 1913), Underwood "was ordered to bed by his physician."[45]

But throughout the legislative push for the reforms, Underwood was continually assisted by President Wilson, who, unlike his predecessor, used the full powers of his office to advance his legislative agenda. Breaking with presidential tradition, Wilson personally appeared before a Joint Session of Congress—the first president since John Adams to do so—to urge the adoption of tariff reform. He regularly consulted with Underwood on both the content and strategy of legislation. Wilson publicly denounced lobbyists' efforts to defeat his reforms. He personally lobbied members of Congress both at the White House and on Capitol Hill, and he frequently appealed to the public for their support. Wilson, indeed, acted as the chief legislative leader of his party in Congress and set the modern standard by which future presidents would be judged in their legislative dealings with Congress.[46]

But, in the final analysis, Underwood needed more than the personal assistance of the president to steer Wilson's program through the House. As a matter of practical importance, Underwood had to exercise his own leadership of the House. For this task, he relied on not only his formal positions of authority but also his knowledge of the legislative process and of the House as an institution. Though Underwood publicly praised Wilson as "a very great leader of men,"[47] privately, according to his son, Oscar W. Underwood, Jr., he "felt that Wilson's chief weakness was his lack of legislative experience," for which Underwood believed he had to continually compensate through his own day-to-day leadership of the House.[48]

Of all the relations Underwood had in the new Congress, none was more agreeable than his relationship with the new Speaker, Champ Clark, with whom, according to Underwood's biographer, he "never quarreled."[49] Underwood and Clark had been colleagues in the House for fourteen years, ever since Clark's election to the House in 1896.[50] Underwood was twelve years younger than the Speaker. They had served together on the Committee on Ways and Means since 1906. Underwood had supported Clark for minority leader to succeed John Sharp Williams in 1908. They had stood side by side in the fight against Speaker Cannon in 1910. And they had worked closely together to reorganize the House after the Democrats gained power in 1911. Looking back on his long association with Clark years later, Underwood recalled there never was "a moment when a spirit of friendship and brotherly love [did] not exist . . . between us."[51]

But from a political standpoint, Clark was the great loser in the transfer of power that took place after the Democrats gained control of the House in 1911. Though Clark became Speaker in the new Congress, he did not inherit the traditional powers of former Speakers, thanks largely to his own revolutionary efforts against Speaker Cannon in 1910. John J. Fitzgerald, the Tammany Hall Democrat from New York, had tried to dissuade Clark from his fight to remove Speaker Cannon from the Rules Committee in 1910. "You are very likely to be the speaker in the next House," Fitzgerald admonished Clark, "and you will want this power. You are simply destroying your coming heritage." But Clark rejected Fitzgerald's advice, telling him:

> I have been in the minority so long that I have seen the advantage and power of the speaker. The Minority Leader is pitted against the speaker as a leader of the majority, and the speaker has all the advantage which his power over members gives him. If I am speaker, I do not want that power. Let it be a fair fight between the leader of the two parties on the floor of the House and the speaker be the umpire instead of majority leader and umpire as well.[52]

When Clark became Speaker in 1911, however—having also given up his power to appoint committees—he discovered that he was not content merely being the "umpire" in the fight between the majority and minority leaders on the floor of the House. He immediately and wholeheartedly threw himself into the partisan struggles of his party. He continually used his procedural authority from the chair to assist Underwood in his floor leadership of the House, and he rivaled even Speaker Cannon in the frequency with which he participated in debate and voted on the House floor.[53] He worked closely with Underwood in the enactment of the reforms in both the Sixty-second and Sixty-third Congresses. He played a pivotal role in mediating a "potentially disastrous intra-party split" on the federal reserve bill in the party caucus in 1914.[54] And on the one measure where Underwood opposed President Wilson (on the Panama Canal tolls exemption bill in 1913), Clark also opposed the president, though not even the combined opposition of the Speaker and the majority leader was enough to defeat a popular Democratic president, determined to have his way on this issue.[55]

The organizational key to Underwood's leadership of the House was his reliance on his party's binding caucus to promote discipline and unity within his party. Underwood used the party caucus in much the same way the leader of a European parliamentary democracy uses the party caucus to achieve unity within the party on matters before a parliament. After a bill had been drafted by the Democratic members of a standing committee (often meeting with Underwood and sometimes President Wilson), it was typically submitted to a closed meeting of the House Democratic caucus, consisting of all Democrats in the House, for an internal party debate and ultimately a vote binding all House Democrats to support the caucus decision on the floor of the House.[56] Each member, regardless of seniority or position, had an opportunity to voice his opinion and influence the party's position in caucus. But once two-thirds of the caucus had made a policy decision, all party members were bound to support it on the floor of the House, unless a member believed the measure was unconstitutional or a contrary pledge had been made to his constituents.

Underwood and other party leaders—primarily Speaker Champ Clark and John Fitzgerald, the chairman of the Appropriations Committee, often referred to as the "caucus cabinet"[57]—used the caucus as a means to measure the relative strength of different opinions within the party. "Let 'em talk," Underwood would say, seeking to give members of his party maximum individual participation in the caucus. "Let 'em have it all out here. Then there will be no kick afterward." And this is generally the way things happened. "Not until the last man had had his say," one observer remarked, "was the vote taken that was to bind them all to united action in the House."[58]

After caucus debate, sometimes lasting for weeks, some such resolution as the following would be presented by Underwood and adopted by the caucus:

> *Resolved*, That the tariff bill passed by the caucus in its amended form is declared to be a party measure and that the members of this caucus are hereby pledged to support the bill in the House of Representatives and to vote against all amendments or motions to recommit the bill. *Provided*, however that the Ways and Means Committee are authorized to propose amendments to the bill that shall not be considered as included in the foregoing inhibition.[59]

Following the adoption of the binding resolution by the caucus, the bill would be sent back to the appropriate standing committee and then, with the cooperation of the Rules Committee, sent to the House floor for a final vote. Once on the House floor, the final vote on a Democratic bill was never in doubt, since the Democrats had already bound themselves to unity in their party caucus.

The caucus system proved to be remarkably successful in holding the Democrats together as a party in both the Sixty-second and Sixty-third Congresses. Only a handful of Democrats voted against their caucus position on the Canadian Reciprocity Act and the individual tariff bills that passed the House in the Sixty-second Congress. And in a study of party unity in the Sixty-third Congress, Elston Roady found that at least 98 percent of the House Democrats supported the caucus resolutions on each of the four major reforms—the Underwood-Simmons Tariff Act, the Federal Reserve Act, the Federal Trade Commission Act, and the Clayton Anti-Trust Act—that Congress enacted into law in the Sixty-third Congress.[60]

The Republicans were furious with the Democrats for using their party caucus to bind members to unity on the floor of the House, a procedure that, for all practical purposes, effectively excluded Republicans from the policymaking process of the House. "Any member who surrenders his action to the control of a caucus whether he be of one party or of the other," an angry Charles A. Lindbergh (R., Minn.) declared, "violates his oath, is a traitor to his constituency, and commits treason against his country."[61]

The Democrats, on the other hand, vigorously defended their use of the binding caucus. Speaking for the majority, Swager Sherley, an influential member of the Appropriations Committee from Kentucky, responded with the classical argument for responsible party government (with which Oscar Underwood and Woodrow Wilson would also have agreed). "If every man was an individualist in the true and full sense of the term," Sherley observed, "government would be impossible and each man would be arrayed against every other. . . . How long do you think it would take the people of America to obtain a result on the tariff, the currency, or some other great issue if it acted simply through individuals and not through parties?"[62]

Underwood's leadership of the House was obviously facilitated by the consensus within his party on the binding caucus as the best way to make party decisions. Even when House Democrats disagreed with the caucus, they usually felt compelled as good Democrats to support the caucus position on the floor of the House. Joseph J. Russell from Missouri said, for example, in announcing his support of the caucus decision on the tariff bill in 1913: "It is a party measure, and as a Democrat I shall vote for it, and am willing to politically sink or swim, survive, or perish, as the fortunes of my party shall decree."[63]

Underwood's leadership of the House also depended upon a friendly and cooperative relationship with committees, particularly committee chairmen. To facilitate his relationship with committees, Underwood used three distinct techniques.

The first was his reliance on the caucus to control committee action. This was done, for example, at the beginning of the Sixty-second Congress in 1911 when Underwood introduced the following resolution that was passed by the Democratic caucus: "*Resolved*: That the Democratic members of the various committees of the House are directed not to report to the House during the first session of the 62nd Congress unless hereafter directed by this caucus, any legislation except with reference to the following matters. . . .[64] To an important degree, therefore, committees served as agents of the Democratic caucus during that period rather than as agents of the House itself. The caucus resolution, however, was not binding on all committees throughout the Sixty-second or Sixty-third Congress, and committees still retained, in some matters, an important measure of autonomy.

The second was Underwood's skillful manipulation of his chairmanship of the Democratic Committee on Committees to maintain harmony and committee cooperation. Theoretically, the job of making committee assignments belonged collectively to all the Democratic members of the Ways and Means Committee, but as a practical matter the job "naturally and inevitably devolved in large measure upon the chairman."[65]

To assist him in maintaining a regional balance in his committee assignments, Underwood kept a large map of congressional districts on the wall of his office.[66] This map was particularly helpful in placing the large number of freshmen on committees in both the Sixty-second and Sixty-third Congresses. There were 77 Democratic freshmen in the Sixty-second Congress and 102 Democratic freshmen in the Sixty-third Congress. Underwood's ability to place such a large number of freshmen on committees, which amounted to a little over one-third of the total Democratic membership in both Congresses, gave him an added measure of influence over the newcomers to Congress.

In selecting committee chairmen, which was also Underwood's responsibility, he was under pressure from many sides to ignore the rule of seniority and select chairmen solely on the basis of ability or party loyalty. But, as one commentator noted, "the consideration of prime importance was harmony. By following the rule of seniority there was a chance to achieve it. Underwood, also Champ Clark, saw that any other course would lead to turmoil."[67]

But there were exceptions to seniority. Cordell Hull, one of Underwood's colleagues on the Committee on Committees from Tennessee (and a future secretary of state under Franklin D. Roosevelt), reported, for example, that the Committee on Committees "turned down William Sulzer [of New York] as chairman of the Military Affairs Committee because he was extravagant." Hull also reported that Edward Pou of North Carolina was removed from the Ways and Means Committee and replaced by Claude Kitchin, from the same state, because "Pou had once voted for a tariff on lumber."[68]

In one instance, Underwood exercised his power to appoint committees in much the same way former Speakers had used this power: to control voting behavior within his party. On April 10, 1913, Underwood, acting with caucus approval, announced to the House that most of the committee assignments would be held up until after the tariff bill cleared the House. "The hope of good committee assignments was, of course," as one observer noted, "designed to keep members 'regular.'"[69]

The third technique Underwood used to gain the cooperation of committees was through his informal, personal power to bargain and compromise with committee chairmen. A friendly relationship between Underwood and the committee chairmen was vital to the success of his party's legislative program, and he acted early in his leadership to establish good relations with committee chairmen.

Underwood's relationship with committee chairmen was no doubt facilitated from the outset by the simple fact that he and most of the committee chairmen came from the same part of the country. Of the fifty-six standing committees in the Sixty-second Congress, for example, thirty-nine of the committee chairmen were from the South, confirming the popular view that the "southern influence predominated in the organization of the House."[70]

Most of the business between Underwood and committee chairmen occurred behind the scenes in informal conversations and in the party caucus away from the glare of publicity. Thomas Logan, who questioned Underwood concerning his relationship with committee chairmen, explained that Underwood did not like to discuss the relationship with committee chairmen because "his success as a leader depends upon his ability to keep his leadership in the background." Logan added: "Mr. Underwood is a diplomatic leader. He tries to avoid any conflict with the rank and file of his party. He seems always to be bowing to their judgment, even when they are accepting his. He makes it seem that every chairman of a committee is the absolute master of the legislative work over which he has supervision."[71]

The slightest indication of possible conflict with committees or between committees prompted Underwood to take the necessary steps to alleviate the situation. In early 1911, for example, a possible conflict between some of the older members and new ones was avoided when Underwood worked out an agreement with committee chairmen to enlarge the key standing committees to accommodate a larger number of Democrats in the new Congress. These difficulties, according to one source, "led to many conferences which disclosed much foreboding that did not reach the public, but it was well known that serious embarrassment, if not open revolt, was avoided by materially enlarging the more important committees."[72]

Also in 1911, Underwood avoided an open revolt within his own party when he yielded to John Fitzgerald's demands to become chairman of the Appropriations Committee. Fitzgerald, the Tory Democrat from New York who had opposed the dismantling of the Speaker's powers, was the senior Democrat on the Appropriations Committee and in line to become chairman of that important committee in the Sixty-second Congress. But some of the Progressives in the country, out to strip the House of any vestige of the old Cannon era, urged Underwood not to give Fitzgerald or any Democrat who had ever sided with Cannon "a position of power for the sake of harmony."[73] The Progressives wanted Albert S. Burleson of Texas, the second-ranking Democrat on the Appropriations Committee and chairman of the Democratic caucus, to become chairman of the Appropriations Committee. Burleson wanted the chairmanship and a majority of the Democrats probably would have voted for Burleson, but Fitzgerald decided to fight for his position. "Go ahead if you want to start something," Fitzgerald warned his colleagues.

> Of all the chairmanships in the House only three are given to northern Democrats, and one of these is the unimportant chairmanship of Invalid Pensions. You have deposed one northern Democrat, [William] Sulzer [of New York, who was the senior Democrat on the Armed Services Committee], from his rights in order to give place to a Southerner. Now, if you want to, go ahead and take the only important chairmanship that goes to a northern Democrat and give it to a Southerner. You won't get away with it without a fight in caucus and another on the floor of the House. And I'm not sure that you'll be able to organize the House after the fight is made.[74]

Underwood appointed Fitzgerald chairman of the Appropriations Committee in both the Sixty-second and Sixty-third Congresses.[75] Despite his past support for Speaker Cannon, Fitzgerald became an active supporter of the progressive Democratic agenda and one of the leaders of the new Democratic House.

A committee of special importance to Underwood's leadership of the House was the Committee on Rules. Though this committee did not become the central leadership committee that Underwood had predicted it would become after the overthrow of Speaker Cannon, it was still a very important committee in the new Congress. "Excepting only the caucus," one observer noted, "the Rules Committee is the most necessary and essential feature of the new floor leader system in the House."[76]

The Democrats wasted no time after gaining control of the House in 1911 to assure that the new Rules Committee (with seven Democrats and four Republicans) was supportive of the Democratic agenda. Underwood and the Committee on Committees carefully selected the Democratic members of the Rules Committee for "their known and proven sympathy with Democratic principles and policies, and for their loyalty to the party."[77] Of the seven Democratic members selected to the Rules Committee (all of whom were newcomers to the committee), five were from the South, including the chairman, Robert L. Henry of Texas. Henry, a great grandson of Patrick Henry, was transferred from the Judiciary Committee in the previous Congress to assume leadership of this important committee. Though Henry was an "agrarian radical," he and the more conservative-minded Underwood cooperated fully in carrying out the party's reform agenda.[78] Henry's cooperation with Underwood and the new majority floor leader system was demonstrated in three significant ways.

First, Henry cooperated with Underwood to ensure that a Democratic bill, which had been debated and approved by the caucus, received a closed rule from the Committee on Rules. That action prohibited Republican amendments on the floor of the House. Second, Henry used the power of the Rules Committee—as one of the three privileged committees of the House (along with the Ways and Means Committee and Appropriations Committee) with the power to report to the House at any time—to delay legislation that Underwood and other party leaders did not wish to consider.[79] Third, Henry cooperated with Underwood and the Democratic caucus in changing the House rules to cope with Republican opposition. This was accomplished, for example, on February 3, 1912, when Henry moved to relegate the Discharge Calendar to a third position behind the Suspension of the Rules and the Unanimous Consent Calendar. Thereafter, any Republican attempt to use the Discharge Calendar to embarrass the Democratic leadership by forcing a bill from a reluctant committee could be prevented by simply suspending the rules or using the Unanimous Consent Calendar.[80]

Underwood's relations with the Republicans in both the Sixty-second and Sixty-third Congresses was similar to his relations with President Taft. Both relations were essentially nonbargaining in nature. There was little compromise or even communication between Underwood and the Republicans. Often in the process of putting together majorities for legislation, particularly in contemporary Congresses, majority leaders are forced to reach out for the support of the minority party. But the ideological division within the Republican Party between the "regulars" and "progressives" and the large Democratic majorities allowed Underwood to virtually ignore the opposition. Thus Underwood's relations with the Republicans were not typical of the bargaining relationships that often exist between the majority leader and the minority party.

Underwood's strategy in dealing with the minority party should be viewed from the two vantage points of on the floor and off the floor. Though Underwood operated with practically every advantage in his favor, he was compelled by the motives of the 1910 revolt to allow the Republicans at least the appearance of effective participation in the decisionmaking process. But as a strong advocate of party government, Underwood was clearly more interested in holding together his own party than in reaching out to the minority.

On the floor of the House, Underwood encouraged the Republicans to debate and criticize majority bills. Underwood attempted to give the floor debate the "appearance of being very democratic" by "permitting full and free discussion."[81] Although the Republicans were usually just speaking to themselves and to their constituencies, they always exploited the opportunity to debate and sharply criticize not only the majority's legislation but also the majority's method of making decisions in the caucus. The Republicans, led by James R. Mann of Illinois (described as "the most clever parliamentarian in the House"[82]), were as consistent in their opposition as they were in their ineffectiveness. Only one Republican amendment was accepted on a major bill.[83]

The Republicans frequently complained that all committees were dominated by the caucus. They complained of presidential pressure on congressmen. They invariably moved to recommit bills to committee, but such motions were defeated. They attempted to overload the Discharge Calendar, but Underwood countered this tactic simply by having the rules changed. A favorite Republican tactic was to attempt to create irregularity and dissension within the Democratic ranks by appealing to Democrats to follow the interests of their own constituencies rather than the wishes of their party. This tactic was equally ineffective.[84]

In his informal relations with the minority party off the floor, there was not much consultation or negotiation between Underwood and Minority Leader Mann. It was not necessary. The important debate and discussion occurred in the caucus. Underwood was unfailingly courteous to Mann, as he was with all his colleagues, and he kept Mann informed on the scheduling of Democratic bills. But Underwood was not overly concerned about effective minority participation in the decisionmaking process. As a Jeffersonian Democrat, Underwood firmly believed in majority rule and the democratic right of the majority—as expressed ideally through the majority party—to enact its will into public policy. That, after all, is what Underwood thought the revolt against Cannon had been about in the first place.

In one important respect, however, Underwood did extend the democratization of the House to the Republicans. He attempted to distribute more influence to the minority party in choosing its own committee members.

Under the old Cannon system, the Speaker had chosen all committees. Cannon had consulted with Democratic Minority Leader John Sharp Williams on minority committee assignments during his first three terms as Speaker, but he did not always follow Williams's recommendations. During Cannon's fourth term as Speaker, the new Democratic minority leader, Champ Clark, was so frustrated with Cannon's veto of minority committee appointments that he informed the Speaker he would not participate in the committee appointment process in the new Congress unless the Speaker accepted all of his minority committee recommendations "without the dotting of an 'i' or the crossing of a 't'." Cannon refused to give Clark total control over minority committee appointments and proceeded to "organize the minority" by himself in the Sixty-first Congress.[85]

In the new system, the minority party still only had the power to "recommend" committee appointments to Underwood, who in consultation with his colleagues on the Democratic Committee on Committees made the final decision. In practice, however, Underwood always accepted the minority party's recommendations. "This is the first time in the history of the House," Underwood proudly told the House as he announced the minority committee assignments at the beginning of the Sixty-second Congress, "when a majority of this House has allowed the Minority Leader to bring a list of committee assignments to their committee and accept his assignment of his own people to represent his own party without the dotting of an 'i' or the crossing of a 't'"—a statement that was greeted by "loud and continued applause on the Democratic side."[86]

Thus, by his deference to the minority—informed and inspired, of course, by his own frustrations in being in the minority for the previous sixteen years—Underwood ironically played an important role in establishing for the minority one of its most basic rights, the right to choose its own committee members, now accepted as part of the modern House. The majority party has continued to set partisan ratios on committees, but the minority has had the right to choose its own committee members since the precedent established by Majority Leader Oscar W. Underwood in 1911.

In the final analysis, Underwood owed his leadership of the House not only to his three formal positions of authority which he skillfully integrated into a unified leadership of the House but also to his own personal traits, which were more in keeping with the emerging democratic norms of the House in the post-Cannon era. Joe Cannon had also held great power in the House. But Uncle Joe's authority as Speaker had not been enough to save him, when his own autocratic personality prevented him from compromising with his colleagues' demands for a more democratic House. Oscar Underwood, too, would have had trouble holding onto power if he had not also been blessed with the personal traits that enabled him to build the trust and confidence of his peers in a more democratic House. For ultimately, as one observer noted, Underwood—the first modern House leader of the twentieth century—was "dependent not upon his power under the rules, but upon his own personality and character, upon the esteem in which he [was] held in the House."[87]

That high esteem was widely reflected in the attitudes of everyone from the Speaker of the House to the lowliest staff member. The Speaker, Champ Clark, described Underwood as "one of the most urbane and patient of mortals—clear-headed, resolute, courageous. The old Latin saying *suaviter in mode, fortiter in re* [gentle in manner, resolute in deed] fits and describes him exactly."[88] Cordell Hull, Underwood's colleague on the Ways and Means Committee, observed that Underwood was "universally conceded to be a splendid statesman and the most capable floor leader within anyone's memory. He never lost his temper. He was able, though not brilliant, possessed common sense and was always on the alert. By his personality he kept everyone united and in good humor."[89] Andrew Martin, who served as an assistant to freshman Carl Hayden in the Sixty-second Congress, remembered Underwood as "always very courteous, the ideal Southern gentleman. He was quiet and tactful, but when he spoke everyone else would listen. When the word spread that Underwood was about to make a speech on the floor of the House," Martin recalled, "practically everyone would go to listen. He was a successful leader because he could control himself and always respected the opinion of others."[90]

Outside observers, too, were quick to recognize the importance of Underwood's personality to his leadership style. De Alva S. Alexander, for example, who had served with Underwood as a Republican representative from western New York from 1897 to 1910, noted that Underwood "brought to the place an attractive personality. His gentle simplicity, easygoing manner and freedom from egotism or personal ambition seemed to deny the sense of high purpose and firmness of mind which his presence conveyed."[91] Even Underwood's most skeptical critic conceded: "Gifted with a personality which so far has made his tyranny pleasant, Underwood has 'got away with it' with admirable skill. Perhaps he would have forced the House to do what it has done since it has been under his thumb, even if he had not had the machine to help him."[92]

In short, Oscar Underwood was, in the words of Arthur B. Krock, "the ideal floor leader" for his time.[93] He was fitted by personality and character, as well as ability, to lead the House after the revolt against Speaker Cannon. The new House required a man who was inclined not to dictate policy as Cannon had done but to bargain and compromise with his peers to reach common agreement. The real measure of Underwood's success was that he truly comprehended the political context in the House and in the nation, which set the boundaries on how a new decisionmaking structure could be established and maintained in the post-Cannon era.

The decisionmaking structure that Underwood worked to establish and maintain in the House from 1911 to 1915 did not survive Underwood's leadership after he left the House in 1915 to go to the Senate. The decentralized system that the Democrats put in place in 1911 was held together by Underwood's leadership and the special circumstances of his time: namely, the widespread public support for the major policy changes advocated by the Democrats, the strong presidential leadership of Woodrow Wilson, the large and supportive Democratic majorities in both houses of Congress, and an especially well-organized House Democratic majority determined to cooperate with a reform-minded president to prove they could govern. The House, though, for a variety of reasons, became increasingly fragmented and difficult to manage after Underwood's departure.

Claude Kitchin of North Carolina succeeded Underwood as majority leader and chairman of the Ways and Means Committee in 1915. Though Kitchin had been one of Underwood's chief lieutenants in the previous Congress, he was unable to sustain Underwood's leadership of the House. Kitchin's leadership was seriously hampered by disagreements he had with President Wilson's war policies. The increasing involvement of the United States in World War I and the policy differences between Wilson and Kitchin, as Randall B. Ripley has noted, "destroyed the usefulness of the binding caucus as a tool for gaining majority party victories."[94]

After the war, the position of majority leader was further weakened when the Democrats separated the majority leadership position from the chairmanship of the Ways and Means Committee, making the chairman of the Ways and Means Committee (who retained his chairmanship of the Committee on Committees until 1974) into an independent authority in his own right. The Speaker, too, gradually regained some of the power and prestige lost in the 1910–1911 revolution. By the mid-1920s the Speaker was once again considered the leader of the majority party in the House, with the majority leader relegated to a secondary role. And committee chairmen, particularly the chairman of the Rules Committee (as Underwood had predicted), became increasingly autonomous and independent leaders of the House.[95]

So, gradually, bit by bit, the centrifugal forces unleashed by the revolt against Speaker Cannon in 1910–1911—held at bay briefly by Underwood at the head of a system of strong party government—worked to make the House the fragmented, unwieldy institution it later became, giving credence to the fear of some of the skeptics at the time of the revolution that "under the new order, power would ultimately be dispensed so widely that there would not be a sufficiently integrated institution, the House, to make the policy effective."[96]

As for Underwood himself, he became a leading member of the U.S. Senate and supported President Wilson in his bitter fight over the League of Nations. From 1920 to 1923, Underwood was the Democratic minority leader in the Senate, making him the first leader since Henry Clay to serve as leader of his party in both houses of Congress. He was a strong critic of the Senate rules, particularly the lack of an effective cloture rule to end the filibuster.[97] In 1924 Underwood was again a candidate for the Democratic nomination for president and possibly could have had the nomination, John F. Kennedy wrote, if he had been willing to make concessions to the Ku Klux Klan, which controlled a large bloc of delegates at the convention.[98] Facing the prospect of a serious challenge to his Senate reelection from Hugo Black, a former Alabama county solicitor (and future Supreme Court justice) who had strong Klan support, Underwood decided to retire from the Senate in 1926. The following year Underwood and his wife moved to Woodlawn, a historic Georgian mansion near Mt. Vernon, Virginia, where Underwood wrote *Drifting Sands of Party Politics* and expounded on his Jeffersonian philosophy of government.[99] He died two years later of a stroke on January 25, 1929, four months short of his sixty-seventh birthday.

NOTES

I would like to thank Charles O. Jones, once again, for his valuable assistance in directing my graduate thesis on Oscar W. Underwood, on which this chapter is partially based. In addition, I wish to thank several other friends and colleagues— Richard F. Fenno, Jr., Paul Ferber, Christine E. Murray, Thomas R. Plough, David E. Price, and Raymond W. Smock—for their helpful comments on earlier drafts of this chapter. I am also very indebted to Louise Novros for her secretarial assistance in completing this project.

1. George Rothwell Brown, *The Leadership of Congress* (Indianapolis: Bobbs-Merrill, 1922), p. 152.

2. *Congressional Record*, March 19, 1910, p. 3433.

3. Brown, *The Leadership of Congress*, p. 176.

4. James S. Fleming, "Re-establishing Leadership in the House of Representatives: The Case of Oscar W. Underwood," *Mid-America: An Historical Review* 54 (October 1972): 234–250; James S. Fleming, "Oscar W. Underwood: Leader of the House of Representatives, 1911–1915 (M.A. thesis, University of Arizona, 1968).

5. C. Dwight Dorough, *Mr. Sam* (New York: Random House, 1962), p. 256.

6. Richard Bolling, *Power in the House: A History of the Leadership of the House of Representatives* (New York: E. P. Dutton, 1968), p. 94.

7. Evans C. Johnson, *Oscar W. Underwood: A Political Biography* (Baton Rouge: Louisiana State University Press, 1980), pp. 20–64.

8. Arthur B. Krock, "Underwood: An Intimate View of the Man, His Traits, Tendencies and Prepossessions," *Harper's Weekly* 56 (June 1, 1912): 10.

9. Burton J. Hendrick, "Oscar W. Underwood: A New Leader from the Old South," *McClure's Magazine* 38 (February 1912): 412.

10. Randall B. Ripley, *Party Leaders in the House of Representatives* (Washington, D.C.: The Brookings Institution, 1967), p. 34.

11. Arthur S. Link, "The Underwood Presidential Movement of 1912," *The Journal of Southern History* 11 (May 1945): 231–232.

12. Ibid., p. 232.

13. Brown, *The Leadership of Congress*, pp. 172–174.

14. Oscar King Davis, "Where Underwood Stands: An Interview with the Democratic Leader of the House," *Outlook* 99 (September 23, 1911): 198.

15. "Caucus Names Clark for Next Speaker," *New York Times*, January 20, 1911, p. 1.

16. Charles Thompson, "Underwood, the Real Power in Congress," *New York Times*, February 26, 1911.

17. De Alva S. Alexander, *History and Procedure of the House of Representatives* (Boston: Houghton Mifflin, 1916), pp. 133–134.

18. Champ Clark, "What the Democrats in Congress Will Do," *Hampton's Magazine* 26 (February 1911): 206.

19. "Caucus Names Clark for Next Speaker," p. 1. The Democrats later increased the number of Democrats on the Ways and Means Committee to fifteen in the Sixty-second Congress and sixteen in the Sixty-third Congress to accommodate larger Democratic majorities in these two Congresses.

20. Arthur Wallace Dunn, *From Harrison to Harding* (New York: G. P. Putnam's Sons), 2: 148.

21. "Caucus Names Clark for Next Speaker," p. 1; W. F. Willoughby, *Principles of Legislative Organization and Administration* (Washington, D.C.: The Brookings Institution, 1934), p. 548; *Congressional Record*, April 5, 1911, pp. 74–80.

22. Fitzgerald had voted to remove the Speaker from the Rules Committee in March 1910, but a year earlier he and twenty-three other Democrats had sided with Speaker Cannon in an important rules fight on the floor of the House. For a discussion of the intraparty conflict in the Democratic Party between the Tory Democrats and "progressives," see Judson C. Welliver and Louis Brownlow, "What Will the Democrats Do?" *Hampton's Magazine* 26 (February 1911): 196–205.

23. "Caucus Names Clark for Next Speaker," p. 1.

24. Ibid.

25. Ripley, *Party Leaders in the House of Representatives*, p. 24.

26. Wilder H. Haines, "The Congressional Caucus of Today," *American Political Science Review* 9 (November 1915): 696–706.

27. George B. Galloway, *History of the House of Representatives* (New York: Thomas Y. Crowell, 1962), pp. 55, 92–93.

28. Ibid., pp. 55–56.

29. Willoughby, *Principles of Legislative Organization and Administration*, pp. 554–555.

30. Dunn, *From Harrison to Harding*, p. 148.

31. Charles O. Jones, "Joseph G. Cannon and Howard W. Smith: An Essay on the Limits of Leadership in the House of Representative," *Journal of Politics* 30 (August 1968): 617–646.

32. William Leavitt Stoddard, "Underwoodism?" *Everybody's Magazine* 28 (June 1913): 802–803.

33. William Howard Taft, *Our Chief Magistrate and His Power* (New York: Columbia University Press, 1916).

34. Randall B. Ripley, *Majority Party Leadership in Congress* (Boston: Little, Brown, 1969), pp. 145–147.

35. Davis, "Where Underwood Stands," p. 200.

36. Before Underwood could exert his leadership over the House, he first had to fight off a determined bid by the titular leader of the Democratic Party, William Jennings Bryan, to control the House. As a former member of the Ways and Means Committee and three-time Democratic presidential candidate, Bryan saw himself, not Oscar Underwood, as the leader of the new House. For a discussion of this bitter feud between Underwood and Bryan and an account of how Underwood was able to fight off Bryan's challenge to his leadership, see Hendrick, "Oscar W. Underwood," pp. 416–417; Link, "The Underwood Presidential Movement of 1912," pp. 232–234; *Congressional Record*, August 2, 1911, pp. 3510–3513.

37. Johnson, *Oscar W. Underwood*, pp. 143–169; Ripley, *Majority Party Leadership in Congress*, pp. 139–141.

38. Hendrick, "Oscar W. Underwood," pp. 404–405.

39. Link, "The Underwood Presidential Movement of 1912."

40. Underwood and Wilson had a good personal relationship, though they did not know each other well before Wilson became president. Wilson had praised Underwood for his leadership of the Sixty-second Congress and even favored Underwood for his vice presidential running mate in 1912, but Underwood declined Wilson's offer, preferring instead to remain in Congress. For a discussion of the Wilson-Underwood relationship, see Johnson, *Oscar W. Underwood*, pp. 193–197.

41. Oscar W. Underwood, *Drifting Sands of Party Politics* (New York: Century, 1928), pp. 311–312.

42. Letter from Woodrow Wilson to A. Mitchell Palmer (chairman of the Democratic caucus in the Sixty-third Congress), February 3, 1913. Arthur S. Link, ed., *The Papers of Woodrow Wilson* (Princeton: Princeton University Press, 1977–1979), 27: 100.

43. James Miller Leake, "Four Years of Congress," *American Political Science Review* 11 (May 1917): 252–283.

44. Brown, *The Leadership of Congress*, p. 183.

45. Johnson, *Oscar W. Underwood*, p. 199.

46. Ripley, *Majority Party Leadership in Congress*, pp. 57–61; Arthur S. Link, *Wilson: The New Freedom* (Princeton: Princeton University Press, 1956), pp. 151–153.

47. Quoted by Johnson, *Oscar W. Underwood*, p. 194.

48. Ibid.

49. Ibid., p. 141.

50. Clark had first been elected to the House in 1892, two years before Underwood. He was defeated for reelection in 1894, before winning again in 1896, giving him a two-year advantage to Underwood in seniority.

51. Quoted by Johnson, *Oscar W. Underwood*, p. 223.

52. Quoted by Dunn, *From Harrison to Harding*, p. 118.

53. Chang-Wei Chiu, *The Speaker of the House of Representatives Since 1896* (New York: Columbia University Press, 1928), pp. 45–58.

54. Ripley, *Majority Party Leadership in Congress*, p. 63.

55. This issue involved repealing the tolls exemption for U.S. ships using the Panama Canal. President Wilson proposed removing the exemption, whereas Underwood and Clark (adhering to the Democratic Party platform) favored its retention. Though Underwood and Clark disagreed with Wilson on this issue, they did not actively work against the president's efforts to repeal the exemption. For the details on this struggle, see Dunn, *From Harrison to Harding*, pp. 240–249.

56. There was some dissension within the House Democrats on the closed nature of the caucus. Some of the Democrats, mostly from the North, favored open caucus meetings. However, they were vigorously opposed in this effort by Underwood and Fitzgerald, who successfully argued that an open caucus would inhibit free discussion within the party and weaken party unity on the floor. For a discussion of this important, internal party division, see Stanley Coben, *A. Mitchell Palmer: Politician* (New York: Columbia University Press, 1963), p. 76.

57. Galloway, *History of the House of Representatives*, p. 141.

58. Davis, "Where Underwood Stands," p. 199.

59. Westel W. Willoughby and Lindsay Rogers, *An Introduction to the Problem of Government* (Garden City, N.Y.: Doubleday, 1921), pp. 343–344.

60. Elston E. Roady, "Party Regularity in the Sixty-third Congress" (Ph.D. diss., University of Illinois, 1951).

61. Quoted in Lynn Haines, *Law Making in America* (Bethesda, Md.: Lynn Haines, 1912), p. 13.

62. Quoted in Willoughby, *Principles of Legislative Organization and Administration*, p. 569.

63. Quoted in Roady, "Party Regularity in the Sixty-third Congress," p. 118.

64. Haines, "The Congressional Caucus of Today," p. 697.

65. Brown, *The Leadership of Congress*, p. 184.

66. Johnson, *Oscar W. Underwood*, p. 138.

67. Robert W. Woolley, "Underwood of Alabama: Democracy's New Chieftain," *American Review of Reviews* 44 (September 1911): 298.

68. Cordell Hull, *The Memoirs of Cordell Hull* (New York: Macmillan, 1948), 1: 63–64.

69. Speaker Thomas Brackett Reed delayed committee appointments in 1897 until the passage of the Dingley tariff bill, and Speaker Joseph G. Cannon also postponed committee appointments in 1909 until the Payne-Aldrich Tariff bill became law. For the specifics on this common leadership technique employed by Underwood and the former Speakers, see Paul D. Hasbrouck, *Party Government in the House of Representatives* (New York: Macmillan, 1927), p. 37.

70. Brown, *The Leadership of Congress*, p. 172.

71. Thomas F. Logan, "What I Am Trying to Do: An Authorized Interview with Honorable Oscar W. Underwood," *World's Work* 23 (March 1912): 540.

72. Alexander, *History and Procedure of the House of Representatives*, p. 82.

73. Welliver and Brownlow, "What Will the Democrats Do?" p. 201.

74. Quoted by Dunn, *From Harrison to Harding*, p. 150.

75. Two years later, Underwood played an important role in having Burleson appointed postmaster general in the first Wilson administration. For an account of the influence Underwood brought to bear on this matter, see Ray Stannard Baker, *Woodrow Wilson: Life and Letters* (Garden City, N.Y.: Doubleday, 1931), 3: 447.

76. Haines, *Law Making in America*, p. 27.

77. Brown, *The Leadership of Congress*, p. 175.

78. Johnson, *Oscar W. Underwood*, pp. 141–142.

79. Haines, *Law Making in America*, p. 23–26.

80. Hasbrouck, *Party Government in the House of Representatives*, pp. 147–148; Fleming, "Re-establishing Leadership in the House of Representatives," p. 243.

81. Roady, "Party Regularity in the Sixty-third Congress," p. 43.

82. Hasbrouck, *Party Government in the House of Representatives*, p. 142.

83. This was an amendment to the Federal Reserve bill endorsing the gold standard in 1913. It was an attempt to embarrass Secretary of State William Jennings Byran, a longtime opponent of the gold standard, but Bryan and the House leaders accepted the amendment.

84. Charles O. Jones, *The Minority Party in Congress* (Boston: Little, Brown, 1970), pp. 57–63; Fleming, "Re-establishing Leadership in the House of Representatives," pp. 245–247.

85. For Cannon's explanation and defense of his committee appointments, see the *Congressional Record*, April 11, 1911, p. 165.

86. Ibid., p. 163.

87. Brown, *The Leadership of Congress*, p. 221.

88. Champ Clark, *My Quarter Century of American Politics* (New York: Harper, 1920), 2: 270.

89. Hull, *The Memoirs of Cordell Hull*, p. 64.

90. Personal interview with Andrew Martin, Tucson, Arizona, January 26, 1967.

91. Alexander, *History and Procedure of the House of Representatives*, pp. 133–134.

92. Stoddard, "Underwoodism?" p. 803.

93. Krock, "Underwood," p. 9.

94. Ripley, *Party Leaders in the House of Representatives*, p. 42.

95. Galloway, *History of the House of Representatives*, pp. 141–159.

96. Bolling, *Power in the House*, p. 101.

97. Johnson, *Oscar W. Underwood*, pp. 226–454.

98. John F. Kennedy, *Profiles in Courage* (New York: Harper, 1956), pp. 226–227.

99. Underwood, *Drifting Sands of Party Politics*.

5

Nicholas Longworth:
The Genial Czar

Donald C. Bacon

Nicholas Longworth became Speaker of the House of Representatives in 1925, at a time when the office was weak and ineffectual. It had been so since 1910, when the House rebelled against the tyranny of Speaker Joseph Cannon and reduced the position to virtual insignificance. Longworth, with charm and canny maneuvering, reclaimed the speakership's lost power. From the moment he was elected, the Ohio Republican ruled with an iron firmness rivaling that of Cannon himself. The surprise was not that the House, despite its earlier experience under an autocratic leader, again trusted its fate to one man. Rather, it was that the individual who acquired such authority, seemingly without half trying, was the improbable Nick Longworth.

It was easy to underestimate Longworth's ability and determination. Many members of Congress and most journalists believed he was more interested in self-amusement than in running the House. Debonair and aristocratic, given to wearing spats and carrying a gold-headed cane, he was anything but a typical politician. He was perpetually cheerful, quick with a joke or witty retort, and unfailingly friendly. He seemed never to have a care and made hard decisions with such ease and detachment that some people wondered if anything at all really mattered to him.

His uniqueness, journalist William Hard once observed, lay in his ability to do serious things in a manner "so light and airy that he might be said to have the specific gravity of feathers." But, Hard quickly added, "in action, when the favorable moment for action has come, he has the weight of lead shot. Then he strikes, and strikes hard."[1]

Longworth's first act as Speaker proved his inner toughness. Surprising even his closest followers, he demanded stiff punishment for the thirteen House Republican liberals, so-called Progressives, who had refused to support the party's presidential ticket in 1924. Not only were they drummed out of the party caucus, they all, including several who had been committee chairmen, were banished to the bottom in seniority on their committees. After that, few doubted Longworth's decisiveness.

Backed by his large majority, Longworth took control of the Republican Steering Committee and Committee on Committees. He placed his own lieutenants on the Rules Committee, which determined when and under what conditions bills came before the House, and rewrote the House rules to in effect eliminate all avenues for bills to reach the floor without his approval. By managing the content and flow of legislation, he helped give the country what most voters of the period seemed to want: consistently balanced budgets, a succession of major tax reductions, and a cautious approach to new programs that would expand the size and role of government.

Longworth came to power when the House was weak and demoralized and vastly overshadowed by the Senate. The Senate usually initiated or rewrote important bills and insisted that the House accept its preferences. Within three years, the roles had been reversed. By 1928, the press was routinely commenting on the House's efficiency and noting that, under Longworth, it had become Congress's dominant branch.

Perhaps more than any other Speaker, Longworth relied on the salubrious effect of his personality to achieve his ends. He consciously used his popularity and reputation for fairness to his advantage. He believed the speakership could be shaped into whatever the holder had the capacity to make of it. Relying on that belief, he wielded power well beyond the limited authority delegated to him under the House rules. "Regardless of the rules, the speakership always will be what the Speaker makes it," he confidently asserted.[2]

Genuinely democratic in his associations, he cultivated members of both parties. They, in turn, called him Nick, as did reporters, lobbyists, and most others.[3] Unlike earlier Speakers, who tended to remain aloof from the rank and file, Longworth reached out to insignificant members. He invited them to join him at the Speaker's big round table in the House restaurant, traditionally off limits to all but the most powerful party leaders, and during House debate he called them to the Speaker's rostrum to hear, in whispered tones, a new joke from his endless repertoire. His warmth extended to Democrats. His staunchest political opponent, Minority Leader John Nance Garner of Texas, was also his closest after-hours social companion. "Don't forget that political adversaries can be as helpful as friends," he told Republicans who questioned his fraternization with the opposition.[4] A reporter who watched Longworth in action over time concluded that "the cement of the House organization is personal relations."[5]

Few Speakers have ruled as confidently and harmoniously as Longworth. Few have accomplished as much, and perhaps none has equaled him in making the difficult task of leading a body of 435 disparate members look so easy. A man of irrepressible playfulness, he made everybody—Republicans and Democrats alike—feel good in his presence. Even those he punished would say, "You can't help liking Nick."

Because they liked Longworth and knew him to have been fair in their own relations with him, his colleagues went along with his requests. When he sought control over legislative scheduling, he got it. When he insisted that his male colleagues show more respect to the women members then coming into Congress for the first time, they complied.

Ironically, Longworth has never received the recognition due him as one of Congress's most innovative and successful leaders. There exists no objective Longworth biography or scholarly study of his exceptional reign as Speaker. The bulk of his papers were inexplicably destroyed upon his death, an act that so far has discouraged any full examination of his career and achievements.

He is usually remembered, if remembered at all, in unflattering terms. He is portrayed as a wealthy dilettante who dabbled in politics and achieved fame of a sort through his marriage to the daughter of Theodore Roosevelt. He is perceived as a talented but indolent leader, an amusing companion with no enemies and few convictions, whose complacency and well-chronicled fondness for after-hours recreation inhibited him from further political advancement.

In a sense, he and his irrepressibly lighthearted approach to life are to blame. His performance as Speaker met all the criteria of strong leadership, save one: He lacked solemnity. "His chief fault is that no matter how deep he becomes he cannot become solemn," wrote columnist Hard.[6] Because he insisted on being himself and refused to approach his job with the outward seriousness expected of a politician, contemporaries belittled his attainments. As he did not seem to take himself seriously, neither did most scholars and journalists, an injustice that time has not rectified.

A Life of Wealth and Privilege

Nicholas Longworth III was born in Cincinnati in 1869. He represented the fourth generation of one of the city's oldest and wealthiest families. His great-grandfather, the first Nicholas Longworth, had been an early settler whose speculation in land earned him the title of "richest man west of the Alleghenies." His grandfather, Joseph Longworth, had been one of Cincinnati's leading benefactors, a donor of land and money for parks and cultural enhancements. His father, Nicholas Longworth II, spent most of his short life on his many hobbies and philanthropies and in the practice of law, serving briefly on the State Supreme Court. Nicholas III shared many of his father's traits, especially a shrewd, analytical mind, a magnetic disposition, a love of music (he played the violin with professional skill), and a zest for life.

Like nearly all his male forebears, including his mother's father, who also had been a prominent jurist, Longworth set out to be a lawyer. After graduating from Harvard University and Cincinnati Law School, he embarked on a legal career only to find the work somehow unsatisfying. He soon drifted into politics. "I like the game of politics because it is exciting, uncertain, and offers a field in which there is a lot of fun and fighting," he explained.[7] He joined the Young Republican Club, where he caught the eye of local party boss George B. Cox, a former saloonkeeper whose corrupt machine had begun to attract national notoriety. Cox sized up Longworth as a born vote getter and, as the scion of one of Cincinnati's leading families, a prestigious addition to his organization. Soon, with Cox's blessing, Longworth was elected to his first public office, the Cincinnati School Board.

In 1899, Cox offered his protégé a seat in the Ohio State Legislature. Longworth served one term each in the Ohio House and Senate and knew immediately that he had found a career in legislative politics. He relished the give-and-take of writing laws. In the crucible of debate he soon learned to articulate his conservative views, particularly on government finance and party responsibility, which changed little over time. He found that he could fight fiercely while keeping his head and sense of humor. No one escaped his good-natured wit, especially the genial but shallow fellow freshman senator named Warren G. Harding. Once, Longworth offered an amendment to a bill only to have Harding jump to his feet and declare, "I want to make a serious speech about this amendment." "If the gentleman intends to make a serious speech," replied Longworth, "I would rather withdraw the amendment.[8]

As a state lawmaker, Longworth showed an ability to grasp complex issues and draft workable legislation. Among his early achievements was a major law that revolutionized the issuance of bonds by Ohio municipalities. The Longworth Act, which even Democrats later described as one of the most successful statutes in Ohio history, remained in force for many years.[9]

On to Congress

Longworth's desire to be a U.S. representative was well known to the citizens of Cincinnati. "He has wished to go to Congress ever since his hair began to grow thinner on top," twitted the *Cincinnati Enquirer*, impolitely calling attention to the thirty-three-year-old politician's rapidly balding pate.[10] In 1902, Boss Cox granted the wish of his promising protégé, whom he had begun to treat like a son.[11]

Longworth was elected as the representative of Ohio's First Congressional District on November 4, 1902. Under then-existing law, the new Congress did not convene until December of the following year. At that time he took his seat in the Fifty-fifth Congress and was assigned to the Committee on Foreign Affairs.

Longworth eased confidently, both politically and socially, into his new life as a congressman. He found his work exhilarating, and with several well-connected relatives in Washington, his evenings filled with desirable social engagements. It was at one such party that the thirty-five-year-old bachelor met President Theodore Roosevelt's twenty-year-old daughter Alice, whose beauty, wit, and spirit made her one of the most acclaimed young women in the land. The pair fell in love and, following a highly publicized courtship, were married in a lavish White House ceremony in 1906.

Insofar as he thought of his goals within the House, Longworth followed the standard course for a new member eager to get ahead. He buckled down to learn the House's rules and precedents as well as its customs and traditions. He assiduously attended the interests of his industrial district by supporting measures, such as the protective tariff, that his constituents deemed vital to their economic well-being. He worked hard on his committee assignments and searched for an issue on which he could become the committee's expert. Perhaps influenced by an uncle in the diplomatic service, he became an advocate for better housing for U.S. ambassadors abroad and eventually saw his proposal to purchase residences for U.S. diplomats become law.[12]

As he grew in experience and confidence, Longworth became more active in House debate. He was not an inspiring orator. His speeches were thoughtful and informative but somewhat stilted. His first speech as a state lawmaker was on the necessity of party unity, a subject to which he would return time and again. Most of his speeches, in fact, dealt with three topics: the value of party government, dangers of political blocs, and benefits of the protective tariff. He was best in the give-and-take of debate, where a witty retort or an apt anecdote could drive home a point better than a long-winded oration. He was known as a hard hitter, respected for the care he took to avoid embarrassing or offending an opponent. Employing irony, rather than sarcasm, he could destroy an opponent's arguments, it was said, with words that left no sting.[13]

In 1907 Longworth was appointed to the Committee on Ways and Means, occupying the seat traditionally set aside for Ohio. With the job came a responsibility to further his state's interests by keeping taxes low and tariffs high enough to assure Ohio producers of a price advantage over foreign competition. His political future would henceforth depend on his providing such protection for Cincinnati-based industries, especially chemical and machine-tool products.

His first task as a Ways and Means member was to help draft the Payne-Aldrich Tariff Act, one of the most complex and controversial enactments of the age. He thought the law, as finally passed, went too far in raising levies on too many products. But he found in working on the bill that he had an aptitude for the intricacies of tariff law. He enjoyed the political give-and-take of tariff writing, and eventually he gained recognition as an expert in that area.

The Payne-Aldrich bill was an eye-opener for Longworth in more ways than one. It was originally conceived as a tariff-reduction measure, which the Republican platform had promised in the 1908 campaign. Instead, the party's archreactionaries, led by Speaker Cannon, brazenly rewrote the bill to raise tariffs even higher. Cannon's arrogance in forcing the House to accept the measure, breaking his party's compact with the electorate, disgusted Longworth.

Only a few months earlier, he had stood by Cannon as the House, in full revolt, rose against the Speaker. When Cannon had tried to resign the office following the revolt, Longworth had joined others in his party to insist that he continue. Now, he decided, Cannon had become an intolerable burden on the House and the party. His announcement that he would oppose Cannon's reelection as Speaker in the next Congress helped other wavering Republicans make up their own minds. Enough of them endorsed Longworth's position to assure that Cannon would be replaced as Speaker in 1911.

The voters in 1910 beat them to it. Disappointed with President Taft, fed up with Cannonism, and enraged over the betrayal on tariff revision, they responded angrily at the polls. Even in his own heavily Republican district, Longworth barely avoided defeat. Other Republican candidates were less fortunate. The Democrats captured control of the House and made substantial gains in the Senate.

Even greater setbacks befell the Republicans in 1912 when former president Roosevelt, running as a third-party candidate, challenged the incumbent Taft for the presidency. The result was a party split with disastrous results for Republicans at all levels. In Cincinnati, Taft's hometown, "regular" Republicans vented their wrath at Roosevelt by casting his son-in-law out of office. Although Longworth regained his seat two years later, his party remained out of power in the House until 1919.

A "New-Breed" Republican

It was a chastened Republican party that reclaimed control of the House in 1919. The party had felt the heat of the electorate in 1910. Now, leaderless and demoralized, members feared that what the voters had done once they could do again. Vanished was the air of confidence, bordering on arrogance, that once distinguished the party in the House.

Gone too were many of the so-called Old Guard from the Cannon era, replaced by younger men, mostly moderates, who believed that the Grand Old Party must renew itself before it could thrive again. Few if any of the newer members wanted a return to Cannonism. They wanted new leaders and a new approach to party organization and House management. Longworth, severing his last remaining ties to the Old Guard, cast his lot with these new-breed Republicans. As a senior party member, accepted by all factions, his voice gave added weight to those calling for far-reaching reform.

He urged colleagues to elect a Speaker who "will picture to the people the spirit of the Republican party of today, and its hopes and aspirations for the morrow." The type of individual he had in mind, he made clear, was not the likes of James Mann, the Illinois reactionary who had served as Cannon's deputy and had led House Republicans during their years in the minority. Furthermore, he said, the party must reexamine all practices, including the sacred seniority system, under which, he said, "utter incompetents" had risen to the head "of our most important committees."[14]

Distrust of a powerful Speaker ran deep in both parties but was more pronounced among Republicans. It was a Republican Speaker, after all, whose abuse of authority had angered voters and fed the insurgency that brought about the Cannon Revolt. The Democrats, picking up where the Republicans left off, virtually destroyed the office when they came to power in 1911. Under the Democrats, the Speaker was an exalted figurehead; he reigned but did not rule.

Since 1917, key Republicans had engaged in spirited debate over how authority should be distributed when and if the party returned to power. Although some yearned for another Cannon, whose authority was never in doubt and under whom the House for years ran as smoothly as a fine-tuned engine, most opposed a return to the old ways. The prevailing sentiment was to avoid any action that might awaken the party's slumbering progressive wing and bring another insurgency. A special committee was created by the Republican conference—the term *caucus* was in disrepute and no longer used in the party's official language—to consider various reform suggestions. Frank Mondell of Wyoming was named chairman. He was joined on the committee by twenty-six senior Republicans, Longworth among them.

The party caucus subsequently adopted several committee recommendations designed to diffuse power and broaden the decisionmaking process. Among them was the creation of a Republican Committee on Committees and the formalization of a five-member Steering Committee to advise party leaders.

Moderates were convinced that if Mann became Speaker, he would seek to rule in the ruthless style of Cannon. When Mann announced his candidacy for Speaker following the 1918 elections and named Uncle Joe Cannon as his manager, his opponents scrambled to find a candidate who could beat him. Attention focused on two challengers: Frederick Gillett of Massachusetts, a docile party elder, and Longworth, not yet fifty years old, the choice of midwestern and independent lawmakers who liked neither Mann nor Gillett.

Hailing Longworth's entry, the *New York Times* described him as the one candidate acceptable to all Republicans, from progressives to Cannon reactionaries.[15] "He has wit, humor, industry, application, a good mind," said the *Times*. "In spite of a certain modesty, he has made his talents acknowledged. He studies public questions carefully. He can think on his feet as well as in his library."[16] It was a rare recognition by the press that the Ohioan had qualities beyond an amiable personality.

Longworth, however, did not have the votes. At least 60 of the 238 Republican members were pledged to Mann and even more were committed to Gillett. The remaining votes were split among a half dozen other contenders. On January 27, Longworth withdrew from the race and threw his support to Gillett.[17] Gillett won with 138 votes to Mann's 69, the remaining votes scattering among three other candidates.[18]

With or without the speakership, Longworth and his reformers expected to control the House by dominating the Committee on Committees, which, under the new party rules, would name the majority floor leader, whips, and chairmen of the fifty or so legislative committees. It would also choose members of the Steering Committee. The Longworth contingent envisioned using the two leadership committees as tools of reform. Armed with the power to reward and punish, they would impose discipline on Republican members and preserve effective party government. What the would-be reformers failed to do, however, was to assess accurately the strength and resourcefulness of Mann and his reactionary followers.

Through a series of adroit maneuvers, the Mann forces gained control of the Committee on Committees and proceeded to fill every leadership position with staunch Old Guard conservatives. For majority floor leader, the most pivotal job in the Republican hierarchy at the time, they picked Frank Mondell, a man with no obvious leadership qualities.

By 1922, Mondell's refusal to cooperate with the Republican administration and his inability to rally his sizable majority for important votes had House Republicans on the verge of open rebellion.[19] In the Harding administration's first year, Mondell actively opposed five of President Harding's major proposals, including a veterans bonus bill and a tax cut. In each case, the *New York Sun* reported, the president was forced to work through Longworth to put his program across in the House.[20] The majority leader's timely decision to run for the Senate in 1922 saved him from almost certain dethronement before the opening of the next Congress.[21]

Soon after the 1922 elections, which left the House Republicans clinging to a slim majority, Longworth announced his candidacy to succeed Mondell as floor leader. Others joined the race, although he was, by far, the top contender. On December 1, 1923, two days before the new Congress was to convene, the Republican caucus elected the Ohioan by voice vote. As it turned out, the selection of Longworth was the only issue on which the badly fractured caucus could agree.

The Republicans needed nearly all of their 225 votes to win the speakership and the right to organize the House, a fact that did not escape the party's newly energized Progressive faction. Numbering about twenty-five, including a half-dozen independents, the dissidents could withhold their votes and thus deprive the Republicans of their majority. They could swing to the Democrats in any close vote. Their intention, they warned, was to go their own way unless certain demands were met. Those demands included more Progressive representation on key committees and rules changes to allow bills, other than those approved by the leadership, to reach the House floor. The caucus convened with party leaders vowing no concessions to the insurgents.

In the party caucus, twenty-four Progressives and independents opposed Gillett for Speaker. He won renomination easily but, without Progressive support, failed to muster the 218 votes needed to assure his reelection by the full House and without which the Republicans could not organize the House.

The matter was still unresolved when Congress convened on December 3. The Progressives carried out their threat, and for four days they shunned the Republican candidate for Speaker, supporting instead their own Republican candidates. The Democrats supported Finis J. Garrett, the minority floor leader. Meanwhile, it fell to Longworth, in his new role as majority leader, to resolve the impasse without appearing to capitulate to the insurgents' demands.

After four days of inconclusive balloting for Speaker, Longworth offered the holdouts a modest concession in exchange for their vote for Gillett. He proposed that the House adopt the old rules for a period of thirty days.[22] Within that time the Rules Committee would study the dissidents' proposed changes and report back to the House. To assure all voices would be heard, he said, the House would debate and be allowed to amend the committee's recommended changes.

Longworth's offer carried no guarantee that the rules would be changed or that more Progressives would go on key committees. Even so, the insurgents declared victory. "We are pleased to see that Mr. Longworth now concedes the necessity for such revision," they said, alleging they never sought more than an opportunity to liberalize the rules. Gillett was elected the next day with Progressive support. "Mr. Longworth has distinguished himself by conducting a superb strategic retreat," observed the *Brooklyn Eagle*.[23]

Majority Leader

It was clear by early 1924 that congressional politics had entered a new period of change and uncertainty. Most of the Old Guard, who had wrested control of the House in 1919, were gone. James Mann died, and Mondell and Cannon both retired in 1923. Republican unity was in shambles. Fueled by the resurgent Progressive movement, party members had begun to divide into blocs representing an array of sectional, ideological, and economic interests. A farm bloc had been formed in 1921 to advocate the interests of agriculture. Other blocs had followed, including a soldiers bloc committed to expanded benefits for veterans, a "wet" bloc intent on the destruction of Prohibition, and even an automobile bloc dedicated to lower taxes for that industry.

A firm believer in strict party rule, Longworth was in good company when he argued that, for the sake of efficient and responsible government, the individual must sacrifice his own independence for the good of the whole. That had been the gospel of Republican politics for decades, and in Longworth's opinion, it had served the nation admirably. Without responsible party government, he said, "I do not believe that a representative democratic republic like ours can long endure."[24] A staple of almost every Longworth speech in the 1920s was his description of the inadequacies of the bloc-ridden parliaments of Europe, which he had visited, and his warning that the bloc system would be disastrous for the United States. He made clear that his highest priority as Republican leader would be to restore and preserve party government in the House of Representatives.

The House wasted little time before testing the new majority leader's mettle. His first decision—to move the administration's tax-reduction bill to the floor ahead of the popular soldier-bonus bill—created a firestorm among members committed to a quick vote on the bonus. Taking the dispute to the caucus, he made a convincing argument that Republicans had a duty to support the president's program. Witnesses said he personally changed some fifteen votes, emerging with a decisive victory. He "displayed a degree of firmness, parliamentary adroitness and personal tact that has not characterized the history of the Republican majority for more than a dozen years," reporter Lewis Seibold wrote.[25]

He did not win every fight. In fact, his small, unruly majority deserted him on his first crucial vote. A coalition of Democrats and Progressive Republicans rebelled against the pro-wealthy tax-rate schedules in Treasury Secretary Andrew Mellon's tax-reduction bill, centerpiece of the administration's 1924 program. The majority leader eventually salvaged that situation by proposing to offset the Mellon rates with sharply reduced rates for low-income taxpayers. The revised bill, which became known as the Longworth Compromise, passed the House in February 1924. "A distinct parliamentary triumph," said the *Cincinnati Times-Star*. Only the *Wall Street Journal* thought otherwise. "Abject cowardice," the paper said of his willingness to settle for less than complete victory.

A bitter blow to the leadership was the House's decision to liberalize its rules, as advocated by the Progressives and most Democrats. Though he personally opposed such tampering, Longworth reluctantly went along with a proposal that eased the so-called discharge rule, under which rank-and-file members theoretically could wrest bills from the committees to which they had been assigned and bring them directly to the floor for debate.[26]

The old rule, written in 1911, required a majority vote of the House to discharge a committee. In practice, the rule was almost useless because the Speaker could simply refuse to recognize a member for such a motion. Under the new rule, approved by a vote of 253 to 114 in January 1924, a bill could be brought to the floor by means of a petition signed by only 150 House members. Although Longworth believed the change weakened "the fundamental rule of them all, the rule of the majority," he accepted it as a victory of sorts.[27] The original amendment called for only 100 signatures. It took all of Longworth's and Rules Committee chairman Bertrand Snell's persuasive powers, and several days of heated floor debate, to convince the House to set the level at 150.[28]

Democrats and Progressives handed the House leadership outright defeat on another controversial rules proposal. The House voted to abolish the so-called Underwood germaneness rule that since 1911 had barred members from offering nongermane amendments to revenue and tariff bills.[29]

In all, some 300 laws, including a tax revision, a soldiers' bonus, European-debt settlements, and immigration restrictions, were enacted in the Sixty-eighth Congress's first session. While the Senate focused on the Teapot Dome scandals, the House acted on 594 measures, nearly double the number passed in the same period of the previous Congress.[30] It was an impressive performance, especially in light of the close division between the two major parties. Longworth received most of the credit, the *Washington Post*, for instance, noting that the rookie floor leader throughout the session had mastered numerous difficulties "by the exercise of tact, persuasiveness, and fertility of resources."[31]

For a leader reputed to prefer play over work, Longworth proved a hard taskmaster. When a lengthy debate was anticipated, he convened the House early. When the legislative calendar became congested, he scheduled night sessions and sent the sergeant-at-arms out to restaurants and speakeasies to arrest stray members and escort them back to the chamber. No one seemed to mind. He drove the members with such good humor that even the dreaded night sessions became evenings of merriment. It was not unusual for members to form impromptu barber shop quartets to entertain colleagues while waiting for the sergeant-at-arms to round up the absentees.[32]

The year 1924 found the United States generally prosperous and satisfied with the Republican administration, which had given them balanced budgets and two tax cuts in four years. Only western farmers, mired in depression, remained a major pocket of dissent. President Calvin Coolidge easily won a full term in 1924, having earlier succeeded Harding, who died in 1923. With this victory Coolidge overcame the divisive third-party candidacy of Robert M. La Follette. The president's victory was accompanied by substantial Republican gains in both houses of Congress. Their new 247 to 183 majority meant that the House leadership no longer had to bargain and beg for Progressive support.

Significantly for Longworth, Frederick Gillett was elected to the Senate. The House speakership, now vacant, could be Longworth's for the asking. His success in leading his party over the past year entitled him to the House's highest office, if he wanted it. The question was, Should he trade his power as majority leader for a prestigious but powerless office? He concluded that, with a few bold maneuvers and the help of friends in key places, he might keep the majority leader's power and be Speaker too. He believed the House, after years of frustration under divided and indecisive leadership, would again accept centralized rule, especially if the ruling authority was a person whose qualities of fairness and sound judgment were already well established.

The time seemed ripe for strong leadership in Congress. President Coolidge's call in his inaugural address for the reassertion of party solidarity and responsibility seemed to reflect the Republican mood. Regular party members in both houses of Congress responded in early 1925 by excluding from the party councils the insurgent leaders who had defiantly opposed Republican policies and candidates in the past and who remained unrepentant. The House Republican Committee on Committees also declared that no one who failed to vote for the Coolidge-Dawes ticket in 1924 would be considered a Republican. The result: In addition to losing their right to participate in the Republican caucus, thirteen Progressives were deprived of their committee assignments.[33] Longworth denied intent to punish anyone and said he hoped their banishment would be only temporary.[34]

Longworth won his party's nomination for Speaker, overcoming a spirited challenge by Martin B. Madden of Illinois, at a secret caucus in February 1925, some nine months before the new Congress was scheduled to convene.[35] His selection so far in advance "was unusual if not unprecedented," said the *New York Times*, noting that "the emphatic victory only confirmed the general belief that his qualifications were superior to those of his rivals."[36]

The Republicans also nominated John Q. Tilson of Connecticut as the new majority leader. Tilson's election was engineered by James Begg, an Ohioan who, as Longworth's most trusted lieutenant, performed sensitive political tasks in Longworth's behalf.[37] Tilson would be indebted to the Speaker for his job. An able parliamentarian, Tilson lacked Longworth's boldness and imagination, but his reserved, businesslike manner complemented the Ohioan's easygoing style.[38] Moreover, he was willing to let Longworth be the boss. They proved a formidable leadership team.

Speaker of the House

Longworth was formally elected Speaker, defeating Democratic nominee Finis Garrett, the following December. In his acceptance speech, the Ohioan stated unequivocally his philosophy and goals, leaving no doubt that he intended to restore the speakership to its former primacy. Signaling that he would act both as Speaker of the House and principal leader of his party, he described his concept of the functions and duties of his office. They divide, he said, into "two general classes," one parliamentary, the other political.

> The first I propose to administer with most rigid impartiality, with an eye single to the maintenance, to the fullest degree, of the dignity and honor of the House, and the rights and privileges of its members. I promise you that there will be no such thing as favoritism in the treatment by the Chair of either parties or individuals.
>
> The political side, to my mind, involves a question of party service. I believe it to be the duty of the Speaker, standing squarely on the platform of his party to assist insofar as he properly can the enactment of legislation in accordance with the declared principles and politics of his party and by the same token to resist the enactment of legislation in variance thereof.
>
> I believe in responsible party government. . . .[39]

The *Philadelphia Public Ledger* summarized Longworth's speech in three words. "I'll Be Boss," proclaimed a headline above an account of the opening-day ceremonies.[40]

"The speakership is a fine thing," Longworth confided to his sister shortly after his election, "better than I had hoped or expected, largely because I was able to take the majority leadership from the floor to the chair, which most Speakers in recent years, except Reed and Cannon, were not able to do."[41]

His demand for Republican solidarity and a halt to the proliferation of special-interest blocs found wide acceptance, except among the radical Progressives, whose votes were no longer essential to the party anyway. The decision to exclude the militants from the caucus the previous February forewarned of the punishment in store for them in the new Congress. For the first time since 1911, the caucus had voted to bind all Republicans to support the party choice for Speaker. The insurgents, Longworth repeated throughout the year, would be welcome back if they would only "change their mind" and begin cooperating. The vote for Speaker, he added, would be the first test of their intentions. Denouncing the rebirth of the binding caucus, the insurgents reasserted their independence and defiantly put forth their own candidate to oppose Longworth.[42]

Having failed the first test, the insurgents went on to oppose Republican-backed changes in the House rules, which Longworth had declared his second test of party loyalty. As a result, the Republican Committee on Committees, "in accordance with the mandate of Czar Nicholas," as a reporter put it, confirmed its earlier decision to deny defiant Progressives their positions on key committees. Progressive leader Nelson lost his seat on Rules, James A. Frear was removed from Ways and Means, and Floria Lampert was replaced as chairman of the Committee on Patents. Other Progressives were allowed to stay on their committees but were dropped to the bottom in seniority.[43]

The effect of the rules changes, adopted over Democratic and Progressive protest, was to rescind the liberalizing amendments adopted by the last Congress. The minimum number of signatures needed on a discharge petition, for instance, was raised from 150 to "a majority of the membership." Some Republicans hostile to the discharge rule had wanted the discharge provision stricken from the rules entirely, but in the end, they settled for restrictive new provisions that made it almost impossible to implement.

Under the new rules, a discharge motion signed by 218 members would still have to be affirmed by a majority vote of the House and seconded in an unrecorded vote by tellers. "Better that the majority should leave out this discharge rule entirely," complained Representative Edward Pou, Democrat of North Carolina, "than to adopt the absurd and impossible rule that is now proposed." Coming only hours after the Speaker's conciliatory address, "which pleased both sides of the aisle," Pou said the Democrats had not expected that "the steamroller would be put into action so soon."[44] The new rule "hermetically seals the door against any bill ever coming out of a committee when the Steering Committee or the majority leaders desire to kill the bill without putting members of this House on record on the measure," added Democrat Charles R. Crisp, accurately describing Longworth's intention.[45]

The elected leadership team headed by Speaker Longworth made up only one of the five major spheres of Republican power in the House. Longworth already controlled three of them: the caucus, the elected leadership team (consisting of the Speaker, majority leader, and whip), and the Steering Committee. He had been one of the original Steering Committee members and as majority leader had served as the committee's ex officio chairman. Although, under party's rules, Speakers were excluded from serving on the committee, Longworth insisted on keeping not only his seat but also his chairmanship.[46] The committee went along. He also demanded that the majority leader and whip be made full participating members. By thus dominating the Steering Committee, he gained substantial influence over the Committee on Committees, whose members were appointed by the Steering Committee. Only the Rules Committee remained to be brought into his orbit.

To consolidate his control, Longworth had the Committee on Committees remove three members from the Rules Committee, including the insurgent Nelson, and replace them with dependable party regulars. The chairmanship remained in the hands of Longworth's longtime ally and Steering Committee colleague, Bertrand Snell of New York. Snell joined Tilson, the Speaker's right-hand man Jim Begg, and Longworth to form an inner circle of advisers. Within a year, the unofficial group would be known as the Big Four and would displace the Steering Committee as the party's principal policy body.[47]

Other Longworth initiatives came rapidly.[48] The Speaker brought in a new parliamentarian, the able Lewis Deschler, an Ohioan, whose encyclopedic knowledge and impartiality would eventually make him a legend in the House. He instructed Tilson to post regularly the legislative schedule for the coming week, ending the old practice of hiding such information from the minority. By initiating a policy of conferring with the minority on holiday recesses and the like, he eliminated a source of partisan hostility. He and Tilson induced chairmen to prepare and publish a calendar of legislation pending before their committees. Armed with that information, never before available, rank-and-file members could learn the nature and status of bills before their own committees and plan their own schedules.

To promote better coordination between committees in scheduling bills for debate, the majority leader's office became a clearinghouse for all committee activity. In addition, the Speaker resumed regular meetings with the president to plan and execute party strategy, reviving a practice that had ended with Theodore Roosevelt's administration.[49]

One of Longworth's early actions was to strike a blow for feminine equality in the House. He declared that the House's three women members were entitled to and would receive respect equal to that of their male counterparts. As a start, he abandoned the practice of addressing a female member as "the gentle lady," a form of address—condescending, many thought—officially used by members since the first woman was elected to the House in 1917. Instead, he began addressing women members as "the gentlewoman," pointing out that if men were addressed as "the gentleman," women should be addressed similarly. When the House's three women members complained that, unlike their male colleagues, they had no lavatory or place to relax, he remedied that situation. With his appointment of Mildred Reeves as the Speaker's secretary, he ended 135 years of having only males in the House's highest staff positions.[50]

Longworth's reforms extended even to the much abused *Congressional Record*, whose clutter and unreliability had long been one of his pet peeves. He barred members from self-serving editing of their remarks in debate, restricted their insertion of undelivered speeches, and refused their requests to insert extraneous material, such as newspaper editorials.[51] Perhaps his most radical innovation was to allow radio broadcasts of major House debates. Although critics found the experimental hookups disappointing, he continued to believe that the burgeoning medium of radio held great promise as a means of demystifying the legislative process and educating the public on major issues.

After serving two months as Speaker, Longworth basked in the adulation of the press. The House's swift enactment of Coolidge's two major requests—another tax reduction and ratification of the European-debt settlements—contrasted sharply with the delay and wrangling that had marked House debate in recent years. Noting that Longworth had solidified his organization "while the Senate has done nothing," journalist Clinton W. Gilbert wrote that, with passage of the tax bill, "the House has become the dominant body."[52]

Gilbert said that, during the House vote on the tax measure, he observed Longworth seated in the rear of the chamber, "watching with satisfaction, knowing that it meant the House was ascending over the Senate in prestige." Two short months, asserted an enthusiastic editorial writer for *Trend* magazine, "has revealed the House as one of the most efficient legislative machines in American history."[53]

The press interpreted Longworth's forceful beginning as unmistakable evidence that House Republicans had abandoned their experiment in committee government. "Signs that we are getting back to truer concepts of government by party are welcome," said the *New York Times*. The newspaper observed that party rule, although not infallible, "is the one great instrument of efficient government which has been devised and without which we should not know how to get along. If we are to have majority rule at all and are to call upon the minority to submit in a law-abiding spirit, it must be by means of a party organization."[54]

Longworth presided "with unusual dignity and justice," wrote political scientist Chang-Wei Chiu in his contemporary analysis of House leadership in the 1920s.[55] Longworth's relaxed demeanor, his deliberate steps to promote civility in an institution that had been torn by hostility for decades, his good-natured teasing of the opposition, and his ability to put politics aside when the fight was over created a new atmosphere. The result was a noticeable gain in bipartisan cooperation. Morale and efficiency rose. Even the quality of debate seemed to improve.

"Czar Nicholas"

Still holding a majority following the 1926 elections, House Republicans held fast to the Coolidge philosophy that government should guard against excessive spending and interfere in people's lives as little as possible.[56] Why burden the country with new programs, especially in a period of unparalleled prosperity and peace, Longworth argued. "The duty of the party in control of the affairs of a Congress lies not only in constructive legislative accomplishment, but equally, and at least as importantly, in the prevention of unwise and dangerous legislation," he once said.[57]

Reporters complained that the House under Longworth's leadership was so efficient and noncontroversial that it had become dull. Even the Progressives had rejoined the Republican fold in return for their old committee assignments. "For the first time in two decades, there is no Republican group [in the House] that can be classified as really insurgent," noted Henry Suydam of the *Brooklyn Eagle*.[58] Only in the Senate, where they held the balance of power, were the Progressives still a force to be reckoned with.

Amid speculation that President Coolidge might not seek reelection in 1928, Longworth's name began cropping up more and more as a leading contender for his party's nomination. In 1927, several potential candidates, including Longworth, begin testing the political waters in various parts of the country. Nick and Alice Longworth were in the midst of a "nonpolitical" tour of the Pacific states, which no Speaker had ever visited while in office, when Coolidge stunned the nation with his famous I-do-not-choose-to-run declaration.

"Now that Coolidge is out of the race, the betting is that the party will swing over to Longworth," said one analyst, ignoring the fact that Longworth was at odds with his party on one crucial issue.[59] That issue was Prohibition, which he had fought since its inception. Indeed, so long as the Prohibition issue remained dormant, the popular Ohioan was widely perceived as the party's leading presidential contender. But then the "drys" began to organize. Temperance activists—Flying Squadrons, as they were known—swarmed across the country urging Republicans to reject Longworth, "a drinking wet all his life."[60] In Ohio, his candidacy was declared unacceptable by the Anti-Saloon League and by his own state party leaders. With the wet versus dry issue dividing Republicans and certain to intensify as the campaign wore on, Longworth saw no choice but to bow out of the race.

"I can say with all honesty and sincerity that I would rather be Speaker of the House of Representatives than head of any other office within the gift of the people," Longworth declared in December 1927, following his reelection to a second term as Speaker. A week later he declared unequivocally that he would not be a candidate for either president or vice president on the Republican ticket. In the 1928 election, the Republican presidential candidate, bone-dry Herbert Hoover, overwhelmed his wet

Democratic opponent, Al Smith of New York. Hoover's win was accompanied by huge Republican gains in Congress. In the Seventy-first Congress, which convened in special session in April 1929, Longworth commanded a Republican majority of more than a hundred seats, the party's largest in decades.

Anxious to help the nation's farmers, President Hoover summoned the lawmakers into extraordinary session to consider two measures.[61] One, aimed at resuscitating long-depressed farm prices, would create a government mechanism to control farm surpluses. The other measure called for modest upward revision of duties on agricultural imports. Longworth, in accepting a third term as Speaker, stated his view that the current tariff act had proved highly successful and needed only minor adjustment. He urged his colleagues to resist the temptation to revise rates in other areas and implored them to keep their changes "to as few in number as possible."[62]

The House, acting with its usual efficiency, needed only a few days to pass Hoover's farm-relief bill. The second bill, sponsored in the House by Willis C. Hawley of Oregon, was waylaid by the high protectionists in the Ways and Means Committee. As sent to the Senate in May 1929, the House bill raised duties on hundreds of items to the highest level in history.[63] The Senate Finance Committee, headed by Reed Smoot of Utah, inserted its changes and sent the bill to the floor. There, in a frenzy of logrolling, the Senate added some twelve hundred amendments, most of them boosting tariffs even higher than the House bill. The Senate also struck out a key provision that would have allowed the president to modify rates up or down as conditions changed. The session ended in November with House-Senate conferees deadlocked in trying to reconcile the two differing bills.

Meanwhile, a stock market crash on October 29 added an ominous note of further uncertainty in the debate over tariff revision. When Congress convened in regular session in December, Hoover renewed his appeal for the measure, citing the worsening economic climate, which, he said, made the bill's passage more imperative than ever. With dubious logic, he said that broad tariff protection was now needed to stimulate domestic industries, which in growing numbers were beginning to scale back operations. Seeking to end the deadlock, he persuaded the Senate to revise portions of its bill. The result, he hoped, would be a bill acceptable to the House as well as to the president. It would be up to Longworth and the House leadership to prevent further changes when the bill came back for a vote in that body.

Longworth sought a straight up-or-down vote, but on a matter of transcendent importance to his party, he could not rally his forces. A number of Republicans, mostly from the Northwest, demanded an opportunity to vote separately on certain changes in the Senate bill. The Steering Com-mittee was no help; it too was divided and could recommend no rule, closed or otherwise, satisfactory to all Republicans.

Longworth finally decided to appease the dissidents by allowing amendments on four items—sugar, cement, lumber, and shingles. On April 2, 1930, the House approved the proposed rule, 240 to 153, only af-ter Longworth "did a great deal of smiling and jesting, negotiating to make it acceptable to the ruthless regulars of his party," radio commenta-tor Hard told his audience that evening.[64] If the Speaker thought his party's huge majority would beat down any changes in the bill, he greatly misread the House's mood.

With much of the press, including many influential Republican news-papers, thundering against the bill, some Republicans failed to show up for the debate. Others, who favored amending the bill, joined with Dem-ocrats to form shifting coalitions. When the lumber schedule came up for debate, Longworth saw right away he had made a mistake.

Instead of raising the duty on lumber from the level set by the Senate, as Ways and Means Chairman Hawley and other lumber-state congress-men had wanted, the House, by a voice vote, accepted an amendment to put lumber on the free list. "Hawley stood in the aisle with his mouth open, mentally paralyzed, speechless," recalled Claude Bowers, who wit-nessed the scene.[65] Longworth, in the chair, waited for the stunned Ore-gonian to demand a roll call. "The ayes . . . seem to . . . have it," the Speaker said slowly, buying time for Hawley to regain his senses. "The ayes . . . seem . . . to . . . have . . . it," he repeated. Hawley remained, said Bowers, "rooted to the spot and still speechless."

Finally, "his face flushed and angry," Longworth asked, "Does the Gen-tleman from Oregon wish to address the chair?" When Hawley still did not respond, the Speaker nodded to another Republican, who requested a recorded vote. The roll call changed nothing. Some twenty Republicans, who would support a tariff on lumber so long as their votes were not recorded, deserted the House leadership. The amendment stood.

The low-tariff forces remained in control for the rest of the day. Sugar duties were reduced, after which farcical wrangling erupted between the lumber bloc and the cement bloc, the former claiming that the latter had reneged on their deal to vote for each other's amendments. "It was a com-edy of errors all around," the Democrat Bowers concluded. Eventually the bill, mangled beyond recognition, was sent to Hoover for his signa-ture. He signed it on June 17. Senator Robert La Follette, Jr., spoke for many Americans when he said it was "the worst tariff bill in the nation's history."[66] It was also to be protectionism's last hurrah.

Surprisingly, Congress took little immediate heed of the rapidly deep-ening depression. With the tariff bill enacted and President Hoover proclaiming that "prosperity is just around the corner," both houses turned to other issues. Nor were economic conditions a major cause of the massive losses incurred by the Republicans in the fall elections. Political scientist Susan F. Stevens's examination of the 1930 congressional elections revealed that voters gave far greater significance to Prohibition, the tariff, and farm policy.[67] In Ohio alone, eight Republican House members were defeated. Longworth had a narrow escape, winning by a mere four thousand votes, after veterans groups turned against him at the polls, claiming he had done too little to help them.[68]

The election left the two major parties almost evenly divided in both houses. Although the Republicans retained a thin majority, much could change before the next Congress convened thirteen months later. Deaths were inevitable. Eleven House members, on average, could be expected to die during an interregnum, more than enough to reverse the 1930 electoral results.[69] Neither party could claim victory.

Which party would organize the Seventy-second Congress was much in doubt as the big clock in the rear of the House Chamber approached noon on March 4, 1931, marking the end of the Seventy-first Congress. Twice the clock had to be moved back to allow scores of lame-duck members to bid mawkish farewells to their colleagues.

When, at last, the Speaker rose from his chair, gavel poised, the House erupted in thunderous applause. House veterans could recall nothing like it. Lucile McArthur, a Longworth staff member, was an observer. "The House membership rose to its feet, wildly beating its hands, and from the Democratic side of the aisle came several prolonged rebel yells that added to the general excitement," she wrote. "Nick stood and waited for it to subside, getting redder and redder with pleasure and gratification. I wept. I couldn't help it. It was such a demonstration of affection."[70]

Longworth closed the session with brief remarks. "Perhaps this is the last time I will address you from this rostrum," he began. "The decision lies with none of us here; it is a decision that rests with an all-wise Providence. . . ." Although he was referring to the uncertain electoral outcome, many would later find his comments prophetic.

Upon final adjournment, members lingered, reluctant to leave. Someone wheeled an old piano into the Chamber. Many gathered around it and began singing sentimental ballads. The remarkable scene concluded with Cliff Woodrum, Democrat of Virginia, leading his colleagues in "Carry Me Back to Old Virginny." For most of those present it was to be their last glimpse of Nick Longworth—carefree, his face crinkled in a broad smile as he accompanied Woodrum lustily on the piano.

Longworth had looked forward to the adjournment. The stress of a contentious lame-duck session, mounting concern that voters in the next election would blame his party for the Depression, and a persistent, painful chest cold had left him exhausted. Still nursing his cold, he traveled to Aiken, South Carolina, shortly after the adjournment to spend a few days at the home of friends. When his illness grew worse, doctors were called. He had developed pneumonia, an often-fatal disease before the discovery of antibiotics. For three days, doctors watched helplessly as his condition deteriorated. Longworth died on April 9. A funeral train, packed with his friends, carried his body back to Cincinnati.

Political analyst Frank R. Kent of the *Baltimore Sun* captured the essence of Longworth's reign. "Without any revision of the rules," Kent wrote, "he completely recovered the power of the speakership and was the undisputed leader of the House with as autocratic control as either Reed or Cannon. It is true he exercised this power with infinitely more tact and grace and gumption and without that touch of offensive arrogance that characterized former House Czars. But he was just as much a Czar. What Mr. Longworth clearly proved was this matter of leadership depends not so much on the rules but on the man."[71]

NOTES

1. William Hard, "Nicholas Longworth," *American Review of Reviews* (April 1925): 373.

2. See William Tyler Page, "Mr. Speaker Longworth," *Scribner's Monthly Magazine* (March 1928): 272–280.

3. Duff Gilfond, "Mr. Speaker," *The American Mercury* (August 1927): 453.

4. Clara Longworth de Chambrun, *The Making of Nicholas Longworth*, (New York: Ray Long and Richard R. Smith, Inc., 1933) p. 204.

5. Clinton W. Gilbert, "The Daily Mirror of Washington," *Philadelphia Public Ledger*, March 2, 1926. Longworth scrapbooks, v. 54, Cincinnati Historical Society.

6. William Hard column, *The Nation*, January 23, 1924. "There is in him a total void at the spot where the American statesman keeps usually that priceless possession of his: a talent for solemnity which would make the British House of Commons flee to the tea terrace."

The notion that solemnity is a requisite for successful service in Congress was best articulated by nineteenth-century Representative Thomas Corwin (R-Ohio). Corwin, the most affable and popular legislator of his time, blamed his humorous nature for his failure to become president. "To succeed in life you must be solemn, solemn as an ass," he told a colleague. "All the great monuments are built over solemn asses." Quoted in Richard Strout, "Foe of the Bon Mot: Politics," *New York Times Magazine*, April 22, 1956, pp. 13, 58–58.

7. J. H. Webb, *Cleveland Plain Dealer*, April 10, 1931. Webb had interviewed Longworth in 1899 on the day Longworth announced his candidacy for the Ohio general assembly. He recalled the quotation years later. Longworth papers, memorial scrapbook, box 4, Cincinnati Historical Society.

8. Gilfond, "Mr. Speaker," p. 456.

9. See *Cleveland World*, April 25, 1902; *Cleveland Leader*, May 1, 1902; *Cleveland Press*, July 29, 1902; *The Ohio State Journal*, Columbus, October 22, 1902; *Cincinnati*

Enquirer, April 10, 1931, in Longworth scrapbook, v. 2, and Longworth papers, memorial scrapbook, box 4, Cincinnati Historical Society.

10. March 28, 1902.

11. Alice Roosevelt Longworth, *Crowded Hours* (New York: Charles Scribner's Sons, 1933), pp. 206–207.

12. The law passed years later under the sponsorship of Frank Lowden, Republican of Illinois. Longworth said it did not matter that he received no credit for its passage. "I don't care who eventually obtains the credit for getting a thing done," he said. "All I care about is getting done the thing that I want." de Chambrun, *The Making of Nicholas Longworth*, p. 185.

13. See Associated Press article, *Arkansas Democrat*, April 9, 1931. Longworth papers, memorial scrapbook, box 4, Cincinnati Historical Society. Also de Chambrun, *The Making of Nicholas Longworth*, p. 281.

14. Longworth speech before the Republican Club of New York. *New York Times*, February 12, 1919.

15. January 13, 1919.

16. Editorial entitled "The Next Speakership," January 15, 1919.

17. *New York Times*, January 28, 1919.

18. *New York Times*, February 28, 1919.

19. "Mondell Faces Loss of Post as House Leader," *The New York Sun*, April 21, 1922. Longworth scrapbooks, v. 50, Cincinnati Historical Society.

20. See also George Rothwell Brown, *The Leadership of Congress* (Indianapolis: Bobbs-Merrill, 1922), p. 203.

21. He was defeated for the Senate.

22. Typewritten statement. Longworth papers, container 1, folder 11. Manuscript Division, Library of Congress.

23. Editorial, December 5, 1923.

24. de Chambrun, *The Making of Nicholas Longworth*, pp. 296–297.

25. *New York Herald*, January 12, 1924.

26. *New York Times*, January 13, 1924.

27. Typewritten speech, dated January 17, 1924. Longworth papers, container 2, folder 1, Manuscript Division, Library of Congress.

28. Paul DeWitt Hasbrouck, *Party Government in the House of Representatives* (New York: Macmillan, 1927), pp. 151–155.

29. *New York Times*, January 15, 1924.

30. Press release, Office of the Majority Leader, July 24, 1924. Longworth scrapbooks, v. 51, Cincinnati Historical Society.

31. *Washington Post*, May 27, 1924.

32. Robert Talley, "So This Is Congress," *Baltimore Post*, May 30, 1924.

33. *New York Times*, March 6, 1925.

34. Longworth statement, January 30, 1925. Longworth papers, container 2, folder 2, Manuscript Division, Library of Congress. See also *New York Times*, March 5, 1925.

35. The vote was 140 to 85.

36. Editorial, March 2, 1925.

37. Unsigned article, "Low Down on the Higher Ups," by "The Gentleman at the Keyhole," *Collier's Magazine*, February 26, 1926.

38. See George Authier, "The New Speaker of the House," *The National Republic*, c. January 1926.

39. *Congressional Record*, December 7, 1926, p. 382.

40. December 8, 1925.

41. de Chambrun, *The Making of Nicholas Longworth*, p. 294.

42. Henry A. Cooper of Wisconsin. See "House Radicals Bolt Longworth on Congress Eve," *New York Times*, December 7, 1925.

43. *New York Times*, December 16, 1925.

44. *Congressional Record*, December 7, 1925, p. 387.

45. Ibid., p. 388.

46. Chang-Wei Chiu, *The Speaker of the House of Representatives Since 1896* (New York: Columbia University Press, 1928), p. 334.

47. *New York Times*, February 22, 1927, p. 21.

48. H. B. Gauss, "House Due to Set Record in Efficiency," *Chicago Daily News*, January 16. 1926. Longworth scrapbooks, v. 54, Cincinnati Historical Society.

49. Randall B. Ripley, *Party Leaders of the House of Representatives* (Washington: The Brookings Institution, 1967), p. 77.

50. *Boston Telegram*, undated, c. 1926. Longworth scrapbooks, v. 54, Cincinnati Historical Society.

51. Clipping from *Chester* [Pennsylvania] *Times*, March 19, 1926. Longworth scrapbooks, v. 54, Cincinnati Historical Society. See also *Congressional Record*, March 24, 1924, p. 4890.

52. "The Daily Mirror of Washington," *Philadelphia Public Ledger*, March 2, 1926. Longworth scrapbooks, v. 54, Cincinnati Historical Society.

53. April 1926.

54. Editorial, February 21, 1926.

55. Chiu, *The Speaker of the House of Representatives Since 1896*, p. 307.

56. See Ernest Sutherland Bates, *The Story of Congress 1789–1935* (New York: Harper & Brothers, 1936), pp. 402–404.

57. Radio address, October 7, 1930. Longworth papers, Manuscript Division, Library of Congress.

58. December 19, 1926.

59. *New Haven* [Connecticut] *Journal Courier*, August 5, 1927. Longworth scrapbooks, v. 57, Cincinnati Historical Society.

60. *New Hampshire Sentinel*, September 29, 1927. Longworth scrapbooks, v. 58, Cincinnati Historical Society.

61. Bates, *The Story of Congress 1789–1935*, pp. 406–407.

62. Longworth remarks prepared for delivery April 15, 1929. Longworth papers, container 2, folder 6, Manuscript Division, Library of Congress.

63. Bates, *The Story of Congress 1789–1935*, p. 407.

64. Transcript of an address by William Hard over the National Broadcasting Company system, April 2, 1930. Longworth scrapbooks, v. 61, Cincinnati Historical Society.

65. See Claude Bowers, *My Life* (New York: Simon and Schuster, 1961), pp. 220–222.

66. Quoted in Donald R. Kennon and Rebecca M. Rogers, *The Committee on Ways and Means: A Bicentennial History 1789–1989* (Washington, DC: U.S. Government Printing Office, 1989), p. 267.

67. Susan F. Stevens, "Congressional Elections of 1930: Politics of Avoidance" (Ph.D. diss., State University of New York at Buffalo, 1980).

68. They got his attention. When Congress convened in December, following the elections, Longworth defied President Hoover by throwing his support to the long-stalled veterans bonus bill. The House was presented with the bizarre spectacle of the Speaker actively opposing the president's position while the majority leader defended it. The bill passed overwhelmingly. "No one doubts that if Mr. Longworth had decided to oppose the bill, he could have kept it from getting to a vote in the House," said Howard Brayman of the *New York Evening Post*, April 9, 1931.

69. This was the estimate of Dr. George Calver, Congress's official physician. See Lucile McArthur, "Idle Moments of a Lady in Waiting," *Saturday Evening Post* (September 19, 1931): 141.

70. Ibid.

71. April 10, 1931.

6

John Nance Garner

Anthony Champagne

Today John Nance Garner is probably best known as Franklin Roosevelt's vice president for two terms, as a vice president who rebelled against what he believed was a left-leaning tendency by Roosevelt, and as a man whom John L. Lewis described as "a labor-baiting, poker-playing, whiskey-drinking, evil old man."[1] Garner, however, had a remarkable career in the House of Representatives prior to being vice president. He was elected to the House of Representatives in 1902 and served until 1933, when he became vice president. Those three decades in the House ultimately led him to the speakership in 1931, and for a while he was believed to be presidential timber. In this chapter I examine Garner the congressman and the congressional leader and attempt to explain his views, his personality, and the power base from which he led the House. To understand Garner requires insights into his early life as well as his congressional life, his district, and the political forces in the Rio Grande Valley that kept him in power in Washington for thirty years.[2]

The Early Garner

Born in 1868 in Blossom Prairie, Texas, not far from the Red River in northeast Texas, John Nance Garner could honestly claim to have been born in a log cabin. Garner's father was a confederate veteran, and his parents were farmers. Although his father was illiterate, he became quite prosperous. As a result, John Nance had greater opportunities for education than most farm boys in post–Civil War Texas. It was not, however, an education sufficient to allow him to succeed at Vanderbilt University, which he left in order to study law in offices in Clarksville, Texas. By 1893, however, Garner had a problem with tuberculosis and sought as the cure for his disease the drier climate of Uvalde, Texas, four hundred miles to the southwest of Clarksville.

Deep in south Texas, Uvalde had been known for its lawlessness. Even when Garner arrived, many people in the area carried sidearms.[3] It was a world of ranches, cattle, and cowboys with a heavy Hispanic influence. It was also a world where an amiable man who could hold his liquor and play a good game of poker fit in with the local political culture. Garner was one of those who fit right in. Not long after arriving in Uvalde, he was appointed county judge and in 1894 was elected to that office. Four years later he was elected to the Texas House of Representatives; two years after that he was reelected. Using his opportunity as chair of the committee that was apportioning Texas in the aftermath of the 1900 Census, Garner created a district from which he thought he could be elected, and in 1902 he was elected to the U.S. Congress as a representative of the Fifteenth Congressional District.[4]

It was a sprawling area. The original district from which he was elected was larger than the state of Pennsylvania. For 150 miles, it ran along the Gulf of Mexico, and then for 400 miles, along the Rio Grande.[5] In land mass, it was the biggest district in Texas. The Fifteenth encompassed twenty-two counties and included the cities of Brownsville, Laredo, and Corpus Christi. Its most populous county had 21,851 inhabitants, and its most rural county had a population of only 792 people. Its total population was 160,694 people. In population, it was the second smallest district in Texas, and its population was almost 30,000 people less than the average Texas congressional district. The Fifteenth was truly wide-open spaces—its population per square mile was 5. Because it was a south Texas district, an area largely unsettled at the time of the Civil War, only 5.8 percent of the population was black, but given its closeness to the Mexican border, its percentage of foreign born was huge—27.2 percent of the population. It was an agricultural district. The value of its livestock was nineteen times the value of its manufactured goods.[6]

Jim Wells's Man in Washington

Garner's early political career cannot be understood merely as the success of an amiable, hard-drinking, poker-playing lawyer who succeeded in politics in Texas ranching country. Garner was elected to Congress because he was the candidate of the large ranchers, landowners, and county political leaders who dominated south Texas politics. The most important of those political bosses was James B. Wells.[7] From 1882 until 1922, Wells was the Democratic chairman in Cameron County. From 1892 to 1900 he was on the State Executive Committee of the Democratic Party. From 1900 to 1904, he was the chair of the Democratic Party State Executive Committee. In 1897, he was appointed a state district judge. He worked with other political leaders such as E. M. House of Austin and delivered votes from the Rio Grande Valley for candidates backed by House. Wells was a crucial supporter over the years of several congressmen, including W. H. Crain, Rudolph Kleberg, and Jeff McLemore.[8] But the most successful Wells protégé was Garner.[9] Other political bosses, most of whom were aligned with Wells, included the notoriously corrupt Archer Parr of Duval County; Judge John Valls of Laredo; Robert Kleberg of Kingsville, who was the attorney for the King and Kennedy ranches; Manuel Guerra of Starr County; Tom Coleman of Dimmit; and Pat Dunn of Nueces County, who was the owner of much of Padre Island.[10]

These political leaders were central to Garner's success. And they were not above engaging in questionable political tactics in behalf of their candidates. Archer Parr was probably the most corrupt. He did not like opposition to his chosen candidates, so oftentimes candidates he opposed got few, if any, votes in Duval County.[11] For example, in the 1926 Democratic primary, Duval County reported 1,342 votes for Garner and 1 vote for Garner's opponent, Sid Hardin.[12]

Garner fully understood that as long as he satisfied the south Texas political bosses, he would be secure in office. Even prior to his first election to Congress, he wrote to Archer Parr, "Have no fears as to what column your county will be in. I leave the whole matter in your hands, and should we be successful you will always find me fighting just as I did at Austin for my friends."[13] Shortly before Garner announced for Congress, he wrote Wells, urging him "to treat me as you would your own boy."[14]

Indeed, Garner left so much of the home front to the south Texas bosses that a continual theme of local press reports and of biographical treatments of Garner is that he rarely campaigned in his district or even visited major parts of his district. Bascom Timmons, for example, wrote that "Garner for thirty years did not canvass his district and franked no speeches home. . . ."[15] Marquis James wrote, "In the thirty years he represented that district Mr. Garner does not appear to have made a dozen campaign speeches in his own behalf."[16] And, though O. C. Fisher claimed that in Garner's first campaign he knew or made himself known to nearly every voter, Garner himself told Fisher, "I didn't have to do much campaigning at home after I got established. I was very fortunate. After I had been there ten years I never had any trouble. I didn't have to pay any attention to my district after that. The people kept me in Congress voluntarily."[17]

In his last ten years in Congress, Garner's main campaign effort appears to have consisted of barbecues that he would give in the back of his home. He built a huge barbecue pit and put in seats for one hundred people.[18] Even in his earlier years in Congress, one finds little evidence of active campaigning by Garner. In 1914, it was claimed that there were five counties in his district that Garner had never visited, that it had been two years since he visited Brownsville and six to eight years since he visited Frio County, which was adjacent to Uvalde. It was also claimed he had only sent two speeches home in ten years.[19] In the 1914 campaign, he did not even go home to vote for himself, although he won with ease.[20]

His dependence on the political bosses, especially Jim Wells, meant that they would back him with winning coalitions against Democratic primary challengers and Republican opponents. In exchange, they wanted patronage, help with constituent problems, and pork barrel projects to aid in the development of the Rio Grande Valley.[21]

At least in his first election to Congress, Wells raised money statewide for Garner's campaign.[22] However, the main source of support for Garner in the district was not money, but votes—largely Mexican American votes controlled by the Wells organization. Garner was once asked how he was able to get the votes of Mexican Americans. His simple explanation: "I had as my campaign manager Judge James Wells of Brownsville. He knew the Mexicans well and they had great confidence in him."[23] It was a bit more complicated than that. Wells and the other bosses used threats, intimidation, personal influence, almost every technique imaginable to muster their forces. Noncitizens often voted, and sometimes Mexican citizens were imported from Mexico to vote.[24]

By 1920, the Wells machine was broken as a result of Wells's declining health and the growth and development of south Texas, but by then Garner's power base was well established, and the local political bosses continued in power. Garner remained loyal to the south Texas bosses, even unsuccessfully intervening while he was vice president to get a charge of income tax evasion dismissed against George Parr, the son of Archer Parr and Archer's successor as Duval County political boss.[25]

In exchange for support, Garner supplied patronage for the machine as well as public works projects for the district. One news clipping reported that Garner had secured larger appropriations for public buildings and a greater number of items than any other congressman. Federal buildings in Del Rio, Eagle Pass, and Laredo as well as authorization of buildings at Uvalde, Corpus Christi, Beeville, and Sequin were the result of Garner's actions. He also secured agricultural soil surveys of sixteen thousand square miles of the district and persuaded the Geological Division of the Interior Department to work there as well, the only district in Texas where they were working. In addition, work had begun on an intercoastal canal and on improvements at Port Aransas, Corpus Christi, and Baffin Bay. Garner had aided in getting good roads and highways in the district.[26] Finally, Garner worked to keep military bases in the district open and to move in additional federal troops to protect banks and cattle from raids from Mexico, which was undergoing revolution.[27] When the War Department threatened to close a cavalry post near Brownsville, Garner successfully lobbied Secretary of War William H. Taft to prevent closure.[28] Wells was especially pleased that Garner had gotten the Department of Agriculture to set up a laboratory in Cameron County to examine the feasibility of introducing certain plants to the region.[29] Garner's most significant effort was beginning the Intercoastal Canal. He was so interested in the canal, which was crucial to water transportation between the coastal parts of his district and the Mississippi River, that he accompanied the Corps of Engineers to his district when the canal was surveyed and rewarded the officer in charge of the survey by appointing his son to West Point.[30] When a Corps of Engineers survey recommended against deepening the Corpus Christi harbor, Garner got the Corps headquarters to reverse the survey recommendation.[31] Garner clearly recognized that he was, in his early years, a pork barrel Congressman. He recalled, "The first few years I was up there, except for working on my 'projects' [government projects in the district] I spent much of my time over in the office building after it was built, playing poker."[32]

Pork for Me; Economy for Others

When Garner first served in Congress, it was 1903; Theodore Roosevelt was president of the United States, and Joe Cannon was beginning his first term as Speaker. The Democrats were in the minority 178 to 208, and they would stay in the minority until 1911, when Champ Clark of Missouri was elected Speaker. Garner was an inconspicuous new member of Congress. Joe Cannon was the dominant member of the House, with powers so great he was often called a Czar.[33]

Garner received largely unimportant committee assignments: the Committee on Expenditures in the State Department and Railways and Canals. The only advantage to such assignments was that Garner was able to use the Committee on Railways and Canals as a forum for pushing a proposal for an Intercoastal Canal.[34] Garner spent his early years in Congress developing networks of friends and allies, not the least of which was Joe Cannon. Garner was a regular at the Boar's Nest, Cannon's hideaway club on K Street; there, it was said, Garner began building a personal fortune at the poker table.[35] Garner's poker-playing ties to Cannon led to extraordinary last-minute approval by the Speaker for an amendment allowing the deepening of the harbor at Corpus Christi, an amendment very important to Garner's district.[36] Those ties also led to Garner's being appointed to a committee in charge of the construction of the first House office building.[37]

After being in the House for two years, Garner was assigned to the Foreign Affairs Committee, still not an important committee but one that was useful for a congressman whose district bordered Mexico. Garner and Nicholas Longworth were assigned to the Foreign Affairs Committee on the same day. Although Longworth was in many ways Garner's opposite—Longworth was well educated, cosmopolitan, and cultured—they were to become fast friends, and during Longworth's speakership, they were to develop one of the most famous working relationships ever between two opposing party leaders.[38]

Within the House, the Czar rule of Cannon was not to last. Garner was a loyal Democrat and supported the revolt against Cannon's rule that ultimately led to the weakening of the Speaker's powers in 1910. In 1911, Democratic leader Champ Clark became Speaker. Thus, for the first time since Garner went to Congress, the Democrats were in control of the House. It was a very different mechanism for leadership than had existed under Cannon. The Rules Committee was no longer controlled by the Speaker. Additionally, the party caucus was used to establish party policy and to bind members of the caucus to support policy. Another development was that seniority was increasingly important as a method for managing diffuse power after the weakening of the speakership. And beginning in the 1890s, there was an increasing trend toward longevity of service, one especially noticeable in the South. Leadership in the Democratic Party was centered in the South. Ronald Peters pointed out that of the 58 standing committees in the Sixty-third Congress, 30 were chaired by southerners and 8 by representatives of border states. Four of the seven Democrats on the Rules Committee were from the South, and one was from a border state.[39]

In 1909 Democratic leader Clark appointed Garner party whip. With Democratic control of the House in 1911, Garner retained the whip position under Oscar Underwood as majority leader. Garner also was appointed to the three-member Committee on Organization that distributed patronage jobs in the newly Democratic House.[40] In 1913, Garner passed up the chairmanship of Foreign Affairs to become a member of the Ways and Means Committee, the tax-writing committee of the House. Democratic members of Ways and Means served as the Committee on Committees for the Democratic members. Within a decade Garner had moved to a leadership position in the party and to one of the most important committees in the House. It was not long before Garner was bragging to his mentor Jim Wells, "You will be happy to know that all hands seem to take more cognizance that I am a member of Congress, than they have heretofore."[41]

Garner, whose political base was built on pork barrel politics, rather ironically began to develop a reputation as a protector of the public purse. Herbert Hoover received intelligence reports on Garner's congressional actions from the Republican National Committee, reports that were gathered largely from materials in the *Congressional Record*. Those reports portrayed Garner as developing a reputation for economy that "was picayunish economy. It was largely grandstand play to the public. . . . [It was] hypocritical . . . when it came to a question of expenditures in his own District." Garner, for example, was accused of continually objecting to small expenditures, such as whether clerks should be paid $125 a month instead of $6 a day, whether canceling machines at the post office should be bought or rented, whether too much money was being spent on furniture in the House office building, and similar matters involving sums of $50 to $3,000. Yet Garner strongly supported an appropriation of $35,795 for the purpose of promoting sugarcane and beets in his district. Garner also tried to vastly increase the appropriations for a government building in Corpus Christi.[42]

Noting Garner's strong interest in securing projects for his district, President Hoover's secretary, Theodore Joslin, received a report from J. Bennett Gordon of the Republican National Committee pointing out that a 1916 article had quoted Garner as making a speech to constituents in which he claimed, "Those fellows from New England and other northern states have plastered their country with unnecessary federal buildings. Now we Democrats are in charge of the House, and I'll tell you right now, every time one of those Yankees gets a ham, I am going to do my best to get a hog."[43] It would not be long, however, before Garner would rise from being a pork barrel congressman, grandstanding for public economy, to become a leader in the movement for a graduated income tax and Wilson's emissary to the House on war measures.

The Garner Style

In some ways, Garner was quite eccentric. He was notoriously thrifty, to a point that his thrift was a joke among his companions.[44] Garner rarely corresponded with people, either not writing them or leaving the task to his wife, Ettie.[45] He granted few formal interviews to the press, although he admitted a small number of correspondents into his personal circle and sometimes used them for his political purposes. Reporters such as Cecil Dickson, Marquis James, and especially Bascom Timmons were as close to him as any politician.[46] Garner disliked public speaking but could be vicious in debate.[47]

Garner had an enormous capacity for making friends, but he had few intimate friends.[48] He tended to keep his own counsel; for instance, it was not until the last moment that he told his closest protégés, such as Sam Rayburn, about his presidential plans.[49]

Once he had established his value to the political bosses in his district, Garner paid little attention to what most politicians would consider fundamental political concerns. Among these were elections, even though he often had Democratic primary opposition and, unlike many southern congressmen, fairly significant Republican opposition.

He enjoyed testing the mettle of men, trying to push them to test the strength of their characters. Once when Lew Deschler was only twenty-five years old and had just started work as a clerk for Speaker Longworth, Garner suddenly accosted him, saying, "Why the hell did you tell Nick Longworth so and so?" Deschler replied that he had not done so, and Garner responded, "The hell you didn't! You sure as hell did!" When Deschler again said he had not told that to Longworth, Garner shouted, "Goddamn it, don't you lie to me! I know you told him that!" Deschler got angry and slammed the desk in front of him, shouting, "Goddamn you, don't you tell me I'm a liar! I didn't tell Nick Longworth that." With that reply, Garner leaned back and said, "Young man, you've got a lot of spunk." Deschler recalled, "Garner was my greatest supporter from that moment on."[50] In a similar vein, Texas congressman John Lyle claimed that "Garner always tested all young new Congressmen and the way he did it . . . he would invite them [over]. . . . He had two different types of whiskey. One was a good whiskey and one was a rather bad whiskey. He had nickel glasses like they used to use in the cafes and he would pour out a full glassful of bad whiskey and hand it to the Congressman and he would see what kind of reaction he had. He would always say, 'Bottoms up' to his good whiskey and he always judged them on whether or not they took it well. [He judged] their character that way."[51]

Arthur Schlesinger, Jr., described Garner as having a "bright, ruddy face, short-cropped white hair, cold blue eyes, and a tight small mouth." He presented, wrote Schlesinger, an appearance of "an infinitely experienced sage and of a newborn baby."[52] Garner was tough talking and hard-hitting. There was, Hardeman and Bacon wrote, a quality of the frontier about him, and he was "painfully truthful, even blunt, ambitious, and felt satisfaction in dealing with national problems." He was rough with people, telling Sam Rayburn, "you've got to bloody your knuckles."[53] In debate, he had as unusual a speaking manner as did Joe Cannon. He spoke in the well of the House, standing almost up against the first Republican row of seats. His face would get progressively redder as he would throw out both arms from his head. He would fully extend his arms with the palms facing one another, then he would raise and lower his body from the knees in violent contortions.[54] At least one of his speeches reminded a reporter of a "camp-meeting" style of speaking.[55]

Prominently displayed above his blue eyes and ruddy cheeks were huge white eyebrows, which added to the overall disheveled appearance of his attire. He was frequently unshaven and was often compared to Joe Cannon in his somewhat seedy appearance.[56] Garner smoked cigars and drank whiskey, mostly Jack Daniels mixed with tap water.[57] It was the whiskey that continually appears in descriptions of Garner and his lifestyle. One author claimed that Garner drank a quart of whiskey a day, starting at 7:00 in the morning. It was claimed that the corners of his living room in Uvalde were stacked with cases of Jack Daniels that had been given him by lobbyists.[58] His Washington office had a large closet that functioned as a liquor cabinet "with many bottles, some in crock jars."[59] John McDuffie wrote Garner in 1944 upon reading an account in which Garner had claimed that he was going to live to be ninety-three and that such an advanced age would be due to drinking bonded bourbon whisky. McDuffie claimed that Garner had "become much more fastidious or ex-

clusive in your taste. I knew when you would drink most anything that
had the least alcoholic content, and on one occasion in your intense desire
to satisfy an overwhelming appetite you paid six brand-new ten-dollar
bills for six quarts of pure Washington water, beautifully labeled as
Scotch."[60]

Whiskey, perhaps some poker, and some conversation were Garner's
way of doing business. He frequently met during the speakership of
Nicholas Longworth in what was called the "Board of Education," where
he would "strike a blow for liberty" and arrange political compromises.
For Garner, politics and alcohol spiced with some poker were the necessary prerequisites of public policy making.

Hardeman and Bacon have written that there was a cruel, hard side to
Garner's personality, and he had an acid tongue that could be turned on
friend and foe alike. One who was not on Garner's side was often seen as
an enemy. And there were some whom he hated passionately, such as
Congressman Finis Garrett. Sam Rayburn, one of the congressmen closest
to Garner, confessed, "I was Garner's lieutenant for fifteen years, and
God, what a chore it was at times. But when the time came for him to
throw his feet out for you, he went all the way."[61]

He was a devoted reader of the *Congressional Record*,[62] and once during
a near fatal bout with pneumonia in the early part of 1925, he tried to read
the *Record* in a fever delirium. After he held the *Record* upside down, John
McDuffie took it from him. McDuffie claimed, "I never had a man to blas-
pheme and curse me as you did." In relating the incident to Congressman
Hatton Sumners, McDuffie explained the fever had driven Garner out of
his head. Sumners disagreed. "Oh, no, John," Sumners said, "he is just being natural."[63]

Heavy-drinking, high-tempered, acid-tongued Garner was to some an
ultraconservative.[64] Others sometimes thought he was "more or less a
Bolshevik."[65] Garner, however, was no wild man. He told Bascom Timmons, "I never did anything by caprice. My acts usually were done deliberately."[66] He also understood, even in the early 1920s, that he was "no
diplomat. I have to go at things in a rough and sometimes, uncouth way.
In politics as well as business I have adopted the old geometrical formula
that the nearest distance between two points is a straight line."[67] Once an
old friend told Garner, "I know you can be rough when you need to, but
generally speaking you've relied on persuasion, it seems to me, more
than anything else. How could you have been so successful in the House
during these years and become the Speaker and have such success in at-
taining your own objectives in the House?" Garner took another sip of
bourbon and said, "I think I would have to attribute my success in having
my own way in the House to the fact that I was always willing to take a
beating in order to have my own way."[68]

The Wilson Era: Early Signs of Leadership

In 1916, Jim Wells wrote Garner, "John, so far as we can glean from the newspapers, we are proud of you, and your attitude in regard to the very important War and Preparedness measures now pending before Congress—but be very careful what you do, as everybody is watching you!"[69] That note presaged the beginnings of a new role for Garner. With preparations for World War I and ultimately with war, Garner assumed the role of liaison between the Wilson administration and the Congress. It was a role assumed almost by default. Speaker Champ Clark had been Wilson's rival for the presidency and felt cheated out of the nomination by the existence of the two-thirds rule. Claude Kitchin was opposed to war and, although Democratic leader, had opposed the war resolution. Garner was whip and supported war measures.[70] However, in the beginnings of the Wilson administration there had been a coolness between Garner and Wilson. Garner had quietly supported Champ Clark for the presidency, but most important, the Jim Wells organization had opposed Wilson. As a result, for a considerable period in the Wilson era, Garner was frozen out of patronage.[71] Apparently it was through the urging of Joseph Tumulty, Wilson's secretary, that Wilson was convinced Garner was a man with whom he could work. And work he did: At least twice a week Garner secretly visited with Wilson. That activity was known in Congress but was not highly publicized.[72] During that time, however, Garner became personally devoted to Wilson. He was later to say, "Woodrow Wilson was as fine a character as ever was. We have never had a better man than Wilson in the White House."[73] It was not only as war liaison with the administration that Garner was beginning to make his mark in those early years. Giving up the Foreign Relations Committee, including an offer of the chairmanship, for a seat on the Ways and Means Committee had proved a wise career move.

It was movement to the Ways and Means Committee that made Garner's career in Congress.[74] That committee had major responsibility for the nation's tax policy, and in Garner's early years on the committee, the income tax was one of the major issues that the committee considered. Garner had long supported a graduated income tax, introducing such legislation as early as 1905. The income tax tended to be supported by southerners who believed that it would be an alternative to high protective tariffs that had been the national government's main source of revenues. Southerners also believed that because per capita income in the South was 40 percent below the national average, the income tax would fall on few in the South. One did not have to be a social reformer to support the tax; mostly it was simply seen as a source for additional revenue.[75] Given that Garner was a Texan and, though not a free trader, was not in favor of the Republican protective tariff for manufactured goods, it should not be surprising that Garner supported the income tax. Although Garner was not on the Ways and Means subcommittee examining the income tax question, he insisted on graduated rates, thus differing from other key Democrats on Ways and Means, such as Oscar Underwood and Cordell Hull, who favored a flat tax in consideration of the 1913 income tax legislation. Garner threatened to go to the party caucus on the issue if the committee insisted on a flat rate.[76] Underwood and Hull were more cautious; they wanted a 1 percent flat tax in order to prevent repeal of the law or its overturn by the Supreme Court.[77]

The passage of an income tax and tariff reduction went hand in hand, since the income tax would replace tariff revenues. The Underwood tariff was the first general tariff reduction since 1857. Traditional Democratic doctrine was in favor of free trade, since the tariff had tended to benefit the northern manufacturing areas of the country. Garner, however, supported a tariff on raw materials. That position allowed Garner to support, for example, a tariff on goat hair that would benefit his district, a large producer of Angora goats. In the debate over the Underwood tariff, Garner's effort to retain the duty on goat hair while putting wool on the free list was subject to Republican derision. More important to his career, his tariff views would add to the tension in his relationship with Claude Kitchin. [78]

Leadership Blocked

With the Republican landslide of 1920, Garner should have been on the road to leadership in the Democratic Party. Champ Clark was defeated, as were Cordell Hull and Henry Rainey. The result was that Claude Kitchin was now party leader, and Garner was the second-ranking Democrat on Ways and Means behind Kitchin. Kitchin's health failed, and in 1921 he decided to leave Washington for a rest. Prior to leaving Washington, Kitchin named Finis Garrett as floor leader, rather than Garner, who was party whip. Different explanations have been offered for the choice of Garrett over Garner. One explanation was that Kitchin resented Garner's leadership role during the Wilson era when Kitchin's opposition to World War I limited his role as the spokesman for the administration in Congress.[79] James Byrnes believed that Kitchin and Garner had angry words over whether Byrnes, who was backed by Kitchin, or Texan James Buchanan, who was backed by Garner, would be appointed to the Appropriations Committee. Garner won the battle because Postmaster General Albert Burleson, also a Texan, used his patronage powers to forward Buchanan's interests. Byrnes believed that Kitchin resented the involvement of Burleson in the battle, was angry with Garner, and, until his illness, never spoke with Garner unless business required it.[80]

Another explanation is that Kitchin, a free trader, distrusted Garner's views, which favored a tariff on raw materials.[81] In a letter to Kitchin in 1922, Garner did try to convey to him, "I don't believe our tariff views differ materially. . . ."[82] But, of course, those views did differ. One press report regarded Kitchin's action as a rebuke to Garner because of Garner's vote in favor of the emergency tariff bill. The report also noted that Carl Hayden's vote for the emergency tariff clearly kept him off the Ways and Means Committee.[83]

Garner's rise to power in the House was frustrated by Garrett's selection. That must have been disturbing to Garner, who once told Bascom Timmons that Speaker Cannon had let Garner take the Speaker's chair on February 25, 1905, as a courtesy when statues of Stephen F. Austin and Sam Houston were unveiled in Statuary Hall in the Capitol. Garner claimed, "When I left the Speaker's chair that day I had made up my mind I was going back as its elected occupant."[84] At almost the same time that Garrett was selected, Jim Wells was weakening physically, his organization was weakening politically, and he was urging Garner to replace Charles Culberson in the U.S. Senate. Some of Garner's biographers believe that he was seriously considering retiring in 1922. He seems to have been overwhelmed by a mixture of feelings about his future at that time. In 1921, for example, perhaps responding to Wells's urging that he run for the Senate, Garner wrote that he thought he was about to be elected Speaker.[85]

Of course, not only was Garner overly optimistic about being elected Speaker in 1922, but the Democrats did not gain control of Congress, although they did have a chance. President Warren Harding's ineffectiveness plus an economic downturn put the Democrats within a dozen seats of a majority and gave them a gain of seventy-eight seats.[86] Bascom Timmons, however, did not believe that it was Garner's ambition to be Speaker that kept him in the House in 1922. He believed it was the challenge of the Ku Klux Klan, a powerful force in Texas and an organization opposed by and opposed to Garner.[87] Writing Claude Kitchin, for example, Garner expressed his concerns about the Klan, "We have an unfortunate state of affairs in Texas—Ku Klux and anti Ku Klux, which means Catholic and anti-Catholic. You know these differences are unhealthy for any State—I fear that it will develop throughout the country."[88]

Although by the 1922 election the Wells organization was in disarray, the county bosses remained. Klan success would have been harmful to the bosses, considering their strong Hispanic base and the antiimmigrant and anti-Catholic views of the Klan. Politically it would have hurt Garner's supporters if he had retired in the face of Klan opposition. Although

Garner did not actively campaign, he made his opposition to the Klan known, and he defeated the Klan-backed opponent. In 1923, after his victory over the Klan, Garner wrote a heartfelt letter to Claude Kitchin discussing his impending retirement. He wrote Kitchin that there was likely to be a battle over the leadership and that he would resolve that problem by withdrawing from any leadership contest.[89]

Not long after Garner wrote Kitchin, Kitchin died, and Garner seemed to forget about retirement. He seriously considered opposing Finis Garrett for the leadership. Hardeman and Bacon believed that there was "keen personal rivalry, even hatred" between the two men. Sam Rayburn, a friend of both men, advised Garner, "You can't win, John."[90] It was advice that Garner recognized as true. James Byrnes, who was a supporter of Garrett, claimed that a few days before the Democratic caucus where the battle for leadership would occur, Garner dropped by Byrnes's office while Byrnes was meeting with Garrett. Garner said, "Finis, I have announced to the press my withdrawal and wish to extend to you my best wishes." While Garrett was trying to express his appreciation of Garner's action, the typically blunt Garner responded, "I want it clearly understood that I am withdrawing only because I know when I am licked."[91]

Finis Garrett served as House minority leader from 1923 until he left the House to run for the Senate from Tennessee in 1928. It was not until Garrett's voluntary departure from the House that Garner was again able to move toward his goal of the speakership. In 1929, Garner became minority leader. At the time, opportunities for Democratic control of the House seemed slim, but economic events took control, and within two years opened the speakership to Garner.

Strangely, it does not appear that Garner completely forgot his dreams of retiring. Sam Rayburn recalled that in 1932, when Garner was talking to Rayburn about his wishes regarding the Democratic nomination for the presidency, Garner said that he had been wanting to leave politics for several terms but that "my people won't let me." Rayburn was surprised by this remark since he was not aware of Garner's wish, but Garner told Rayburn that he thought four years as vice president would be a nice way to ease out of politics.[92]

Garner and the Politics of the 1920s

During the 1920s, Garner made his reputation as a critic of Republican revenue policies. Rarely was he able to defeat Republicans, but through modifications of their bills and through alliances with insurgent Republicans, he was able to moderate the strongly probusiness stance of Republican legislation. During the 1920s, Garner faced two major Republican tariff bills—the Fordney-McCumber bill in 1922 and the Hawley-Smoot bill in 1929. Garner's tactic in regard to the former bill was not to oppose it in its entirety but instead to fight for certain schedules and rate changes.

In April 1921, Joseph Fordney introduced a tariff bill that provided for a widespread increase in the protective tariff. It also abandoned the old method of determining the tariff according to foreign values and introduced a new method known as "American valuation." American valuation required determination of differences in the costs of production in the United States and abroad before rates could be fixed.[93]

In one of his more colorful exhibitions on the floor, Garner attacked the American valuation system as one that would create the highest tariff in U.S. history and that would be impossible to calculate. Seizing a straw hat to illustrate his point, he challenged Republicans to determine what its rates would be.[94] However, Garner supported the protection of raw materials through a tariff, a view opposed by Kitchin, who was a free trader. Kitchin sent a telegram to his colleagues in 1921 from his sickbed urging them to oppose any form of protectionism.[95]

Free trade Democrats sometimes claimed that Garner was essentially a Republican on the tariff issue.[96] That there was some validity to that point is suggested by what happened in 1928 when Garner had Democratic opposition in his district on the tariff issue. He released a letter from former Republican congressman Joseph W. Fordney, who argued that Garner's tariff position was in the best interest of his district and that Garner's position on the tariff should therefore be supported by his district.[97]

Kitchin's telegram insisting on free trade was an attack on Garner's views. Garner, however, believed that even though he could not beat the Republicans, he could delay the legislation, modify the bill, and make it a 1922 campaign issue. Garner was able, through a recommittal motion instructing the Ways and Means Committee to abandon an embargo on dye and to put fertilizers on the free list, to break Republican ranks by appealing to the Republican farm bloc. It was the first time a tariff bill had ever been recommitted, and it was done with 102 Republican votes.[98] Ultimately a modified Fordney-McCumber tariff was passed following the instructions of the recommittal motion and eliminating the American valuation system.

In a letter to Kitchin, Garner tried to explain that he had opposed even more efforts to protect raw materials, such as sugar, wool, and metal. His goal in the tariff battle, he argued, was "that the strategic and effective thing to do was to divide the republicans and alienate as many as possible from the regular organization."[99] Kitchin may not have appreciated Garner's tariff strategy, but Garner's personal friend and political opponent, Nicholas Longworth of Ohio, surely understood. Commenting on Garner's success in modifying the Republican tariff and splitting House Republicans, Longworth said, "The gentleman from Texas is the greatest fisherman since Izaak Walton. With the able assistance of the gentleman from Minnesota, Mr. Knutson, who acted as basket carrier, Mr. Garner cast his line . . . and hooked more than 100 Republicans. Let him take what satisfaction he desires from it. He will never do so well on this side again."[100] It was a strategy with potential, Garner wrote to Kitchin, because Harding was ineffective and because "I don't believe there has ever been a more united minority than we had during the past Congress, and I know there never was a more disorganized majority."[101]

Garner was to continue his strategy of promoting a tariff on raw materials, but in May 1929, when the Hawley tariff bill was debated in the House, the Democrats did not put up the kind of opposition one had come to expect from them on protective tariffs, and Garner was not successful in breaking loose the Republican farm bloc.[102] Although the Hawley tariff had a fourteen-month journey through Congress, Garner only railed against it.[103] He was unable to affect the legislation as he had the Fordney-McCumber tariff. What was clear was that the Hawley tariff would pass. Garner voted no on the tariff but made sure that mohair and Bermuda onions, major products of his district, were included in the tariff schedules.[104]

The tariff was just one side of the Republican economic policies. The other side was tax reform, which consisted of efforts to reduce the surtax on incomes and efforts to reduce inheritance and estate taxes. These tax reduction programs were largely the result of budget surpluses coupled with the probusiness philosophy of Secretary of the Treasury Andrew Mellon. Mellon made numerous tax reduction proposals, with some of the most notable battles over tax policy occurring in 1921, 1924, 1925, and 1927. In these battles, Mellon proposed such policies as repeal of the excess profits tax, reduction in the maximum income surtax rates, and reduction or elimination of gift and inheritance taxes. Garner, on the other hand, favored lower taxes on lower-income people, less drastic reductions in the surtax than Mellon, and retention of gift and inheritance taxes.[105]

One of the richest men in America, Treasury Secretary Mellon dominated tax policy in the 1920s. It was a policy that stressed tax reduction on the theory that reductions would release funds that would be used for investment. That investment, in turn, would increase prosperity.[106] In 1921, Mellon proposed, among other things, reduction of the surtax from 65 percent to 25 percent. Garner favored a 32 percent surtax, but Kitchin opposed any tax reduction until the war debt was paid. Going to the Democratic caucus, Garner won with his reduction plan. Fiorello LaGuardia and other Progressive Republicans joined the Democrats in the battle over the surtax. When the Senate set the surtax at 50 percent, Garner, raiding the Progressive Republicans again, got the House to accept that figure, even though the conference report recommended a 40 percent surtax.

In 1924, Mellon again pushed for tax reduction, with part of his plan being a 25 percent surtax, and Garner countered with a proposal for a 44 percent surtax. Ultimately, Garner was able, with Democratic caucus approval of his plan and often with Progressive Republican support, to get a 40 percent surtax, to lower taxes for those with small incomes, to keep corporate taxes unchanged, and to increase estate taxes.[107] Garner's performance was impressive enough that the opposition researcher for Herbert Hoover, who wrote up reports for each session of Congress in which Garner sat, wrote admiringly of Garner for the first time. He wrote,

> "In this session, however, he exhibited real leadership. . . . [H]e held his Democratic minority in line almost to a man and obtained the support of the so-called progressive element of the Republicans to the end that he defeated the Administration tax bill, known as 'the Mellon plan' and substituted therefor the rates of the so-called 'Garner plan'. The main difference between these two plans was that the Garner plan taxed wealth much more heavily than did the Mellon plan. This was done through higher rates in surtaxes and in corporation taxes, as well as in inheritance, estate, gift and like taxes."[108]

In October 1925, Mellon tried again—this time proposing a surtax of 20 percent and the reduction and eventual repeal of inheritance and gift taxes. Compromising, Garner supported the lower surtax in exchange for higher personal exemptions and continuation of the estate tax, although he was opposed by Henry Rainey, who would later be majority leader when Garner was Speaker.[109] Garner's defense of estate taxes was based in part on a sectional appeal, much like his earlier support of the income tax was based on the belief that it would not significantly affect southerners. Garner claimed, "All the thirteen southern states put together paid less than 6 $\frac{1}{2}$ percent of the inheritance tax for the last ten years, while New York paid five times more than all the southern states put together. Yet gentlemen from those states are opposed to any such tax as that. You are unwilling to go up and get Ogden Mills' money. You do not want this economic system by which you collect according to wealth."[110] In spite of Senate repeal of the estate tax, Garner obtained passage of his version. He told the House that in conference committee he had insisted that without an estate tax, the bill would not become law.[111]

In 1926, Garner tried unsuccessfully to force the administration's hand on tax relief by proposing a reduction of corporate taxes in proportion to the budget surpluses and repealing taxes on automobiles and amusement tickets.[112] In 1927 the administration wanted further surtax reductions and repeal of the estate tax. Garner proposed an alternative of dropping the corporate tax from 13.5 percent to 11 percent, repealing the auto and amusement excise taxes, and lowering the surtax on low-income persons. However, he opposed changes in the estate tax or in the high income surtax. Ultimately the result was a 12 percent corporate tax, repeal of the excise tax on autos and amusement tickets, and no repeal of estate taxes.[113]

In the tax reduction battles of the 1920s, Garner tried to position the Democratic Party in favor of tax reduction *and* taxation based on the ability to pay. Although he never proposed redistributing wealth or using taxation as a way of remedying social problems and went along with the conservative mood of the country, at the same time he tried to present the Democratic Party as a party representing the masses and the Republicans as the party of wealth.[114] He was able to use the strong southern base of the Democratic Party to support these objectives, since the South would pay little of the high income surtaxes and estate taxes. He was often able to use the Democratic caucus to strengthen his position, and he could reach out to insurgent Republicans who rebelled at the eastern wealth that Andrew Mellon represented. However, Garner could only delay, maneuver, and compromise. He could not completely block the Mellon proposals.

Garner was not always opposing Republican policies in the open battleground of the House floor. He was a man with whom one could deal; he would trade votes and compromise. As things developed, in the late 1920s, the Republicans also had a leader who was willing to deal and compromise. That leader was Nicholas Longworth of Ohio, a long-standing personal friend of Garner's, a friend going back to his days on the Foreign Affairs Committee. Although it is difficult to imagine more different men than Garner and the aristocratic Longworth, the fact remains that theirs was one of the great congressional friendships. Often they were able to iron out issues and work out compromises in the privacy of the so-called Board of Education, where they and their allies would retire at the end of the legislative day for drinks and conversation.

For Garner these negotiation sessions allowed him to have a Democratic voice in policymaking and to do so without expending the political currency necessary to fight pitched battles in committees and on the floor. For Longworth, these sessions could reduce delay in legislating. He also could avoid the battles and Garner's continual probing of his forces in an effort to drive the Progressive Republicans from the regulars.[115]

These negotiation sessions were confidential affairs. Bascom Timmons, who attended many of the sessions, claimed that all understandings between the two men were precise ones, with no ambiguity. However, Timmons did not divulge any negotiation other than a trivial one involving U.S. embassies.[116] There were limits to these negotiations. Many of the major issues of the 1920s, such as the tariff or tax reduction, were issues where at least the major points had to be fought on the floor. Even though Garner and Longworth had great influence within their parties, neither was a czar in the image of earlier congressional leaders such as Reed or Cannon.

The Speakership

As the 1930 elections approached, Garner and Nicholas Longworth teased one another about their prospects of being Speaker, joking over which would have use of the Speaker's car. Longworth's unexpected death in 1931 turned the race into even more of a close call, owing to the deaths of several congressmen.[117] The election results initially showed the Republicans still in control with a majority of two. However, during the interim before the next session of Congress convened after the election, fourteen members died. Republican fatalities exceeded Democrats, and when the Seventy-second Congress convened, Garner was elected Speaker by a vote of 218 to 208 for Bert Snell, Longworth's successor. Five additional votes were cast for George Schneider, a Progressive Republican.[118]

In the aftermath of Longworth's death, but prior to the next session of Congress, Democrats gave thought to how and whether they could organize the House. William Bankhead was quick to size up the political possibilities resulting from Longworth's death, and though he expressed grief, he thought Longworth's passing offered a tremendous opportunity to control the next House. Longworth's death, Bankhead believed, "will doubtless throw the Republicans into considerable confusion." He urged that Progressive Republicans be approached to aid the Democrats in capturing the House.[119]

Garner responded with expressions of grief but quickly moved to Bankhead's major point. Although he thought there were Republicans who would like to see him Speaker, Garner wrote, they would not cross party lines any more than Democrats who disliked him would vote for a Republican for Speaker. But Garner believed the Democrats should organize the House. He wrote, "I believe we are capable of legislating for the country and I never yet have ran [*sic*] away from a responsibility."[120] Some of Garner's allies—for instance, John McDuffie—thought that politically it would probably be better for the Democrats not to organize the House in 1931, but that seemed unavoidable.[121] Rayburn, who was also aware of the concerns that Democrats not share in the responsibility for the economic crisis prior to the 1932 presidential election, made it clear to McDuffie what had been obvious to Garner: "Since it seems we have a majority in the House, the question of whether we organize is no longer debatable."[122]

With Democratic control of the House by a narrow majority, the question became what policies Speaker Garner thought were appropriate. His ideas, as he expressed them in a letter to McDuffie, were remarkably orthodox. Garner wanted to reduce government salaries and increase the income tax. He wanted to increase the inheritance tax. His primary goal was a simple one: The budget must be balanced.[123] Given that overpowering objective, there was not much difference between Garner's thinking and that of Herbert Hoover. Indeed, Jordan Schwarz has stated, "Notwithstanding the desperate condition, the Democratic Party offered few alternatives to the policies of the party in power."[124] Garner supported many of Hoover's policies, to such a point that Hoover wrote that Garner was "a man of real statesmanship when he took off his political pistols."[125] The major focus of disagreement between Garner and the Hoover administration was that Garner was somewhat more sensitive to the human needs created by the Depression and more aware than Hoover that the 1930 elections were a demand by voters for greater governmental involvement in the economy.[126]

Garner's speakership was held together by a bare majority. During that period tensions existed in the Democratic Party, although not as great as in the aftermath of Garner's speakership. For years the party had been primarily a southern party, and Garner was part of that southern domination that in large part was based on the seniority of southern representatives. Northern Democrats felt excluded from the leadership, and Garner was perfectly content to continue that practice of exclusion. For example, he backed Alabama Congressman John McDuffie for the majority leadership against Tammany Hall–backed John J. O'Connor of New York and Illinois Congressman Henry Rainey. Rainey won the leadership position, but Garner never accepted Rainey within his leadership circle. He let it be known that he considered Rainey "loose-lipped," and he rarely invited Rainey to the gossip and strategy sessions at the Board of Education meetings. Garner preferred to ignore the majority leader as much as possible and to work with the southern committee chairmen to accomplish his goals. In that preference, he opposed the concept of a party steering committee that would have diffused power from the Speaker and the committee chairs.[127] Instead, Garner worked through southerners, often committee chairmen and often Texans. Among his key allies were Texans Marvin Jones, James Buchanan, Sam Rayburn, Hatton Sumners, and Joseph Mansfield; North Carolinians Lindsey Warren and dean of the House Edward Pou; John Collier of Mississippi, chair of the Ways and Means Committee; Charles Crisp of Georgia, second-ranking member of the Ways and Means Committee; John McDuffie, the Democratic whip, and William Bankhead, both of Alabama; and Missourians Clarence Cannon and Jacob Milligan.[128] These men were either committee chairs or high in the order of seniority. They were not willing to voluntarily relinquish power. When William Bankhead, for example, picked up on a newspaper report that Edward Pou would relinquish his claim to the chairmanship of the Rules Committee to a northern Democrat, he immediately wired Garner that he hoped the report was false, and if true, that he wanted the job.[129]

Garner's thin majority and his conservative base of support in the House, coupled with his own conservative inclinations, made it difficult for him to initiate an alternative to the Hoover program. The razor-thin majority did allow Garner to effectively plead for party harmony, but he could not innovate too greatly. The narrowness of his majority also encouraged him to reach out to dissident Progressive Republicans, as he had during the late 1920s. He was often able to work through Fiorello LaGuardia, whom he called "Frijole," who was able to deliver about fifteen dissident Republicans to the Garner side.[130]

Garner had a somewhat more inflationary approach than did Hoover, but he was a disappointment to liberals such as Rexford Tugwell, who saw Garner as a "confused Texan" who was "so conservative and so lacking in imagination that nothing had occurred to him that Hoover had not thought of first. . . . And anyway Garner was known to be more worried about balancing the budget than about unemployment. He was hopelessly sterile as a leader. . . ."[131] Although Tugwell's evaluation of Garner is very harsh, Garner did not offer, indeed could not offer, a clear alternative to Hoover's policies. His brief speakership can perhaps best be understood by examining the politics surrounding two major policies that he supported: the national sales tax and the public works bill.

One measure of the intensity of the economic crisis of the Hoover presidency is unemployment. In 1929, unemployment was 3.2 percent of the civilian workforce. In 1930, unemployment was at 8.7 percent, and by 1932 it was 24.9 percent. On top of that, underemployment was massive. Many employers, for example, tried to avoid firing workers by working them only three or four days a week. Hoover's response to this economic crisis was to urge voluntary or state and local relief efforts. He opposed large public works projects and an expanded federal role in the economy. In the face of depression, Hoover's solution was to study the problem and attempt to build confidence in the nation by claiming prosperity was imminent. In his view, the budget had to be balanced even if through national sales taxes. The major exception to Hoover's retrenchment efforts was the Reconstruction Finance Corporation, which issued loans to banks and other credit institutions in an effort to save them from ruin. The major theme of Hoover's policies, however, was not contrary to Garner's: The budget must be balanced.[132]

Garner's support for a national sales tax is surprising in light of his views on a sales tax that was proposed by Republicans in 1920 as a way to finance the veterans' bonus. Garner claimed then that the sales tax was a plan "to place a tax on the backs and bellies of the people instead of taking [it] from the pockets of the best able to pay."[133] However, Garner was committed to a balanced budget, and to achieve that balance he agreed with Secretary of the Treasury Ogden Mills to a sales tax on all but food and cheaper clothing. Charles Crisp, acting chairman of the Ways and Means Committee, claimed that the committee was in complete accord with that view. It was a tax policy that was also supported by financier and leading Democratic donor Bernard Baruch and by William Randolph Hearst, who had begun booming Garner for president less than one month before Garner endorsed the tax.

Within the Ways and Means Committee, only Robert Doughton of North Carolina dissented, and Garner anticipated no problems in passage of the sales tax. Because there had been complaints that the recent Glass-Stegall bill had been subject to a gag rule, Garner promised unlimited discussion of the sales tax. Not only did Garner fail to anticipate problems and fan the flames of controversy by allowing unlimited discussion, but he absented himself from the floor fight and committed himself without the benefit of a Democratic caucus vote. It proved to be an extraordinary failure of leadership, because Progressive Republicans and Democrats revolted and overwhelmingly beat back the legislation. Garner seemed to put the blame for the failure on Charles Crisp, but others saw Garner's behavior as, in the words of Walter Lippman, "just plain stupid." Lippman may have offered the best explanation for Garner's actions on the sales tax. Others have hinted that Garner never really was committed to the tax and that this was a payoff to Hearst for his endorsement. What needs to be stressed, however, is Garner's orthodoxy in economic views and his support for a balanced budget above all else. Indeed, in salvaging what he could from the sales tax fiasco by giving a "camp-meeting" speech to the House, he stressed that the primary objective of the House had to be to balance the budget. That theatrical speech, in which he asked all members in favor of balancing the budget to rise from their seats (and where all in the House did rise), played well in the press, but it could not hide Garner's failure to control the House. His leadership in the House as well as his presidential prospects were considerably weakened.[134]

Amazingly, in the lame-duck Congress after the election of 1932, Garner again endorsed an administration proposal for a sales tax, only to have to withdraw that endorsement at Roosevelt's insistence. Some thought Roosevelt betrayed Garner, but others believe Garner endorsed the tax without first consulting with Roosevelt. If the latter explanation is the case, it is further evidence of the lengths to which Garner was willing to go to achieve his budget-balancing goal.[135]

Ahead of the goal of budget balancing was maintaining power and winning elections, however. By May 1932, the Depression had deepened, and the Democratic convention and the 1932 elections were fast approaching. Garner, in the face of considerable demand for action in relief programs, proposed his public works program, a program that Herbert Hoover called "the most gigantic pork barrel bill ever proposed to the American Congress. It is an unexampled raid on the public treasury."[136] Although Hoover had supported public works that were "productive" or revenue generating, Garner's plan included numerous "nonproductive" public works, including the construction of a large number of post offices around the country. Garner had argued with Hoover in favor of "nonproductive" public works in early March, and the debate intensified when Garner proposed his bill. Garner, along with many others, was convinced by April 1932 that the Depression was intensifying. More than that, however, a public works bill offered Garner a chance to recapture control over the House that he had lost with the sales tax battle, and it offered Democrats in general a popular proposal with which to battle Hoover and the Republicans as the election approached.[137]

In rough outline, his proposal provided for $1.2 billion for projects such as public buildings, post offices, highways, waterways, and flood control; a $1 billion increase in Reconstruction Finance Corporation capitalization; and $100 million for discretionary spending by the President.[138] Garner had learned from his experience with the sales tax. He carefully laid the groundwork for the bill. He called Majority Leader Henry Rainey; Joseph Byrns; Lindsey Warren of North Carolina; John McDuffie of Alabama; Cliff Woodrum of Virginia; John Collier of Mississippi; Charles Crisp of Georgia; Sam Rayburn of Texas; William Bankhead of Alabama; and Christopher Sullivan of New York into a conference room. Garner asked each for his candid opinion on the bill, standing in front of each man as he spoke. Only McDuffie and Warren spoke against the bill, although Byrns was undecided. Garner told the group that he would have abandoned the public works bill if a majority of them had opposed it, but that now he would attempt to bind the Democrats in a caucus.[139] Garner received a Democratic caucus vote in support of the public works bill in early June; he limited debate on the bill to three hours, with a rule that also stipulated that only Ways and Means Committee members could offer amendments; and he reached into Progressive Republican ranks as he had prior to the sales tax battles to pick up LaGuardia-led Republicans.

Rather than being the passive Speaker of the sales tax battle, Garner wished to be directly involved in the battles over public works, even proposing to Republican leader Bert Snell that they be the public works conferees with the Senate rather than following the traditional conference appointment mechanisms. Snell, however, rejected the proposal, an action that led to an explosion of the famed Garner temper. As Jordan Schwarz described the encounter, "The gentlemen exchanged words, then began pounding a desk with their fists and filled the office with loud epithets that sent secretaries running into the halls. 'I hate a man without guts,' Garner bellowed. Snell countered, 'Well you've run aplenty yourself this season.' For a moment Garner could not find a come-back, and when he did, reporters regretted that it was unprintable."[140]

It was also Garner who took the lead in negotiations with Herbert Hoover over the provisions in the conference report and Garner who held out against any further concessions being made to Hoover.[141] In July 1932, the public works bill was passed and, as had been widely anticipated, was vetoed by President Hoover, although a compromise public works measure was passed before Congress adjourned.

Garner's presidential candidacy, begun in January 1932 by William Randolph Hearst, gave him California and Texas at the Democratic convention. But, as Garner well knew, Franklin Roosevelt was the man to beat. On the third ballot, Roosevelt had 683 votes and Garner had 101. Votes for other candidates ranged from 190 for Al Smith to 8 for Newton Baker. With the two-thirds rule still in effect, Roosevelt needed 770 votes for the nomination. A deal was struck, and Garner released his delegates who backed Roosevelt. Garner received the vice presidential nomination. With Hoover blamed for the Depression, the Roosevelt-Garner ticket carried forty-two of forty-eight states.

Garner served as Roosevelt's vice president for eight years, and in the early years was especially valuable to FDR as a crucial congressional lobbyist for the administration. However, as the years passed, Garner became increasingly disenchanted with the New Deal. He thought the administration was not firmly against sit-down strikes, and he opposed the Wage and Hour bill, the Court Packing Plan of 1937, and Roosevelt's effort to purge the Democratic Party in 1938. Most important, he opposed Roosevelt's plan to seek a third term. By 1937, Garner's relationship with FDR began its long, deteriorating slide.

Garner made a run for the Democratic nomination in 1940, embittered over Roosevelt's break with the two-term tradition. When that effort failed, Garner retired to his home in Uvalde, Texas.

Conclusion

Garner has been described as being a product of the seniority system.[142] That, of course, he was. His career in Congress spanned three decades. To understand Garner, however, it is crucial to separate out several threads in his career and in the development of Congress. Garner, as long as he satisfied Jim Wells and the local political bosses of his sprawling district with pork barrel projects, was essentially a free agent. Though he had Republican opposition as well as Democratic Party opposition, he rarely faced a major threat to his career. Even the threat of a Klan opponent that was coupled with the demise of the Wells organization was, at best, only a mild disturbance for Garner. With an absence of district concerns, Garner could concentrate upon building the networks and reputation within the House that would benefit him in the long haul and allow him to fulfill the ambition to be Speaker.

In spite of his disappointment at being displaced by Finis Garrett and his inclinations to retire in the early 1920s, the point is that he never had to retire. His district allowed him to outlast both Finis Garrett and the Republican control of the House in the 1920s. Garner also had a tough, forceful personality that was coupled with an impressive capacity for friendships. He has been described as having a "natural talent for making friends, drinking whiskey, and playing poker."[143] In the first third of the twentieth century, those social skills were probably as important as media skills are today.

Garner also was a pragmatist. He was someone with whom other politicians could work. He would compromise and cut deals. Ideological impurity was not a problem for Garner. He might be against the Smoot-Hawley tariff in general, for example, but if there was to be a tariff, he wanted Bermuda onions and mohair in the tariff schedule. He could be for government economy and for pork. He could fight surtax reduction one year and support it later to avoid estate tax reduction. He could rail against the nefarious schemes of the Republicans in general and Nick Longworth in particular and then walk arm in arm with Longworth off the House floor to "strike a blow for liberty" in the Board of Education.

Garner was also a Texan at a time when Texans were powers in Congress and at a time when southerners represented a dominant wing of the Democratic Party. Garner's father was a Confederate veteran, and Garner was born in a slaveholding area of Texas. His closest political friends in the House were southerners. His economic views, especially regarding the income tax and the estate tax and his opposition to a protective tariff for manufacture only, were views beneficial to the South.[144]

In terms of institutional forces within the Congress and their effect upon Garner as a political leader, it is clear that Garner's career as a leader was based on his service on the Ways and Means Committee,[145] at that time a springboard to power not only because it was the tax-writing committee but also because revenue issues were the most important issues of his era. Additionally, at that time the Democratic members of the Ways and Means Committee functioned as the party's Committee on Committees, and that status added to the power of his position. The Committee on Committees position helped Garner make loyal friends in the House, and when his well-placed allies gained seniority, Garner enhanced his power base.

For twelve consecutive years of Garner's career, the Democratic Party was out of power; in some years, as in 1920, the party suffered major defeat. Those defeats cleared the party of most members more senior to Garner and no doubt added to his claims to power. By the time Garner did gain power, he had seen the speakership go through distinctive periods—from the Cannon era when the Speaker was so powerful that his rule was called Czar rule to the rise of the Democratic caucus as a major force for policymaking within the Democratic Party. When Garner attained the speakership, the binding caucus still existed and was used by him.

Under Garner, the House was also beginning to enter a relatively new phase in which the Speaker functioned as a broker, a negotiator who put together coalitions and compromises by working with and through committee chairs. At times Garner struggled against further diffusion of power in the House, opposing, for example, a steering and policy committee. Owing to Garner's contempt for Majority Leader Henry Rainey, Garner attempted to function both as Speaker and majority leader and was generally successful in ignoring the majority leader. The relationship with Rainey, however, also reflected deep-seated divisions between southern and northern wings of the Democratic Party. Garner represented the more conservative southern wing, Rainey the liberal northern wing. Those sectional differences would become a wide gulf by Roosevelt's second term.

For many of Garner's years of leadership, he was in the minority and sought to drive a wedge into the Republican Party, separating the Progressive Republicans from the regulars. Even when Garner was Speaker, his slight majority provided an incentive for him to keep lines of communication open to Progressive Republicans. It was quite the opposite from the leadership era of Sam Rayburn, who was mostly in the majority and had to deal with Republicans trying to drive a wedge between southern and northern Democrats.

During his two years as Speaker, Garner was puzzled by the Depression, and his major proposed solutions to it, such as a balanced budget and smaller government, were both orthodox and ineffectual. Rather than being an innovator and a person of vision, Garner was a deal maker, a pragmatist who functioned more effectively opposing a policy agenda than in setting one of his own.

NOTES

1. Neil MacNeil, *Forge of Democracy* (New York: David McKay, 1963), p. 80.
2. Richard Fenno has emphasized that one cannot understand members of Congress and congressional politics without understanding the nature of the dis-

trict that keeps (or fails to keep) the members in office. See Richard F. Fenno, Jr., *Home Style* (Boston: Little, Brown, 1978).

3. O. C. Fisher, *Cactus Jack* (Waco, Tex.: Texian Press, 1978), pp. 8–9.

4. Fisher, *Cactus Jack*, pp. 8–20; Bascom Timmons, *Garner of Texas* (New York: Harper and Bros., 1948), pp. 15–26.

5. For biographical treatments of Garner's life, see Fisher, *Cactus Jack;* Timmons, *Garner of Texas;* and Marquis James, *Mr. Garner of Texas* (Indianapolis: Bobbs-Merrill, 1939). A discussion of the district is found in the special supplement of the *Uvalde Leader-News*, November 23, 1958, John Nance Garner Museum, Uvalde, Texas. The occasion for printing the supplement was to commemorate Garner's ninetieth birthday.

6. Data on the district are from Stanley B. Parsons, Michael J. Dubin, and Karen Toombs Parsons, *United States Congressional Districts, 1883–1913* (New York: Greenwood Press, 1990).

7. Joe Robert Baulch, *James B. Wells: South Texas Economic and Political Leader* (Ph.D. diss., Texas Tech University, 1974); see generally, Evan Anders, *Boss Rule in South Texas* (Austin: University of Texas Press, 1982).

8. Baulch, *James B. Wells*, pp. 365–366.

9. Alwyn Barr, "John Nance Garner's First Campaign for Congress," *West Texas Historical Association Yearbook* 48 (1972): 105–110.

10. See generally, Anders, *Boss Rule in South Texas;* Baulch, *James B. Wells;* and Fisher, *Cactus Jack*, pp. 20–21.

11. Anders, *Boss Rule in South Texas*, p. 193. Anders wrote that often "solid minorities failed to satisfy the Duval chieftain. Often he strived for unanimity in the vote count."

12. Untitled, John Nance Garner Scrapbook 11–18–13 to 3–4–25 [*sic*], Center for American History, University of Texas at Austin.

13. John Nance Garner to Archer Parr, November 20, 1901, John Nance Garner Museum, Uvalde, Texas.

14. Quoted in Barr, "John Nance Garner's First Campaign for Congress," p. 106.

15. Timmons, *Garner of Texas*, p. 286.

16. James, *Mr. Garner of Texas*, p. 83.

17. Fisher, *Cactus Jack*, p. 22.

18. Ibid.

19. "Maney Announces He Is a Candidate Against Garner," John Nance Garner Scrapbook, Center for American History, University of Texas at Austin.

20. "John Garner Plans Visit to Corpus Christi Shortly," John Nance Garner Scrapbook, Center for American History, University of Texas at Austin.

21. Anders, *Boss Rule in South Texas*, pp. 121–123.

22. Barr, "John Nance Garner's First Campaign for Congress," p. 110. See also the following letters to James B. Wells, all in the James B. Wells Papers, Center for American History, University of Texas, Austin, Texas: J. A. Kemp, November 1, 1902; Monta J. Moore, October 22, 1902; J. W. McKnight, October 30, 1902; B. H. Carleton, November 2, 1902; W. H. Clendenin, October 22, 1902; James E. Luch, October 23, 1902; Edward M. House, October 8, 1902.

23. Fisher, *Cactus Jack*, p. 20.

24. Anders, *Boss Rule in South Texas*, pp. 12–19.

25. Ronnie Dugger, *The Politician: The Life and Times of Lyndon Johnson* (New York: W. W. Norton, 1982), pp. 322–323. An interesting treatment of Garner's actions in Parr's behalf is William Robert Smith interview by Michael Gillette, Lyndon B. Johnson Library, Austin, Texas, November 9, 1983, pp. 4–5.

26. "Hornby Praises Garner's Work," in John Nance Garner Scrapbook No. 1, November 18, 1913/April 4, 1925, Center for American History, University of Texas, Austin, Texas.

27. Timmons, *Garner of Texas*, pp. 36–38.

28. Ibid., pp. 36–37.

29. Baulch, *James B. Wells*, p. 253.

30. Fisher, *Cactus Jack*, p. 25.

31. Timmons, *Garner of Texas*, pp. 61–62.

32. Fisher, *Cactus Jack*, p. 26.

33. George Rothwell Brown, "Heraldings," January 11, 1932, John Nance Garner Scrapbooks 12–08–1931/02–20–1932, Center for American History, University of Texas, Austin, Texas.

34. Timmons, *Garner of Texas*, pp. 39–40.

35. D. B. Hardeman and Donald C. Bacon, *Rayburn: A Biography* (Austin: Texas Monthly Press, 1987), pp. 107–108.

36. Timmons, *Garner of Texas*, pp. 61–62.

37. Fisher, *Cactus Jack*, p. 30.

38. MacNeil, *Forge of Democracy*, pp. 79–84.

39. Ronald M. Peters, Jr., *The American Speakership* (Baltimore: The Johns Hopkins University Press, 1990), p. 97.

40. Anders, *Boss Rule in South Texas*, p. 122.

41. John Nance Garner to James B. Wells, January 17, 1915, James B. Wells Papers, Center for American History, University of Texas, Austin, Texas.

42. "Notes on Remarks of John N. Garner—Sixty-Second Congress," President's Individuals File—Garner, John Nance, Herbert Hoover Presidential Library, West Branch, Iowa.

43. Attachment titled "Garner's Pork Barrel Philosophy" attached to memorandum from J. Bennett Gordon to Mr. Joslin, July 20, 1932, President's Individuals File—Garner, John Nance, Herbert Hoover Presidential Library, West Branch, Iowa. Garner claimed he was misquoted by a reporter of a speech he gave at Pleasanton, Texas, in Atascosa County and that what he had actually said was: "Too often the disposition of the people is this: If a man from Massachusetts gets a hog in an appropriation bill, they expect a man from Texas will at least try to get a ham." See Fisher, *Cactus Jack*, p. 33.

44. John McDuffie to John Nance Garner, May 18, 1949, John McDuffie Papers, W. S. Hoole Special Collections, University of Alabama, Montgomery, Alabama.

45. See especially James, *Mr. Garner of Texas*, pp. 133–136. Garner incorrectly claimed that he never wrote letters more than one page in length when he did write. Fisher, *Cactus Jack*, p. x. John McDuffie for one recognized the extent to which Garner depended on his wife, Ettie. McDuffie wrote, "After all, Mr. Garner

owed much of his success to Mrs. Garner, whom I often-times designated as 'Congressman.'" John McDuffie to Bascom N. Timmons, December 20, 1948, John McDuffie Papers, W. S. Hoole Special Collections, University of Alabama, Montgomery, Alabama.

46. James, *Mr. Garner of Texas*, is essentially a Garner campaign biography. Bascom Timmons was one of Garner's closest friends, so close that Garner chose Timmons to be his spokesman at the 1940 Democratic convention. See Fisher, *Cactus Jack*, p. 149. Cecil Dickson was often used by Garner as a witness when Garner felt he needed someone he trusted to listen in on a conference. See Fisher, *Cactus Jack*, vii.

47. *Congressional Record*, April 6, 1922, pp. 5119–5120.

48. Hardeman and Bacon, *Rayburn*, p. 136.

49. Ibid., p. 137.

50. Larry Hufford, ed., *D.B.: Reminiscences of D.B. Hardeman* (Austin: AAR/Tantalus, 1984), p. 41.

51. John E. Lyle interview by Anthony Champagne, May 1980, the Sam Rayburn Library, Bonham, Texas, p. 4.

52. Arthur M. Schlesinger, Jr., *The Crisis of the Old Order, 1919–1933* (Boston: Houghton Mifflin, 1956), p. 227.

53. Hardeman and Bacon, *Rayburn*, pp. 70, 115, 136.

54. Timmons, *Garner of Texas*, p. 90.

55. Frank Kent, "The Great Game of Politics," *Baltimore Sun*, March 29, 1932, John Nance Garner Scrapbook No. 3, March 1, 1932–April 18, 1932, Center for American History, University of Texas, Austin, Texas.

56. Owen P. White, "Cactus Jack," *Collier's Weekly*, January 23, 1932, John Nance Garner Scrapbook, 12–08–1931/2–20–1932, Center for American History, University of Texas, Austin, Texas.

57. Rayburn claimed Garner was so thrifty that he would not buy ice and that was why Garner drank his whisky with tap water. Hardeman and Bacon, *Rayburn*, p. 114.

58. James Reston, Jr., *The Lone Star: The Life of John Connally* (New York: Harper and Row, 1989), p. 41.

59. Hardeman and Bacon, *Rayburn*, pp. 485–486, note 8.

60. John McDuffie to John Nance Garner, November 6, 1944, John McDuffie Papers, W. S. Hoole Special Collections, University of Alabama, Montgomery, Alabama.

61. Hardeman and Bacon, *Rayburn*, p. 136. Emanuel Celler of New York once rose to the floor and began to speak with the traditional language, "Mr. Speaker, reserving the right to object. . . ." At that point, the temperamental Garner cut Celler off saying, "There is not reason to object" and then cut Celler off by banging his gavel. When another Democrat made a motion Garner opposed, even though "yeas" outnumbered "nays," Garner held the motion defeated and moved on. In the early Hoover administration, when Garner was more Hoover ally than opponent, Garner told Majority Leader Rainey and Ways and Means chairman Collier that they should keep quiet about their personal views on tax policy. They did. If you were a stranger calling on Garner, it would not be unusual for him to

greet you by saying, "What the hell do you want?" See Raymond Clapper, "Garner Rule in House Is Iron-Fisted," *Dallas Journal*, January 26, 1932, John Nance Garner Scrapbook, 12–08–1931/2–20–1932, Center for American History, University of Texas, Austin, Texas.

62. According to Timmons, Garner believed that reading the *Congressional Record* and committee reports would teach one the congressional trade. See Timmons, *Garner of Texas*, p. 112.

63. John McDuffie to John Nance Garner, November 6, 1944, John McDuffie Papers, W. S. Hoole Special Collections, University of Alabama, Montgomery, Alabama.

64. Rexford G. Tugwell, *The Democratic Roosevelt* (Garden City, N.J.: Doubleday, 1957), p. 226.

65. John McDuffie to John Nance Garner, July 23, 1940, John McDuffie Papers, W. S. Hoole Special Collections, University of Alabama, Montgomery, Alabama.

66. Timmons, *Garner of Texas*, p. 286.

67. John Nance Garner to Claude Kitchin, October 5, 1922, Claude Kitchin Papers, University of North Carolina, Chapel Hill, North Carolina.

68. Robert J. Smith oral history by Michael Gillette, May 15, 1979, Lyndon B. Johnson Library, Austin, Texas, tape 1, p. 11.

69. James B. Wells to John Nance Garner, March 2, 1916, James B. Wells Papers, Center for American History, University of Texas, Austin, Texas.

70. Fisher, *Cactus Jack*, p. 49.

71. Anders, *Boss Rule in South Texas*, pp. 198–199. Timmons claimed that Garner's (and therefore the Wells machine's) patronage problems led to a showdown battle with Secretary William McAdoo and with President Wilson in which Garner claimed that he "got the worst dressing down from Wilson I ever got from anyone." Timmons, *Garner of Texas*, pp. 74–75.

72. That Garner's work in behalf of the Wilson administration was behind the scenes is illustrated by reports on Garner's record that were compiled for President Hoover. In a review of Garner's work through an examination of the *Congressional Record* during the Sixty-fifth Congress, the so-called War Congress, a concluding paragraph noted, "That a man who afterward became the floor leader of his party in the House and then Speaker, and now nominated for Vice President, should have contributed so little to the discussion and determination of the tremendous issues that were before Congress during the period of the World War, is sufficient commentary in itself as to his grasp of public issues and his contribution toward their solution." See "Notes on Remarks of John N. Garner Sixty-Fourth Congress," President's Individuals File—Garner, John Nance, Herbert Hoover Library, West Branch, Iowa.

73. Fisher, *Cactus Jack*, p. 49. One should not assume, however, that Garner's personal admiration of Wilson made him a dedicated advocate of the New Freedom. Reviewing Texas congressional leadership from 1913 to 1917, Dewey Grantham described Garner as giving "promise of being a conservative of conservatives." Garner opposed a freight tax in 1914 that would have increased revenue following a decline in customs receipts. Garner was the only Texan who voted

against the Wilson administration's trust program, including the Rayburn Railroad Securities Bill. Voting along with all or most of the Texas delegation, Garner also opposed the prohibition amendment in 1913 and the Susan B. Anthony Amendment in 1914. See Dewey W. Grantham, Jr., "Texas Congressional Leaders and the New Freedom, 1913–1917," *The Southwestern Historical Quarterly* 53 (July 1949): 39, 41–43.

74. MacNeil, *Forge of Democracy*, p. 163.

75. John Wylie Hillje, "The Progressive Movement and the Graduated Income Tax, 1913–1919" (Ph.D. diss., The University of Texas, 1966), pp. 23, 30–31.

76. Roy G. Blakey and Gladys C. Blakey, *The Federal Income Tax* (London: Longmans, Green, 1940), p. 75.

77. Hillje, "The Progressive Movement," p. 28.

78. Soreno Payne attacked Garner's mohair tariff claiming, "There are about 3,000,000 goats in the United States of which about 2,999,999 are in Texas." J. Hampton Moore even criticized Garner in verse:

> *Of all the creatures in the land,*
> *Of pedigrees supremely grand,*
> *There's none that do respect command*
> *Like Garner's goat of Texas.*
> *The modest sheep may browse around*
> *From Maine way to Puget Sound*
> *But they don't count a cent a pound*
> *With Garner's goat of Texas.*
> *The noble steer may be of use*
> *If freed from tyrant trust abuse;*
> *But even that would be the deuce*
> *To Garner's goat of Texas.*
> *If you want wool, the wool is fair;*
> *If you want hair, the wool is hair;*
> *If you want meat, the meat is there!*
> *That's Garner's goat of Texas.*
> *So while you kick the wool off sheep,*
> *And beef and mutton make so cheap,*
> *Protective tariff now will keep*
> *The Garner goat of Texas.*
> *Browse on, thou mild-eyed ruminant*
> *Thou are the casual nexus*
> *That binds protection to free trade*
> *Thou Garner goat of Texas.*
> *Oh, wondrous breed of Lone Star State,*
> *Premier of wool and hair, thy rate*
> *Of 10 per cent is truly great—*
> *Thou Garner goat of Texas.*

Garner proved his quickness in debate, however, responding,

> *Mr. Speaker:*
> *Hampie Moore is a hell of a poet—*
> *He don't know a sheep from a goat.*

See, for example, Timmons, *Garner of Texas*, pp. 77–79. It was an exchange John McDuffie recalled with obvious enjoyment years later in a letter to Bascom Timmons. McDuffie wrote, "On his [Garner's] eightieth birthday I sent him a telegram as follows:

> *Here's hoping you'll reach your 93,*
> *Then be as happy as you can be.*
> *Like Hampie Moore, I'm a hell-of-a-poet*
> *(After reading this, am sure you know it);*
> *But at least I know a sheep from a go-at!*
> *Many happy returns!!*

See John McDuffie to Bascom Timmons, December 20, 1948, John McDuffie Papers, W. S. Hoole Special Collections, University of Alabama, Montgomery, Alabama.

79. Timmons, *Garner of Texas*, p. 88.

80. James F. Byrnes, *All in One Lifetime* (New York: Harper & Brothers, 1958), pp. 32–33.

81. Timmons, *Garner of Texas*, p. 88.

82. John Nance Garner to Claude Kitchin, October 5, 1922, Claude Kitchin Papers, University of North Carolina, Chapel Hill, North Carolina.

83. "Stand on Tariff Beats Hayden for Democratic Post," John Nance Garner Scrapbook, 11–18–1913/3–04–1925, Center for American History, University of Texas, Austin, Texas.

84. Timmons, *Garner of Texas*, p. 42.

85. Baulch, *James B. Wells*, p. 361. Garner was not the only one mentioning the speakership at that time; Bascom Timmons, Garner's reporter-ally, was writing about the possibility. Timmons, however, also wrote that Finis Garrett, Henry Rainey, and Cordell Hull were possibilities as well. See Bascom Timmons, "Garner Is Boomed to Next Speaker," *Ft. Worth Record*, November 8, 1922, John Nance Garner Scrapbook, 11–18–1913/3–04–1925, Center for American History, University of Texas, Austin, Texas. At the same time he was thinking about being Speaker, he was considering retirement; Timmons, *Garner of Texas*, p. 95. Congressman John Box of Texas took Garner's retirement seriously enough that he made it known that he would like to replace Garner as whip. See John C. Box to Claude Kitchin, Henry D. Flood, Finis J. Garrett, and John N. Garner, March 5, 1921, Claude Kitchin Papers, University of North Carolina, Chapel Hill, North Carolina.

86. David Burner, *The Politics of Provincialism: The Democratic Party in Transition 1918–1932* (New York: Alfred A. Knopf, 1970), p. 104.

87. Timmons, *Garner of Texas*, p. 95.

88. John Nance Garner to Claude Kitchin, October 5, 1922, Claude Kitchin Papers, University of North Carolina, Chapel Hill, North Carolina.

89. John Nance Garner to Claude Kitchin, January 6, 1923, Claude Kitchin Papers, University of North Carolina, Chapel Hill, North Carolina.

90. Hardeman and Bacon, *Rayburn*, p. 136.

91. Byrnes, *All in One Lifetime*, pp. 34–35.

92. Hardeman and Bacon, *Rayburn*, p. 138.

93. Michael J. Romano, "The Emergence of John Nance Garner as a Figure in American National Politics, 1924–1941" (Ph.D. diss., St. John's University, 1973), p. 24.

94. "Garner Opens Democrat Drive on Tariff Bill," John Nance Garner Scrapbook, 11–18–1913/3–04–1925, Center for American History, University of Texas, Austin, Texas.

95. Romano, "The Emergence of John Nance Garner," p. 26.

96. Schlesinger, *The Crisis of the Old Order, 1919–1933*, p. 228.

97. Fordney's remarkable letter is as follows:

I understand that you have opposition in your district based on your position on the tariff. I am quite surprised at this, because in my service with you for 10 years on the ways and means committee, I always found that you took particular care to see that farm and ranch products were well taken care of in the way of protection.

While you and I did not always agree on rates to be placed on manufactured products, I always found you ready to boost farm products, especially the products of Texas. There is no better evidence of this fact than the rates provided for on some of the Texas products in the Underwood tariff law, for instance, angora goat hair. By you alone was the duty provided for in that bill on this product.

If you were having opposition from a republican in your district I could understand how claims of this kind could be made against you, but to have such opposition from a democrat is beyond my comprehension.

I wish you people to understand from me that there never was a man in congress bearing democratic sentiments that gave more earnest attention to the welfare of the farmer than you have. I would like to meet the fellow on the same platform that would take exception to your work in congress in the interest of farm products.

I think I could explain to the satisfaction of your constituency that you are entitled to their most earnest support.

See "Fordney Defends Garner's Stand on Farm Tariffs," a memorandum citing as its source the *Houston Chronicle*, April 13, 1928, in the President's Individuals File— Garner, John Nance, Herbert Hoover Presidential Library, West Branch, Iowa.

98. Timmons, *Garner of Texas*, p. 96.

99. John Nance Garner to Claude Kitchin, October 5, 1922, Claude Kitchin Papers, University of North Carolina, Chapel Hill, North Carolina.

100. Timmons, *Garner of Texas*, p. 96.

101. John Nance Garner to Claude Kitchin, October 5, 1922, Claude Kitchin Papers, University of North Carolina, Chapel Hill, North Carolina.

102. Garner accused Majority Leader Tilson of using rules in the House that strangled debate on Smoot-Hawley and prevented opposition from Democrats and Progressive Republicans. He claimed Tilson was engaging in "czarism," which had once before caused the House to revolt "before despotic leadership. . . ." See "Bureau of Publicity, Democratic National Committee Press Release," November 8, 1929, President's Individuals Files—Garner, John Nance, Herbert Hoover Presidential Library, West Branch, Iowa.

103. The delay in passing Smoot-Hawley was primarily in the Senate. Speaker Longworth claimed that the delay made the Democratic Party responsible for the Depression. Garner, on the other hand, argued that the tariff had been rushed through the House but that the Senate had an obligation "to debate a measure whose final enactment meant the imposition upon American taxpayers of something like an additional tax burden of a billion dollars annually." See "Bureau of Publicity, Democratic National Committee Press Release," October 7, 1930, President's Individuals File—Garner, John Nance, Herbert Hoover Presidential Library, West Branch, Iowa.

104. Garner wrote Joseph W. Fordney, saying, "You did not put enough duty on onions in your bill, so we are trying to get a 50% increase—had hearings here on the matter last month." See John Nance Garner to Joseph W. Fordney, March 5, 1928, President's Individuals File—Garner, John Nance, Herbert Hoover Presidential Library, West Branch, Iowa. See also Schlesinger, *The Crisis of the Old Order, 1919–1933*, p. 228.

105. Romano, "The Emergence of John Nance Garner," pp. 31–75.

106. For an interesting treatment of Mellon, see Robert S. Allen, *Washington Merry-Go-Round* (New York: Horace Liveright, 1931), pp. 163–183.

107. Romano, "The Emergence of John Nance Garner," pp. 31–52.

108. "Notes on Remarks of John N. Garner 68th Congress," President's Individuals File—Garner, John Nance, Herbert Hoover Presidential Library, West Branch, Iowa.

109. Garner never published a speech he gave on the floor on December 8, 1925, in which he denounced Rainey's position, but Rainey did publish his reply on December 9, in which he accused Garner of completely surrendering to the Republicans even though earlier he had opposed the Mellon Plan and had "made a real fight for the common people of this country." See "Remarks of John N. Garner 69th Congress, 1st Session, Dec. 7, 1925—July 3, 1926," President's Individuals File—Garner, John Nance, Herbert Hoover Presidential Library, West Branch, Iowa.

110. "Notes on Remarks of John N. Garner Sixty-Ninth Congress," President's Individuals File—Garner, John Nance, Herbert Hoover Presidential Library, West Branch, Iowa.

111. Romano, "The Emergence of John Nance Garner," p. 64.

112. Ibid., pp. 65–66.

113. Ibid., pp. 67–73.

114. Ibid., pp. 74–75.

115. Richard B. Cheney and Lynne V. Cheney, *Kings of the Hill* (New York: Continuum, 1983), pp. 156–157; Peters, *The American Speakership*, pp. 104–106.

116. Timmons, *Garner of Texas*, p. 123.

117. Ibid., pp. 129–130.

118. Alfred Steinberg, *Sam Rayburn: A Biography* (New York: Hawthorn Books, 1975), p. 89.

119. William B. Bankhead to John N. Garner, May 21, 1931, William B. Bankhead Papers, Record as a U.S. Representative, 1917–1940, Correspondence, March–November 1931, State of Alabama Department of Archives and History, Montgomery, Alabama.

120. John Nance Garner to William B. Bankhead, May 25, 1931, William B. Bankhead Papers, Record as a U.S. Representative, 1917–1940, Correspondence, March–November 1931, State of Alabama Department of Archives and History, Montgomery, Alabama.

121. John McDuffie, June 15, 1931, John McDuffie Papers, W. S. Hoole Special Collections, University of Alabama, Montgomery, Alabama.

122. Sam Rayburn to John McDuffie, November 6, 1931, John McDuffie Papers, W. S. Hoole Special Collections, University of Alabama, Montgomery, Alabama.

123. John Nance Garner to John McDuffie, September 24, 1931, John McDuffie Papers, W. S. Hoole Special Collections, University of Alabama, Montgomery, Alabama.

124. Jordan A. Schwarz, "John Nance Garner and the Sales Tax Rebellion of 1932," *Journal of Southern History* 30 (May 1964): 162.

125. Ibid.

126. Jordan A. Schwarz, *The Interregnum of Despair* (Urbana: University of Illinois Press, 1970), p. 236.

127. Peters, *The American Speakership*, pp. 114–118.

128. George Rothwell Brown, "Heraldings," January 11, 1932, John Nance Garner Scrapbook, 12–08–31 to 2–20–32, Center for American History, University of Texas, Austin, Texas. See also Fisher, *Cactus Jack*, p. 69; James, *Mr. Garner of Texas*, p. 111; and Hardeman and Bacon, *Rayburn*, p. 114.

129. William B. Bankhead to John N. Garner, telegram, November 13, 1931, William B. Bankhead Papers, Record as a U.S. Representative, 1917–1940, Correspondence, March–November 1931, State of Alabama Department of Archives and History, Montgomery, Alabama.

130. Fisher, *Cactus Jack*, p. 78.

131. Rexford G. Tugwell, *The Democratic Roosevelt* (Garden City, N.Y.: Doubleday, 1957), p. 226.

132. Jordan Schwarz, *The New Dealers* (New York: Alfred A. Knopf, 1993), pp. 43–56.

133. Romano, "The Emergence of John Nance Garner," p. 18.

134. Bascom Timmons should have known better when he wrote about Garner's sales tax speech, "Garner had made the speech of his life, restored his leadership and brought the House back to order. Backwoods evangelism had triumphed." See Timmons, *Garner of Texas*, p. 149. The best treatment of the sales tax battle is Schwarz, "John Nance Garner and the Sales Tax Rebellion of 1932," pp. 162–180. Lippman is quoted in Schwarz.

135. Schwarz, "John Nance Garner and the Sales Tax Rebellion of 1932," p. 179.

136. Unauthored and undated memorandum titled "Garner Attacks President and Denies His Own Relief Program Is 'Pork' Legislation," President's Individuals File—Garner, John Nance, Herbert Hoover Presidential Library, West Branch, Iowa.

137. Schwarz, *The Interregnum of Despair,* pp. 142–178.

138. Timmons, *Garner of Texas,* p. 151.

139. Ibid., p. 150.

140. Schwarz, *The Interregnum of Despair,* p. 170.

141. *Congressional Record,* July 6, 1932, p. 15120.

142. See generally, Romano, "The Emergence of John Nance Garner."

143. Grantham, "Texas Congressional Leaders," p. 39.

144. It is instructive that in the early stages of the Garner boom for the 1932 Democratic presidential nomination, Ettie Garner in an interview tried to discount the connection to the South. She declared, "We are not Southerners. We are Southwesterners." See "The Rising Star of Texas," *Corpus Christi Caller,* January 27, 1932, John Nance Garner Scrapbook, 12–08–1931/2–20–1932, Center for American History, University of Texas, Austin, Texas.

145. MacNeil, *Forge of Democracy,* p. 163.

7

The Speaker and the Presidents: Sam Rayburn, the White House, and the Legislative Process, 1941–1961

Lewis L. Gould and Nancy Beck Young

Speaker Sam Rayburn's leadership of the House of Representatives has become legendary in the history of U.S. politics. His wise sayings to new members are often quoted. He declared to new member James Roosevelt in 1955: "If you want to get along you better go along."[1] After the Republican victory in 1994, Speaker Newt Gingrich harked back to Rayburn as an example of congressional comity he hoped to emulate. Rayburn's apparent dominance of the House and its proceedings during the 1950s is often contrasted with the modern lack of discipline and cohesion among the Democrats. As a result, the Speaker's personal character, his devotion to the House as an institution, and his political friendships have all received extensive historical coverage.

In the process, Rayburn has become a legislative icon, the embodiment of a lawmaker. Yet when he is thought about, it is usually in comparative terms. When authors consider Sam Rayburn in relation to his protégé Lyndon Johnson, Rayburn's moralism emerges in contrast to Johnson's alleged cynicism and ruthlessness. Or Rayburn's leadership style is juxtaposed with that of a modern Speaker, whether it be Jim Wright, Tom Foley, or Newt Gingrich.[2]

An odd aspect of Rayburn's existing historical reputation is that his legislative performance as Speaker of the House has rarely been analyzed in any detail. The literature on Rayburn is striking for its general consideration of numerous aspects that are ancillary to his basic role as Speaker. As long as Rayburn's career is treated as a set of discrete episodes, the full impact of his service as a Speaker will not come into focus. What is most required now is a detailed and sophisticated scrutiny of Rayburn's entire career in a way that does justice to the complexity of the man and his times.

In this chapter we look at Rayburn's performance during World War II and his relationship with President Dwight D. Eisenhower in the 1950s. We argue that Sam Rayburn's reputed and legendary dominance of the House during his years as Speaker overstates the power that he actually wielded and underemphasizes how much Rayburn had to struggle to push legislation through. Moreover, much of Rayburn's success hinged on the political context in which he worked. The nature of a specific issue, the size of the Democratic majority, the exercise of presidential leadership—all these influenced whether Rayburn succeeded or failed in a particular lawmaking episode.

The essential picture of Rayburn as a politician is correct. He was a dedicated lawmaker deeply involved in the details of enacting legislation, he exemplified the congressional concept of the workhorse rather than the show horse, and his love for the House left him with little time for family or social life. But these general impressions do not convey how Rayburn managed legislation, the depth of his commitment to the Democratic Party, or the skill with which he worked to achieve his ends. A sense of Rayburn the lawmaker in action is what this chapter seeks to provide.

When Dwight D. Eisenhower took the oath of office as president of the United States on January 20, 1953, Samuel Taliaferro Rayburn had been a member of Congress for four decades. In the years before 1955 Sam Rayburn had accumulated a reputation for fairness and integrity of leadership. Born January 6, 1882, in Tennessee, Rayburn grew up in Texas. At fifteen, Rayburn stood in the rain to hear Joseph Weldon Bailey, a representative and later senator from Texas, give a speech. Rayburn often recalled that "it must have been under the spell of Bailey's oratory that I decided to become Speaker."[3]

Ten years later Rayburn was elected to the state legislature where he served for six years. He became known as a staunch defender of the controversial Bailey, whose enemies charged him with corruption in office when he was up for reelection in 1907. Rayburn defended his childhood hero, who regained his Senate seat. Just as Bailey had encouraged him, Rayburn would later nurture such political protégés as Lyndon Johnson and Lloyd M. Bentsen, Jr. The hardworking Rayburn served as speaker of the Texas House of Representatives during his final two years in Austin.

Rayburn was elected to the House of Representatives in 1912 and gained a seat on the Interstate and Foreign Commerce Committee. He endeavored to pass a measure to grant the Interstate Commerce Commission the power to oversee the bonds and stocks that interstate railroads issued. Rayburn's proposal encountered the opposition of President Woodrow Wilson and was not enacted. Close ties to Congressman John Nance Garner and tireless attention to his work helped Rayburn gain friends among Democratic House leaders during his first three terms.

The Republican victory in the 1918 congressional elections halted Rayburn's formal rise to power for more than a decade. During the 1920s, Rayburn's ties to Garner became stronger as the younger man mastered the legislative process and the ways of the House. When the Democrats regained control of Congress in 1930, Rayburn became chair of the Interstate and Foreign Commerce Committee. The election of Franklin D. Roosevelt as president in 1932 brought Rayburn closer to the center of congressional power. Thereafter he engineered the passage of several key bills, including the Securities Act, the Federal Communications Act, the Securities and Exchange Act, the Public Utilities Holding Company Act, and the Rural Electrification Act.

Elected majority leader in January 1937, Rayburn faced a rebellious Congress increasingly under the spell of conservative Democrats. That condition defined Rayburn's leadership style from his earliest days in power. When Rayburn became Speaker on September 16, 1940, after the death of William B. Bankhead, he had to lead the House in light of the partisan and ideological alignments that he confronted. The experience of being Speaker during World War II shaped Rayburn's subsequent performance in the 1950s.

What this meant to Rayburn, was, first, that he never could count on an easy victory. In the 1940s he put Roosevelt's war program through after close roll-call votes. The struggles of the World War II era honed Rayburn's skill at compromise and his instinct to seek the middle ground. Second, this use of compromise as an approach left Rayburn vulnerable to attacks from the left and right within his own party. The more conciliatory a tone he took, the more likely the Speaker was to face liberal and conservative challenges. The war years are an underexamined phase of Rayburn's career, but they were crucial to the formation of the leadership techniques that he used later during Eisenhower's presidency.

Rayburn believed that the executive and legislative branches of government were equal in stature and significance. When speaking of his long service in Washington, the Texas Democrat often observed that he had served *with* eight presidents, not *under* them. Biographers of Rayburn have yet to assess the impact of the Speaker's independence on public policy. In December 1940, Franklin D. Roosevelt wrote to Rayburn and his majority leader, John W. McCormack, asking for increased cooperation in the coming session of Congress, but Rayburn believed he had already proven his mettle to the White House. Later, despite Rayburn's close relationship with Harry S. Truman, he did not hesitate to criticize White House policies. For example, in August 1952, the Speaker warned the president that an extra session of Congress would not produce "a stronger [price] controls law" but would "probably do nothing at all."[4]

An incident from early in Rayburn's tenure as Speaker set the tone for the problems he faced throughout the war years. Congress had authorized a peacetime draft in 1940. Rayburn agreed that "the quickest, safest and most Democratic way to raise an army is by selective service." When the draft was enacted, Roosevelt declared the term of service would be only one year. By the summer of 1941, even though conditions in Europe had worsened rather than improved, the term of service for the previous year's draftees was about to expire. The administration wanted draftees held over for the duration of the present emergency. Administration partisans prepared legislation to extend the terms of the draft. Lister Hill (D-Ala.) managed the draft extension bill in the Senate and explained the administration's goals: "We want Congress to declare a flat state of emergency for the psychological effect on Congress and the rest of the people. But we don't want that emergency to apply to anything but this matter of holding the Army together. It's all a matter of finding the right words. . . . If we don't find them some of these people will talk all summer about what the President might or might not do under a declaration of emergency." Rayburn knew that he needed the votes of twenty Republicans to balance projected Democratic defections. The measure passed by a vote of 203 to 202 only after Rayburn resorted to personal lobbying and the stern and quick use of his parliamentary powers. But the debate left a bitter taste in the Speaker's mouth.[5]

In his fascinating memorandums, Frank McNaughton, the *Time* correspondent who covered Congress during the war, pictured Rayburn as angry with the partisan fight that Republicans waged against the draft extension bill in August 1941. Calling the Republicans "God-damned sons-of-bitches," he argued to McNaughton that the minority party acted the way they did because their predictions that Roosevelt would lead the country into war had proven incorrect. Rayburn contended, "This makes them look like a bunch of god-damned liars and fools. Of course they hate it. They are just damned also disappointed. They'd like to have us in the war so they could go out and say, 'We told you so.' Hell's fire, who wants to take this country into war? The Democrats don't. The President doesn't." Rayburn asserted that "what we are trying to do is build up our defense so that no one will attack us, and these political minded bastards keep yelling about war. The Republicans are gambling on a repetition of 1920—a long, desperate gamble that the war will be over in 1942, and they are trying to catch the backwash for 1944."[6]

As he continued his attack, Rayburn spoke of war as a definite event in the future, not a possibility. Rayburn realized the House would pass a war declaration without incident, but he doubted the results in the more isolationist Senate. He recognized that Democrats were divided in their support for Roosevelt but believed that public support for national defense would win out. Rayburn trusted that Congress would hear from constituents such as the one who wrote him that "the Veterans of Foreign Wars know what war is [and] we offer our services if needed." Rayburn's bitterness toward the GOP surfaced when he cut off Republican access to the floor to make antiadministration speeches.[7]

Shortly after passing the draft extension bill by one vote, Congress left town for a month-long holiday. Rayburn told reporters, "When I start to the ranch the road gets narrower and narrower every mile I go. At the end of the narrowest road I know, there's the gate, and there's no telephone out there." Instead of granting itself a recess, a "watchdog squad" remained in Washington and reconvened every three days only to vote another three-day adjournment. One national journalist noted that Congress, "exhausted as it is, bedeviled and rudderless . . . doesn't trust Franklin D. Roosevelt, [and] wants to get back quick if it thinks necessary." Rayburn returned from the break convinced that "God damn it, don't ever let anybody tell you the people down in my state . . . are isolationists. They are ready to go, now, at the drop of a hat. They are for the president and they want to see this sonofab [*sic*] Hitler whipped and whipped damned good."[8]

In the remaining days of 1941, Rayburn faced even greater tests of his leadership. Between 1935 and 1937 Congress had passed three neutrality laws that reflected the inward-mindedness of most depression-era Americans. But with the war raging in Europe, internationalist sentiments, stemming from the White House, emerged in what became a piecemeal campaign to repeal those laws. In late September 1941, Rayburn believed that Congress would approve the arming of merchant ships without much opposition but that repeal of neutrality laws would generate opposition. "You know how it is. There's a lot of sentimental appeal in the word neutrality. The isolationists would get up and holler like hell about neutrality, and the public would get wrought up about it. If we go at it the other way just leave the act on the books and cut the guts out of it with amendments, at least they can't holler that we are doing away with neutrality."[9]

In early October 1941, Rayburn and McCormack had yet to hear anything definite from the White House on the subject of neutrality legislation and were quite angry to be out of the loop. At McCormack's behest, Rayburn pushed Roosevelt to allow the House to be the first, rather than the Senate, to consider repealing the provision of the Neutrality Act that prevented the arming of merchant ships. Rayburn believed that since the House rules prevented long debates, he could get the measure passed before the isolationists gathered strength. Indeed the House acted by the middle of October, but the Senate did not vote for three more weeks, when they also struck the sections of the Neutrality Act prohibiting U.S. merchant ships from entering belligerent ports. Rayburn and McCormack realized that House passage of the revision of the Neutrality Act permitting armed U.S. merchant ships to enter belligerent ports would be close. Although they had gotten a 121-vote margin of victory on the arming of merchant vessels, the House leaders realized the next vote would more likely resemble the narrow one-vote win on draft extension. Indeed, passage by an 18-vote majority came only after Rayburn took the floor for debate, read a letter from the president, and promised a floor vote on anti-strike legislation.[10]

Increased government control of the domestic economy became another pressing issue for Congress in the months prior to Pearl Harbor. Even before price control legislation was introduced in Congress in August 1941, Rayburn had grown weary with the process. Agriculture's demands for inflation and labor's concern about wage controls resulted in his declaration that the measure is "the kind of bill on which there will be pretty full hearings." Rayburn doubted that the measure would pass, and he remained skeptical about the possibility of getting any price control legislation through Congress in early October 1941. McNaughton noted that "the administration has been playing its entire anti-inflation program like an eighth-grade orchestra stumbling through Beethoven's Ninth Symphony." Rayburn realized the futility of adding wage control to the price control bill. He knew the Republicans would then attack the Democrats as antilabor. Furthermore, Rayburn was frustrated with the lack of communication from the White House about strategy. Rayburn vowed "to get some kind of bill through the house, but God knows what it will be."[11]

The price control bill up for vote on the House floor contained an amendment that provided farmers with parity price protection at the 1919–1929 average. When asked whether he would force congressmen with farm constituents to vote against this amendment, Rayburn replied: "Hell's fire, I'm not going to ask these farm boys to cut their throats by voting against the Brown amendment. Damned if I will do it. With that in there it will be a hell of a lot better bill than what the Senate will pass. If these farm boys were to exempt wages in the bill, and then vote against the Brown amendment, there'd be a lot of them that wouldn't come back. I'm not going to ask them to do it." The Speaker held true to his word. After the bill passed the House, Rayburn assured a constituent that "there is no way of [the legislation] touching cotton or any other farm products until they have reached 110% parity or the market price on October 1, 1941, or the highest average of 1919–1929."[12]

After the war declarations were passed on December 8, 1941, Rayburn's pragmatic leadership style emerged as he guided the president's program through the House. Despite the prevailing notion that Congress moved like a steamroller to mobilize for the war effort, a careful examination of the record reveals the degree of difficulty Rayburn faced in ensuring both domestic and military readiness. For example, contrary to the wishes of the leadership, members of the House passed a bill limiting provisions of the draft to those men aged 21 to 44. Rayburn and others realized the foolishness of this vote. They knew that as with the initial draft legislation and the neutrality laws, Congress would later be required to come back and correct its mistakes.[13]

In addition to facing a difficult struggle with Republicans over Roosevelt's war program, Rayburn battled with the press over public perceptions of Congress. At the same time that the Speaker was privately irate with the politicization of war issues by Republicans, he launched an increasingly vocal public defense of Congress as an institution. In March 1942 when Rayburn told the press that "Congress is being criticized, but Congress has given the President every new law he has asked for defense purposes," the media and members of Congress interpreted Rayburn's statement as an attack on the pending antistrike bill that Howard Worth Smith had introduced. Yet Rayburn countered, "I made not one utterance about legislation, prospective or otherwise, any sort of legislation, and I did not have in mind anything with reference to the wage-and-hour legislation." In fact, the Speaker wrote a Texas woman earlier that month, "There is no one that is more distressed about any element of labor trouble than I am. We in the House have been determined for some time to try to do something about it and, although it seems to have been forgotten, on December 3, 1941, the House passed a very strong bill known as the Smith anti-strike bill and sent it to the Senate, where it has not yet been acted upon." Rayburn stressed that the Smith bill "would in my opinion have cleared up most of our labor disputes. This bill really has teeth in it."[14]

By the end of May 1942, Congress was ready to pass new legislation stiffening the libel laws and to initiate investigations into the behavior of the press. The outburst of anger from the legislative branch resulted from critical newspaper treatment of Congress. Rayburn told McNaughton, "You can't make Ham Fishes out of everybody in Congress. It's true before the war there was a hell of a lot of politics and backbiting, but don't forget this—the President got every bill and every damned dime that he asked, and it always took a majority of Congress to give it to him." The Speaker asserted, "There may be bad men in this Congress, but the record shows that the majority of them have been good men. Maybe not all statesmen, but there are great men in this Congress, and I'm not going to see them take this pounding indefinitely. If the newspapers and columnists keep hammering us, I'm going to get me 30 minutes of radio time and take this direct to the people." In fact, Rayburn defended Congress in a public appearance at Muhlenburg College in Allentown, Pennsylvania, later that month. But attacks on Congress did not abate. The *New York Times* editorialized that "Congress has for generations been a rather irresponsible body, chiefly because of its bad internal organization."[15]

Economic controls remained a political problem for Rayburn and the administration throughout the war. Rayburn's handling of the problem reveals much about his loyalty to Congress as an institution. When asked whether Congress would fund a plan by Leon Henderson, director of the Office of Price Administration, to combat farm price inflation with subsidies, Rayburn responded, "We couldn't give any assurances of any kind. We can't bind this House to anything in advance. You take this goddamned Henderson with his high manners, riding rough-shod over Congress, refusing to answer mail or give Congressmen information. And all this talk about nationwide gasoline rationing. He is one of these fellows that wants to make the whole country suffer," argued the Speaker. "If we're swimming in gasoline in Texas, make us use just so much because there is a shortage somewhere else. . . . Personally, I think there's got to be subsidies of some kind. The situation is getting dangerous and you've got to have subsidies. But I don't know what this House will do about giving Leon Henderson subsidy money. You saw what they did to his appropriation."[16]

In an off-the-record interview, Rayburn told McNaughton that Roosevelt was "pretty worked up" over the failures of price control "and he ought to be. I told him that if he sent anything up here, it would have to be forceful. . . . He'd have to send a message to the Congress, and make it a hard, ringing one. . . . The President very definitely has in mind legislation to freeze wages. Of course there's got to be legislation. We've got to do something or we're going to have the god-damnedest blowup this country ever saw, and it'll cost us billions of dollars." In a meeting with Roosevelt, Rayburn and McCormack warned the president that any wage control legislation faced stiff congressional opposition from a coalition of farm state and labor state representatives. Urging the use of presidential war powers, the two congressional leaders advised Roosevelt to act alone on the problem of spiraling wages and prices. Instead, Roosevelt challenged Congress to act on the problem before October 1. Rayburn and other leaders responded with anger at this attack on their institution. Congress returned after a month-long vacation and passed a joint resolution giving the executive branch legislative sanction for increased wartime control over the economy. The president blasted Congress in a press conference for parochial thinking. Rayburn told one reporter that it was "a hell of a thing to do, and it has got to stop. We have a hard enough time up here carrying the load for him without any blasts like that, that are totally undeserved and uncalled for. Hell, we put this bill through for him, and he's getting just about what he wants. And then he kicks us this way." The Speaker complained that the House Banking and Currency Committee was prepared to kill the bill and would have had he not pressured them to report it out to the House floor. Rayburn called Harry Hopkins at the White House, warning him that "the blood pressure is pretty high up here now, and another one or two like that and Congress will just rebel against these tactics. These fellows will start hitting back."[17]

Indeed, political posturing in Congress only got worse as time passed. When asked what impact the 1942 midterm elections would have on the complexion of Congress, Rayburn asserted that either party could gain ten or more seats. "There is no big trend yet. Look at the primaries. Most of the men, in every case, were renominated by their parties. The people in many cases, even with the isolationists, just went out and voted for the man in Congress, regardless of his record, on the theory that he had been here and knew what was going on." The Speaker used Hamilton Fish as an example of his point. Fish had never endeared himself to Rayburn, and the Speaker believed the New York Republican was vulnerable until "they started getting all this stuff out about the President and Wendell

Willkie conferring and planning to beat Fish, and the people just said 'By God he can't be that bad. I've been voting for him for 20 years and I know him better than they do.' Ham Fish is coming back. Whenever everybody starts jumping on a man, then the public is going to vote for him, particularly if they've been voting for him for a long time." Privately dissatisfied with the conduct of the war, Rayburn predicted that after the elections were over, Congress would demand investigations and voice its objections during the executive session portion of committee hearings.[18]

Despite Republican gains of forty-six seats in the Seventy-eighth Congress, Rayburn insisted on retaining a five-vote Democratic majority on the Rules and the Ways and Means Committees. Regarding the general tone of the next Congress, Rayburn declared, "I doubt that there will be much domestic legislation put before Congress. We'll probably have only the war program, with the regular appropriations. There will be a tax bill, but outside of that, I doubt that the domestic program will amount to much. There won't be any trouble over the military appropriations. We know that. The Republicans are going to go along with us. They can't do otherwise. . . . We will have a technical majority, but for all practical purposes, we haven't even a working majority." Privately, though, the Speaker remained optimistic about the coming Congress. He told John J. Cochran that "the result of the election and the closeness of the majority does not weigh upon me as heavily as the loss of a score or more of the finest fellows who ever served in Congress. You will remember when we had a majority of four in the House and kept things going in good shape, and I think we can go along very well." In fact, Rayburn told the new Congress in January 1943 that they would assume a much more central role in the war effort and that there would be no more rubber stamp for the administration. He declared, "It shall be my unwavering determination to protect and defend the rights, the prerogatives and the power of the House of Representatives. We must have teamwork between the executive departments and the legislative branch of government. That cooperation must be mutual and accepted by all."[19]

Rayburn opposed Roosevelt's introduction of a program for postwar domestic reform legislation to Congress. The Speaker believed that Congress should devote its attention to the war effort. "This will lie around a long time. Parts of it will be picked up and enacted, others discarded. Congress will move slowly, perhaps over a period of several years. Eventually you'll find that pretty much of this program will become law. It's something to shoot for over the years. And it is popular, or will be when the people understand it." Yet the Speaker argued that "we've got plenty to do without it. There's the bituminous coal act that we've got to extend, the reciprocal trade program, and then a tax bill. This is a tremendously costly and controversial program. When your house is afire, you don't generally start in to building an addition to it." Throughout 1943 Rayburn and McCormack fought a rearguard action in Congress to save the president's war program. Much of the tension within the legislative branch stemmed from Republican assumptions that Roosevelt would run for a fourth term; they therefore began their campaign against his reelection.[20]

Before the war ended, Rayburn had established a clear pattern for his guidance of Congress. Searching for middle ground and compromise, the Texas Democrat had little patience for overtly partisan and what he termed mean-spirited attacks from the opposition. In the process, Rayburn developed a strong institutional defense of the Democratic agenda and of Congress. After Republicans gained control of the House in the 1946 midterm elections, Rayburn did not relish the thought of becoming minority leader. He wrote to Truman on November 10, indicating he would not accept the post. "I will be freer to take the floor when your program really needs me than to be in the position of yapping with every little fellow who jumps up on the republican side—and God knows there will be plenty of them if I read correctly the returns." Rayburn asked that he be included in White House strategy sessions because "my one desire is to serve." Truman understood Rayburn's position and agreed that "you and I can do an excellent job of strategy in any position which you choose to occupy in the new Congress." Yet the president encouraged Rayburn to take the minority leader's job, which he eventually did. The ensuing years of Democratic exile from power only intensified Rayburn's understanding of the interworkings of Washington politics. His willingness to receive southern Democrats who supported the Dixiecrats in 1948 back into the Democratic fold shows his understanding of the relationship between party loyalty and congressional effectiveness.[21]

The techniques of leadership that Rayburn developed during World War II and the immediate postwar years carried over into his relationship with Dwight D. Eisenhower in the 1950s. To better understand the relationship between the Republican president and the Democratic Speaker, analysis of several key episodes—including Rayburn's push for a twenty-dollar tax credit in 1955, his ongoing fight with the president over western water projects, and his role in the Landrum-Griffin labor legislation from 1959—is warranted. In February 1955, the Democratic House, under Rayburn's leadership, narrowly passed a twenty-dollar tax credit for all U.S. taxpayers. The House action has been given brief coverage as a source of friction between Eisenhower and Rayburn, which it certainly was, but the overall treatment of the incident has been cursory and superficial.[22] In fact, the tax battle of early 1955 represented more than a passing moment of tension between president and Speaker. It became a prolonged struggle on Capitol Hill that dominated the headlines for more than a month. An examination of Rayburn's performance on this subject indicates how complex his role as a legislative leader was and how much energy and thought he devoted to initiatives that his biographers have often ignored.

The events of early 1955 reflect another circumstance that Rayburn biographers have yet to confront. As manager of one of the two branches of Congress, Rayburn faced interlocking issues that often overlapped in their mutual effects. In the case of the twenty-dollar tax credit, these other matters included the personal situation between Rayburn and Dwight Eisenhower at the time, the Speaker's ambitions for change in natural gas policy, and the imminence of the 1956 election.

The House Democratic leadership announced its proposal to give a twenty-dollar tax credit for each taxpayer and dependent on February 19, 1955. The disclosure triggered an intense dispute between Eisenhower and Rayburn. What has not been previously addressed is where this tax-cutting policy originated. The impulse that led Rayburn to propose the tax credit sprang from both a look backward at the previous session and the anticipation of what the Republicans might do as the 1956 presidential election neared.[23]

In 1954, the Republican Congress had enacted a tax cut measure that granted substantial reductions to business, stockholders, and upper-income individuals. Secretary of the Treasury George M. Humphrey called the law "the largest single tax cut in history." President Eisenhower mentioned the 1954 tax bill in his State of the Union address and in his budget message to Congress. "The basic tax law was revised," he said, "to relieve hardships for millions of Americans and to reduce tax barriers to economic growth." In 1955, however, "in view of the prospective deficit, we cannot afford to have any further loss of revenue this year through reductions in taxes." The Republicans would not be lowering taxes in 1955, but, said the president, "I am hopeful that such reductions can be made next year."[24]

For Sam Rayburn and many House Democrats, the 1954 tax cut had one fundamental defect. It had been tilted toward the wealthy. "A great many of us think," he wrote, "that most of this went to the high income people and very little to the low income group." As he told another correspondent from Texas, "the last tax bill more nearly took care of the fat cats than it did the average citizen." The concern that Eisenhower expressed about the deficit also did not impress Rayburn. "Last year, when they knew there was a large deficit, they reduced taxes by the billions, and most of it went to the big folks. I think it is time for the little folks to have a cut." Finally, the Speaker and his allies in the House leadership expected the GOP to propose an election-year tax cut in 1956, and they hoped to preempt the Republicans.[25]

Rayburn's attempt to extend a tax credit to lower-income earners had roots in the 1954 congressional campaign. In a nationwide television and radio broadcast on September 10, 1954, the minority leader of House Democrats singled out the 1954 tax legislation for special criticism. "Eight out of every 10 taxpayers, were brushed off with only the lamb's share," he said, "and a mighty skimpy lamb's share it was." Instead, Rayburn proposed, "We Democrats ought to get the Republican Congress to increase the personal exemption on income taxes from $600 to $700." After the Democratic victory in 1954, party leaders talked about what one of them called "lower tax relief." These ideas circulated around Sam Rayburn and new Senate Majority Leader Lyndon Johnson.[26]

Rayburn gave an oblique public signal of his intentions in early January when he announced at the time of the State of the Union message that, although he concurred with the president's intention to postpone reductions in corporate and excise taxes, his decision "did not bind him or the Democrats not to seek other tax reductions, possibly by increasing the personal income-tax exemption." The comment passed largely unnoticed, and harmony seemed to prevail when Rayburn and the Democrats helped the president win renewal of the Reciprocal Trade Agreements Act in February over the opposition of many Republicans.[27]

It was a political surprise when, after a meeting with Speaker Rayburn on February 19, House Democrats declared that the twenty-dollar credit would be introduced by the Ways and Means Committee during the following week. The tax credit amendment represented a shrewd political stroke: It put the Democrats in the position of favoring tax relief for average Americans, a stance that the Republicans had often exploited while styling the Democrats as big spenders. As a Floridian told Rayburn, "Most assuredly it is the little fellow who needs relief because he has so little to begin with." It also made Rayburn's party the first to advocate tax relief before the 1956 election. The Speaker referred back to Eisenhower's State of the Union message about tax cuts in 1956 and said: "This may be a forerunner."[28]

Since the Democrats held a 232 to 203 majority in the House, a tax credit amendment also offered the potential of giving the opposition a political victory on behalf of a popular cause early in the new Congress. Accordingly, the Democrats added their tax credit as an amendment to a bill to extend the corporate tax rate and other existing excise taxes. If the tax credit stayed in the bill, it would be very difficult for Eisenhower to veto the measure as a whole.[29]

A distracting element in the political equation between Speaker Rayburn and Eisenhower at the time, moreover, was the sense of grievance that Rayburn felt at not having received personal copies of Eisenhower's messages to Congress since the start of the new session. In fact, the White House was sending the messages to the office of the House majority leader, John McCormack, where they were being handled. As it happened, a clerk in McCormack's office had failed to send them on to the Speaker, but that was not known in mid-February when Rayburn considered that he was being slighted. The resulting tension played into the tax credit battle.[30]

The Democrats acted quickly in mid-February 1955. On February 21, the Ways and Means Committee met in closed session to approve the tax credit. Secretary of the Treasury George M. Humphrey attended the lengthy meeting but made little headway in trying to dissuade the Democratic majority from acting. They voted 15 to 10 to send the tax credit amendment to the House floor. Humphrey called the action "one hundred per cent political" and charged that it was "not responsible financial management of the Federal Government." The committee chairman, Jere Cooper of Tennessee, countered that "whatever the President may have in mind by way of tax reduction next year, we will be sure that low-income tax payers will be taken care of."[31]

The Democratic maneuver caught the Republicans by surprise, and angry GOP leaders assembled at the White House on Tuesday, February 22, to plot their response. The resentment against Sam Rayburn permeated the gathering. Humphrey led off with the comment "that Rayburn was playing politics up to his ears and was ready for anything and would try to do everything possible to disrupt the President's program." Eisenhower chimed in that "it was almost unbelievable how Rayburn and his people were playing with the interests of the United States."[32]

As the discussion of the tax issues ended, the president told the meeting that he thought "it's about time that I personally went after Rayburn. I know many of his constituents and have a lot of good friends in Texas. I think I should get those friends to go after him and ask him what the hell he is trying to do up here in Washington." Eisenhower said Republicans should warn Rayburn that if he persisted in his tactics the president might not sign some natural gas bills that the Speaker wanted.[33]

With a presidential press conference scheduled for the following day, Eisenhower instructed aides to draft language for him to use in criticizing the tax credit. James Hagerty responded with some tart comments about the Democrats. When he met with reporters, however, the president did not use the Hagerty text. Instead, he described the Democratic measure as "reaching some kinds of heights in fiscal irresponsibility." Rayburn retorted, "It's too bad when the people who have been passing all his legislation get so irresponsible so fast."[34]

During the press meeting, Sarah McClendon of the *El Paso Times* said that there seemed to be "no channel of communication" between the White House and the Speaker's office. Reporters said that the president was "flushing angrily" when he answered: "I doubt that the Speaker has to bring me any complaints about my office through a roundabout source of communication." Eisenhower said that he and Rayburn had been "personal friends for years" and that all Rayburn had to do was call him on the telephone. Majority leader John McCormack responded that "the initiative ought to come from the President." The next day, the Speaker and the White House worked out an arrangement whereby Rayburn would get his own copy of presidential messages well in advance, but it was clear that Eisenhower felt his honesty had been challenged.[35]

Despite the presidential denunciation of the tax credit idea, the Democratic leadership in the House canvassed its members about the proposal that was, as they framed it, "designed for the benefit of the small taxpayer." The tally showed 172 in favor, 7 against, and 53 not voting or undecided. The leadership then asked the assistant whips to speak with all of their members who were away to stress that it was "vitally important" to be present on February 24 when the vote occurred. "We want all the Members here," wrote McCormack, "so that we will know what we can do to help the low income tax group."[36]

The House Democrats prevailed when the key vote took place in a heated session of the House on February 25, with 417 members of the House present. During the partisan debate, Republican Charles Halleck of Indiana charged that the tax credit initiative was no more than a Democratic effort to buy votes, which might in fact violate the Corrupt Practices Act. An angry Rayburn fired back: "I am no shoddy dealer. I am not trying to blackmail anybody, and I am not trying to buy votes—and you who have made these statements will live to regret it." Republican Dan Reed of New York moved to recommit the section of the bill with the tax credit (in effect killing it), and the crucial vote followed.[37]

The first tally had Reed's motion defeated by a vote of 192 in favor to 197 against. Leaders on both sides of the aisle delayed the final counting as they rounded up absent members and pressed others to change their vote. When the result came, the Reed motion lost, 205 in favor to 210 against. Sixteen southern Democrats deserted the Speaker to support the White House, but five northeastern Republicans provided the decisive votes to give Rayburn his narrow victory.[38]

When Eisenhower received the news of the vote, he told Hagerty to be sure to "keep a list of those 5 Republicans and if you ever see at any time that anyone in the White House wants me to see any one of them, you bring it to my attention and I'll stop it." The president also sent congratulations to the GOP House leaders for their hard fight against Rayburn.[39]

The House passed the bill as amended and sent it to the Senate, where the tax credit faced an uncertain destiny. The outcome in his chamber pleased Rayburn. "We really gave the Republicans a surprise and a pretty good licking last week," he wrote to a leader of Texas liberals. "They are mighty mad that we stole this thunder from them because I am sure they expected President Eisenhower to recommend some tax readjustments next year." Among the House leadership on the Republican side, suspicion of Rayburn remained as strong as ever. Charles Halleck of Indiana told the White House that "Rayburn was inspired by both thin skin & desire for votes."[40]

Rayburn's initiative drew strong newspaper criticism. The *New York Times* called his idea a "flagrantly political proposal" and said that "politics had its heyday yesterday on Capitol Hill." At home, a liberal Democrat in Texas, Ralph Yarborough, praised the tax credit because "it restores the Democratic Party to its time-honored traditional position as the party that looks out for the little man." As Rayburn put it, "It all adds up to the proposition that when this administration gets ready to get on a business basis we are ready to go along with them, but we do not believe in special privileges for anybody. We never have believed in them."[41]

When the tax credit measure reached the Senate in March 1955, the alliance of Republicans and southern Democrats that Rayburn had faced in the House derailed the Speaker's program. In the Senate Finance Committee, a majority voted nine to six against the tax credit. Democrats Walter George of Georgia and Harry Byrd of Virginia joined seven Republicans in rejecting the twenty-dollar cut. When the overall tax bill came to the floor, Majority Leader Lyndon Johnson proposed a variant of the Rayburn proposal that would have accorded a tax reduction to those with annual incomes under five thousand dollars and rescinded some of the benefits in the 1954 tax bill that favored the wealthy. Johnson's action made the bill into a major confrontation between the two parties over fiscal policy, but the president and the Republicans prevailed by a vote of fifty to forty-four when five southern Democrats joined the GOP minority.[42]

A disappointed Sam Rayburn said that "the Democrats made a fight for the measure, but some of those in the Senate never would yield." As a result, the tax credit idea was dead. "However," added Rayburn, "we will live to fight another day." Several months later, newspaper reports had the Speaker still "simmering" at the administration's criticism of the tax credit proposal. He promised that if tax cutting occurred in 1956, the Democrats would take care of the little fellow.[43]

The twenty-dollar tax credit battle in 1955 was not a Rayburn victory, but it revealed much about his priorities as a Democratic leader. He used his power as Speaker to frame an issue around which the new Democratic majorities in the Congress might rally. Despite the historical impression that Rayburn invariably cooperated with Eisenhower during the 1950s, the tax credit controversy represented an occasion when the Speaker confronted the president in a partisan way on an issue that defined a difference between the two parties. The episode also reveals that Rayburn and Eisenhower were no more than formal "friends" in a political sense and that an undercurrent of tension marked their relationship. Most of all, the tax battle indicates that Rayburn's legislative performance was far more complex and intricate than has been previously understood. Until there is a coherent narrative of his record on major policy issues during the 1950s, the historical understanding of his achievements as a politician will be incomplete.

Rayburn and Eisenhower also clashed in a less visible legislative arena when they differed over an obscure reclamation project in Colorado. The interaction between the two men over the Fryingpan-Arkansas project illustrates the complex relationship between the Speaker and the president. In this case, Rayburn frustrated Eisenhower, and the water project, which the president badly wanted, was not acted upon in the House between 1953 and 1960. Authorization for the Fryingpan project did not occur until the Kennedy administration, and actual construction took place in the years after Rayburn's death.[44]

The concept of a Fryingpan-Arkansas project had originated during the 1930s to move water from the western slope of the Colorado Rockies, where rainfall was more abundant, through a tunnel under the Continental Divide into arid eastern Colorado. The water would be directed into the Arkansas River and used to irrigate land along the banks as it flowed toward Kansas, Arkansas, and ultimately the Mississippi River. Fryingpan Creek in western Colorado would be the source of the water, hence the name of the project. As conceived, the project aimed to provide water for irrigation in eastern Colorado, supply electric power for the same region, and serve the water needs of Colorado Springs as well as communities along the Arkansas River. The genesis of the project went back to the 1930s, and the planning for it had been completed during the Truman administration in 1951. When the Eisenhower administration took office in 1953, the new secretary of the interior, Douglas McKay, also gave Fryingpan his endorsement.[45]

Rayburn's announced position on Fryingpan varied during the 1950s. He supported water projects in general, especially those for Texas, but he viewed them differently when they might affect his own state adversely. Since the Rio Grande had its headwaters in Colorado, Rayburn and his Texas colleagues looked warily at any scheme that might reduce the flow of water to the river that formed the border with Mexico.[46]

Dwight D. Eisenhower had argued during the 1952 campaign that "we need river basin development to the highest degree" but had stated that it should occur through a federal-state partnership rather than through the direct action of the national government alone. He sounded the same theme in his budget message to Congress in February 1953. Washington should promote reclamation projects, but the president warned against "exclusive dependence on Federal bureaucracy." At the outset of the administration, when issues of governmental economy loomed large, the policy was to restrict work on existing reclamation projects and to limit new ones from being started.[47]

By early 1954, however, the Eisenhower administration had decided to proceed with an Upper Colorado Basin project. This planned endeavor involved several western states and as many as six dams. Because of its importance and complexity, the Upper Colorado attracted the most public attention. Eisenhower also had become convinced of the merits of Fryingpan. During the summer of 1953, the president vacationed in Denver and returned there in 1954. While in the area, he heard from proponents of Fryingpan and became an enthusiastic convert to its construction. In the years that followed, he spoke out for it in his budget messages and State of the Union speeches, and he prodded Republican congressional leaders to get it enacted.[48]

There was no difficulty in the Senate. The upper house passed the bill either unanimously or by comfortable margins time and again. Prospects in the House were less promising. The supporters of Fryingpan had problems even getting their bill up for consideration on the House floor. There was substantial opposition within the Rules Committee, including the ranking Democrat, Howard W. Smith of Virginia, and the bill languished in the Rules panel. Finally, in July 1954, as the congressional session wound down, the Rules Committee offered a rule to structure the debate on Fryingpan. The Interior Committee had held hearings in 1953 and approved the measure. It reached the House in the hectic rush to adjourn during an election year.[49]

Rayburn opposed Fryingpan at this time. "I couldn't support the so-called Fryingpan Bill because it was an expenditure of $172,000,000, and it was doubtful that there would be any water left in the upper Colorado after California and Mexico got their share." He indicated that he could support the adoption of "a full program with reference to the whole river." Led by economy-minded Republicans, the California delegation, and Howard Smith, the House—by a vote of 195 against to 188 in favor—decided not to grant a rule. The Fryingpan project was dead for another year. Rayburn's lack of support frustrated the president's goal.[50]

As 1955 opened, Eisenhower returned to his advocacy of the Fryingpan project. His budget message contained an endorsement of the proposal, and he followed its legislative progress closely from the White House. In a meeting with Republican congressional leaders on May 10, 1955, the status of Fryingpan came up. House Minority Leader Joe Martin (R-Mass.) reported that "Rayburn is against Fryingpan," prompting one senator to ask why. Eisenhower's legislative aide, Jerry Persons, responded with a wry question that further revealed the internal White House attitude toward the Speaker: "Just to be difficult?"[51]

Three weeks later, Fryingpan came up again at a White House session of Republican lawmakers. "Where is Fryingpan?" asked the president, who also inquired about the Blue River near Denver and the Upper Colorado Basin Project. Jerry Persons observed that "Rayburn & Dems will not allow a partnership bill out—afraid of its success being demonstrated." Eisenhower came back with "what we're willing to do in this country in the name of politics is terrifying."[52] Joe Martin commented that "Fryingpan may get out of [committee]," but it would be "flagged in Rules." The president added that he "would certainly like to see 4 or 5 of these [projects] get started. Esp. Colo[rado] River. —shows we are willing to do where no private is available."[53]

As for the Speaker in 1955, his general opposition continued, but he assured one Coloradan who wrote to him, "I will keep my eye on it, and I want you to know that I will try to do the just and fair thing when it comes up in the House for consideration." As Speaker once again, Rayburn had a number of dam projects to consider. The Upper Colorado River Basin project contained the controversial Echo Park dam in the Dinosaur National Monument of Utah and Colorado that conservationists very much disliked. Rayburn told Joe Martin, who passed it on to the White House, that "the House would never approve the Echo Park dam." On the other hand, if Echo Park were taken out of the Upper Colorado plan, he said, "I will do all that I can to forward this project if and when it comes before the House of Representatives." By the summer of 1955, Rayburn knew that "if and when" in the case of both Fryingpan and the Upper Colorado River legislation meant the following year.[54]

President Eisenhower once again raised the visibility of the Fryingpan proposal when he "strongly" recommended it in his State of the Union message of January 5, 1956. By this time, Fryingpan's fortunes were intertwined with yet another controversial western dam project. The Hells Canyon Dam in Idaho had become the focus of an acrimonious dispute between Republicans who were working to have the Idaho Power Company build the dam and western Democrats, such as Senators Richard Neuberger and Wayne Morse of Oregon, who wanted the government to construct the facility. Senate Majority Leader Lyndon Johnson regarded support for a federally built dam at Hells Canyon as a key element in the Democratic campaign to carry northwestern states in 1956. As a result, the issue was joined in Congress during the spring.[55]

Some on Capitol Hill wished to link Hells Canyon and Fryingpan into a single package. Rayburn was not among them. He told his correspondents, "I think we are going to get the Fryingpan Bill up before this session of Congress is over," but he resisted attempts to tie the two projects together. That pleased the Coloradans. But there was a quid pro quo for Rayburn's support for Fryingpan. As he said to a Colorado leader, "I am certainly going to help out on Fryingpan, and would appreciate you people helping out a little on Hells Canyon." Indeed, the Speaker now claimed, "I have been supporting this project all along."[56]

Fryingpan came up in the House on July 26, 1956, in the form of debate over whether the legislation should be granted a rule for further debate. It was two days until adjournment. The Senate had once again passed a bill to authorize the project by a unanimous vote on July 12. Nonetheless, the proponents of Fryingpan in the House had received a setback when the Senate voted against a federally constructed dam at Hells Canyon. The Colorado project came to the floor without the support of the Rules Committee and its chairman. Indeed, Howard Smith told his colleagues, "There have been some funny things going on around here." In a departure from his "hidden-hand" style, President Eisenhower called Minority Leader Martin that morning "and said he hoped the bill would pass," news which Martin shared with the House.[57]

Rayburn's role in these events is somewhat conjectural. Two days later he said, "I did get a rule out of the Committee for the consideration of the Fryingpan legislation, but there was so much opposition in the House that it was defeated, and we will have to try to get back to it next session." After spirited debate, the vote in 1956 was 179 in favor of granting a rule and 194 against.[58]

Another two years went by before Fryingpan again reached the House floor in any form. President Eisenhower again recommended the project in his 1957 budget message. The Interior Committee held hearings in May and July 1957, but the legislation received no further action until just before adjournment in August 1958. On the 15th, the House Rules Committee granted the Fryingpan bill a rule, and the possibility of direct consideration arose. The chairman of the Interior Committee, Wayne Aspinall of Colorado, asked for a whip check on the measure. The poll showed 36 Democratic votes in favor, 59 against, 4 leaning toward the bill, and 10 leaning against, with 108 members either absent or undecided. As a result, the House did not consider the bill before Congress adjourned.[59]

For Dwight Eisenhower, there was no doubt in his mind who was responsible for the inaction on Fryingpan. His personal secretary, Ann Whitman, recalled an occasion when the president's special counsel asked him to sign a water project bill in which Rayburn was interested. "Eisenhower tartly asked why he should sign the measure when the administration's Fryingpan-Arkansas water project, approved by the Senate, had been defeated in the Democratic-controlled House." The aide noted that the Speaker "had helped with foreign aid, etc. President very reluctantly signed."[60] During the Kennedy administration and after Sam Rayburn's illness, which later proved fatal, had commenced, Fryingpan passed the Congress and was constructed. This single water project, however, illustrates how complex the Rayburn-Eisenhower relationship was in its day-to-day operations during the 1950s.

The tensions between Rayburn and Eisenhower climaxed during the 1959 fight for the controversial labor reform legislation, the Landrum-Griffin Act, an episode from the Speaker's career that deserves greater scrutiny. Scholars have argued that Rayburn's relationship with Eisenhower was one of cooperation or even Democratic domination. Furthermore, Sam Houston Johnson, the brother of the Senate majority leader, remembered that "Eisenhower couldn't buy toilet paper without Lyndon Johnson and Sam Rayburn's approval since 1955." Evaluating Rayburn for the 1950s, scholars have emphasized his apparent dominance of the congressional scene. A more thorough analysis of his activities in that period, however, reveals that the Speaker faced challenges from Eisenhower and the Republicans, from liberals in his own party, and from conservative Democrats in Congress. The GOP distrusted the Speaker. For example, Joe Martin declared in a 1957 meeting with Eisenhower and other Republican leaders about the fate of a tax program for helping small business, "I wouldn't be lulled to sleep by anything Mr. Rayburn says—because he's playing politics this year. That may be an understatement!" Furthermore, when the question of reappointing Robert Bartley, Rayburn's brother-in-law, to the Federal Communications Commission came up in March 1958, an Eisenhower partisan argued, "Bob is a good boy, but why reward the Speaker, who certainly would not return the favor? Why offend the millions of Eisenhower Democrats who hate Rayburn's guts? Bob's reappointment would add credence to the popular belief that Sam Rayburn has more power now than he had under Truman."[61]

At the same time, Rayburn heard more and more voices within the Democratic Party urging a greater commitment to a more activist agenda. In April 1955 Rayburn heard from a West Virginian, who stated: "Many of us democrats are discouraged by the lack of liberal legislation." With memories of his wartime problems still fresh in his mind, Rayburn replied that "most of the things that have been done here during the Republican Administration have been the renewing and extending of liberal legislation that was enacted during the past Democratic Administrations. We are going along with the President when we think it is in the interest of the Country.... [But] we are giving them a pretty good licking" when we disagree. To another critic Rayburn explained, "I said in the campaign of 1954 when we were electing a Democratic Senate and House that we were not going to follow the gruesome, mean example set by the Republicans by building up hate against Eisenhower just because he was president and member of another party, as they built up hate against Roosevelt and Truman."[62]

The election of 1956 proved an important turning point for Rayburn and congressional Democrats. After Eisenhower's reelection, Rayburn told Truman that the GOP's failure to carry Congress was "about the biggest Republican defeat that I have seen in many years. The nation wanted Mr. Eisenhower, at least they voted for him, but they certainly did not want the Republicans as they proved by their votes. It shows that we still have a virile Democratic Party, and with the proper leadership in the years to come we will be the Party in power again." Indeed, Rayburn believed that with proper leadership, the Democrats could control both the executive and legislative branches of government after the 1960 elections. Truman exhorted Johnson: "I think you and Sam are in the places where you can put the Democratic Party in the lead where it belongs. You can rest assured you are not going to get any leadership from the White House."[63] However, would the Rayburn version of moderate action prove popular with the leaders of the Democratic Party?

Soon after the 1956 elections Paul Butler, the new chair of the Democratic National Committee, proposed that the congressional leadership be included on the Democratic Advisory Council (DAC), a party-sponsored policymaking board primarily of nonelected leaders. Rayburn, Johnson, and Majority Whip Carl Albert of Oklahoma declined. Rayburn refused the invitation because he believed partisan political activity interfered with his duties as Speaker. By 1957 tension between Rayburn and Butler's DAC heightened. Paul Butler addressed the Democratic Congressional Club on May 15, 1957, and stressed that the DAC was "not antagonistic to the Congress." Yet Butler argued that there was no room for conservatives in Democratic Party ranks. So what would be the reaction of other national Democrats to this growing feud between Rayburn and Butler? Charles S. Murphy, one of Truman's personal advisers, assured the former president that "now that we don't have you in the White House . . . , we need this kind of thing ever so much more. It is natural for the Congressional leaders to be skeptical about this just as it is natural for them to disagree with the Executive about many things, and it needs to be handled so as to make sure it does not impinge on their prerogatives. I think that has been done, although the leaders still are not enthusiastic about the Advisory Council."[64]

Debate over civil rights policy proved a major sticking point for Rayburn and Butler as they feuded for control of the Democratic message. After Butler became chairman of the Democratic National Committee, he consistently advocated a more liberal policy for the Democratic Party, which involved, in part, a stronger stand on civil rights. Rayburn, though, believed such positions would isolate the party from its traditional southern base. In October 1958 Rayburn replied to Butler's criticisms that the Democratic Party should abandon its ties to white southerners by asserting: "Mr. Paul Butler knows before now that I think he is talking too much and not very sensibly at that. I assure you that I agree with nothing he said about the South and its importance to the Democratic Party, now and in the future." Yet the midterm elections in 1958 only weakened Rayburn's position. Liberal Democrats picked up additional votes in the House and intensified their drive for a greater voice in House affairs.[65]

By July 1959 the tensions between Butler and Rayburn came to a head in an incident that students of the Speaker's life have so far ignored. On Sunday, July 5, Butler appeared on the "Celebrity Parade" news program and attacked the Speaker's leadership capabilities. Joseph MacCaffrey moderated the affair, which included interviews with Butler and Congressman John Brademas. Both guests advocated a strong stand on civil rights. Butler declared that his DAC "[has] to try to influence the Democratic leadership of the Congress to come along with the national program, rather than the more conservative and moderate program which they are trying to follow." After his July 5 television interview, Butler denied that he had made a "personal attack upon any Democrat," yet at the same time he argued that "public response by telegraph and mail correspondence has supported the position I have taken on behalf of our Party by an exact ratio of 6 $\frac{1}{2}$ to 1." Yet Albert told a constituent in Oklahoma, "I simply cannot believe that this is a true indication of how the general public feels. When these controversies come up, I feel those who approve of one's stand are more prone to write than those who do not." At a later meeting with the Burro Club, Democrats supporting the leadership reminded Butler that he had said, "I'm hopeful that the attitudes and policies of the leadership will change. . . . I am inclined to believe that we won in 1958 not so much because of public satisfaction with the record of the Democratic Congress . . . as we won upon a negative vote against the Administration because of the lack of positive and aggressive leadership."[66]

A Texas Democrat defended Rayburn: "We cannot understand why Butler should be permitted to spit into the Democratic milk." Rayburn argued that Butler was "running wild" and had "fallen into the hands of the most radical left-wing elements of the Party—including his Advisory Council and the ADA [Americans for Democratic Action]." He defended the Democratic leadership by saying, "We are not here for the principal purpose of passing legislation that the President doesn't like. It is our duty here to pass legislation in the interest of the country, and then let the President do as he pleases . . . and let Paul Butler rave as much as he desires."[67]

After Butler's televised comments, House and Senate Democrats arranged for an internal poll of the support for Rayburn and Johnson as leaders of the party in Congress. The process became an unusual semi-public referendum on the Speaker and his leadership, with members of Congress vetting their positions in the national press. Robert G. Spivack, the Washington correspondent of the *New York Post*, conducted the survey. Although Rayburn received predictable support from the South and the West, some of the younger members did not declare their enthusiasm for the Speaker as readily as did their senior colleagues. That Rayburn had to resort to this kind of public affirmation of his authority was an indication that his power was not what it had been. Carl Albert gave the Speaker's office regular reports about the Spivack poll of congressional Democrats. Frank Chelf, a Democrat from Kentucky, told Spivack that "our Congressional leaders are taking the only possible route to a successful program via compromise and mutual understanding by working together and what's more, being realistic because there are some things in the platform that, while they read well and sound better, really are not very practical." Robert Byrd added that "it should not be our objective merely to strive to establish a voting record for the forthcoming political campaign." Furthermore, John E. Moss of California argued, Congress should not feel compelled to follow the dictates of a national party platform because "Congress is a more contemporary body than a national convention." A Texas Democrat put the matter even more bluntly to Butler: "It ill becomes a political accident like yourself to speak in derogatory terms about the great Sam Rayburn. I freely predict that when your bones are forgotten dust the name of Sam Rayburn will live on enshrined in the hearts of the American people."[68]

Against the backdrop of this intraparty political struggle, Rayburn faced one of the most difficult tests of his congressional leadership. As part of his planned race for the presidency in 1960, John F. Kennedy had been advocating legislation providing for increased penalties for labor racketeering. How would Rayburn handle this political demand that had the potential of further dividing the party along liberal, labor, and conservative lines? Rayburn's role in the labor racketeering legislation fight contrasts with the public persona he had developed. In the mid-1950s he told an interviewer, "I honestly believe that teamwork is the way to get work done. If I'm on the team, I'll either play with it, or get off." But labor reform legislation had been a constant problem for Congress in the late 1950s that did not lend itself to cooperation. When the Senate Republican Policy Committee issued a document on labor's political contributions, labor leaders, including Walter Reuther, expressed their anger with Johnson and Rayburn for not answering the argument. A Johnson staffer, however, noted that the Republican Policy Committee routinely issued such statements and that to answer them would give them greater public scrutiny than they deserved.[69]

Indeed, Rayburn did not handle this policy debate with great skill. Rayburn stalled action on the Kennedy-Ives bill in 1958 until August 18, when the House refused to consider the proposal under a suspension of the rules. The Speaker was "unhappy" with accusations he had killed the bill. Kennedy, despite his advocacy of the bill, came to Rayburn's defense. The Labor Department, meanwhile, debated what role the administration should take with regard to Rayburn's delaying tactics. Secretary of Labor James Mitchell criticized House members for "[surrendering] against the Democratic leadership." Mitchell's staff presented three options for Republicans. First, the GOP could limit its attacks on Rayburn, hope that no legislation passed, and use that against Democrats in the midterm elections. Another option involved heavy lobbying for labor legislation and downplaying Kennedy's contribution to any bill that resulted. Finally, Labor Department officials suggested pushing for compromise on the Kennedy-Ives bill.[70]

In early January 1959 Rayburn explained his actions on the Kennedy-Ives bill. "I did hold up this bill until the report on a Labor Welfare Bill was filed. Until they acted on the welfare bill, I did not think it would be wise to send the second bill to the Committee because I feared the welfare bill might get tangled up in an argument over the Kennedy-Ives bill, thus, resulting in no bill at all." The Speaker complained that "after the Republicans had gone around accusing the Democrats of doing nothing to pass this legislation, only 41 out of the 201 Republicans in the House voted for it."[71] In the end, though, Rayburn's strategy simply provided Republicans with ammunition in the 1959 fight while further weakening his base within the Democratic Party.

Republicans saw their opportunity and pressured the divisions within the Democratic Party. Barry Goldwater told a Texas audience: "I look to the leadership of Lyndon Johnson and Sam Rayburn to do something about Hoffa and Ruther [*sic*]. . . . If I know Lyndon and the Speaker, Mr. Rayburn, they'll do something about these bums! If they don't, it will be a day they will never forget!" Eisenhower told Congress in January 1959 that "complete and effective labor-management legislation, not a piecemeal program, is essential to assure the American public that true, responsible collective bargaining can be carried on with full protection to the rights and freedoms of workers and with adequate guarantees of the public interest."[72]

Rayburn tried during the first half of 1959 to find a way to frame labor legislation that would not split the Democrats in Congress, but he lacked the ultimate clout that Eisenhower possessed. Furthermore Rayburn suffered as a result of the divisions both within the Democratic Party and within organized labor. Indeed, the real problem for Democrats was getting a bill out that contained stiffer penalties but also protected the interests of organized labor. George Reedy, a Johnson aide, told his boss, "Our basic difficulty—which is not understood by Meany—is that we cannot afford to have a Democratic Congress pass a *truly* anti-labor bill. And yet, that is almost certainly what he will get from the House—and perhaps from the Senate—if Title VI remains in the bill." Rayburn told one Texan, "It is just too bad that some people in the labor movement do things to cast reflection on all others. This rackets game among some of those high in the unions is a distressing thing to all of us here. We are most seriously considering bringing forward legislation that will put the racketeer out of business whether he is in the Teamsters Union or belongs to any other order of labor." Yet the Speaker realized that "there is no law that we could pass that would keep Hoffa, you, me, or anyone else from saying anything we wanted to say that would not be treasonable. I think Hoffa has already found he went too far and has been trying to straddle out of it ever since." In the middle of July, Rayburn met with George Meany "and some of the other labor maharajahs." Rayburn's aide, D. B. Hardeman, remembered that "Meany said . . . Hoffa some time ago had a meeting of all the attorneys representing the Teamsters, and they couldn't find a hotel room large enough to hold them—there were over 500."[73]

At the end of July, House Republicans appealed to Eisenhower, saying,

"We do not have the votes to pass the Landrum-Griffin bill [a new version of the Kennedy-Ives bill]. It is the consensus of the undersigned that a personal [television] plea from you to the American people to get behind the substitute bill could make it possible for this bill to become law. It is estimated that Bob Kennedy, on his two recent [television] appearances, had a viewing audience of 50 million people. The mail response to his appearances is the largest since Truman fired MacArthur. If we did not feel that the American people are entitled to know the truth, we would not be making this request of you, Mr. President."[74]

In the summer of 1959, while House Republicans appealed to Eisenhower for a televised statement, Rayburn was still dithering about what kind of statement he might issue. Roscoe Drummond recommended that Rayburn write a letter to every Democrat in the House on the eve of the vote on the labor bill and use the prestige of office to pass the measure. Drummond believed the letter should be released to the press to increase its prestige. Reedy, not sure whether the Speaker would accept such a plan, argued: "If he could be persuaded, it would cut through the fog and give the House members some elbow room. If the Speaker won't do it, the idea should be rejected out of hand." Reedy believed such a letter from Rayburn would "put Halleck in the position of being 'tough' on American workingmen and women should he try to argue against the letter."[75]

In early August Rayburn issued a public statement on the controversy surrounding the various labor legislation proposals in Congress. "I have said many, many times that legislation shouldn't be passed to punish somebody. It shouldn't be passed in heat or anger, and I am not accusing anybody of this on this bill. . . . There has been a great deal of talk about weak bills and strong bills. I am supporting the Committee bill. I think it does a splendid job. It controls racketeering, hot cargo, and extortion or shakedown picketing." Yet in his correspondence, Rayburn made clear that he believed the Landrum-Griffin substitute was intended as punishment.[76]

On August 6, 1959, the president made a case for the legislation in a nationally televised speech. Eisenhower asked Americans, "Has [Congress] . . . measured up to the minimum requirements I outlined to protect the American people? I regret to say that, as yet, the answer is no—definitely no." Tallies from the White House mail room indicated that the mail was "running 24 to 1 in support of the President's position." The Speaker replied with a request for equal time to air the Democratic argument, but the major networks initially declined. Yet Rayburn prevailed and responded to the president on August 10 with his own nationwide radio address. The Speaker argued, "The middle road—the road of reason and fair play—is a hard one to walk, but more often than not it is the path of common sense and justice. When a bill is being fought by both Jimmy Hoffa and the labor haters, that in itself is a pretty good recommendation." In a meeting with his legislative leaders on the Hill, Eisenhower noted that "Sam is making pitch about equal time—networks." Halleck praised the president's speech, but Eisenhower focused on Rayburn's response. The House minority leader then suggested that it was "about time we call these bills what they are: the Hoffa bill." Eisenhower agreed that might be some help.[77]

Indeed, Eisenhower won in the confrontation between president and Speaker, with Rayburn left looking ineffectual and contributing to the impression that he was on the decline. Furthermore, Ann Whitman noted in her diary that "the House passed the Landrum-Griffin labor bill (the one advocated by the President on television a week previously) against specifically Sam Rayburn and the Jimmy Hoffa lobby." Despite his loss, the Speaker retained the middle ground when he assured a constituent that the entire Congress opposed racketeering and explained that "the Senate passed a so-called Labor Bill and the House passed one that was somewhat different. The two bills are now in conference where I am hoping that a good compromise will be reached that will straighten out some things that have been happening in both labor and management so that the American people might have a little better chance."[78]

The battle over Landrum-Griffin demonstrated from the legislative perspective what the Butler feud showed from the political angle: Rayburn's influence in Congress and with his party was under siege. Indeed, Rayburn's problems with Congress moved into the national spotlight. *Newsweek* noted in September 1959 that "time was, on Capitol Hill, when Sam Rayburn's word made the nation's laws"; after listing his major defeats in the Eighty-sixth Congress on the increased gas tax, civil rights, and labor legislation, the magazine went on to ask "given the 284–153 majority the Democrats have in the House, why had Rayburn slipped so badly?" Indeed the writers for *Newsweek* provided the following answers for Rayburn's difficulties—miscalculations, ties to Johnson's presidential ambitions, and the presence of Charles Halleck as minority leader instead of the weaker Joe Martin. When a California Democrat complained about Rayburn's "dictatorial manner," the Speaker replied simply, "I have received your letter." Far from being a dictator, Rayburn's troubles lay with his World War II–era understanding of the importance of moderation in the face of a new generation of assertive Democrats. Closer to the point, one man complained that Rayburn "sat back and allowed the Republicans . . . to make a mockery of a free labor movement." Indeed, in November a jaded Rayburn gave a different assessment for his recent defeat. "Some labor leaders do not know who their friends are. A good many of them go on the say-so of other people and, of course, the representatives of the industries are mighty dumb on many occasions and on many issues."[79]

In the last year of his speakership, Rayburn's fortunes rebounded with the election of John F. Kennedy to the presidency and the celebrated, if narrow, victory in the fight to expand the House Rules Committee in early 1961. Yet when the battle for control of the House was joined, a favorable outcome for the Speaker was far from certain. The 1960 election had swelled the Republican ranks with an additional twenty-one members. The Rules Committee retained power over which legislation moved on to a vote in the full House and which legislation never emerged from the committee system. The battle pitted two powerful House icons, the moderate Rayburn and the conservative Rules Committee Chairman Howard Smith, against each other in a battle for prestige and influence. The prize was nothing less than control over the work of the House. Smith voiced the prejudices of conservative southern Democrats who opposed such measures as civil rights. Rayburn wanted mastery of the House chamber, and Kennedy feared for his legislative agenda at the hands of the recalcitrant Smith. Despite the eight-to-four split between Democrats and Republicans on the Rules Committee, a conservative coalition reflecting the interests of the GOP and southern Democrats usually controlled the committee because of the seniority system. Smith and William Colmer (D-Miss.) regularly joined with the four Republicans.[80]

Questions about Rayburn's leadership; the passage of civil rights, housing, education, and minimum wage legislation; and Democratic presidential politics converged early in 1960. On the heels of the Landrum-Griffin battle, the Democratic Speaker appeared less powerful in comparison with his Senate counterpart, Johnson, who was mounting a race for the White House. One liberal journal, *The New Republic*, editorialized its concerns that a Democratic victory in 1960 hinged on passage of civil rights and other liberal legislation. The editors argued that although Johnson would prevail in the Senate, if only because of his presidential ambitions, "seventy-eight-year-old Speaker Rayburn is no longer the master in his house. The combination that the new Minority Leader, Charles Halleck of Indiana, has formed with right-wing Southern Democrats led by Howard Smith of Virginia is proving too much for him." Under Halleck's tenure the minority party took a more partisan tack on House affairs, as exemplified by the appointment of conservative Republicans to the Rules Committee in place of departing moderates. Advocating the restructuring of Rules away from the seniority system so that it provided instead for majority policy initiatives, *The New Republic* suggested a strategy whereby Rayburn could bypass Smith and his Rules Committee, which controlled access to the House floor, but doubted the move would ever be made. What *The New Republic* and other liberal opinion makers wanted was a return to the all-powerful Rayburn that existed only in legend.[81]

Rayburn had had problems with Smith and the Rules Committee throughout his years as Speaker. One Rayburn backer explained that "no man was ever more abused or frustrated by another man than Mr. Rayburn was by the second best legislator in the House, Howard Smith." In 1944, Rayburn complained that Smith had used his committee for legislative instead of procedural activities. In 1955, Rayburn recognized that the "Committee on Rules is a pretty ticklish thing." House liberals had asked for relief from the restrictive practices of the Rules Committee in 1958. The Democratic Party platform, adopted in July 1960, urged several reforms, including civil rights, housing, minimum wage, education, and health care legislation. Kennedy and Johnson wanted a special session of Congress to pass these items and to boost their campaign. But in August 1960, criticism of the Rules Committee climaxed when the southern Democrat–Republican coalition halted all consideration of liberal legislation in the special session. Richard Bolling (D-Mo.), a member of the Rules Committee and a Rayburn ally, precipitated the controversy by calling measures for committee votes he knew the Smith coalition would defeat.[82]

In the weeks after the election, Democrats discussed the appropriate strategy with regard to the House Rules Committee. Stewart Udall, an Arizona congressman who would become secretary of the interior in the new administration, advised a Kennedy aide that any reform plan for the Rules Committee would survive only if it had Rayburn's support. Udall argued, "The only plan which has a fighting chance in the House must be the Rayburn plan." Yet Udall worried because "the Speaker has been notoriously 'soft' in matters of discipline. . . . I hope our August fiasco has stiffened him and strongly feel that forceful presidential urging will be required to make him lead this fight."[83]

Aware of the pressure on Rayburn for action, supporters of Smith and the Rules Committee lobbied hard for their cause. The Southern States Industrial Council, a group that billed itself as "the voice of the conservative South," opposed efforts to "emasculate the Rules Committee . . . because such changes . . . would open the door to all sorts of vicious legislation." Smith and Halleck met after the election and plotted strategy to prevent changes to the Rules Committee. Both Smith and Colmer cautioned conservatives of the liberal attacks on the structure of their committee.[84]

In early December, Rayburn worried that Smith and Colmer were "trying to raise a ruckus in Washington about Committee assignments, especially the Committee on Rules." To prevent these problems from distracting the new Congress, Rayburn suggested that the caucus delay the naming of any committees beyond the Ways and Means, which functioned as the Committee on Committees. "I want as little done at the caucus as possible for obvious reasons because if we start naming sitting members of other committees we get into a ruckus about some of them." Clarence Cannon (D-Mo.), the chairman of the Appropriations Committee, advised Rayburn that after an informal survey he expected "every Democrat to get together on a program which we can all endorse" after Kennedy's inauguration. To Cliff Davis (D-Tenn.), Rayburn reported Smith and Colmer's overtures to Halleck and the Republican leadership, then asserted, "but I know that friends like you are going to tell them that in the caucus and otherwise you are going to stand by the Speaker. I think their little group can be smothered out pretty fast."[85]

Believing it the least offensive route to a productive session of Congress, Rayburn considered replacing Colmer because the Mississippi Democrat had bolted the national ticket in the November election. Furthermore, Rayburn reasoned, the decision to purge was a matter for the caucus, whereas the enlargement plan would go to the House floor. For all the problems Smith and the conservative coalition made for Rayburn, the Speaker remained protective of his turf. Rayburn indicated the Rules Committee problem was "utterly" an internal House matter and advised the president-elect to remain aloof. As the new year unfolded, Rayburn debated between enlarging the Rules panel and removing Colmer. The Speaker met with the committee chair in early January, and Smith dismissed talk of enlarging his committee. At that point, Rayburn spoke of purging Colmer and found a more cooperative Smith, who wanted to retain his Mississippi colleague on the committee. By the middle of January, Rayburn backed off Colmer. Instead he sought an enlarged committee when Carl Vinson (D-Ga.) and Francis E. Walter (D-Pa.) promised help with procuring southern Democratic votes for the enlargement resolution. Rayburn believed that alternative was a "painless way" to disarm the conservatives and "the way to embarrass nobody if they didn't want to be embarrassed." A resolution providing for three new members went to the Democratic caucus, where Rayburn, using party discipline, pushed for nonbinding instructions that Rules Committee Democrats bring the matter to the House floor.[86]

As the opening of the Eighty-seventh Congress drew near, Rayburn explained the controversy. "The issue is very simple. Shall the elected leadership of the House run its affairs, or shall the chairman of one committee run them?" The Democratic Party caucus approved the plan on January 18, and the Rules Committee reported the resolution to the floor on January 24. Yet the probability of victory was far from certain. Halleck applied tremendous pressure to stave off the enlargement proposal, even grabbing, shaking, and spitting at one unlucky Republican who supported the expansion proposal. Opposition strength increased as the vote approached. Business leaders waged a letter-writing campaign to Congress.[87]

Rayburn attended the first weekly leadership breakfast meeting at the White House on the 25th. Kennedy asked about the pending vote to enlarge the Rules Committee. Because Carl Albert's office had run a whip check, Rayburn admitted to a shocked audience: "Yes, as a matter of fact, I don't think we have the votes. It's very, very difficult, and we've had compromise after compromise on what to do with the Rules Committee, but now this expansion and the assignment of these new members to the Rules Committee would give us, as we saw it, just a majority, that's all, to bring your program to the floor." After the meeting concluded, Kennedy and his legislative liaison, Lawrence O'Brien, agreed that Rayburn must postpone the vote. Kennedy called the Speaker, invited him back to the White House, and urged him to delay the vote for a week. After taking a head count, administration officials had estimated the enlargement proposal would fail by seven votes on a best-case scenario. Although administration partisans believed the Speaker had lost touch with the pulse of his chamber, Bolling argued, "we developed as good a counting system in Rayburn's last four or five years as there ever has been in the House." Indeed, Carl Albert ran several whip checks for the Speaker, and frantic telegrams went out to uncommitted and absent Democrats seeking their support. Furthermore, the House leadership kept a list of likely Democratic opposition to the Rules change. Nevertheless, when Rayburn postponed the House vote from January 27 to the 31st, Halleck argued, "the New Frontier is having trouble with its first round-up."[88]

Announcement of the postponement triggered more suggestions for compromise. On January 27, Vinson and Walter met with Smith and sought a compromise. Smith assumed their failure to reply the following day meant the rejection of his plan. Smith and those Democrats who fought the Rayburn initiative had agreed to let stand for debate the five major planks of the Kennedy program—federal medical care, federal aid to education, federal housing program, an increased minimum wage, and area redevelopment. The Rules Committee chairman said he would also make the appointment of conference committees easier and pass from the committee a resolution providing for changes in its composition. On the latter point Smith argued that the leadership could pass the measure immediately "or adopt the wiser course of waiting until the Committee on Rules in the opinion of the Leadership, acts in a manner contrary to the wishes of the House." Smith asserted that "those of us who oppose this packing scheme have offered every honorable solution for the sake of harmony." Recognizing the ploy for what it was, Rayburn rejected the Smith offer and noted the administration "may have forty bills!"[89]

By this point the fight had gone too far for a compromise. Rayburn told members who broached that subject: "Hell no. We're going to vote. I've met with Howard three times and he won't give an inch. The only way to avoid a vote is for me to abdicate and I won't do it. If they lick me, that's that. For the next three months, I'll have those who vote against me come to my office, and there'll be more ass-kicking than they ever dreamed possible." Hard edged and ready for a fight, Rayburn went to work securing the needed votes. Over the years he had accumulated numerous chits, and it was in this fight that the Speaker called for his favors. Bolling, Frank Thompson of New Jersey, Udall, and Robert F. Kennedy lobbied hard for the initiative. Furthermore, organizations such as the American Federation of Labor–Congress of Industrial Organizations (AFL-CIO) joined the fight.[90]

When the final vote arrived, Rayburn's leadership team was "precise on the number" in the "most intensively counted thing outside the Landrum-Griffin Bill." Rayburn prevailed by a vote of 217 to 212, which meant the addition of two Democrats and one Republican to the Rules panel and the end of six-to-six votes that had killed liberal legislation for decades. Debate lasted for one hour, and Rayburn made one of his few speeches from the floor. He asserted: "Let us move [the Kennedy] program. Let us be sure that we can move it. And the only way that we can be sure that this program will move when great committees report bills, the only way it can move, in my opinion, my beloved colleagues, is to adopt this resolution today." Twenty-two Republicans joined 195 Democrats in the affirmative, whereas 148 Republicans and 62 Democrats said no. The following day, some southern Democrats who bolted the Speaker found their plum committee assignments from the past sessions revoked.[91]

Naturally enough, the vote elicited praise and blame. One newspaper argued: "If the Administration thinks it has received an all-clear signal, we rate Tuesday's 5-vote mandate with Mr. Kennedy's 113,000 votes mandate of Nov. 8." An Oklahoman told Carl Albert he believed Rayburn handled the Rules Committee fight "masterfully. . . . I think his gambit was indeed risky insofar as sacrificing his own career was concerned when he had a cinch to accomplish the same thing otherwise. Speaker Rayburn is a true statesman. . . . We need the South. God bless them! Let's give them a little time and keep them on our side now and forever more."[92]

Who was responsible for the five-vote victory? Bolling argued that Rayburn "probably wouldn't have won that rules-packing fight without the Kennedy apparatus, but nobody could have won the fight without the Rayburn effort." Rayburn, though, interpreted his victory as a victory for a strong speakership. "When the House revolted against Speaker Cannon in 1910, they cut the Speaker's powers too much. Ever since I have been Speaker, I have been trying to get some of that power back for the office."[93] Although the vote affirmed Rayburn's power in 1961, its long-term consequences were less bright.

Kennedy knew the victory might prove Pyrrhic. "With Rayburn's own reputation at stake, with all of the pressures and appeals a new president could make, we won by five votes. That shows what we're up against." Even after the Rules Committee victory, O'Brien described what the administration perceived as "continuing serious problems in the House. Every major vote was by a short margin." Furthermore, in the years after Rayburn's death, some liberals complained that the Speaker's "regime snuffed out individualism."[94] This criticism reflected from another perspective the same frustrations that produced the Rules fight in the first place, namely a dissatisfaction with the seniority system and the bloodless style of leadership Rayburn personified. Therefore the challenges to Rayburn's authority as Speaker and his narrow triumphs demonstrate just how fine a line the Texan walked in an era in which the political culture he knew so well came increasingly under attack. It is only from an appreciation of the complex problems Rayburn faced that a sophisticated understanding of his years as Speaker can be developed.

By the time of his death in November 1961, Sam Rayburn had once again become a legislative icon in U.S. politics. During the several decades that have followed since Rayburn's passing, biographers and students of Congress have correctly stressed the many significant achievements of the Speaker's long career. He has been transformed into an idealized paragon of congressional excellence who can be held up as a historical contrast with his less-accomplished successors.

However, the scholarly deification of Rayburn has had the unintended consequence of reducing his legislative record to a series of adages and character sketches. Believing that all has been said about Rayburn and that his papers are sparse and unrevealing, historians and political scientists have regarded his life as a closed volume about which all the essential work has been done. Precisely the opposite is the case. It is time to move beyond Sam Rayburn as a statue frozen in history and to look anew at a master lawmaker, his victories and defeats, with the same intelligence, thoroughness, and insight that Rayburn himself brought to Capitol Hill.

NOTES

1. James Roosevelt Interview, March 26, 1979, Former Members of Congress, Inc., Project on "The Modern Congress in American History," Library of Congress.

2. Anne Marie Kilday, "Rayburn Invoked in Crime Bill Debate," *Dallas Morning News*, August 28, 1994, in which Speaker Tom Foley said: "I'm tired of hearing about Mr. Sam."

3. Quoted in Lewis L. Gould, "Mr. Sam and Three Senators," *Discovery* 13 (1993): 7–11.

4. Sam Rayburn (hereafter SR) to Harry S. Truman, August 12, 1952, in President's Secretary's Files, "Rayburn, Sam," Box 134, Harry S. Truman Papers, Harry S. Truman Library (hereafter HSTP, HSTL); *Public Papers of the Presidents of the United States: Harry S. Truman, 1952–1953* (Washington, D.C.: Government Printing Office, 1966), pp. 510–511.

5. SR to Henry Garvin, September 3, 1940, in Box 3R279, Sam Rayburn Papers, Center for American History, University of Texas at Austin (hereafter SRP) (first quote); *New York Times*, July 16, 1941, August 6, 1941; Lister Hill quoted in Jerry Greene to David Hulburd, July 25, 1941, in "Reports of Flanagan, Wilfrid Flescher, Kendell Foss, Jerry Greene," Box 18, Frank McNaughton Papers, HSTL; *New York Times*, August 12, 1941; *Congressional Record*, 77th Cong., 1st sess. (August 12, 1941): 6995–7077.

6. SR quoted in McNaughton to Hulburd, August 15, 1941, in "Frank McNaughton Reports, January-August 1941," Box 1, McNaughton Papers, HSTL.

7. For Rayburn's views on the likelihood of war, see McNaughton to Hulburd, August 15, 1941, in "Frank McNaughton Reports, January-August 1941"; McNaughton to Hulburd, December 4, 1941, in "Frank McNaughton Reports, December 1941," Box 1, McNaughton Papers, HSTL; see J. A. Benton to SR, August 9, 1941, in Box 3R285, SRP, for the quote.

8. *New York Times*, August 16, 1941 (first quote); McNaughton to Hulburd, August 15, 1941, in "Frank McNaughton Reports, January-August 1941," Box 1, McNaughton Papers, HSTL (second quote); SR quoted in McNaughton to Hulburd, September 18, 1941, in "Frank McNaughton Reports, September 1941," Box 1, McNaughton Papers, HSTL.

9. SR quoted in McNaughton to Hulburd, September 27, 1941, in "Frank McNaughton Reports, September 1941," Box 1, McNaughton Papers, HSTL.

10. McNaughton to Hulburd, October 3, 1941, in "Frank McNaughton Reports, October 1941," Box 1, McNaughton Papers, HSTL; *New York Times*, October 8, 1941; McNaughton to Hulburd, October 10, 1941, in "Frank McNaughton Reports, October 1941," Box 1, McNaughton Papers, HSTL; *Congressional Record*, 77th

Cong., 1st sess. (October 17, 1941): 8007–8042; (November 7, 1941): 8592–8680; Mc-Naughton to Hulburd, November 7, 1941, in "Frank McNaughton Reports, November 1941," Box 1, McNaughton Papers, HSTL; *New York Times*, November 9, 1941, November 11, 1941, November 13, 1941; *Congressional Record, 77*th Cong., 1st sess. (October 17, 1941): 8007–8042; (November 13, 1941): 8826–8891; *New York Times*, November 14, 1941, November 18, 1941.

11. SR quoted in Frank McNaughton to Hulburd, August 1, 1941, in "Frank McNaughton Reports, January-August 1941," McNaughton to Hulburd, October 3, 1941, in "Frank McNaughton Reports, October 1941" (second quote); SR quoted in McNaughton to Hulburd, November 6, 1941, in "Frank McNaughton Reports, November 1941," Box 1, McNaughton Papers, HSTL.

12. SR quoted in McNaughton to David Hulburd, November 21, 1941, in "Frank McNaughton Reports, November 1941," Box 1, McNaughton Papers, HSTL; SR to E. P. Litchfield, December 1, 1941, in Box 3R285, SRP (second quote); *New York Times*, November 27, 1941, November 28, 1941; *Congressional Record, 77*th Cong., 1st sess. (November 28, 1941): 9198–9247.

13. McNaughton to Hulburd, December 17, 1941, in "Frank McNaughton Reports, December 1941," Box 1, McNaughton Papers, HSTL.

14. SR quoted in McNaughton to Hulburd, March 20, 1942, in "Frank McNaughton Reports, March 1942," Box 2, McNaughton Papers, HSTL; SR to Mrs. William G. Holmes, March 13, 1942, in Box 3R290, SRP (second and third quotes). Rayburn sent several similar letters out to other constituents and concerned citizens. See the correspondence in Box 3R290; *Congressional Record, 77*th Cong., 1st sess. (December 3, 1941): 9363–9398.

15. SR quoted in McNaughton to James McConaughy, May 28, 1942, in "Frank McNaughton Reports, April-June 1942," Box 2, McNaughton Papers, HSTL; *New York Times*, May 31, 1942, June 17, 1942 (second quote).

16. SR quoted in McNaughton to McConaughy, July 3, 1942, in "Frank McNaughton Reports, July-August 1942," Box 2, McNaughton Papers, HSTL.

17. SR quoted in McNaughton to McConaughy, July 16, 1942, McNaughton to McConaughy, July 24, 1942, in "Frank McNaughton Reports, July-August 1942"; Franklin D. Roosevelt, *The Public Papers and Addresses of Franklin D. Roosevelt, with a Special Introduction and Explanatory Notes by President Roosevelt*, vol. 11, *Humanity on the Defensive, 1942* (New York: Harper and Brothers, 1950), pp. 364, 384–396; SR quoted in McNaughton to McConaughy, September 9, 1942, September 11, 1942, both in "Frank McNaughton Reports, September 1942"; SR quoted in McNaughton to McConaughy, October 2, 1942, in "Frank McNaughton Reports, October 1942"; all in Box 2, McNaughton Papers, HSTL.

18. SR quoted in McNaughton to McConaughy, September 10, 1942, in "Frank McNaughton Reports, September 1942," McNaughton to McConaughy, October 29, 1942, in "Frank McNaughton Reports, October 1942," Box 2, McNaughton Papers, HSTL.

19. SR quoted in McNaughton to McConaughy, November 20, 1942, in "Frank McNaughton Reports, November 15–30, 1942," Box 3, McNaughton Papers, HSTL; *New York Times*, January 6, 1943; SR to John J. Cochran, November 11, 1942,

in Box 3R290, SRP (second quote); McNaughton to McConaughy, January 7, 1943, in "Frank McNaughton Reports, January 1943," Box 3, McNaughton Papers, HSTL; *New York Times*, January 7, 1943, January 8, 1943.

20. SR quoted in McNaughton to McConaughy, March 13, 1943, in "Frank McNaughton Reports, March 1943," Box 3, McNaughton to McConaughy, May 28, 1943, in "Frank McNaughton Reports, May 1943," Box 4, McNaughton Papers, HSTL.

21. SR to Truman, November 10, 1946 (first quote); Truman to SR, November 13, 1946 (second quote), in President's Secretary's Files, "Rayburn, Sam," Box 134, HSTP; McNaughton to Bob Hagy, November 12, 1948, in "Frank McNaughton Reports, October-November 1948," Box 14, McNaughton Papers, HSTL.

22. D. B. Hardeman and Donald C. Bacon, *Rayburn: A Biography* (Austin: Texas Monthly Press, 1987), p. 393, mentions the tax credit proposal briefly. Stephen E. Ambrose, *Eisenhower*, vol. 2, *The President* (New York: Simon and Schuster, 1984), pp. 252–253, treats the episode from Eisenhower's point of view in a single paragraph; Robert Dallek, *Lone Star Rising: Lyndon Johnson and His Times, 1908–1960* (New York: Oxford University Press, 1991), p. 469, examines the tax credit battle from Johnson's vantage point; Ivan W. Morgan, *Eisenhower Versus "The Spenders": The Eisenhower Administration, the Democrats and the Budget, 1953–1960* (New York: St. Martin's Press, 1990), pp. 37–38, is based on newspaper accounts and looks at Rayburn's role very quickly.

23. *New York Times*, February 20, 1955.

24. Senate Committee on Finance, *$20 Texas Credit: Hearings Before the Committee on Finance, United States Senate*, 84th Cong., 1st sess., 1955, p. 13; *Public Papers of the Presidents of the United States: Dwight D. Eisenhower, 1955* (Washington, D.C.: Government Printing Office, 1959), pp. 17 (third quote), 97 (second quote).

25. SR to R. B. Chandler, February 4, 1955, SR to O. O. Ford, March 3, 1955, SR to Reginald Kiefer, March 4, 1955, Box 3R421, SRP.

26. SR Speech, September 10, 1954, Sam Rayburn, Correspondence, 1954–1961, Box 115, Post-Presidential Files, Charles S. Murphy to Stephen A. Mitchell, November 5, 1954, Box 105, Charles S. Murphy Correspondence, 1953–1954, Post-Presidential Files, HSTP, HSTL.

27. *New York Times*, January 4, 1955; Carl Albert, with Danney Goble, *Little Giant: The Life and Times of Speaker Carl Albert* (Norman: University of Oklahoma Press, 1990), p. 210.

28. *New York Times*, February 20, 1955; N. G. Sherouse to SR, March 2, 1955, Box 3R421, SRP.

29. Morgan, *Eisenhower Versus "The Spenders,"* p. 37.

30. *New York Times*, February 24, 1955.

31. Ibid., February 22, 1955.

32. James C. Hagerty Diary, February 22, 1955, Box 1a, Dwight D. Eisenhower Library, Abilene, Kansas, hereafter DDEL (quotations); there are further notes of the February 22, 1955, meeting in Legislative Meetings Series, Office of the Staff Secretary, White House Box 2, DDEL. Eisenhower said of Rayburn in these notes that "he's complete partisan & obliged to members."

33. Hagerty Diary, February 22, 1955.

34. Hagerty Diary, February 22, 1955, has his acerbic comments prepared for Eisenhower; for what the president actually stated, see *Public Papers of the Presidents of the United States: Dwight D. Eisenhower, 1955*, p. 282; *New York Times*, February 24, 1955, for Rayburn's response.

35. *Public Papers of the Presidents of the United States: Dwight D. Eisenhower, 1955*, p. 291; *New York Times*, February 24, 25, 1955.

36. Carl Albert to Torbert McDonald, February 21, 1955, John McCormack to Carl Albert, February 22, 1955, and "Whip Poll on $20 Tax Credit," Legislative Series, Box 26, Folder 59, Carl Albert Papers, Carl Albert Congressional Research and Studies Center Congressional Archives, University of Oklahoma, Norman, Oklahoma, hereafter CAP.

37. *New York Times*, February 25, 1955; for Rayburn's comments, see *Congressional Record*, 84th Cong., 1st sess. (February 25, 1955): 2170.

38. *New York Times*, February 26, 1955, for the congressional vote totals.

39. Hagerty Diary, February 25, 1955, Box 1a, DDEL.

40. SR to Kathleen Voigt, March 4, 1955, Box 3R421, SRP; notes on meeting of March 1, 1955, Legislative Meetings Series, Office of the Staff Secretary, Box 2, DDEL.

41. "The Tax Handout," *New York Times*, February 26, 1955; Ralph Yarborough to SR, March 12, 1955, SR to Yarborough, March 25, 1955, Box 3R421, SRP.

42. Dallek, *Lone Star Rising*, p. 469; Morgan, *Eisenhower Versus "The Spenders,"* p. 38.

43. SR to N. G. Sherouse, March 25, 1955, Box 3R421, SRP; *New York Times*, August 28, 1955.

44. For general background on the Fryingpan-Arkansas water project, see House of Representatives, *Fryingpan-Arkansas Project, Colorado*, 87th Cong., 1st sess., 1961, H. Rept. 694; Roscoe Fleming, "Water and Politics: From the Frying Pan into a Colorado-California Feud," *Frontier*, October 1954, pp. 7–8; "Frying Pan Project," *Life*, March 14, 1955. There is additional background on the project in Daniel Tyler, *The Last Water Hole in the West: The Colorado–Big Thompson Project and the Northern Colorado Water Conservancy District* (Niwot: University Press of Colorado, 1992), pp. 292–295.

45. House Committee on Interior and Insular Affairs, *Fryingpan-Arkansas Project, Colorado: Hearings Before the Subcommittee on Irrigation and Reclamation of the Committee on Interior and Insular Affairs on H.R. 236*, 83d Cong., 1st sess., 1953, pp. 1–2, 6–7, 12–19; James Earl Sherow, *Watering the Valley: Development Along the High Plains Arkansas River, 1870–1950* (Lawrence: University Press of Kansas, 1990), pp. 130, 170, 171.

46. Rayburn's attitude toward public power comes through in his September 10, 1954, speech cited in Note 26.

47. Elmo Richardson, *Dams, Parks and Politics: Resource Development and Preservation in the Truman-Eisenhower Era* (Lexington: University Press of Kentucky, 1973), pp. 74 (quotations), 114–115.

48. *Public Papers of the Presidents of the United States: Dwight D. Eisenhower, 1954* (Washington, D.C.: Government Printing Office), pp. 454, 659; *Congressional*

Record, 84th Cong., 2d sess (July 26, 1956): 14800, where Joe Martin referred to the president's "personal inspection" of the project.

49. *Congressional Record*, 83d Cong., 2d sess (July 28, 1954): 12449; *Public Papers of the Presidents of the United States: Dwight D. Eisenhower, 1954*, p. 659; Joseph Shelley to SR, July 20, 1954, Elmo J. Osborne to SR, July 22, 1954, Box 3R422, SRP.

50. SR to Elmer J. Osborne, July 31, 1954, Box 3R422, SRP; *Congressional Record*, 83d Cong., 2d sess. (July 28, 1954): 12453.

51. *Public Papers of the Presidents of the United States: Dwight D. Eisenhower, 1955*, p. 159; Meeting of May 10, 1955, Office of the Staff Secretary, Legislative Meeting Series, Box 2, DDEL.

52. Meeting of June 1, 1955, Office of the Staff Secretary, Legislative Meeting Series, Box 3, DDEL.

53. Ibid.

54. SR to Maxon L. Bevens, April 19, 1955, Box 3R422, SR to Isaac Smoot, August 1, 1955, Box 3R435, SRP; L. A. Minnick to Director Hughes, June 1, 1955, White House Central File, Subject Series Congress, Box 18, DDEL.

55. *Public Papers of the Presidents of the United States: Dwight D. Eisenhower, 1956* (Washington, D.C.: Government Printing Office, 1956), p. 16; Alva B. Adams to SR, May 15, 1956 (quotation), James W. Meyers to SR, April 30, 1956, Box 3R435, SRP; Richardson, *Dams, Parks and Politics*, pp. 123–126; Mason Drukman, "Oregon's Most Famous Feud: Wayne Morse Versus Richard Neuberger," *Oregon Historical Quarterly* 95 (Fall 1994): 328–331; Johnson bracketed the Hells Canyon dam with the Fryingpan-Arkansas project in a speech of November 21, 1955, announcing his legislative program for 1956 after his recovery from his 1955 heart attack. See *Congressional Record*, 84th Cong., 2d sess. (January 17, 1956): 630.

56. SR to James W. Meyers, May 11, 1956 (first quote), SR to Alva B. Adams, May 17, 1956 (second quote), SR to John B. Farley, July 3, 1956 (third quote), Box 3R435, SRP.

57. *Congressional Record*, 84th Cong., 2d sess. (July 23, 1956): 14798 (Martin quote), 14801 (Smith quote).

58. SR to Ike Griffin, July 28, 1956, Box 3R435, SRP; *Congressional Record*, 84th Cong., 2d sess. (July 23, 1956): 14801–14802.

59. *Public Papers of the Presidents: Dwight D. Eisenhower, 1957* (Washington, D.C.: Government Printing Office, 1957), p. 56; House Committee on Interior and Insular Affairs, *Fryingpan-Arkansas Project, Colo.: Hearings Before the Subcommittee on Irrigation and Reclamation of the Committee on Interior and Insular Affairs on H.R. 594*, 85th Cong., 1st sess. 1957; *Congressional Record*, 85th Cong., 2d sess. (August 15, 1958): 17907, Daily Digest, August 15, 1958, D581–D582, reporting action of Rules Committee; Wayne Aspinall to Carl Albert, August 15, 1958, Clair Engle to "Dear Colleague," August 16, 1958, Whip Poll of the Fryingpan-Arkansas Project, August 18, 1958, Legislative, Box 34, Folder 12, CAP.

60. Robert J. Donovan, *Confidential Secretary: Ann Whitman's 20 Years with Eisenhower and Rockefeller* (New York: E. P. Dutton, 1988), p. 76.

61. Transcript, Sam Houston Johnson Oral History Interview No. 3, June 9, 1976, by Michael L. Gillette, p. 4, Lyndon B. Johnson Library, Austin, Texas (hereafter cited as LBJL); Minutes of June 4, 1959, meeting, Box 4, Legislative Meetings

Series, Records of the Office of the Staff Secretary, DDEL; Wingate H. Lucas to Gerald C. Morgan, March 10, 1958, and Morgan to Lucas, March 13, 1958, both in White House Central Files—General File 41-A Endorsements, "Bartley, Robert T.," Box 380, DDEL.

62. Tom Zink to SR, April 27, 1955, SR to Zink, May 7, 1955; SR to Mrs. George Cox, June 1, 1955, all in Box 3R421, SRP.

63. SR to Truman, November 14, 1956, in Post-Presidential File, "Rayburn, Sam correspondence, 1954–61," Box 115, Truman to Lyndon B. Johnson, November 29, 1956, in Post-Presidential File, "Johnson, Lyndon B.—correspondence, 1955–58," Box 22, HSTP, HSTL.

64. Lyndon B. Johnson to SR, December 3, 1956, in "Rayburn, Sam, 2 of 4," Box 52, Lyndon B. Johnson Archives (hereafter cited as LBJA), LBJL; Carl Albert to Paul M. Butler, December 7, 1956, E. C. Gathings to Albert, December 11, 1956, both in Folder 7, Box 9, Series General "A," CAP; SR to Butler, December 8, 1956, in "Rayburn, Sam, 2 of 4," Box 52, LBJA, LBJL; Truman to Butler, December 13, 1956, in Post-Presidential File, "I. Political File, Advisory Council—Democratic National Committee—correspondence," Box 691, HSTP, HSTL; Minutes of the Meeting 84th–85th Democratic Congress Club, May 15, 1957, in Folder 10, Box 11, Series General "A," CAP; Charles S. Murphy to Harry S. Truman, August 7, 1957, in Post-Presidential File, "Democratic National Committee—Paul Butler," Box 65, HSTP, HSTL.

65. SR to Karl G. Hunt, October 25, 1958, in Box 3R463, SRP. For an idea of the involvement of the DAC in public policy debate, see *New York Times*, February 2, 1958, February 3, 1958, October 22, 1958, October 23, 1958, December 7, 1958, December 8, 1958, December 9, 1958.

66. *New York Times*, June 15, 1959, July 7, 1959; transcript of "Celebrity Parade," attached to Butler to Albert, July 15, 1959, in Folder 44, Box 15, Series General, CAP; Butler to SR, July 15, 1959, in Box 3R480, SRP; Albert to Charles B. Duffy, July 18, 1959, in Folder 44, Box 15, Series General, CAP; Butler quoted in "Some Highlights of Mr. Paul Butler's Appearance Before the Burro Club, July 21, 1959," in Box 3R461, SRP.

67. Earl B. Mayfield to SR, July 7, 1959, in Box 3R480, SR to D. W. Gilmore, July 8, 1959, in Box 3R461, SRP.

68. *New York Times*, July 11, 1959, July 12, 1959, July 14, 1959, July 16, 1959, July 17, 1959, July 18, 1959, July 19, 1959, July 20, 1959, July 21, 1959, July 22, 1959, July 25, 1959; "Carl Albert Called in the Following Report on the Spivack Wire," in Box 3R463, SRP; Frank Chelf to Robert G. Spivack, July 11, 1959; Robert Byrd to Spivack, July 11, 1959; John E. Moss to Spivack, July 13, 1959, all in Folder 44, Box 15, Series General, CAP; R. D. McCain to Paul Butler, July 11, 1959, in "McCain, R. D.," Box 51A, Wright Patman Papers, LBJL.

69. Quoted in Edward Boyd, "Mr. Speaker, The Dynamo of Capitol Hill," *American Magazine* (April 1955): 98. For a detailed account of labor legislation in the 1950s, see R. Alton Lee, *Eisenhower and Landrum-Griffin: A Study in Labor-Management Politics* (Lexington: University Press of Kentucky, 1990); George Reedy to Johnson, July 29, 1958, in "Reedy: Labor 1 of 2," Box 428, Senate Papers, LBJL.

70. *New York Times*, June 19, 1958, June 23, 1958, July 18, 1958, July 31, 1958, August 3, 1958; *Congressional Record*, 85th Cong., 2d sess. (August 18, 1958):

18260–18288; Confidential Memorandum, "Position on Labor Legislation," in "1958—Secretary's Personal File—Confidential—Miscellaneous (2)," Box 37, James P. Mitchell Papers, DDEL.

71. SR to Frank H. Jonas, January 14, 1959, in Box 3R478, SRP.

72. GFD to Buzz, January 16, 1959, in "Reedy: Memos January 1959," Box 428, Senate Papers, LBJL; Dwight D. Eisenhower to the Congress of the United States, January 28, 1959, in "Labor Legislation," Box 12, Bryce Harlow Papers, DDEL.

73. *New York Times*, August 4, 1959; Reedy to Johnson, [January 1959], in "Reedy: Memos January 1959," Box 428, Senate Papers, LBJL; SR to L. L. Medley, April 13, 1959, SR to C. Andrade, May 22, 1959, both in Box 3R478, SRP; D. B. Hardeman to Maury Maverick, Jr., July 14, 1959, in "Maury Maverick, Jr., 1958–60," Box 14, D. B. Hardeman Papers, LBJL.

74. Carroll D. Kearns et al., to Eisenhower, July 31, 1959, in White House Central Files—Official File 124, Box 631, DDEL.

75. Reedy to Johnson, August 1, 1959, in "Reedy: Memos August 1959," Box 430, Senate Papers, LBJL.

76. "Speaker Rayburn's Comments on Proposed Labor Legislation," August 3, 1959, SR to Fred L. Kemp, August 5, 1959, both in Box 3R478, SRP.

77. *New York Times*, August 6, 1959, August 7, 1959; *Public Papers of the Presidents of the United States: Dwight D. Eisenhower, 1959* (Washington, D.C.: Government Printing Office, 1960), pp. 569–570; William J. Hopkins to General Persons, August 10, 1959, in "Diary, August 1959 (2)," Box 11, Ann Whitman Diary Series, Ann Whitman File, DDE Papers as President, DDEL; *New York Times*, August 8, 1959, August 11, 1959; "As Speaker Rayburn Sees the Labor Issue," *U.S. News and World Report* (August 24, 1959): 90; Minutes of August 11, 1959 meeting, Box 6, Legislative Meetings Series, Records of the Office of the Staff Secretary, DDEL.

78. *New York Times*, August 14, 1959, August 15, 1959; Diary, Week August 7–15, 1959, in "Diary, August 1959 (2)," Box 11, Ann Whitman Diary Series, Ann Whitman File, DDE Papers as President, DDEL; *Congressional Record*, 86th Cong., 1st sess. (August 13, 1959): 15824–15868; (August 14, 1959): 15882–15892; SR to William J. Whitten, August 28, 1959, in 3R478, SRP; *Congressional Record*, 86th Cong., 1st sess. (September 4, 1959): 18115–18154.

79. "A Leader with Troubles: Division in the Ranks," *U.S. News and World Report* (September 7, 1959): 48; "Mr. Sam's Skid," *Newsweek* (September 7, 1959): 36, 38; Harold Orr to SR, April 28, 1959, SR to Orr, May 1, 1959, both in Box 3R480, SRP; Lowell D. Blanton to SR and Johnson, October 21, 1959, in Post-Presidential File, "Johnson, Lyndon B.—correspondence, 1958–63," Box 22, HSTP, HSTL; SR to Robert Oliver, November 9, 1959, in Box 3R480, SRP.

80. James N. Giglio, *The Presidency of John F. Kennedy* (Lawrence: University Press of Kansas, 1991), p. 37; Tom Wicker, *JFK and LBJ: The Influence of Personality upon Politics* (Chicago: Ivan R. Dee, 1991), pp. 30–39.

81. "It's Up to Mr. Sam," *The New Republic* 142 (February 8, 1960): 3–4; Hardeman and Bacon, *Rayburn: A Biography*, p. 449.

82. Transcript, Richard Bolling Oral History Interview, February 27, 1969, by Paige Mulhollan, p. 30, LBJL; Bruce J. Dierenfield, *Keeper of the Rules: Congressman Howard W. Smith of Virginia* (Charlottesville: University Press of Virginia, 1987),

pp. 104, 124–125, 136, 144, 162, 165–166, 172; SR to Bob Sikes, August 29, 1955, Box 3R420, Chet Holifield to SR, December 16, 1958, in Box 3R461, both in SRP; *New York Times*, August 29, 1960; Dallek, *Lone Star Rising*, p. 584.

83. Stewart Udall to Kenneth O'Donnell, November 22, 1960, Folder 1, Box 87, Stewart Udall Papers, University of Arizona Special Collections.

84. J. Clifford Miller, Jr., to Dear Member, November 29, 1960, in Folder 67, Box 42, Legislative Series, CAP; Dierenfield, *Keeper of the Rules*, pp. 176–177; Hardeman and Bacon, *Rayburn: A Biography*, p. 451.

85. SR to Clarence Cannon, December 2, 1960, Cannon to SR, December 8, 1960, both in Box 3U44, SR to Clifford Davis, December 7, 1960, in Box 3U45, all in SRP.

86. *New York Times*, November 13, 1960; Hardeman and Bacon, *Rayburn: A Biography*, p. 454; *New York Times*, December 20, 1960, January 9, 1961, January 12, 1961, January 13, 1961, January 18, 1961.

87. Hardeman and Bacon, *Rayburn: A Biography*, pp. 451 (Rayburn quote), 458; *New York Times*, January 19, 1961, January 25, 1961.

88. SR quoted in Transcript, Lawrence O'Brien Oral History Interview No. 1, September 18, 1985, by Michael L. Gillette, pp. 39–43; Bolling Oral History Interview, February 27, 1969, p. 4, both in LBJL; Albert to Philip J. Philbin, January 23, 1961; Albert to Jim Wright, January 23, 1961; Albert to Thaddeus J. Dulsk, January 23, 1961; Albert to William A. Burrett, January 24, 1961; Albert to Robert Nix, January 24, 1961; Whip Polls; all in Folder 80, Box 58; "Anticipated Democratic Votes Against Rules Change" [January 25, 1961], in Folder 76, Box 53, all in Legislative Series, CAP; *New York Times*, January 26, 1961.

89. Smith to Carl Vinson and Francis E. Walter, January 28, 1961, in Folder 76, Box 53, Legislative Series, CAP; *New York Times*, January 27, 1961; Rayburn quoted in Dierenfield, *Keeper of the Rules*, p. 177.

90. Rayburn quoted in Hardeman and Bacon, *Rayburn: A Biography*, p. 459; Bolling Oral History Interview, February 27, 1969, p. 17, LBJL; *New York Times*, January 29, 1961.

91. Bolling Oral History Interview, February 27, 1969, p. 4, LBJL; *Congressional Record*, 87th Cong., 1st sess. (January 31, 1961): 1580; *New York Times*, February 1, 1961, February 2, 1961.

92. *Tulsa World*, February 2, 1961; Aaron M. Mixon, Jr., to Albert, February 24, 1961, Folder 75, Box 53, Legislative Series, CAP.

93. Bolling Oral History Interview, February 27, 1969, p. 27, LBJL; Rayburn quoted in Hardeman and Bacon, *Rayburn: A Biography*, p. 451.

94. Kennedy quoted in John Morton Blum, *Years of Discord: American Politics and Society, 1961–1974* (New York: W. W. Norton, 1991), pp. 31–32; O'Brien Oral History Interview No. 1, September 18, 1985, pp. 100–104, LBJL; Frank Thompson, Jr., to Udall, February 26, 1963, in Folder 13, Box 107, Stewart Udall Papers, University of Arizona Special Collections.

8

Hale Boggs:
The Southerner as
National Democrat

Patrick J. Maney

President Bill Clinton still talks about the time he spent with Hale Boggs. It was an ephemeral moment in the Louisiana congressman's hectic schedule. Always in demand as a speaker, Boggs had traveled to San Antonio in October 1972 to address a gathering honoring House colleague Henry Gonzales. Clinton, then serving as the Texas coordinator for George McGovern's presidential campaign, was in the audience. After the talk he introduced himself to Boggs. The next day, Clinton drove the majority leader to the airport for the return flight to Washington. They talked politics on the way. The two were an odd couple: One was a bushy-haired, twenty-seven-year-old Yale law student and antiwar sympathizer; the other a fifty-eight-year-old congressman and staunch defender of U.S. involvement in Vietnam. Clinton was a political neophyte, Boggs a consummate insider who'd first been elected to the House six years before Clinton was born. Despite differences in age and politics, the future president sensed an immediate kinship with the elder statesman. Several days later Clinton called the congressman's office in Washington to encourage Boggs to make another trip to Texas. "Mr. Clinton was very enthusiastic about the good that Mr. Boggs could do," Boggs's secretary noted in a memo.[1]

What was it about Boggs that so intrigued the ambitious young Clinton? The older man's storied charm and charisma doubtless had something to do with it. But the real attraction was that Boggs, with the help of wife Lindy, had practically written the book on how to mesh national aspirations with the fast-changing racial realities of southern politics. His career taught lessons that southern moderates of Clinton's generation, who were looking for alternatives to the George Wallaces of their native region, were anxious to learn: How does one play a constructive role in Washington and still get elected back home?

Early Life, 1914–1940

Born in 1914, the third of six children, Thomas Hale Boggs grew up on the Mississippi Gulf Coast and in the New Orleans area. The Great Depression hit the family hard. His father, a bank cashier, found himself out of work for long stretches of time. To make ends meet, the family opened a tourist camp on their Mississippi property, but visitors were few and far between during those years of hard times. Long after Boggs became a successful politician, writer Larry L. King sensed in the man a "hard core" that had taken form during these early years—"some sly, tough, intelligent power, an essence hinting that if times got hard and he had no other choice, then Hale Boggs might go on the road and very successfully sell lightning rods." Boggs never had to sell lightning rods, but in the 1930s he did help put himself through Tulane University, where he graduated Phi Beta Kappa and earned a law degree, by peddling chewing gum and mail-order suits to fellow students.[2]

Boggs earned his greatest renown at Tulane as editor of the school newspaper, the *Hullabaloo*, where his coworkers included future notables Lindy Claiborne and Howard K. Smith. Believing, as many did, that greedy munitions makers and Wall Street financiers had pushed the United States into World War I, Boggs editorialized against rearmament and war. Not since "the mass murder scene that someone ironically described as a war to end war," he wrote in a typical piece, "has there been more need for student antiwar meetings and strikes."[3]

But Boggs was no radical. His antiwar views were fully in line with public opinion during the 1930s. Moreover, on matters relating to race relations, he gave no indication that he dissented from the prevailing Jim Crow practices of his native region. And when he wasn't railing at warmongers, he was extolling the virtues of fraternity life. An enthusiastic member of Beta Theta Pi, he subscribed to the view that "once a Beta, always a Beta, everywhere a Beta."[4]

"As long as I can remember," Boggs later recalled, "I wanted to be a member of Congress." The opportunity presented itself in the late 1930s, when Louisiana was rocked by a series of scandals perpetrated by the political descendants of the state's most famous politician, Huey Long, and shocking even by Louisiana's notoriously flexible standards. Boggs helped organize the People's League to oust the wrongdoers from office. In 1940, he himself won election to Congress on the promise of reform.[5] But he failed to secure a firm foothold in his New Orleans–area district, and in 1942 he went down to defeat. A year later he entered the Naval Reserve and served out World War II in Washington as a legal officer in the War Shipping Administration.[6]

Rise to Prominence, 1946–1960

In 1946, Boggs regained his seat—this time for good. From the beginning, he left no doubts that he aspired to a position of leadership. He arranged for introductions to key members of Congress, and he campaigned for the best committee assignments. He courted his colleagues, from the powerful to the lowly, as assiduously as he did his most influential constituents back home. Most important, he endeared himself to legendary House Speaker Sam Rayburn, of Texas, who took Boggs under his wing and groomed him for leadership. In the late afternoons, Rayburn would invite Boggs to a small room on the first floor of the Capitol, behind the members' dining room. This was the so-called Board of Education, and there, over scotch and bourbon, the Speaker would review the day's events and plot future courses of action with his top lieutenants. In addition to

Boggs, these included Carl Albert of Oklahoma, Wilbur Mills of Arkansas, Richard Bolling of Missouri, and, until his election to the Senate, Lyndon Johnson of Texas. To be invited to these sessions was, in the words of Carl Albert, "the prize most cherished by every member, freshman and veteran alike." Boggs had a standing invitation. Rayburn was also a frequent visitor to the Boggs home. A bachelor who had had a short and unhappy marriage, Rayburn would invite himself out in the evenings for dinner with the family.[7]

In 1949, Rayburn gave Boggs's career an additional boost by awarding him a seat on the most powerful committee in Congress, Ways and Means, which had jurisdiction over tax and trade legislation, social security, and a host of other critical matters. Boggs's new assignment was partly an award for having remained loyal to the Democratic party during the Dixiecrat revolt of 1948, and it helped him in his district by ensuring a steady flow of campaign contributions from oil companies eager to preserve the oil depletion allowance and from a multitude of other interests that stood to gain or lose from the actions of the principal tax-writing committee of Congress. Equally important, as a member of Ways and Means, Boggs automatically became a member of his party's Committee on Committees, which put him in a position to collect a lot of IOUs from his colleagues.[8] In his quest for standing, Boggs was aided immeasurably by wife Lindy, whom he had met at Tulane and married shortly thereafter. Descended from an old Louisiana family and a long line of politicians (including William C. C. Claiborne, Louisiana's first governor), Lindy quickly became one of the best known and most popular persons in Washington.

In 1955 Rayburn and Majority Leader John McCormack of Massachusetts designated Carl Albert as the majority whip. For Boggs, they created a new position in the leadership, the post of deputy whip. The way Rayburn operated, both the whip and deputy whip positions were largely honorary. Albert had so little to do in his new job that one of his top aides got bored and asked to be reassigned to the home office. As for Boggs, as one insider put it, "no staff, no nothing, just a paper job. But Albert didn't have anything to do, so Boggs had double nothing to do."[9] But it was the perception that counted, and on that score Boggs appeared to be climbing his way up the leadership ladder.

Boggs was also making his mark on the floor. In an era of increasing legislative specialization, he carved out for himself an expertise in international trade and taxation. A focus on overseas commerce made sense for a congressman who represented a port city. But it also meshed nicely with his personal interests. He took a real interest in foreign affairs, and unlike many of his colleagues, he loved to travel abroad. So Boggs schooled himself in the intricacies of international trade until he could speak more knowledgeably on the subject than just about anyone else on Capitol Hill. He believed that expanded trade was critical to economic growth, and he devoted himself to reducing trade barriers and lessening the tax burdens on the overseas investments of U.S. companies. Hale Boggs never became a household name. But by the late 1950s, he had made himself known to expansion-minded corporate executives throughout the country.[10]

Louisiana

While Boggs was making a name for himself in Washington he was also securing himself in his district. This was no easy task if for no other reason than that his district was in Louisiana, and Louisiana was—and probably still is—the toughest testing ground in all of American politics. Visiting politicians like Daniel Rostenkowski of Illinois still recall their first trip to New Orleans: "First of all, I didn't know anyone had elections on weekends," said Rostenkowski. "And then there was cheating in one of the parishes. It gets rough in Chicago, but I've never seen anything like what goes on down there."[11]

Surviving Louisiana's Darwinian politics was tough enough. But Boggs's national ambitions made the task all the more difficult, for some of the positions his House leadership role obliged him to take inevitably put him at odds with powerful constituents. There's no better example of the truth of Tip O'Neill's old chestnut about all politics being local than the career of Hale Boggs.

Boggs managed the tension between national ambition and local realities by developing a multifaceted strategy, the main component of which was broadening his electoral base. The truly notable thing about this broadening effort was his quiet recruitment of African Americans—long before the Voting Rights Act—into his electoral coalition. When Boggs first ran for Congress in 1940, fewer than a thousand blacks were registered to vote in the entire state, and even their votes were meaningless because Louisiana barred them from participating in the only election that really counted, the Democratic primary. But in 1944, the Supreme Court, in *Smith v. Allwright*, outlawed the white primary. Elsewhere in the South, white leaders promptly erected new barriers or strengthened old ones to prevent black citizens from taking advantage of the court's decision. In some parishes in Louisiana, white registrars simply turned out the lights and locked up the doors when they saw blacks coming to sign up to vote.[12]

But in south Louisiana, African Americans encountered less resistance to voting than in most places in the South. This was probably due to the area's more tolerant French-Catholic culture and the fact that blacks con-

stituted a small enough percentage of the electorate that they didn't un-
duly alarm whites.[13] Following the *Smith* decision, blacks registered to
vote in growing numbers. In 1946, when Boggs regained his seat in Congress, 3,000 African Americans in his district were eligible to vote. By
1956, nearly 23,000 blacks, composing 16 percent of the entire electorate,
had been added to the rolls.[14] Fully a decade before the passage of the
Voting Rights Act of 1965, Boggs was one of a small number of Deep
South congressmen with a significant percentage of registered black voters.[15]

Boggs was not the only southern politician to court black voters. But he
was more adept at it than most, and he inspired trust and respect from his
new constituents. He was "the first decent white politician I knew in
Louisiana," recalled black civil rights activist Avery Alexander. "He was
actually elected to office without calling us by that 'N' name and talking
about keeping us down."[16]

Boggs also broadened his base by reaching out to white, blue-collar
workers. He had begun his career as a crusader for good government,
which played well in the silk stocking neighborhoods of his district but
had limited appeal elsewhere. So he began to take more of an interest in
issues of concern to ordinary working people, issues like decent wages
and affordable housing. He forged a close alliance with organized labor,
which had a larger presence in the New Orleans area than in most other
areas in the South. All the while he refrained from the tried-and-true way
of getting white votes, that of playing the race card. Instead he appealed
to economic self-interest.[17]

So it was that Hale Boggs created and sustained a biracial coalition—
this at a time when most of the South was still in the grip of Jim Crow. No
wonder young Bill Clinton later viewed Boggs as a useful role model for
Clinton's own beckoning future.

The way in which Boggs held his biracial coalition together was also
instructive for any aspiring politician. He did so by closely adhering to
the first law of electoral politics: service your constituents. However
much some southerners might complain about federal intervention, they
welcomed the material benefits Washington bestowed on them. And few
regions of the country needed federal assistance as much as south
Louisiana, with its fragile economy and flood and hurricane–prone environment. Over the years Boggs was instrumental in delivering thousands
of jobs and securing generous appropriations for levee and canal projects.
In the 1960s, after a couple of devastating hurricanes hit the area, he authored federal flood insurance without which many residents might have
had to settle elsewhere. Funds flowed more freely during Democratic administrations than Republican, but Boggs was always able to get something out of Washington. He attended to the needs of individual con-

stituents as well. No problem was too small for his office to handle. His staff proved so effective at getting things done that citizens from neighboring districts soon began bringing their problems to his office. Boggs's door was always open, and he told his aides that even if a letter writer did not live in his district, there was a good chance a friend or relative did.[18]

The close attention to constituent affairs built up a fund of political capital on which Boggs was able to draw when national ambitions angered voters at home. And in the populist culture of Louisiana, where the Longs had made a career of attacking elites, constituent service also signaled that Boggs hadn't gotten too big or too important to care about the everyday concerns of local citizens.

Finally, Boggs took steps to protect his right flank from the white segregationists who loomed large in his district. When circumstances required, he could wave the rebel flag with the best of them. He would talk about his love for the South and boast of his great-uncle who had been a brigadier general in the Confederacy. He would appeal to local feeling by saying southerners didn't need outsiders telling them how to run their lives. In 1956 he joined a hundred legislators from the Deep South to sign the infamous Southern Manifesto, which condemned the Supreme Court's landmark *Brown* decision of 1954 and encouraged the states to resist integrating their public schools.[19]

Boggs also became a militant Cold Warrior. It would have been practically impossible to find an elected official anywhere who wasn't opposed to communism. But for Boggs the issue took on added urgency because many of his constituents considered communism a code word for integration.[20] During the Cold War, Boggs vigorously supported the efforts of the Truman administration and its successors to contain the power and influence of the Soviet Union. An early and steadfast supporter of U.S. intervention in Southeast Asia, he became, during the 1960s, one of the principal congressional defenders of U.S. involvement in Vietnam.

Broadening his electoral base, servicing his constituents, and protecting his right flank—those were the components of the political survival strategy Boggs put into place during his rise to prominence. He made only one major misstep. In 1951, he ran for governor of Louisiana and lost. It was a bizarre campaign, even by Louisiana standards. In the early going, one of Boggs's foes, a surrogate for archsegregationist Leander Perez, tried to get Boggs thrown out of the race on the bogus grounds that he had been a communist at Tulane. Boggs survived but only after lengthy and costly legal proceedings. Then he faced a more formidable challenge in the person of the roughish but wily incumbent governor, Earl Long, Huey's younger brother, who was unable to succeed himself and was backing another candidate. Feigning sympathy for the beleaguered

Boggs, Long told audiences in heavily Protestant north Louisiana that Boggs couldn't possibly be a communist because he was a Catholic. And not just a run-of-the-mill Catholic, either, for he was as close as he could be to the archbishop of New Orleans and even had a brother who was a Jesuit priest. To north Louisianians, being Catholic was about as bad as being communist, so Boggs was finished in that part of the state. The unhappy experience convinced him that as a Catholic and a New Orleanian, he had no chance to pick up enough votes in the rural and Protestant parts of Louisiana to win a statewide election. That ruled out any future tries for either governor or U.S. senator. So Boggs concluded that his future lay in the House of Representatives, not in Louisiana. That he didn't reach that conclusion earlier may explain why Sam Rayburn passed him over in favor of Carl Albert for the whip position.[21]

Following his defeat, Boggs intensified his drive for national standing. In 1952 and 1956, he helped coordinate the southern campaigns of Democratic presidential candidate Adlai Stevenson. The former Illinois governor lost both times, but Boggs turned the unsuccessful campaigns to his own personal advantage. He established useful contacts with party officials around the country, and he further identified himself as a national Democrat. His very presence in the campaign may also have helped keep the southern and northern wings of the Democratic party from breaking apart over civil rights as they had in 1948.[22]

Boggs and JFK, 1960–1963

Boggs really came into his own during the 1960s, beginning with the Kennedy administration. Of the six presidents he served with, John F. Kennedy was his favorite. "Boggs liked class," an insider recalled, "and Kennedy had class." "There was just magic between them," added Lindy.[23]

They had known each other since 1947, when Kennedy entered and Boggs reentered the House. At the Democratic convention in 1956, Boggs had buttonholed delegates on behalf of Kennedy's unsuccessful campaign for the vice presidential nomination. And in 1960, Boggs was one of the first southern legislators to back the Massachusetts senator for president.[24]

Boggs had hoped to be permanent chairman of the Los Angeles convention that nominated Kennedy, but at the last minute he lost out to another southerner, Governor LeRoy Collins of Florida. Although deeply disappointed to lose star billing, Boggs nevertheless played a key role at the convention by helping Lyndon Johnson get the vice presidential nomination.[25]

Although Boggs and Kennedy came from vastly different backgrounds, they had much in common. They shared a common religious affiliation, of course, and although neither was particularly devout, each had experienced the sting of anti-Catholic bigotry. They were keenly intelligent but also possessed an analytical cast of mind that is unusual in politicians. They were avid readers with a preference for historical biography. Boggs had the more mercurial personality of the two, but both were basically nonideological problem solvers with little enthusiasm for lost causes. They assumed that rational solutions existed for most problems but that progress was achieved in incremental steps over long periods of time.

When Kennedy took office in 1961, Boggs found himself in a strategically important position. The Democrats had won the presidency but had lost twenty seats in the House, nearly all of which had been held by northern liberals. This meant that southerners, whose own ranks had been diminishing in recent years, held the balance of power. As one Kennedy aide later noted, to sustain a bare Democratic majority in the House, the administration not only needed the votes of every northern, western, and border state member—a tall order in itself—but also of more than half of all southerners.[26] Domination of key committees further enhanced southern clout. So, as a Kennedy ally, Boggs would be called upon to deliver as many of the all-important southern votes as possible.

The first call was not long in coming. To have any chance of success, the administration first had to get its legislative agenda through the ultraconservative House Rules Committee, which in recent years had become a kind of black hole into which liberal bills entered, never to be seen again. Shortly after Kennedy's inauguration, Speaker Rayburn proposed enlarging the committee from twelve to fifteen members.[27] For help in the ensuing fight, Rayburn turned to his top leaders, including Boggs.

If the Louisiana lawmaker hoped that the Rules fight would go unnoticed back home, he was disappointed. He received more mail—almost all of it opposed to expansion—than on any previous matter. Stirred up by urgent-sounding editorials in the *Times Picayune*, the largest newspaper in the district, many of Boggs's white constituents warned that "packing" the committee would have dire consequences: Kennedy would become a dictator; the South would find itself at the mercy of a new generation of northern carpetbaggers; individual rights would be extinguished; and worst of all, a refurbished Rules Committee would throw open the doors to civil rights.[28]

Publicly, Boggs said as little as possible about the issue. Behind the scenes, however, he worked hard for enlargement, especially within his own state's delegation. In the end, five out of eight Louisiana congressmen voted with the administration. Elsewhere in the South, fewer than half of the legislators supported the measure. Since the proposal passed by only five votes—the exact number Louisiana provided—the state's delegation could claim credit (and receive blame) for the outcome. In fact, a leader of the opposition, Rules Committee member William Colmer of Mississippi, believed that Louisiana was decisive. Boggs privately boasted that he had delivered his colleagues. When he saw the head of Kennedy's congressional liaison office, Lawrence F. O'Brien, Boggs held up five fingers and said, "Got 'em." Boggs probably exaggerated. One member of the delegation may have supported the reform measure only after assurances that the administration would appoint one of his political supporters to a federal job. Nevertheless, Boggs emerged from the Rules fight with his reputation enhanced. He had demonstrated to his colleagues and to the administration that he could take the heat back home and still deliver the votes in Washington.[29]

Kennedy's first year in office opened with a victory for Boggs but ended with a great loss. In December 1961, Sam Rayburn died. Except for the four years Republicans had controlled the House, Rayburn had been Speaker since 1940. Rayburn's control was never as great as legend later had it, as the closeness of the Rules fight demonstrated. Still, he had been a dominant Speaker, who, in the eyes of many members—Democrats and Republicans alike—defined the office. Rayburn's death ushered in a new period in the House's history during which power became more decentralized, the legislative agenda more issue oriented, and fixtures like the seniority system more vulnerable to attack.

For Boggs, Rayburn's death was a deep personal blow. "Mr. Sam" had been Boggs's benefactor—and more. Boggs later likened their relationship to that of a father and son, and in truth, Boggs probably had been closer to Rayburn than to his own father. Now he was on his own.

With Rayburn's death, Boggs moved up a notch in the leadership. In January 1962, John McCormack of Massachusetts, the longtime floor leader, ascended to the speakership; Carl Albert, the whip, easily bested Missouri's Richard Bolling for majority leadership. McCormack and Albert then named Boggs to the whip position. Boggs had actually figured in early newspaper speculation as a candidate for Speaker or majority leader. But he was willing to bide his time. McCormack was seventy years old, and some insiders believed that he would serve only a year or two and then step down.[30] Then Boggs would be in a position to move up to majority leader or even Speaker. In fact, one of his supporters urged him to keep an eye on the top spot. "If you maintain a reasonable sort of 'balance' in handling controversial issues," this backer counseled, "you can develop enough support to 'leap frog' Carl Albert or anybody else when McCormack relinquishes the Speaker's job."[31]

Loosely modeled after the whip system in the British Parliament, the position Boggs assumed in January 1962 had formally originated in the late nineteenth century. The main job of the majority whip was to poll Democratic members to see how they intended to vote on major pieces of legislation. In this effort, he was helped by a number of assistant whips, each of whom was responsible for tallying votes in specific geographic regions. The whip would report the results to the Speaker and the floor leader, who would then devise a strategy for achieving the desired outcome. The whip might also serve as the floor leader's right hand, lining up votes or filling in for the leader when he was away or helping manage debates on the floor. The whip might perform all of these functions or none of them. It depended almost entirely on the individuals involved.

For an ambitious man like Boggs, with scarcely concealed ambitions to be Speaker, being whip was trickier than it seemed. He doubtless took an expansive view of the job. He wanted to do everything every previous whip had done—and more. But he also had to be careful not to appear to encroach on the territory of the Speaker and the floor leader, who, for the time being at least, held the key to Boggs's future advancement. So at first the new whip moved cautiously.[32]

Eventually Boggs became an active whip and a full-fledged member of the leadership. With the help of his assistant, D. B. Hardeman, who'd been Rayburn's right-hand man, Boggs did the counts, participated in strategy sessions with Kennedy's legislative team, and accompanied Albert and McCormack to the White House for the Tuesday morning leadership meetings with the president.

But Boggs's importance exceeded the formal position that he held. With Rayburn gone, Boggs was the only southerner in the leadership. As such, he represented a link to a critical but increasingly shaky component of the Democratic coalition.

In May 1962, Kennedy underscored Boggs's importance by visiting New Orleans, where the lawmaker faced a tough fight for reelection because of his vote to enlarge the Rules Committee. Even before the trip, Kennedy had tried to persuade Samuel I. Newhouse, whose newspaper empire had recently acquired the *Times Picayune,* to let up on Boggs.[33] Now Kennedy was going to visit Boggs's home personally to help him shore up his popularity. But the trip also had political advantages for Kennedy. If he could draw big and enthusiastic crowds in the Crescent City, he might persuade wavering southern Democrats that he was still worth backing. But if there were mutual advantages to be derived from the trip, there were also mutual risks. The president's visit would further identify Boggs with the national administration, and his enemies were already saying that he was more interested in carrying water for the Kennedys than in serving the interests of his constituents. As for Kennedy, if he got a bad or even a mixed reception, southern legislators would be confirmed in their fear that the president was political poison.

Kennedy's 1962 trip was a triumph. In the heart of Dixie, Mardi Gras–size crowds lined the streets to cheer the president. There was hardly a protest to be heard. The only untoward event occurred out of public view. After much negotiation the Louisiana congressional delegation agreed to accompany the president from Washington to the Crescent City aboard Air Force One. As they were boarding the plane in Washington, several congressmen—including F. Edward Hébert, who represented the district adjoining Boggs's—reputedly complained because Kennedy's assistant press secretary, who happened to be black, was also scheduled to be onboard. Boggs's colleagues apparently feared being photographed getting off the plane in New Orleans with a black man. After tense, last-minute negotiations, Press Secretary Pierre Salinger agreed to leave his assistant behind. The rest of the trip came off without a hitch.[34]

Boggs went on to win reelection, beating back tough challengers in the primary and in the general election. But if Kennedy hoped that his warm reception in New Orleans would help break the legislative logjam, he was mistaken. Congress rebuffed most of his initiatives. The main obstacle was the conservative coalition of Republicans and conservative southern Democrats, who, when they combined, seemed invincible. Kennedy had some legislative triumphs, including the creation of the Peace Corps and the Alliance for Progress, passage of the Trade Expansion Act of 1962, and an increase in the minimum wage. But his record displayed conspicuous omissions, especially in the areas of health care for the elderly and civil rights. Many factors contributed to Kennedy's legislative woes, including his slim margin of victory (and subsequent lack of a mandate); his preoccupation with foreign affairs; and, despite a highly competent congressional liaison staff, his impatience in dealing with legislators and legislative matters. But above all it was the conservative coalition that doomed most of Kennedy's initiatives. And the coalition, especially its southern Democratic contingent, stiffened its resistance to the administration as racial tensions increased in late 1962 and 1963.[35]

By that time, Kennedy's popularity among whites in south Louisiana was rapidly diminishing. To judge from Boggs's mail, the turning point came in September 1962, when Kennedy dispatched federal troops to Oxford, Mississippi, to restore order after white mobs went on a rampage to protest the admission to the University of Mississippi of James Meredith, an African American student. Many of Boggs's constituents reacted as though Kennedy had sent a reincarnated General Sherman on another march through the South.[36]

As Kennedy's fortunes declined, Boggs increased his support for the administration, unlike most of his southern colleagues. In 1961 he had voted with the president 66 percent of the time; by 1963 he was voting with Kennedy 84 percent of the time. Only a dozen southerners could match his record of party loyalty.[37]

Boggs also began defending Kennedy more openly in public, as he did most notably on August 29, 1963, at a labor gathering in New Orleans. Some members of the all-white audience were in a foul mood to start with because of the previous day's March on Washington, during which Martin Luther King, Jr., had delivered his "I Have a Dream" speech. The trouble began when Boggs predicted that Kennedy would be reelected in 1964. Some listeners jumped to their feet and booed at the mention of the president's name. As Boggs went on to defend the record of the administration at home and abroad, there was more jeering. He enumerated all of the benefits local citizens received from the federal government, from jobs in the space and shipbuilding industries to the money to build sewage treatment plants. But many in the audience were in no mood to hear Boggs praise Washington. "Shut up," some shouted. Boggs himself became impatient and angry and, from the sounds of it, also began to feel the effects of predinner drinks. At one point he egged the crowd on even more by calling the March on Washington a "great exercise in Americanism." Not to be outdone, the following speaker, longtime state AFL-CIO head Victor Bussie, called Kennedy the greatest president in his lifetime and said it was a good thing the South had lost the Civil War.[38]

Three months later, Kennedy was dead. Boggs's first instinct was to blame ardent segregationists. Shortly after he heard the news from Dallas, he ran into William Colmer, his archconservative colleague from Mississippi, who was talking with a friend in front of the Rayburn Building. "Your people, your Ross Barnetts are the people that crucified this man," Boggs told Colmer, with reference to Mississippi's segregationist governor. Later that day, over the objections of D. B. Hardeman, Boggs put out a press release implying that right-wingers in New Orleans and elsewhere were responsible for the president's death. "The radicals and haters . . . have had their way," he wrote. "They are the ones who really pulled the trigger which killed a great American, but they will not prevail."[39]

Boggs's reaction to Kennedy's death—his instinctive tendency to blame fellow white southerners—was not typical. But then, Hale Boggs was not a typical southern politician.

Boggs, LBJ, and the Great Society, 1963–1968

Boggs enjoyed a close relationship with Lyndon Johnson in large part because of the closeness of their wives and families. Charmed by Lindy, Lyndon and Lady Bird Johnson liked to be in company of the Boggses. The two families celebrated their birthdays together and attended the weddings of their children. Boggs was part of a select group that could have his call put right through to the president or have it returned within the hour. Or he could take the president aside at dinner and tell him what was on his mind.

As in most Washington relationships, Boggs and Johnson periodically took each other's measure. Boggs admired Johnson, to be sure. But there may have been times when he mused about the circumstances that had put Johnson in the White House rather than himself. And Johnson, for his part, tended to be more demanding—and critical—of those closest to him than of others. He may also have suspected that Boggs remained at heart a Kennedy man. So, even though the president and the whip were close, a current of tension ran through their relationship.[40]

Boggs's role in Johnson's first major action, the creation of the Warren Commission, suggested something of the nature of their relationship. When Johnson took office, Boggs was one of many who urged him to appoint a blue-ribbon panel to investigate the Kennedy assassination and make a report to the public. Cool to the idea at first, Johnson eventually supported it, and he so informed Boggs, although in confidence. On November 29, one week after the assassination, Boggs was on the House floor when Charles Goodell of New York called for a congressional investigation. To ward off such a move, Boggs announced, "on the highest authority," that the president intended to appoint a blue-ribbon panel to conduct the inquiry. Johnson, who was still working out the details of the investigation, was annoyed by the premature disclosure of his intentions. "Talking to the leaders is just like talking into a big microphone," Johnson grumbled to confidant Abe Fortas. And when Fortas suggested that Boggs be appointed to the commission, Johnson said, "He's talking all the damn time. He's a good fellow, but he's done announced it in the House." Johnson nevertheless did name Boggs to the Warren Commission.[41]

Upon becoming president, Johnson moved swiftly to achieve passage of a far-reaching domestic program that he called the Great Society. Legislative activity came in two major spurts. In 1964, Congress passed a tax cut to stimulate the economy, a package of antipoverty measures, and the landmark Civil Rights Act of 1964 outlawing racial discrimination in public accommodations such as hotels and restaurants. In 1965, following the Democratic landslide of the previous November, Congress passed the Voting Rights Act, created Medicare and Medicaid, liberalized immigration, provided federal aid to education, and enacted a host of other measures. By the time it was done, Congress had passed over 435 bills. There had been nothing like it since the New Deal. And in some respects the legislative outpouring of the 1960s was more impressive than that of the 1930s because no crisis comparable to the Great Depression was driving events.

During the Johnson years, Boggs was an integral part of the most sophisticated legislative machinery that any president, before or since, has assembled. To be sure, Boggs did not directly involve himself in the formulation of most Great Society bills. According to his best friend in the House, Dan Rostenkowski, who served with him on Ways and Means, Boggs was not a legislative technician like, say, Wilbur Mills, who would work his way, line by line, through the tax codes. As Rostenkowski put it, "the Wilbur Mills types would make the snow balls, and Boggs would throw them."[42] Boggs's two principal contributions to the Great Society were defending legislation on the floor of the House and in the media and working behind the scenes to secure the votes for passage.

Of all of the leaders in the House, recalled David Bunn, a member of Johnson's House liaison staff from 1965 to 1967, "Boggs was the most helpful." McCormack and Albert did their part, Bunn said, "but it was really Hale Boggs who produced the votes not only in terms of getting people to the floor but also in pointing out to them all the reasons why they should support the president's program." Boggs got parliamentary results by employing a modified version of the legendary "Johnson treatment." During important votes, he would stand in the chamber and listen as the clerk called the names. If someone voted differently than expected, Boggs would spring into action. "All of a sudden you could see something click in his mind," recalls aide Richard Rivers. "He would move through the members in the chamber like a lion through high grass. He would go to the area where the voice had come from, and he would pounce." Arms locked, he and the errant member would disappear into the cloakroom for four or five minutes. After returning to the chamber, the chastened legislator would usually change his vote.[43]

Despite appearances, Boggs was rarely heavy-handed in his dealings with colleagues. "He tried to get us to move faster than we were willing to move," recalled Mississippi Democrat C. V. "Sonny" Montgomery. "But if you didn't vote with him, he didn't rant and rave like some of them had done over the years." Tom Bevill of Alabama remembered that during his first years in the House, Boggs would come up to him and say, "Now in your part of the country you may have to vote the other way on this, but we need your vote if you see where you can do it." Another member, Jake Pickle of Texas, recalled that Boggs would never ask a colleague to vote differently than he himself was willing to vote. "Hale provided cover for us," Pickle said. "If he voted for a bill, coming from New Orleans as he did, it was easier for us to vote for it."[44]

If someone didn't vote as Boggs wanted him to, he did not seek revenge. He belonged to the "no permanent friends, no permanent enemies" school of politics. The way he saw it, tomorrow was another vote, so why permanently alienate potential allies? Yet Boggs was tough and he was partisan, and if he didn't punish bad behavior, neither did he reward it. Democratic members who deserted the administration could expect Boggs to tell them that if they wanted to vote with the Republicans, they could get their cherished committee assignments from the Republicans.[45]

An effective behind-the-scenes operator, Boggs performed even better on center stage. He was one of a small handful of legislators who, in the view of Capitol insiders, could actually affect the outcome of a vote with a speech. "He really did understand the legislation," said Johnson aide Bunn, "and he had a mind that could absorb and deal with the technical parts of bills." Frequently the leadership would call upon him to close the debate for the administration's side.[46]

Boggs was one of an even smaller handful of legislators who used television to his great advantage. As a political medium of communications, television came into its own during the 1960s. Kennedy had made television an integral part of the presidency, becoming the first chief executive to hold live news conferences and to preempt prime-time programming to address the nation. Members of Congress caught on more slowly. Boggs was an exception. He understood instinctively that what worked on the stump or even on the floor of the House did not work on television. So when he went on the air, he learned to modulate his voice, control his gestures, and to speak in conversational tones.

Boggs continually amazed his staff with his ability to perform flawlessly on television with little or no preparation. It helped that he was a quick study. One time, for example, one of the networks wanted to interview him about a breaking story. As the makeup was being applied, Boggs leafed through a statement his press secretary, Richard Rivers, had given him at the last minute. Then, Rivers remembered, "They flipped the lights on, he gave me the text and turned to the camera, and in pure Hale Boggs prose, drawing on some of the material I had provided, he spoke for 12 minutes and 52 seconds in tight, cogent, coherent, concise prose." "I've been around a lot of public speakers," Rivers said, "and I've never known anyone else who had those powers of retention and presentation."[47] To be sure, Boggs was not always in top form. But at his best, he had few rivals.

In time, Boggs's television presence and reputation as a moderate made him Lyndon Johnson's most effective congressional spokesman on Vietnam. In 1966, for example, Boggs drew praise, even from critics of the war, for his defense of the administration on a CBS roundtable debate moderated by correspondent Eric Sevareid. "Rarely have I heard a United States Congressman express his views in a more mature, reasonable, and well informed manner than you have done," wrote David R. Obey, then a member of the Wisconsin legislature. "You are an excellent spokesman for the Administration—the most able I have heard to date."[48]

Boggs's leadership, during the Johnson administration and later, was a collaborative affair in which family and staff played key roles. Above all there was his wife, Lindy. At once the supportive wife, hosting a thousand parties and teas and rising at four in the morning to bake coffee cakes for the weekly whip meetings, she was also a shrewd behind-the-scenes adviser. She managed his toughest reelection campaigns. She widened his circle of acquaintances, in New Orleans and in Washington. And it was she who soothed wounded feelings left in the wake of his political battles. "He could never remember my name," recalled a family acquaintance. "But Lindy—Lindy remembered everybody." This same person said that "Hale Boggs was twenty percent Hale and eighty percent Lindy." Concluded Boggs's administrative assistant in the whip's office, Gary Hymel, "You can quibble over the percentages, but there's no question that she was essential to his career."[49]

Boggs's children also played a part in shaping their father's career by exposing him to people and ideas he would otherwise not have encountered. Young people were always visiting the house on Bradley Boulevard, and Boggs never knew who he would be meeting at the dinner table. One time it might be Allard Lowenstein, who later earned fame as a civil rights and antiwar activist and to whom Boggs's daughter Barbara was briefly engaged. Another time it might be Barney Frank. It was almost impossible for a generation gap to develop. Although Boggs steadfastly supported the Vietnam War, he had to know that many of those who opposed it were not wild-eyed radicals but young people like his own children and their friends.[50]

Civil Rights

It was the Mississippi-born Boggs's identification with civil rights that earned him his greatest notoriety. Before the mid-1960s, he had automatically voted against all civil rights measures with the exception of Rules Committee enlargement, which many of his white constituents considered just as bad.

In 1964, he considered supporting the Civil Rights Act and polled his inner circle of advisers and friends. With one exception, they told him it wasn't worth the risk—that he would almost surely go down to defeat and his constituents, black and white, would be worse off with some segregationist in the seat. The one exception was Lindy, who urged him to take the risk.[51] In the end, Boggs opposed the bill. During the debate he temporarily relinquished his whip position to supporters of the measure, who created a "buddy" system to track the vote.[52]

But if support for civil rights was risky at home, Boggs soon found that continued opposition also carried hazards. By 1964, some of his black supporters, especially the younger ones among them, were beginning to feel that he was taking them for granted. "We wish to serve notice on you," three prominent black leaders wrote him in 1964, "that unless there are some changes of attitude as well as of practice in the future administration of your position, we shall be compelled to use any and every means at our disposal to let Negroes, as well as the entire country, know that their confidence in you is misplaced."[53] Boggs continued to enjoy strong support in the black community. But he had no way of knowing how long it would be before this kind of critical sentiment would spread.

Meanwhile, following the 1964 election, some of Boggs's colleagues, believing that a key member of the leadership should not have opposed the Civil Rights Act, reportedly were plotting to oust him as whip. McCormack, Albert, and Boggs foiled the plot, which, because the whip position was appointive and not elective, had stood little chance of succeeding in the first place. Nevertheless, the dissatisfaction of his colleagues, combined with the previously expressed complaints of some black supporters in his home district, prompted Boggs to rethink his public posture on civil rights.[54]

The next test was not long in coming. In the summer of 1965, in the wake of the dramatic march of Martin Luther King, Jr., from Selma to Montgomery, President Johnson threw the full weight of his administration behind a bill to guarantee African Americans the ballot. Boggs surveyed the situation back home as best he could. No vote for civil rights was hazard free, of course, but he did find some encouraging signs. In one poll, 88 percent of respondents said everyone should be able to vote regardless of race. Boggs also received assurances from Louisiana's popular governor, John McKeithen, that he would continue to support Boggs even if Boggs cast his first vote for civil rights. In the end, Boggs decided to support the voting rights bill, and he so informed his family the night before the roll call. Lindy and twenty-one-year-old daughter Cokie were pleased. But they wanted him to do more than vote yes. They wanted him to give a speech. "Look," Boggs told them, "I'll vote for it. Just leave me alone." They persisted. "I'm not speaking for it," he repeated. "Okay? Just get off my back."[55]

The next day, Boggs kept his resolve not to speak until Louisiana colleague Joe D. Waggonner took the floor in opposition. The bill was unnecessary, Waggonner said, because there wasn't enough discrimination in Louisiana to warrant such drastic action.

Statements like Waggonner's were par for the course in civil rights debates, and Boggs had heard them a hundred times. But now, with an impeccable sense of timing, he decided to respond. As one who was proud of his southern heritage, Boggs said, he wished he could agree with his colleague about the lack of discrimination in Louisiana. But he could not. Waggonner surely knew there were places in Louisiana where persons were denied the right to vote because of the color of their skin. "I shall support this bill, drastic though it may be," Boggs concluded, "because I believe the fundamental right to vote must be part of this great experiment in human progress, under freedom, which is America."

It was the speech of his life, and when he finished wave after wave of applause swept the floor and the galleries. Colleagues showered him with praise. A speech that "will ring through the ages," said Emanuel Celler of New York, the bill's floor manager. A newspaper editor in Wisconsin thought Boggs deserved a new chapter in John F. Kennedy's *Profiles in Courage*. An Iowa resident wrote him, "You may not get reelected in Louisiana but you have made history all over the USA." He added, "Is your life safe at home?" Black constituents, including those who had been critical of him just months before, commended him for having "the courage of his convictions."[56]

But the people who responded most enthusiastically to Boggs's speech were southern white moderates—the very sort of people that young Bill Clinton would soon be grooming himself to join. Finally, many of them thought, a southerner had said what they had wanted to say but hadn't dared to. Now maybe the rest of the country would realize that not all southern whites were bigoted rednecks. "I've never been prouder of anyone than I was of Hale Boggs when he made that speech," recalled federal judge Fred Cassibry. "I always suspected that there were more people out there who felt like I did about civil rights. But until Boggs made that speech they were afraid to speak up."[57]

Boggs had always been in demand as a speaker. But following the Voting Rights Act, the invitations poured into his office. Now he began to say things in public that he would never have dreamed of saying before. The day was at hand, he told southern audiences, when their political leaders would forego appeals to race. "You don't insult people who can go out and vote against you," he said. Reflecting the liberal optimism of the 1960s, Boggs predicted: "As Negroes attain full citizenship, we are going to be able to get this issue out of politics. Then we can go on to important things, like housing and employment." Boggs met friendly receptions just about everywhere he went. But he was especially popular on southern college campuses, where he was viewed as part of a new breed of southern politician.[58]

Dark Days, 1968–1970

Boggs's career had its ups and downs. The Voting Rights Act and its aftermath were among the high points. And there were others. But events in the late 1960s and early 1970s brought him, in roller-coaster fashion, to a low point. The downward plunge began in 1968—not just for Boggs but for the country.

For the United States, 1968 was the year of shocks. In January the Tet offensive in Vietnam convinced most Americans that the long war in Vietnam was futile. In March, Lyndon Johnson, under attack by antiwar forces within his own party, stunned the nation (and the Boggs family, including son Thomas, who was helping manage Johnson's reelection campaign in Wisconsin) by pulling out of the presidential race. In April, Martin Luther King, Jr., was gunned down in Memphis. In the days that followed, the worst riots in U.S. history broke out in cities throughout the country. From the living quarters of the White House, Lyndon Johnson could see smoke rising from burning buildings a few blocks away. In June, Robert F. Kennedy, a leading contender for the Democratic presidential nomination, was shot and killed in Los Angeles, just minutes after declaring victory in the hard-fought California primary. Then in August, at the Democratic national convention in Chicago, bloody battles erupted in the streets between police and antiwar protesters.

The United States appeared to be coming apart at the seams. Not since the Civil War a century before had there been such concern—in the United States and abroad—about the survival of the United States and its institutions.

The tumultuous events of 1968 played themselves out in Boggs's own life. The Tet offensive convinced some of his key supporters that the United States needed to cut its losses and get out of Vietnam. Until 1968, Boggs's steadfast support of the war had counted as a plus in his district. Now, for the first time, he was under pressure to reexamine his prowar views.[59] President Johnson's decision to step down caught Boggs by surprise. Some persons close to him suspected that he felt let down, perhaps even betrayed, by the president he had supported so loyally, especially on Vietnam. More disappointments followed. Since 1960, when Boggs had lost his bid to chair the Democratic national convention—the convention that had nominated John F. Kennedy—he had hoped for another chance. In 1968 he lost out again, this time to House Majority Leader Carl Albert. Boggs's consolation prize, if you could call it that, was to serve as Lyndon Johnson's handpicked choice to chair the platform committee. He thus found himself in the unenviable position of trying to fashion a compromise between irreconcilable prowar and antiwar factions within the party. Actually, according to son Thomas, Boggs almost pulled it off. Working behind the scenes, he came close to uniting warring groups behind a compromise plank. All that was needed was President Johnson's assent, and Boggs had reason to think that it would be forthcoming. But at the last moment, Johnson withheld his support and thus ended any chance of compromise. (The president, says Thomas Boggs, who was involved in the negotiations, must have had "one scotch too many" when he made his decision.[60])

In the end, Boggs, though closely identified with LBJ and the war, earned praise even from antiwar activists for the fairness with which he had conducted the platform hearings.[61] The convention itself, of course, was a disaster, and just about everyone who took part in it, including Boggs, came away with a tarnished image.

The worst was yet to come. Boggs returned from Chicago only to find himself in the middle of the toughest campaign of his career. He faced a revitalized Republican party and a formidable foe, David C. Treen, who had devoted his career to ousting Boggs from Congress. Earlier in the year, Boggs had supported a bill to ban discrimination in housing, and now Treen warned that as a result of Boggs's vote, undesirable elements would be moving into middle-class, suburban white neighborhoods. Boggs, for his part, ran on the slogan "Boggs Delivers." You may not like everything I've done, he was saying, but look how the district has bene-fited from my being in Washington. And indeed Boggs could point to an impressive list of federal grants and programs that he had brought to southeast Louisiana.[62]

The 1968 campaign turned into a bare-knuckled, ugly affair with ex-cesses on both sides. Lindy Boggs served as campaign manager, and never before had her fence-mending skills been more needed. Boggs won the election with only 51 percent of the vote. He had little reason to re-joice. Richard Nixon had ended nearly a decade of Democratic rule in the White House, and the demographics of Boggs's own race suggested that he would face uphill reelection fights for the foreseeable future. Worse still, his prospects for advancement within the leadership suddenly ap-peared in jeopardy. An unwritten rule holds that top congressional lead-ers must come from safe districts. Otherwise they would have to spend too much time campaigning for reelection to perform leadership duties and to maintain a national perspective. Following the election, Boggs briefly considered a bold, all-or-nothing gamble to rectify his perilous sit-uation. He would challenge McCormack for the speakership. But he thought better of it.[63]

A final indignity added to Boggs's woes. In 1969, a U.S. attorney tar-geted Boggs in a federal corruption probe. The charge was that Boggs had used his influence to secure for a Baltimore contractor a generous appro-priation for a Capitol building project. In exchange, the contractor had re-modeled Boggs's Bradley Boulevard home at a fraction of the true cost.[64] Suddenly, after nearly twenty-five years in Congress, Boggs's future looked bleak.

By this time, too, people were noticing that Boggs just wasn't himself. And there were an increasing number of incidents: uncharacteristically rambling press conferences and nearly incoherent speeches on the floor. One time, a colleague recalled, "Boggs came on to the floor—his face was flushed. His arms were pumping up and down. He was speaking loudly, but not making much sense." Capitol Hill secretaries had once voted Boggs the most charming man in the Congress. Now he might brush past colleagues without so much as a nod. "What's wrong with Hale?" they kept asking one another. "Oh, he's just been drinking again," was the usual response.[65] A few people suspected that the problem ran deeper than drink, but they could never quite put their finger on what ailed Boggs.

Majority Leader's Race, 1970–1971

On May 20, 1970, in the midst of Boggs's dark period, John McCormack called a press conference to announce that he was stepping down as Speaker. It was a measure of how far Boggs's star had fallen that he learned of McCormack's pending announcement not from the Speaker but from a reporter. Then, during the press conference itself, McCormack singled out Carl Albert, heir-apparent to the speakership, for praise. He barely mentioned Boggs.[66]

In slighting the majority whip, McCormack was not alone. As they handicapped the upcoming race for majority leader, reporters and columnists discounted Boggs's chances or ignored him altogether, even though he should have been the front runner by virtue of his position, prominence, and years of service. Such was the state of Boggs's fortunes.

Boggs's apparent vulnerability attracted a wide field of contenders. The first to declare was Morris Udall of Arizona, a liberal, who probably would have entered the race even if Boggs had appeared to be stronger. First elected to the House in 1961, the forty-eight-year-old Udall was an ex–professional basketball player whose brother, Stewart, had served as Kennedy's secretary of the interior. Witty and bright—some thought him Lincolnesque—Udall had a loyal corps of followers among younger, reform-minded members. Next to enter the race was twelve-year veteran James G. O'Hara of Michigan. With close ties to labor and civil rights activists, the forty-five-year-old was the most liberal of the contenders. Wayne L. Hays of Ohio and B. F. Sisk of California later completed the field.

The uncertainty of the outcome generated more press coverage than was usual for such internal matters. But important issues were at stake. Since the 1960s, critics had been taking Congress to task for having fallen out of step with the times, and now they viewed the majority leader's contest as a referendum on reform. In general, observers identified Udall and, to a lesser extent, O'Hara with change and the other candidates, including Boggs, with the status quo.[67]

Boggs got off to a stumbling start. But he regained his footing and waged a skillful campaign, employing, in the parlance of political scientists, both "inside" and "outside" strategies.[68] He began by working inside the House. Starting with the Louisiana delegation, moving next to other southern delegations, and then fanning out through the rest of the membership, Boggs asked his colleagues for their support. Senior committee chairs and senior members of state delegations received priority treatment. First thing in the morning, Gary Hymel, a former New Orleans reporter who had become Boggs's top aide in 1965, would give Boggs the names of four or five members to see that day. The next morning, Hymel

would supply another list. "I got to be something of a nag," Hymel recalls. To fellow southerners, Boggs stressed his southern roots and reminded them that should he lose, the Deep South would be without an
elected leader in either house for the first time in decades. To southerners
and committee chairs he emphasized the importance of the seniority system, which Udall and the Young Turks supposedly wanted to reform.[69]
The Boggses also held their celebrated garden parties. Members privately
joked at the obviousness of the invitations. But even they had to admit
that these events showcased some of Boggs's greatest assets—his charm,
his graciousness, and his wife, Lindy.

Some of his colleagues required more than personal appeals. Certainly
there was no love lost between Boggs and fellow Louisianian Joe D. Waggonner, especially after Waggonner had provided the occasion for
Boggs's famous voting rights address. Waggonner supported Boggs but
only after being assured that he would get Boggs's seat on Ways and
Means.

For Boggs, several developments proved key. One was the endorsement of Wilbur Mills of Arkansas, chairman of Ways and Means and one
of the most respected and influential members of Congress. Mills, whose
intellect rivaled Boggs's, helped hold the southern delegations in line for
Boggs. Another important development was the late entry into the race of
B. F. Sisk of California, who apparently came in at the urging of Mississippi's William Colmer, Florida's Robert Sikes, and a few other disaffected southerners who wanted a conservative alternative to Boggs. Their
strategy backfired. When Boggs heard the news of Sisk's candidacy, he
was jubilant. "It's over. I've won," he told aides. His reasoning was this:
Although he and Sisk had comparable voting records, the Californian
had a reputation of being more conservative. Certainly he lacked Boggs's
personal identification with the Great Society. No longer the most conservative candidate in the race, Boggs now found himself more palatable to
northern liberals.[70]

One other factor was critical. Although Carl Albert remained neutral,
retiring Speaker McCormack did not. In 1969, Udall had challenged Mc-
Cormack's speakership—not with any hope of winning but to express his
dissatisfaction with the status quo. At the time, McCormack had shaken
Udall's hand as if to say, "No hard feelings." But there were hard feelings,
and when it appeared that Udall might have a chance of winning the majority leader's race, McCormack threw the weight of his influence behind
Boggs, or at least against Udall. Above all, McCormack gave Boggs a
chance to help himself by presiding over the floor as much as possible.
Boggs took full advantage of the opportunity and performed like the
leader of old. His steady behavior did much to reassure members whose
support had been wavering.

In addition to an inside strategy, Boggs brought outside influence to bear. For starters, he used his contacts in the press to generate a string of favorable columns and editorials. In some parts of the country, newspaper editors visited local congressmen in Boggs's behalf.[71] Lobbyists played a role. "In the South," Morris Udall later recalled with a mixture of awe and bitterness, "the Boggs people put the heat on recalcitrants through lobbyists for various industries: oil, tobacco, textiles, and so on. They snatched six or eight votes from me there. . . . Boggs had people all over Washington—lawyers and lobbyists and bureaucrats—dating back to the New Deal, and almost all of them knew somebody to pressure for him."[72]

As the vote approached, some of the clouds that had been hovering over Boggs began to lift. The previous year, the Louisiana legislature had redrawn the lines of Boggs's district so as to eliminate the threat to his re-election. Boggs denied that the changes amounted to a gerrymander, but they did. In fact, aide Gary Hymel later admitted that he had sat down with a map of south Louisiana and a precinct-by-precinct tally sheet from the last election—the election Boggs almost lost. Then he simply sketched out a new district, leaving out areas of major Republican strength and adding areas of Democratic strength. Map in hand, Hymel had spent two weeks in Baton Rouge working with Boggs's allies in the legislature to get the new district approved. The effort paid off. In November 1970, Boggs's refashioned district gave him 69 percent of the vote as compared to 51 percent two years before. Once again, he had an essential prerequisite for a leadership position—a safe district. Boggs's prospects brightened further when, in 1970, Attorney General John Mitchell found insufficient evidence to indict Boggs in the Baltimore contractor case.[73]

On Tuesday, January 19, 1971, the majority leader's contest came to an end. As expected, Carl Albert ascended to the speakership. Then Boggs defeated Udall on the second ballot, 140 to 88. In the aftermath of the election, Udall and much of the press interpreted the outcome as a triumph of the establishment, a victory of Goliath over David. There was a large element of truth to that assessment. In the final accounting, the powers that be—both inside and outside the Congress—had thrown their support to Boggs. But to stress the traditional nature of Boggs's victory is to obscure an impressive aspect of his win. Of all the candidates, Boggs had displayed the broadest appeal. The South had been his base, but he had gathered a significant number of votes from members representing all other regions of the country. He could claim impressive support from southern conservatives and northern liberals, white segregationists and blacks, old-line committee chairs afraid of losing their positions and incoming freshmen looking to make a name for themselves.[74]

Majority Leader, 1971–1972

Boggs had a stormy first year as majority leader. His first act was a precursor of things to come. By tradition, the floor leader selected the whip with the approval of the speaker. Boggs's choice for whip was Dan Rostenkowski of Chicago, who had worked as hard as any member for Boggs's election. Moreover, Boggs had promised to support him for the job. But Rostenkowski and Albert had had a falling-out, and now Albert vetoed his selection as whip. As a concession to the reformers, Albert wanted to have someone like Udall fill the position. But Boggs wouldn't hear of it. Finally, Boggs compiled a list of eight persons who would be loyal to him but also provide geographic and ideological balance. Boggs took the list to Albert, who crossed out three names. From those remaining, Boggs chose Thomas P. "Tip" O'Neill of Massachusetts, who had played an unexpectedly important role in Boggs's election, helping to deliver a large number of northeastern votes. Not everyone took the folksy, storytelling O'Neill seriously. But Boggs did, and O'Neill more than repaid Boggs's confidence in him.[75]

As a result of the previous November's off-year elections, Boggs commanded the largest majority in the House since the heyday of the Great Society, with Democrats outnumbering Republicans 254 to 180. Admittedly, the first two years of the Nixon administration, although overshadowed by Vietnam, had produced some impressive reforms, including the Occupational Safety and Health Act, establishment of the Environmental Protection Agency, extension of the Voting Rights Act, and a constitutional amendment lowering the voting age from twenty-one to eighteen. But what had appeared to be a continuation of the Great Society, although in truncated form, was actually its final chapter. In his 1971 State of the Union address, President Nixon announced his intention to "reverse the flow of power and resources from the States and communities to Washington, and start power and resources flowing back from Washington to the States and communities and, more important, to the people all across America." He christened his idea revenue sharing, and he called for the federal government to distribute billions of dollars to the states with no strings attached.[76]

Boggs's relationship with Nixon was correct and formal. They had known each other since the 1940s, and had generally been on good terms. But when Nixon became president he ended the practice followed by Presidents Kennedy and Johnson and no longer invited the majority whip to his regular meetings with congressional leaders. So when Boggs became floor leader, he had reason, beyond differences of party and policy, to be wary of the president.[77]

Boggs pursued a twofold approach toward Nixon. He supported the president on foreign policy, including his conduct of the Vietnam War. But domestic matters were another matter. Boggs criticized revenue sharing, calling it "fool's gold," and he led the attack on Nixon's efforts to impound, or refuse to spend, money that Congress had already appropriated. Boggs also hammered the administration for its handling of the economy, which by the early 1970s was beset both by rising unemployment and rising inflation. Economists were as baffled as everyone else by these seemingly contradictory trends, and they dubbed the new phenomenon "stagflation." Boggs advocated wage and price controls to curb inflation (which the administration eventually implemented) and the expansion of public works to reduce unemployment (which the administration rejected).[78]

Boggs's immediate problem, however, was not the Nixon administration but dissension within his own ranks. Factionalism was nothing new for the Democrats. But the events of the late 1960s and early 1970s, particularly the war, brought the party to the breaking point. There was, of course, the Dixiecrat contingent that was quick to join the Republicans on a number of important issues. But the greatest challenge came from a band of reformers, many of whom had supported Udall in the majority leader's race. The previous year, they had scored an important victory with the passage of the Legislative Reorganization Act of 1970, which sought to make legislators more accountable for their actions. Among other things, the act had ended the practice whereby members of the House could vote on controversial amendments without having to go on the record. There had been other reforms, most of which Boggs had supported. But now the dissenters wanted more than procedural changes. They wanted a greater say in shaping party policy, especially on the Vietnam War. In the spring of 1971, with the backing of Boggs's own whip, Tip O'Neill, they tried to get the Democratic caucus to go on record in support of the withdrawal of all U.S. troops in Vietnam by the end of the year. Boggs, saying that Nixon was doing an "outstanding" job in foreign affairs, opposed the effort to set a date for withdrawal.[79] But when Boggs and Albert tried to block the resolution by discouraging attendance at regularly scheduled meetings of the caucus, outraged members threatened to rebel. Herman Badillo, a freshman representing a poor Puerto Rican district in New York, protested to Boggs: "I, for one, did not seek election to the House of Representatives to merely ratify whatever may be put in front of me by the party leadership." He added that unless the leadership gave all members a greater voice in party deliberations, they "would be replaced by Members who can spell democratic with a small 'd.'" Parren J. Mitchell, Maryland's sole black representative, echoed the complaint: "Like other new members, I am feeling increasingly frustrated, increasingly alienated, increasingly embittered because our own

Caucus will not confront crucial issues and will not even permit debate on them when the power bloc concluded that it will not allow a Caucus meeting to take place."[80]

Once again, Boggs found himself in the role of conciliator, trying to bridge divergent factions in his party. Wisconsin's David Obey, in his third year in Congress and generally sympathetic with the reformers, remembered Boggs's cautionary warning: "You don't have to tear down the House to reform it."[81]

Boggs also found himself at odds with Speaker Albert. Things came to a head when Albert allowed an important bill increasing Social Security benefits to come up for a vote on a day when Boggs had assured the members that no roll calls would be taken. Scheduling votes is normally the responsibility of the floor leader, but in this instance the Speaker acted on his own. Boggs himself was absent for the vote, and the next day, embarrassed and angry, he had to apologize to his colleagues for inadvertently misleading them.[82]

Boggs and Albert were still trying to establish themselves in their new jobs, so a certain amount of friction was to be expected. But the trouble between them went deeper. They had much in common, to be sure. Both were exceptionally bright (Albert was a Rhodes Scholar), ambitious, and in agreement on most issues. Groomed for leadership by Sam Rayburn, both had inherited their mentor's reverence for the House as an institution. But the very fact that they shared many traits and experiences made them natural rivals. Both had eyed the speakership from their first days in Congress, and the fact that Albert achieved their mutual goal first did not lessen their rivalry. Despite similarities, they had very different personalities and styles of leadership. Albert was cautious and deliberate, a worrier, who—a pundit once said—had the look of someone forever wondering if he'd remembered to turn off the stove before leaving home. Boggs thought him indecisive. On the other hand, Boggs was forceful and aggressive and could be explosively impulsive.

Boggs and the Federal Bureau of Investigation

On the morning of April 5, 1971, Boggs delivered a brief speech on the floor of the House that ignited a firestorm. His speech was as follows: "When the FBI [Federal Bureau of Investigation] taps the telephones of Members of this body and Members of the Senate, when the FBI stations agents on college campuses to infiltrate college organizations, when the FBI adopts the tactics of the Soviet Union and Hitler's Gestapo, then it is time—it is way past time, Mr. Speaker—that the present Director thereof no longer be the Director. The way Mr. Hoover is running the FBI today, it is no longer a free country." Boggs caught everyone by surprise, including his own staff. By the time reporters reached his office for details of the sensational charges, the congressman and his aides had left, separately, for RFK Stadium where the Washington Senators were playing the first baseball game of the season. There Boggs joined former vice president, now senator, Hubert Humphrey of Minnesota and reputedly told Humphrey that he had just driven another nail into the coffin of FBI director J. Edgar Hoover. The next day, Boggs issued a statement saying that he had reason to believe that the FBI had tapped his telephone and the telephones of other members of Congress. He would provide the proof, he said, in an upcoming speech on the floor of the House.[83]

The reaction was immediate and intense. Attorney General John Mitchell categorically denied Boggs's charges. Deputy Attorney General Richard Kleindienst said that Boggs "must have been sick or not in possession of his faculties" when he made his speech. On the advice of President Nixon, J. Edgar Hoover refrained from public comment. Privately, however, he launched a counteroffensive. He told his contacts on the Hill, in the Justice Department, and in the press that Boggs had either been drunk when he made the speech or suffering from a massive hangover.[84]

In truth, Boggs had recently been involved in another series of embarrassing incidents, supposedly while under the influence. Three weeks earlier, he'd been knocked to the floor in a bathroom brawl at the annual Gridiron Club dinner in Washington. Then, just a couple of days before his speech criticizing Hoover, Boggs had gotten involved in a bizarre incident at a Florida fund-raiser for a colleague. He'd reportedly gotten so out of control that local law enforcement officials had tried to lock him in a room to keep him from creating a scene.[85]

These and other incidents provided plenty of ammunition for Hoover and his allies. President Nixon, for his part, told Chief of Staff H. R. Haldeman that "we should attack Boggs on his drunkenness and try to destroy him."[86] In fact, there was no evidence that Boggs had been drinking when he made his speech.

Boggs also had his defenders. In the days following the speech, several colleagues came up to him and said that they, too, suspected that their phones were being tapped. And although the first mail that poured into Boggs's office was overwhelmingly hostile, within a week or two pro and con letters were running about even.[87]

Boggs's follow-up floor speech, written with the help of former LBJ adviser Horace Busby, was anticlimactic. In it Boggs said that in 1970 he and his family had heard strange noises on their home phone. The telephone company sent out an investigator, who told Boggs that a tap had been placed on the phone but that it had been removed prior to the inspection. The telephone company subsequently denied the whole story, saying that their repairman had found no evidence of a tap. Most observers, including critics of the FBI, concluded that Boggs had failed to prove his charges.[88]

So what was the truth of the matter? FBI files, later released under the Freedom of Information Act, neither proved nor disproved Boggs's allegations. On the one hand, those files contained no evidence that the FBI had tapped his phone or kept him under surveillance by other means. On the other hand, those same internal records demonstrated that J. Edgar Hoover's private denials were not as unequivocal as his public ones. When asked by Deputy Attorney General Kleindienst if someone within the FBI might have tapped the phones of Boggs or other members of Congress, Hoover said he seriously doubted it. But he added—intriguingly for a man whose control over his agency was reputed to be absolute— "You can't ever tell as we used to have so few employees and now have about 20,000 today. . . ."[89]

Whatever the facts in the case, the subsequent disclosure of FBI abuses made believers out of many, including those who had been skeptical at the time. Recalled conservative Mississippi congressman Sonny Montgomery, who'd been one of the doubters: "Boggs was probably right. In fact, they were probably bugging a lot of us."[90]

Boggs never knew it, but his accusations may have led to a major change in FBI policy. In 1956 the Bureau had begun a top secret domestic security operation code-named COINTELPRO (Counter Intelligence Program), the purpose of which was to employ "dirty tricks" to destroy the American Communist Party. By the 1970s, however, COINTELPRO was primarily targeting civil rights and antiwar groups. Boggs's attack on the FBI, combined with other events, probably convinced Hoover that it was just a matter of time before his sure-to-be-controversial domestic operation was exposed. On April 28, 1971, three weeks after Boggs's first speech, he quietly terminated COINTELPRO.[91]

Death and Legacies

By 1972, the furor over Boggs's clash with the FBI had subsided. So, too, had much of the criticism of Boggs as floor leader. By 1972, his position was so secure that most commentators were predicting that it was just a matter of time before he ascended to the speakership.

The end came suddenly. A week after his return from San Antonio and his chance meeting with Bill Clinton, Boggs was off again, this time to Alaska to campaign for freshman congressman Nick Begich. On Sunday morning, October 15, after a late-night session and only a few hours of sleep, he flew to Anchorage. That night, at a fund-raiser for Begich, it was clear that Boggs still wanted to be thought of as a southerner who had supported civil rights. "Just as I didn't think the people of the Territory of Alaska should be second class citizens," he said, "I didn't think that the people who had a color of skin different than mine that lived in my community should be second class citizens. So I voted that way." The next day, Boggs and Begich headed toward Juneau on a private plane for another campaign appearance. The plane disappeared without a trace. Despite the largest search-and-rescue operation in U.S. history, neither the plane nor its occupants were ever found.[92] In January 1973, Lindy Boggs succeeded her husband in the House, where she served until 1990.

Although Hale Boggs's leadership was cut short, he left his mark on national life. He directly foreshadowed the emergence of the moderate, biracial politics that Jimmy Carter and then Bill Clinton came to exemplify. Hale Boggs's adroit balancing of regional pressures and national ambition also make him a role model for southerners like Bill Clinton who came of age in the late 1960s and early '70s.

Yet, as President Clinton learned, by the mid-1990s, biracial coalitions of the kind Hale Boggs pioneered became harder to sustain. The widening income gulf between city and suburb raised racial polarization to dangerous levels. A faith in the ability of an activist federal government to improve the life chances and well-being of ordinary men and women waned. This antistatist sentiment, which ran wide and deep in the white electorate, limited the ability of southern Democratic moderates to hold their base together by distributing federal largesse as Boggs had done. Whether even Hale Boggs could pull it off today is an open question. But in his time, he was a master of the politics of biracialism.

NOTES

For their generous help in the preparation of this chapter, I wish to thank Lawrence N. Powell, Gary Hymel, Roger H. Davidson, Robert L. Peabody, Donald A. Ritchie, and Richard Rivers.

1. Clinton talked at length about his meeting with Boggs during a campaign appearance in New Orleans in 1992. Secretary quoted in memo, October 10, 1972, T. Hale Boggs Papers, Special Collections, Howard-Tilton Memorial Library, Tulane University, New Orleans (hereafter referred to as the Boggs Papers).

2. On Boggs's early life, see correspondence, clippings, and scrapbooks in boxes containing youth and early career materials, Boggs Papers. See also Scott E. Balius, "The Courage of His Convictions: Hale Boggs and Civil Rights" (M.A. thesis, Tulane University, 1992), pp. 4–8. Larry L. King, "The Road to Power in Congress," *Harper's Magazine* 242 (June 1971): 42.

3. "Front Row," *Tulane University Hullabaloo,* September 28, 1935; "Speakers Battle on Stand," *New Orleans States,* April 22, 1936, p. 1.

4. T. Hale Boggs, "There's a Scene Where Brothers Greet," n.d., Personal, Political, Navy Correspondence, Boggs Papers.

5. Boggs quoted in Harry Kelly, "Boggs Profile," Subject file—House of Representatives, Boggs Papers. On his first campaign for office, see Scrapbooks 2 and 3, Boggs Papers.

6. Boggs to Campbell Palfrey, May 26, 1941, 1940 campaign file, Boggs Papers; "Four Walk Out on Long Eulogy," clipping, Scrapbook 3; military records, Personal, Political, Navy correspondence, Boggs Papers.

7. Neil MacNeil, *Forge of Democracy: The House of Representatives* (New York: David McKay Company, 1963), pp. 81–83; Carl Albert, *Little Giant: The Life and Times of Speaker Carl Albert* (Norman: University of Oklahoma Press, 1990), p. 171; Lindy Boggs, *Washington Through a Purple Veil: Memoirs of a Southern Woman* (New York: Harcourt Brace, 1994), pp. 139–141.

8. One need only look at the letters from newly elected members to Boggs to appreciate the importance of a position on the Committee on Committees. See files of House of Representatives, Boggs Papers.

9. Quoted in Barbara Sinclair, *Majority Leadership in the U.S. House* (Baltimore: Johns Hopkins University Press, 1983), p. 55.

10. Thomas Boggs, interview with author, Washington, D.C., May 24, 1995 (hereafter cited as Thomas Boggs May interview). For Boggs's role in foreign trade matters, see, for example, the files concerning the reciprocal trade agreement in 1958. See, too, MacNeil, *Forge of Democracy*, pp. 325–326.

11. Daniel Rostenkowski, interview with author, Washington, D.C., September 22, 1994 (hereafter cited as Rostenkowski interview).

12. James Bolner, ed., *Louisiana Politics: Festival in a Labyrinth* (Baton Rouge: Louisiana State University Press, 1982), p. 299. On discriminatory voting practices in Louisiana, see U.S. Commission on Civil Rights, *Voting: 1961 Commission on Civil Rights Report* (Washington, D.C., 1961), pp. 39–72. See also Richard Polenberg, *One Nation Divisible: Class, Race, and Ethnicity in the United States Since 1938* (New York: Penguin, 1980), p. 159.

13. James H. Fenton and Denneth N. Vines, "Negro Registration in Louisiana," *American Political Science Review* 51 (1957): 704–713; Richard L. Engstrom, Stanley A. Halpin, Jr., Jean A. Hill, and Victoria M. Caridas-Butterworth, "Louisiana," in Chandler Davidson and Bernard Grofman, eds., *Quiet Revolution in the South: The Impact of the Voting Rights Act, 1965–1990* (Princeton, N.J.: Princeton University Press, 1994), p. 107. This tolerance did not, however, extend to integration.

14. "Number of Registered Voters by Congressional Districts," enclosed in Clarence K. Jones, Jr., to Boggs, April 2, 1965, Campaign files, Boggs Papers.

15. Comparative figures are hard to come by, but it's doubtful that more than a handful of Boggs's colleagues in the House had as many black voters in their districts. Figures are scarce because Louisiana was almost alone among southern states in maintaining detailed records on the racial characteristics of voting registration before the 1960s. Even then, most states did not compile these data by congressional district. By 1960, the first date for which I could find South-wide statistics, a dozen or more congressional districts had as many or more registered black voters as Boggs's. U.S. Commission on Civil Rights, *Voting;* U.S. Commission on Civil Rights, *Political Participation* (Washington, D.C., 1968).

16. Avery Alexander, interview with author, New Orleans, December 1994. See also Arnold R. Hirsch, "Simply a Matter of Black and White: The Transformation of Race and Politics in Twentieth-Century New Orleans," in Arnold R. Hirsch and

Joseph Logsdon, eds., *Creole New Orleans: Race and Americanization* (Baton Rouge: Louisiana State University Press, 1992), p. 273.

17. "CIO's Kroll Denounces Dixiecrats," n.d., Scrapbook 7, Boggs Papers; Victor Bussie, President of Louisiana AFL-CIO, interview with author, New Orleans, August 18, 1995 (hereafter cited as Bussie interview). On Boggs's relationship with labor, see Patrick J. Maney, "Hale Boggs, Organized Labor, and the Politics of Race in South Louisiana, 1940–1972," in Robert H. Zieger, ed., *Southern Labor in Transition: 1940–1995* (Knoxville: University of Tennessee Press, 1997).

18. Harry Lee, interview with author, Metairie, Louisiana, November 15, 1994; Gary Hymel, interviews with author, Washington, D.C., July 7 and December 6, 1994 (hereafter cited as Hymel interviews); and Richard Rivers, interview with author, Washington, D.C., July 8, 1994 (hereafter cited as Rivers July interview). The Boggs Papers contain a massive number of "case" files concerning constituent problems. One need only compare these files with those of his Louisiana colleague, F. Edward Hébert, to see how much more involved Boggs was in constituent affairs. The Hébert Papers are also at Tulane University.

19. "Ike Criticized in Louisiana," *New Orleans Times Picayune* [1957], Scrapbook 16; Boggs to Robert M. Stewart, October 23, 1957, Subject file; "Boggs Assails Civil Rights Legislation" [1957], Scrapbook 16; all in Boggs Papers.

20. See, for example, Mrs. Emmett Herring to Dwight D. Eisenhower, February 9, 1956, Subject files, Boggs Papers.

21. For details of the governor's race, see Boggs governor's campaign file, Boggs Papers. It might also be noted that Boggs polled many fewer votes in his home base of Orleans Parish, and that, too, contributed to his defeat.

Before that unsuccessful campaign, the Boggs family had divided its time between New Orleans and Washington. The children went to school half of the year one place and half of the year the other. But after the election, Boggs moved his family to Washington, where they soon bought a house on Bradley Boulevard in Bethesda and the children went to school all year round. Cokie Roberts, interview with author, Washington, D.C., September 20, 1994 (hereafter cited as Cokie Roberts interview).

22. For Boggs's role in the campaign, see 1952 and 1956 campaign files, Boggs Papers. See also "George Dixon, Representative from Louisiana Gains Spotlight with Adlai," September 1956, clipping, Scrapbook 15, Boggs Papers; Fred Cassibry, interview with author, New Orleans, February 20, 1995 (hereafter cited as Cassibry February interview); Bill Monroe, interview with author, Alexandria, Virginia, December 2, 1994 (hereafter cited as Monroe interview). Both Cassibry and Monroe attended the 1956 Democratic National Convention that nominated Stevenson a second time, Cassibry as a member of the platform committee and Monroe as a reporter. Both recalled Boggs's key role in shaping a compromise on the civil rights plank of the platform.

23. Richard Rivers, interview with author, Washington, D.C., December 6, 1994; Lindy Boggs, interviews with author, New Orleans, 1994, 1995, and 1996 (hereafter cited as Lindy Boggs interviews).

24. Lindy Boggs interviews. Account of Boggs at 1956 Democratic convention provided by Bussie interview; Cassibry February interview and interview with

author, New Orleans, July 6, 1995; Monroe interview. Bussie attended the convention as president of the state AFL-CIO, Cassibry as a member of the Democratic platform committee, Monroe as a New Orleans newsman.

25. Boggs's role was to help persuade Sam Rayburn to support LBJ as Kennedy's running mate. Rayburn initially opposed Johnson's candidacy because he believed that it would wreck the career of his fellow Texan. Without Rayburn's support, Johnson probably would have turned down JFK's offer of the second spot on the ticket. But Boggs apparently convinced Rayburn that Kennedy was likely to lose the South and the election without LBJ on the ticket. "Do you want Nixon to be President of the United States?" Boggs asked. "You know I don't want that to happen," Rayburn replied. "Well," said Boggs, "unless you approve of Lyndon taking the nomination, that's what's going to happen." See "'Lame Duck' Trio in Key Posts for Convention," June 5, 1960, and other clippings, 1960 Campaign file; transcript, Hale Boggs interview on the *Today Show,* September 1, 1965; both in Boggs Papers; Herbert S. Parmet, *JFK: The Presidency of John F. Kennedy* (New York: Penguin Books, 1983), pp. 26–27.

26. Arthur M. Schlesinger, Jr., *A Thousand Days: John F. Kennedy in the White House* (Boston: Houghton Mifflin, 1965), pp. 708–709.

27. For background on the Rules Committee fight, see MacNeil, *Forge of Democracy,* pp. 410–448.

28. Legislative file, 1961–1965, Boggs Papers.

29. William M. Colmer, interview transcript, October 27, 1978, Former Members of Congress, Oral History, Library of Congress; Argyll Campbell, interview with author, Washington, D.C., December 3, 1994 (hereafter cited as Campbell interview); David Bunn, interview with author, Washington, D.C., December 6, 1994 (hereafter cited as Bunn interview). Campbell, Boggs's aide, witnessed the O'Brien exchange. Bunn, who worked in the Kennedy administration, said that he helped arrange the federal job for Boggs's Louisiana colleague.

30. "Rep. Bolling Faces Big Odds in Bid to Become Speaker," *Dallas Morning News,* November 23, 1961, p. 12, Scrapbook 22, Boggs Papers.

31. Memo, "H of R Speakership" [1961]. Although this memo is unsigned, or at least the signature was removed, the content clearly indicates that the writer was a supporter and adviser to Boggs. Subject file, 1961, Boggs Papers.

32. When Boggs became whip, Donald C. Bacon, a congressional fellow assigned to the whip's office, recalled that Boggs didn't exactly know what to do with the position. There were no hard-and-fast rules, so he went from day to day, feeling his way. Bacon, interview with author, Washington, D.C., September 20, 1994.

33. Thomas Maier, *Newhouse: All the Glitter, Power, and Glory of America's Richest Media Empire and the Secretive Man Behind It* (New York: St. Martin's Press, 1994).

34. Accounts of JFK's trip, in Scrapbooks, Boggs Papers; Campbell interview.

35. Standard accounts of the Kennedy administration include Schlesinger, *A Thousand Days,* and Parmet, *JFK: The Presidency of John F. Kennedy.*

36. The tone and the volume of the letters Boggs received from constituents suggest that the crisis at the University of Mississippi was a turning point in the way people in his district viewed Kennedy.

37. Congressional Quarterly Service, *Congressional Quarterly Almanac*, vols. 17–19 (Washington, D.C., 1961–1963).

38. Tape recording of labor meeting, August 29, 1963, Boggs Papers.

39. William Colmer, interview transcript, October 27, 1978, Former Members of Congress, Oral History, Library of Congress; press release, November 22, 1963, Press Release file, Boggs Papers; D. B. Hardeman, interview, April 22, 1969, Oral History Collection, Lyndon Baines Johnson Library, Austin, Texas (hereafter cited as LBJ Library).

40. Lindy Boggs interviews.

41. Telephone conversations between Lyndon B. Johnson and Hale Boggs and Abe Fortas, November 29, 1963, LBJ Library.

42. Rostenkowski interview.

43. Bunn interview; Rivers July interview; Campbell interview.

44. Sonny Montgomery, Tom Bevill, and Jake Pickle, interviews with author, Washington, D.C., September 22, 1994.

45. Hymel interviews.

46. Bunn interview; MacNeil, *Forge of Democracy*, pp. 325–326; Neil MacNeil, interview with author, Bethesda, Maryland, July 12, 1994 (hereafter cited as MacNeil interview).

47. Rivers July interview.

48. David R. Obey to Boggs, January 31, 1966, Boggs Papers.

49. Rev. Thomas Clancy (family friend), interview with author, New Orleans, June 27, 1994 (hereafter cited as Clancy interview); Hymel interviews.

50. Clancy interview; Steve Roberts (Boggs's son-in-law), interview with author, Washington, D.C., December 5, 1994.

51. Campbell interview; Monroe interview; Lindy Boggs interviews.

52. Charles and Barbara Whalen, *The Longest Debate: A Legislative History of the 1964 Civil Rights Act* (New York: New American Library, 1986 [1985]), p. 110.

53. Robert F. Collins, Nils R. Douglas, and Lolis E. Elie to Boggs, November 11, 1964, Campaign files, Box 7, Boggs Papers.

54. Clippings, Scrapbook 29, Boggs Papers.

55. Argyll Campbell to Boggs, June 29, 1965, Campaign file, Box 8, Boggs Papers; Press Release, March 18, 1965, Press Release file, Boggs Papers; Cokie Roberts interview.

56. "A Profile in Courage," *Sheboygan (Wisconsin) Press*, July 14, 1965, clipping; Sam T. Morrison to Boggs, July 19, 1965; and Revius O. Ortique, Jr., to Boggs, July 14, 1965, all in Legislation file, Boggs Papers.

57. Cassibry February interview.

58. Boggs quoted in "A Way Our Congressmen Will Never Be," *Chapel Hill Weekly*, November 1965, clipping, Box 9, Boggs Papers.

59. See, for example, Peter H. Beer to Boggs, March 12, 1968, Subject files—Vietnam, 1968, Boggs Papers; Lindy Boggs interviews.

60. Thomas Boggs May interview. Whether any agreement could have survived the supercharged atmosphere of the Chicago convention is questionable. Eugene McCarthy, a leader of the antiwar movement, discounted the possibility of a compromise. It was his view that he had already compromised enough before the con-

vention ever began. Without McCarthy's support any agreement would have been short-lived. Eugene J. McCarthy, telephone interview with author, July 1995. For a more skeptical view of Boggs's role as platform chair, see Lewis Chester, Godfrey Hodgson, and Bruce Page, *An American Melodrama: The Presidential Campaign of 1968* (New York: Viking Press, 1969), pp. 531–536.

61. Wilson Wyatt to Boggs, August 30, 1968; Elaine Freed to Boggs, September 2, 1968; Richard Gephardt to Boggs, September 4, 1968; all in Campaign Box 10, Boggs Papers.

62. Federal Government—Grant Administration, Boggs Papers.

63. Boggs to S. I. Newhouse, November 16, 1968, Boggs Papers; Balius, "The Courage of His Convictions," p. 164.

64. Andrew J. Glass, "Congressional Report/Uncommitted Democrats Hold Key to Choice of New House Majority Leader," *National Journal* 3 (January 9, 1971): 70.

65. MacNeil interview; Rostenkowski interview; colleague quoted in Robert L. Peabody, *Leadership in Congress: Stability, Succession, and Change* (Boston: Little, Brown, 1976), p. 157; Hymel interviews.

66. The following account of the leadership race draws heavily upon Peabody, *Leadership in Congress*, pp. 149–233.

67. See, for example, "Udall and O'Hara," *The New Republic*, January 16, 1971; John Fischer, "The Coming Upheaval in Congress," *Harper's Magazine*; and Americans for Democratic Action, Press Release, January 16, 1971, all in Scrapbook 46, Boggs Papers.

68. Nelson W. Polsby, "Two Strategies of Influence: Choosing a Majority Leader, 1962," in Robert L. Peabody and Nelson W. Polsby, eds., *New Perspectives on the House of Representatives* (Baltimore: Johns Hopkins University Press, 1992 [1963]), pp. 260–291.

69. King, "The Road to Power in Congress."

70. Hymel interviews.

71. Boggs to Ashton Phelps, November 13, 1970; Ashton Phelps to David Starr, November 30, 1970; Subject file—House of Representatives, 1970; and G. Duncan Bauman to Ashton Phelps, December 7, 1970; all in House of Representatives Subject file, 1971, Boggs Papers.

72. Quoted in Abner J. Mikva and Patti B. Saris, *The American Congress: The First Branch* (New York: Franklin Watts, 1983), pp. 97–98. When asked about Udall's statement two decades later, Boggs's son Thomas, who helped orchestrate the outside strategy, said, "There is a lot of truth to it." But the younger Boggs added that his father's race had taught him a lesson: It was probably best for lobbyists to stay out of leadership races because a lot of members resent being told by outsiders how they ought to vote on internal matters. In his father's case, however, Boggs believed that outsiders probably helped more than they hurt. Thomas Hale Boggs, Jr., interview with author, Washington, D.C., July 12, 1994.

73. Richard L. Engstrom, "The Hale Boggs Gerrymander: Congressional Redistricting, 1969," *Louisiana History* 21 (Winter 1980): 59–66; Hymel interviews; Boggs's Federal Bureau of Investigation (FBI) files obtained from FBI, Department of Justice, Washington, D.C.

74. Hymel interviews.

75. Peabody, *Leadership in Congress*, pp. 217–219; Rostenkowski interview; and Hymel interviews.

76. Quoted in Stephen E. Ambrose, *Nixon: The Triumph of a Politician 1962–72* (New York: Simon and Schuster, 1989), p. 432.

77. Lindy Boggs interviews.

78. Majority Leader files, Boggs Papers.

79. "Boggs Scores Democrats' Move for Viet Pullout by End of '71," *Washington Post*, March 13, 1971, p. A6.

80. Herman Badillo to Carl Albert, April 21, 1971, and Parren J. Mitchell to Boggs, May 19, 1971, Subject file, 1971, Boggs Papers.

81. David Obey, interview with author, Wausau, Wisconsin, July 30, 1994.

82. Clipping, Majority Leader files, Boggs Papers.

83. "Boggs Demands Firing of Hoover," *Washington Post*, April 6, 1971, pp. A1, 9; "Congress Wiretaps Denied," *Washington Post*, April 7, 1971, p. 1; "Justice Department Asks Hill Inquiry on FBI," *Washington Post*, April 8, 1971, pp. 1, 10. Boggs's comment to Humphrey cited in Boggs's FBI files, obtained from FBI, Department of Justice, Washington, D.C.

84. Memo, J. Edgar Hoover to Mr. Tolson and Mr. Bishop, April 6, 1971, file 94–37804, FBI files of T. Hale Boggs, Federal Bureau of Investigation, Washington, D.C.

85. *Congressional Quarterly*, August 6, 1971, pp. 1641–1642; clippings, Boggs's FBI files, obtained from FBI, Department of Justice, Washington, D.C.

86. H. R. Haldeman, *The Haldeman Diaries* (New York: G. P. Putnam's Sons, 1994), p. 267.

87. FBI file, 1971, Boggs Papers.

88. *Congressional Record*, April 22, 1971, pp. 2911–2916. Criticisms of Boggs include Jack Anderson, "McCormack Left a Power Vacuum," *Washington Post*, March 10, 1972, p. D19.

89. Hoover quoted in Boggs's FBI files, obtained from FBI, Department of Justice, Washington, D.C.

90. Sonny Montgomery, interview with author, Washington, D.C., September 22, 1994.

91. Boggs's speech was not the only factor in Hoover's decision. On March 8, 1971, an FBI field office in Media, Pennsylvania, was broken into, and files detailing COINTELPRO activities were stolen. So Hoover had additional reason to fear that the cover was about to be blown on COINTELPRO. See Richard Gid Powers, *Secrecy and Power: The Life of J. Edgar Hoover* (New York: Free Press, 1987), pp. 464–467.

92. Balius, "The Courage of His Convictions," pp. 178–179.

9

Gerald R. Ford: Minority Leader of the House of Representatives, 1965–1973

James M. Cannon

Think where man's glory most begins and ends
And say my glory was I had such friends.

—William Butler Yeats, *The Municipal Gallery Revisited*

As it was with so many advancements in the public life of Gerald Ford, he became Republican leader of the House of Representatives because of his friends. It was not his ambition but his good nature—an agreeable blend of openness and self-confidence, competence and directness—that elevated Ford above the more aggressive and better known of his peers, again and again. More than anything else, the likable character of the man was the key to his success, not only as a member and leader in the House but throughout his life.

Ford's public record of legislative accomplishments is modest. He served in the House for almost twenty-four years, nine as minority leader. He served well, but as a workhorse, never as a show horse. His most lasting contributions are unsung, buried in old committee reports providing money for national defense, secret intelligence, foreign aid: the complex business of national security.

His great strength was that of a man everyone could count on. He was always there, always ready to help other members turn their constituents' needs and political visions into laws that would work. His talent was to conciliate, to find the middle ground. As a leader his greatest skill lay in his quiet ability to find the acceptable compromise between warring factions and outsized egos. He is best remembered for integrity and good will; he brought an era of civility to the democratic process.

House Speaker Thomas P. O'Neill, as ardent a Democrat as Ford was a Republican, said of Ford: "He was the All-American nice guy. After 5 o'clock, we were the best of friends. Jerry understood, as I did, that democracy works best when the opponents flail away at each other in public, then sit down in a room and work it out."[1]

O'Neill's observation reflects the essence of Ford's political career: Ford made friends, and his friends made him. He quickly mastered the art of allocating federal money, so his friends made him a power in the House. After House Republicans suffered a terrible political defeat, a band of activists turned to Ford to lead them back to victory. In the national crisis after Watergate, Ford's friends, Democratic and Republican, made him vice president and then president.

Patterns

The qualities and values that brought Ford success in public life can be traced directly to a childhood that began in peril. He was born in Omaha,

Nebraska, July 14, 1913, into a family of great wealth. His paternal grand-father owned banks, vast tracts of land, a stagecoach line, railroad stock, and warehouses. But the child's father, Leslie King, was a spoiled wastrel, dissolute, dishonest, and abusive. A few days after his son was born, King came into the nursery with a butcher knife and threatened to kill his wife and baby. Courageous and resourceful, the new mother wrapped her six-teen-day-old son in a blanket, found a carriage for hire, and rode across the Missouri River bridge to the railroad station in Council Bluffs, Iowa, where her parents had come from Illinois to take her away.

For a proper young woman, Dorothy Gardner King's broken marriage was a brutal end to innocence. Yet she came out of the experience with a resolute self-confidence and sunny optimism that remained with her all her life. She imparted these and many other good qualities to her son.

In Grand Rapids, Michigan, where her parents had taken her and her son to live, she began a new life. Divorce was rare in 1913, but an Omaha court found King guilty of extreme cruelty, granted custody of the child to the mother, and ordered King to pay alimony and child support. But King refused to pay anything.[2]

A year after she moved to Grand Rapids, Dorothy met Gerald Ford at a church social. He was a paint salesman, honest and hardworking, kind and considerate, a man of integrity and character—everything her first husband was not. After a proper courtship, Dorothy Gardner married Jerry Ford, and her two-year-old son grew up as Jerry Ford, Jr., believ-ing—until he was a teenager—that "Dad" was his true father.[3]

> From his mother Ford drew energy, self-discipline, and a sure and abiding sense of morality. From her, and from his stepfather, he learned to trust and to be worthy of trust. Both taught, practiced, and enforced honesty, fairness, and self-reliance; a respect for learning; and the obligation of every citizen to take part in public affairs. In times of setback and misfortune, both demon-strated cheerful hope and resolution in putting things right again. Their good habits, their strong values, became those of the son.[4]

From early boyhood throughout his political career, Ford's progress fol-lowed a consistent pattern: People believed in him, saw in him the promise and the possibilities, and took the initiative at pivotal moments to boost him higher. For some the motivation was his earnest sense of duty; for others, it was his genial outlook, his habit of hard work, or his deeply embedded desire to learn.

As an Eagle Scout, Ford proved his leadership as swimming coach and camp counselor. He did his job so well that one summer his scoutmaster persuaded the governor of Michigan to choose Ford as one of eight Eagle Scouts to guide tourists in Lake Mackinac. In Grand Rapids, a discerning coach at South High School took the gangly Ford in hand and made him a football star. The principal of South High, aware that Ford could not afford college, arranged for his honor student to meet the football coach at the University of Michigan. Coach Harry Kipke was so impressed that he got Ford a job waiting on tables so he could enter college and play football. Ford's ability on the field and exemplary conduct off the field prompted Kipke to recommend Ford to a coach at Yale. At Yale, a lone professor believed Ford could make it through Yale Law School and gave him a chance. In the Navy during World War II, a crusty old sea captain found in Ford an apt student of gunnery and navigation and brought him to the bridge of the aircraft carrier USS *Monterey* to be part of the ship's command in battle. In Grand Rapids after the war, the best lawyer in the city taught Ford the hands-on practice of law and encouraged him to run for Congress.

All this support from Ford's friends was neither luck nor happenstance. Ford knew himself well and capitalized on this quality that attracted others. Over the years he deliberately cultivated those who could help him, people who would educate and train him and open opportunities. In candor and with pride Ford once said: "I have always been able to develop allegiances with good people. I don't know how to define it, or why I have it, but I have a capability of getting people to like to work with me. I am very proud of it. I know I have had a lot of good luck. But I have always believed what my Dad used to say, 'The harder you work, the better your luck.' "[5]

World War II changed Ford's life, as it did the lives of millions of other Americans who endured hardship and survived battle. "Before the war I was a typical Midwest isolationist," Ford said. "I returned understanding we could never be isolated again. My country was obligated to lead in this new world."[6]

In 1947 Ford decided to run for Congress. Except for his mother and stepfather, nobody gave him much of a chance to win. The representative for the Fifth District of Michigan was an entrenched Republican, Bartel Jonkman. He had a Dutch name and a Dutch identity in a part of western Michigan where the Dutch dominated politics. Ford's motives were strong. Jonkman was an unrelenting isolationist, vehement in opposition to the Marshall Plan and the United Nations. He had been put in office and kept in office by a corrupt Republican political boss.

Political corruption was anathema to Ford. Convinced that he and his supporters were obligated to clean up his party, Ford ran as a reformer. With other political neophytes he developed a plan to outorganize and outwork the incumbent. By driving to all the small towns and farms in the district, by walking door-to-door in every part of Grand Rapids, by speaking wherever he could find even a handful of people to listen, Ford won 23,632 votes in the September Republican primary, almost 10,000 more than the incumbent. In the November general election, Ford defeated the Democratic candidate and was elected to the Eighty-first Congress with more than 60 percent of the vote.

Allies for the Future

From his first day in the House, Ford continued his habit of making friends who would affect his future. He first took the oath of office at noon on January 3, 1949. Moments later, a slender, black-haired man walked up to Ford and held out his hand. "I'm Dick Nixon, from California," he said. "I heard about your big win in Michigan, and I want to say hello and welcome you to the House." Ford was surprised that anyone outside Michigan had ever heard of him.[7]

By inheritance and by geography Ford was conservative. He had been brought up to believe in self-reliance for the individual and the community: The less government, the better. One of his first votes reflected that commitment. Representative John Rankin and other Democrats were promoting a bill that would provide all veterans of World War II a pension of one hundred dollars a month, even if they had never been in combat. The proposed benefit was popular, but Ford considered it a needless giveaway and a poor investment of public money.

His opposition to the veterans pension bill took him into an inner political alliance that would shape and advance his House career. "A group of us, about fifteen and almost all World War II veterans ourselves, established the Chowder and Marching Society, initially with the sole purpose of solid opposition to John Rankin and his pension for veterans," Ford said. "That's how Chowder and Marching got started. It included Dick Nixon, John Byrnes, Glenn Davis, Thruston Morton, Charlie Potter, among others. The organization continues to this day, and out of that group came two presidents, senators and others who were leaders in Republican politics."[8]

Chowder and Marching was Ford's first alliance in Washington. By design and by numbers, power is diffused in the House; no member's original idea or act of legislation will bear his stamp at the end of the process. Decisions are made by alliances—within a committee, within a party, across party lines—but always in the dynamics of political interests. Ford realized that politics worked in the House as it had in Grand Rapids—"You had to make allegiances to get something done."[9]

By defeating an incumbent Republican in a primary, Ford had offended other Republicans in the Michigan delegation. But he found a friend in Earl Michener, the senior Republican of the delegation. Michener was an old-timer in the House—he had first been elected in 1918—and had earned the respect of the senior Democrats and Republicans who ran the

House. Ford would often sit with Michener on the House floor and just listen to him.

"Jerry," Michener told Ford, "you can become one of two kinds of Members in the House. You can either be a floor man, and learn how to handle debate, rules, procedures; or you can become a committee expert. If it's the latter, pick an area of your committee on which you want to be an expert. Learn more about that subject than anyone else in the House of Representatives, so that when you speak on it, people listen."

Michener put in a good word for Ford with John Taber, senior Republican on the House Appropriations Committee, and with the revered Speaker of the House, Sam Rayburn. Ford invested hours in sitting with and listening to Taber, a tight-fisted old curmudgeon from upstate New York who was admissions officer for any Republican aspiring to the Appropriations Committee. On most issues Ford was as conservative as Taber and often voted with him. Taber liked that.[10]

Ford's courtship of Taber paid off. In the second year of Ford's first term, Michigan's only member on the House Appropriations Committee resigned from the House to run for governor. Ford asked John Taber to grant him the committee assignment. "Jerry," Taber replied, "if the Michigan delegation will vote for you, I want you on the committee."[11]

That was a problem for Ford. He had offended other members of the delegation by opposing a big public works project for Michigan. To win their support, he might have to change his position and support what he felt was pork barrel politics and a waste of federal money. Ford talked it over with Betty Ford, his young wife and most trusted political counselor. She reminded him of his commitment during his campaign to vote his conscience. He had not forgotten that pledge, he told her, but he wanted that seat on the Appropriations Committee and thought it would offer greater opportunities to serve the country. Betty Ford replied:

"Frankly, Jerry, if you're not going to vote your conscience, you're no good as a Congressman. And you might as well quit. You always say you've got to vote for what you think is right, and if that means you have to sacrifice getting on the Appropriations Committee, that's too bad."

Ford stuck to his position on the public works project, still persuaded his fellow Republicans from Michigan to support his bid, and won the seat on the Appropriations Committee. "And that," Ford said, "was the greatest break in the world—to get on one of the three best committees in the House before the end of my first term. Appropriations was where the power was, and I said to myself, 'That's going to be my specialty—how the government spends money.'"[12]

Deliberately, Ford chose obscurity. To the Capitol press, the appropriations process was dull and unworthy of regular attention. But members prized its seats and knew its importance. They dealt with the reality that the thirty Democrats and twenty Republicans who then made up the Appropriations Committee held the ultimate power of the U.S. government—the power to spend money. "For me," Ford said, "it was the place to be. I began to learn how the Federal government really works." It was also the place where Ford first began to earn a reputation among the House leaders for hard work and steadiness and for being a man who always kept his word.[13]

In early 1952 Ford and eighteen other Republicans in the House signed a letter to General Dwight Eisenhower urging him to run for the Republican nomination for president and pledging their support. Ford opposed Senator Robert Taft; he considered Taft too liberal on domestic policy, particularly on public housing and federal aid to education.[14]

With Eisenhower's election as president, the Republicans also won control of the Senate and House. John Taber, the new chairman of House Appropriations, appointed Ford one of eleven members of the defense subcommittee and chairman of the Army Subcommittee on Appropriations. As a Navy veteran, Ford would have preferred to manage Navy appropriations. But Taber told him: "You've got too many friends in the Navy. All those damn admirals will be after you, and you won't resist them. But if you're with the Army, you will tell the generals to go to hell."[15]

Taber was right. Ford turned out to be a rigorous examiner of military spending.

[Representative] Mel Laird, who served on Appropriations with Ford, said that Ford excelled at asking questions. To quiz a Defense Department witness, Ford devised his own catechism for any new weapon: "Number one, how did you decide what the costs would be? Number two, give me your schedule for the four key things—research, development, production, and deployment. Number three, give me your cost estimates in the interim." The next year, when the same witness or his successor came before the committee, Ford would bring out his notes from the previous year and ask, "This is what you told us last year where you would be. Now tell me where you are."[16]

To find out for himself how the Army was spending its money, Ford inspected U.S. troops and weapons in Korea. He went on to Saigon to find out how well the French were using U.S. military aid. After visiting the front lines and talking with the French commanders and troops, Ford noted in his diary that the French had neither a political strategy for bringing democratic government to Vietnam nor a military strategy for winning their war against the Communists.[17]

Ford came home convinced that no country on the mainland or rim of Asia was secure from the expansionist ambitions of the USSR, Red China, or both.

The trip reinforced Ford's belief that the United States had a compelling national security interest in preventing Communist expansion in Asia, and a moral obligation to assist the creation of democratic governments there. Like most World War II veterans who had been part of the American military might that defeated Japanese and German aggression, Ford believed in the postwar decades that U.S. military power was invincible. And like most, he believed that America should be prepared to use that power to advance the cause of free peoples everywhere.[18]

Ford's work on Defense Appropriations so impressed George Mahon, who chaired the subcommittee after the Democrats regained control of the House in 1955, that Mahon not only relied on Ford but saw that he was regularly promoted. "I was impressed by his calm judgment and steady hand," Mahon said. Ford, he added, was always well prepared, was never partisan on national security issues, and could even understand "the intricacies of nuclear strategic capabilities."[19]

Ford's reputation as a solid and dependable worker also earned him the respect of Speaker Sam Rayburn, who rarely talked to young Republicans. Rayburn directed that Ford be brought onto the supersecret committee that authorized all Central Intelligence Agency (CIA) spending and major operations. Rayburn and Senate Majority Leader Lyndon Johnson chose Ford as one of two House Republicans to serve on the bipartisan House-Senate committee to form the National Aeronautics and Space Administration that would manage the U.S. program to overtake the Russians in the race for preeminence in space.[20]

By 1961 Ford was also beginning to be recognized outside Congress. That year the American Political Science Association gave him its Congressional Distinguished Service Award with the commendation: "A moderate conservative who is highly respected by his colleagues of both parties, he symbolizes the hard-working, competent legislator who eschews the more colorful, publicity seeking roles in favor of a solid record of achievement in the real work of the House: Committee work."[21]

Until October 1962, Ford and his fellow House Republicans expected to win a substantial number of seats in the upcoming congressional elections. Two years earlier, despite John Kennedy's presidential victory, the Republicans gained 20 seats, and were up to 174 in the Congress. Ford hoped his party would win even more seats in the off-year elections. But the Cuban missile crisis, resolved just before the election, changed popular opinion about Kennedy's presidency. Instead of the twenty seats the Republicans hoped to gain, they got only two new ones.

A small committee of the disappointed—Melvin Laird of Wisconsin, Charles Goodell of New York, Robert Griffin of Michigan—came to see Ford. Goodell spoke bluntly: "Damn it. We have to make a change."[22] They asked Ford to run against Charles Hoeven, the aging chairman of the House Republican Conference, who ranked third in the Republican leadership hierarchy. The conference was supposed to provide practical legislative proposals and campaign issues to House Republicans, but Ford's visitors argued that Hoeven did nothing to help Republicans.

Ford thought it over, talked to his wife, and agreed to challenge Hoeven. "By itself, the Conference chairmanship was of little importance," he said, "but these young guys wanted change and they wanted a leader. If I defeated Charlie Hoeven, and I felt sure I could, this would be recognition. I would get a head start on the possibility of becoming Republican Leader." And that, Ford calculated, could lead to Speaker of the House.[23] Ford won by 86 to 78; he was on the way to becoming leader.

Ten months later, with the assassination of President Kennedy, politics in the United States entered a new age. The new president, Lyndon Johnson, brought into the White House his commanding energy and his own agenda. As Senate majority leader, Johnson had used fear and reward to exercise political power; as president, he was ready to use fear, reward, and all the other political forces at a president's command to impose his convictions on the country. He resolved to guarantee civil rights to all races, to end poverty, to expand Social Security benefits, to initiate federal medical care and federal money for education—to create his Great Society.[24]

In 1964 the conservatives of the Republican Party nominated Senator Barry Goldwater of Arizona to run against President Johnson. In winning the nomination, Goldwater's followers not only demolished the party's moderates, Governor George Romney of Michigan and Governor Nelson Rockefeller of New York, but also captured the Republican Party's philosophy and reputation. By their extremism of rhetoric and their politics of exclusion, the conservatives alienated Republican moderates and millions of independent voters.

Consequently, the presidential campaign of 1964 was never a serious contest. Johnson had flaws, notably his war in Vietnam; but the record of his one year in office and his promise of the Great Society to come reassured the public mind. Johnson won in a landslide, with 61 percent of the popular vote and 486 of 538 electoral votes. Goldwater had arrived on the national stage too early. The conservative idea was ascending, but U.S. voters were not yet ready to elect a conservative president.

After the election, political historian Theodore White wrote that the Republican Party suffered "from a general condition—a continuing failure to capture the imagination of the American people [and] from a specific political ailment—the lack of any agreed purpose for their Party."[25] With Goldwater's rejection, the Republican Party came out of the election in desperate condition: They had less than half the Senate—32 seats to the Democrats' 68—and less than half the House—140 seats to the Democrats' 295.[26]

Time for a Change

Ford, in Grand Rapids on election night, watched in disbelief as the Johnson numbers went up and as his Republican House colleagues went
down in defeat. The Goldwater campaign and Election Day debacle had
cost his party thirty-six seats in the House. Near midnight, Ford was so
angry that he got in his car and drove fourteen hours to Washington,
stopping only for gasoline.[27]

Something, he knew, must be done to save his party and provide responsible opposition to the combined force of President Johnson's will and his
commanding Democratic majorities in Congress. Ford had some ideas and
put them together in an article for *Fortune* magazine, aptly titled "What Can
Save the GOP?" Looking back at the election, Ford observed—and history
would later affirm his judgment—that the 1964 presidential election was
not so much a victory for Johnson but more a vote against the Goldwater-
Miller ticket—"the first negative landslide in American history."

> Fortunately, the 1964 election returns—dismal as they were—suggest only
> severe shock, not a fatal wound. The Republican Party is very much alive,
> and it retains a deep reserve of recuperative powers in its basic organization
> and philosophy. . . . I believe the basic Republican position we must regain is
> the high middle road of moderation. We welcome into the party Republicans
> of every reasonable viewpoint. But we must firmly resist the takeover of our
> party by any elements that are not interested in building a party but only in
> advancing their own narrow views. . . . We must come forward on a planned
> and thoughtful basis with attractive, workable alternatives to Administra-
> tion proposals. Our aim should be an affirmative and specific Republican
> legislative program for the Eighty-ninth Congress.[28]

To support the concept, Ford set forth the issues where Republicans
would focus their experts and counterproposals: foreign policy, defense,
social legislation and particularly Social Security and the new Medicare,
labor law, farm price supports, tax cuts, and spending cuts. Ford also
committed his party to a realistic effort to balance the federal budget.[29]

Two weeks after the 1964 election, Representative Thomas B. Curtis of
Missouri sent an eight-page letter to all his Republican colleagues calling
for change: "Yes, I am dissatisfied with our leadership in the House, not
necessarily our leaders, however." Curtis was not openly calling for the
overthrow of Republican leader Charles Halleck of Indiana, but that was
the message that got through. "I threw a lighted match into some tinder,
and it caught fire," Curtis said.[30]

Republican moderates who had survived the Democratic sweep in the
House were already meeting in twos and threes to discuss a challenge to
Halleck. Their first choice was Representative Melvin Laird of Wiscon-

sin—astute, creative, very much a leader. But the more the Young Turks talked, the more they realized that Laird was so devious by nature and controversial by reputation that he could not win.[31]

In mid-November three young Republicans marched in to see Ford. "When they came in—Griffin, Goodell, Rumsfeld," Ford said, "they said something had to be done. Their voices were vigorous. They were determined to act. They said that the Republicans could not tolerate the kind of leadership they had. It was too old. It had a bad image. It didn't have any imagination."[32] They pulled no punches in their criticism of Halleck. With his habit of heavy drinking, often before he came to the floor, his dour appearance on television, and his lack of initiative, he had lost the respect necessary to lead the party. They were there to test Ford's reaction to the proposal that he challenge Halleck for the leadership.

"They told me they had two or three other people in mind," Ford said, "and they wanted to know my reaction. They didn't say right then and there that they would push me, but they wanted to know my views." After an hour of discussion, Ford said: "Well, I agree with you that something must be done. I am interested, but I don't want to make a commitment until I think about it and talk to Betty."[33]

Ford did think about it. With his usual deliberate approach to any major decision, he weighed the merits of running or not running. He respected Halleck. He knew it would not be easy to win a majority of the 140 Republican votes necessary to defeat him.

> "Charlie was one of the toughest, best infighters I ever knew in the political arena," Ford said. "He was a good speaker. He was very bright. He knew politics in and out. He lived politics all his life. But the image he portrayed on TV and in the media was totally negative. As a spokesman for the party he had gone through so many tough political battles over the years, and had so many disappointments, that in many ways he had become sour on politics, sour on a lot of things. And he just didn't have the affirmative, aggressive approach that we felt was needed to turn things around."[34]

Debating the merits of challenging Halleck, Ford saw that if he won, he would stand only one step away from becoming Speaker. But there was a compelling argument against victory: Under the House rules, a leader must give up his committees, so Ford would lose his beloved seat on the Appropriations Committee. And as it happened, the two Republicans senior to Ford on the committee had been defeated—so Ford was in line to become ranking member on Appropriations. It was possible, he thought, that he could do more good as the leader of the Republican minority on Appropriations than he could in the better-known role of House minority leader. After weighing the merits of each course, Ford decided to run for leader. His wife and two older sons agreed.[35]

Before he told anyone else, however, Ford first consulted his close friend and frequent political counselor, Melvin Laird. The crafty, ever ambitious Laird liked the idea. "Go for Leader," Laird said to Ford. "I'll go for your job. We'll both win." Ford told Halleck, face to face, that he was considering a challenge for the leadership.[36]

Despite his political wounds, Halleck was still a formidable fighter. Many Republicans in the House were in his political debt, and Halleck called in all obligations. On Saturday, December 19, 1964, Ford held a press conference to announce he would challenge Halleck. He promised to lead "a fighting, forward-looking party seeking responsible and constructive solutions to national problems."

The lead switched from Halleck to Ford and back again. Halleck held the better cards—incumbency, his record of holding the party together, and all the favors he had done for his colleagues. But Ford's team of Young Turks had better organization, more energy, and the message of hope.[37] In his personal appeals for votes, Ford said, "I made my argument on a reasonable, constructive basis, not one that was critical of Charlie Halleck. My approach was to be positive, hopeful."[38]

In lining up the votes, Ford's friends knew it would be close. On Monday, January 4, 1965, the first day of the Eighty-ninth Congress, all 140 Republicans caucused in the spacious, paneled hearing room of the House Ways and Means Committee. After a flawed first ballot, and a tense second ballot, Ford won 73 to 67, and Halleck stood to move that the election be unanimous. "In the end," Ford said, "Bob Dole persuaded three other Kansas Republicans to vote with him, and those four votes probably saved the day."[39]

As he had promised in his campaign, Ford took the first steps to improve the organization and operation of the House leadership. Leslie Arends of Illinois continued as Republican whip and joined Ford's new team—even though Arends had worked hard for Halleck's reelection. Laird was elected chairman of the Republican Conference, third in the Republican hierarchy.

To create and promote new Republican initiatives, Ford appointed a new Planning and Research Committee and named Charles Goodell of New York to be chairman. At Ford's direction, Goodell was to set up and manage task forces on each of the major domestic and foreign policy issues the Republicans knew they were about to confront.[40]

Ford Versus Johnson:
Leading the Minority in Opposition

Ford, charged with leading the opposition to a president with a resounding electoral mandate, braced himself to confront a tide of new proposals.

President Johnson, in his 1965 State of the Union Address, proclaimed: "We are only at the beginning of the Great Society." With unbounded ambition, Johnson set for himself and Congress a nine-point national agenda: education for every child in the United States, a major new attack on disease, a commitment to improve the nation's cities, an end to air and water pollution, redevelopment of poor regions of the country, a greater effort to stop crime, additional measures to guarantee the right to vote, federal support for the arts, and "an all-out campaign against waste and inefficiency."[41] He sent up bills in what *Congressional Quarterly* called "a seemingly endless stream."[42] And Congress rolled over Ford and the Senate Republicans to pass most of them.

Johnson signed into law bills providing Medicare for those on Social Security, a housing program that included rent subsidies for poor families, a one-billion-dollar program to provide jobs and economic growth in Appalachia, new protections for civil rights, and immigration reform that eliminated national quotas. Johnson doubled the money for his poverty programs, raised Social Security benefits and taxes, and won passage of Lady Bird Johnson's proposal to beautify highways in the United States.

To overcome objections that educators and congressmen had against government aid to church schools, Johnson persuaded the National Education Association and the National Catholic Welfare Conference to support his new plan to provide the aid to children, especially poor children, and not schools. He moved his Elementary and Secondary Education Act through Congress quickly, passing the word: "Approve the bill and worry about perfecting details later."[43]

Ford, outnumbered two to one, devised a strategy that offered alternatives and protected his fellow Republicans.

> "We used a technique of laying our program out in the general debate," he said. "When we got to the amendment phase, we would offer our program as a substitute for the Johnson proposal. If we lost in the Committee of the Whole, then we would usually offer it as a motion to recommit and get a vote on that. And if we lost on the motion to recommit, our Republican Members had a choice: They could vote against the Johnson program and say we did our best to come up with a better alternative. Or they could vote for it and make the same argument. Usually we lost; but when you're only 140 out of 435, you don't expect to win many."[44]

Ford and his House Republicans lost on alternatives such as federal revenue sharing, an economic growth plan, and expansion of voting rights protection to the people of all states. With some of their alternatives, particularly on civil rights and voting rights, House Republicans did manage to make changes that improved the quality and practicality of new laws.[45]

Even as he opposed Johnson, some of Ford's own supporters thought he should fight harder.

"You had to kick him in the ass usually to get him to do anything," Laird said. "You had to keep prodding him to meet with the newspaper people to tell them about our alternatives, to sell our programs. If I set up these luncheons with reporters, he would do them—and do a great job." Ford was reluctant to court the press. He liked reporters, but he did not initiate any press interview that might suggest he was looking for personal publicity.[46]

The votes and the momentum were with President Johnson. In a dramatic national address, he pledged to guarantee the vote to blacks in parts of the South where it had long been denied and followed up with the Voting Rights Act of 1965. It was passed, and it worked. Before the next federal election, 500,000 new black voters were registered in eleven southern states. In time this act changed the political balance of power in the old Confederacy and transformed the Democratic and Republican Parties.

Ford thought President Johnson was driven to show that he, a Southerner, could get social legislation through Congress that Kennedy, a Northern liberal, had not been able to pass. Compelled to prove that he was the more effective President, Johnson "moved too fast on a whole raft of broad-based social legislation—the Poverty Program, the Job Corps, a number of Civil Rights proposals, Federal Aid to Education," Ford said. "He put the pressure on his two-to-one majorities in the House and Senate to enact legislative programs hook, line, and sinker without thorough hearings and debate. We passed some very loose legislation. Congress gave the bureaucracy too much control. So some of the well-intentioned programs fell flat on their face, the Poverty Program being in many aspects the best example."[47]

In the public mind, and even more so among the press, House Republican leader Ford stood in the shadow of his towering counterpart in the Senate, Everett McKinley Dirksen. Ford knew Dirksen well; they had served together in the House for one term, and Ford always enjoyed being in Dirksen's presence. Dirksen had, in his then six years as Senate Republican leader, combined his enormous legislative abilities with consummate skill in public performances to earn his standing as one of the great powers in Washington. He and Lyndon Johnson had been devoted friends and working allies in the Senate; after Johnson became president, the bonds held.

Ford admired Dirksen, knew he could learn from Dirksen, and set out to earn his friendship. Ford asked for and followed Dirksen's advice. "Ev responded extremely well, and instead of being bitter because I had defeated his dear friend Charlie Halleck, he sort of brought me to his bosom," Ford said. "I found Everett Dirksen to be one of the most competent political figures I ever met. He was the last of the Titans on the Hill."[48]

Despite President Johnson's great legislative successes in domestic programs during the first year of his full term, there was one issue on which the opposition to Johnson's policies was ominous and increasing: Vietnam. On the war in Vietnam, Ford differed strongly from Johnson—not on the fact that the United States had entered the war but that President Johnson himself was not doing enough to win it. Twelve years earlier, Ford had returned from Vietnam and Korea convinced that the United States should use its military power to block communist expansion in Asia; nothing since had changed his mind. Consequently, Ford believed that President Johnson should not only prosecute the war but also pay for it. "President Johnson believed we could have guns and butter without a tax increase," Ford said. "I was convinced then that he was planting the seeds for inflation and economic distress."

In 1965, not long after he became Minority Leader, Ford told President Johnson in a White House meeting: "We went in Vietnam to win, and militarily we must do what we have to do to win." It was a deliberate act by Ford; he wanted to tell the President face-to-face where he stood on Vietnam before he carried his arguments into a public forum. . . .

Some time later Johnson called the Congressional Leaders to the White House to discuss whether he should order the withdrawal of all American dependents from Vietnam. "Mr. President," Ford said, "I think the presence of U.S. dependents inhibits our capability to carry out military missions. Their presence indicates to the enemy that we don't take this conflict seriously. I strongly urge you to take the dependents out. I believe you should move forward with a military plan and win the war."

Johnson's response to the Congressional leaders was that he could not risk military action that would provoke the People's Republic of China to become more directly involved, as they had in Korea. Nor, the President said, could he make any military move that might encourage the Soviet Union to increase their military aid to North Vietnam—or take aggressive action elsewhere in the world.

In a one-on-one meeting with the President at another time, Ford urged Johnson to bomb Hanoi with everything short of nuclear weapons and to move enough U.S. forces into Cambodia to stop the use of sanctuaries. "Use our full non-nuclear capability," Ford told the President. "I will support you publicly if you make that decision." If the Vietnam War drags on, Ford said to Johnson, "I don't believe that Congress or the public will continue to support it."[49]

Ford's point was more accurate than he realized. The country was weary of Vietnam. In the congressional elections of 1966, the public provided the first and best real measure of President Johnson's record in the conduct of domestic and international affairs. The Democrats lost three seats in the Senate and forty-seven in the House.[50]

Ford was elated. He had campaigned tirelessly across the country to elect new Republican members. Now, in the new Congress, he would have 187 Republicans, enough to mobilize coalitions that could check some of Johnson's costly new social initiatives. Ever optimistic, Ford calculated that if his friend Richard Nixon should be nominated in 1968, the party could win not only the White House but enough new House seats—thirty-one was the magic number—to make Ford Speaker.[51]

In the late 1960s the United States entered an era of violence that was to cause permanent damage to national self-esteem. Television brought this violence into U.S. living rooms. Riots in the slums and ghettos of U.S. cities led the nightly news. Two more leaders were assassinated—Martin Luther King, Jr., and Senator Robert Kennedy. Violence in Vietnam went on and on; every day U.S. soldiers were being wounded and killed. More and more older Americans opposed the Vietnam War; more and more young men refused to obey the law that required them to serve in uniform. President Johnson's prestige and political power plummeted.

Congress, always alert to the public standing of the president and even more conscious of how popular opinion might affect them in the next election, paid less and less attention to the programs and appeals from the White House. The situation in Congress, reported *Congressional Quarterly*, was "largely one of stalemate."[52]

Ford, who had repeatedly stated his concerns about Vietnam to Johnson in private, took his case to the public. In a carefully prepared address in the House, Ford asked: "Why are we pulling our best punches in Vietnam? Is there no end, no other answer except more men, more men, more men? . . . What *is* their mission?" Citing the Defense Department's own numbers—12,000 dead, 75,000 wounded, 480,000 U.S. troops in Vietnam and plans to send another 45,000—Ford asked, "Is there any clear, coherent and credible military plan for bringing this bloody business to a conclusion?" From his own experience on Defense Appropriations and his continuing close working relationships with Defense officials, Ford believed that a combined strategy of air and ground military power and diplomatic initiatives could force an end to the fighting in Vietnam.[53]

It was unusual for Ford, as leader, to take such a strong public position on a major political issue, but he felt it was his duty to say what he believed. He had taken care, many times, to give the president his views in private. He was convinced that Vietnam was tearing the country apart.

The president, furious at Ford's attack, set out to diminish Ford and succeeded.

"Dumb," Johnson called Ford. "Jerry played football too many times without a helmet," Johnson would gleefully tell confidantes. Johnson's charges that Ford was a dolt and a stumblebum stuck. Ford heard all the stories. So did his friends, and they insisted he strike back in a personal attack on Johnson. Ford said no, partly because revenge was not in his character, partly because he understood that Johnson was already wounded, stung to wrath by the poison of popular criticism of the War in Vietnam.[54]

As candidates and parties maneuvered and organized for the Campaign of 1968, Congress became even more cantankerous and independent. Johnson's dominion over the House and Senate ended. In March 1968, after a disappointing showing in the New Hampshire primary, Johnson announced that he would not again run for president.

In the summer the Republicans nominated former vice president Richard Nixon, and the Democrats chose incumbent vice president Hubert Humphrey. Alabama governor George Wallace ran as an independent. After a contentious campaign, Nixon won by a thin plurality, 43.4 percent of the popular vote over Humphrey's 42.7 percent and Wallace's 13 percent. The Republicans gained five seats in the Senate, but the Nixon margin was so low that his party picked up only four seats in the House.[55] Ford was disappointed. In the Ninety-first Congress he would have only 192 Republicans he could count on to support President-elect Nixon and his programs.

In the final days of the Johnson presidency, Ford got a call from the White House: The president would like to see him. In the Oval Office, with no one else present, Johnson began a monologue about his sadness over the loss of lives in Vietnam and the failure of liberals to appreciate the Johnson record in civil rights and social gains. Suddenly, Johnson said: "Jerry, you and I have had a lot of head-to-head confrontations. I've been pretty tough on you, and you've been a little rough on me at times. But I never doubted your integrity." "Mr. President," Ford said, "I never doubted your integrity. I didn't like some of the things you said about me, and obviously you didn't like some of the things I said about you. But I never questioned your loyalty or your patriotism." Johnson leaned forward, brought his face within inches of Ford's, and said: "I never doubted yours." Ford said later it was as close as Johnson could come to apologizing for his ridicule of Ford.[56]

Ford and Nixon: Leading the Minority in Support

Even before the celebrations that attended President Nixon's inauguration, Ford was ready and waiting to get to work. "As Minority Leader under a Democratic administration, my responsibility had been to propose Republican alternatives," he said. "Now my job was to push Nixon's programs through the House. Ev Dirksen had to do the same thing on the Senate floor."[57]

Ford and Dirksen discussed their plans and waited to hear from President Nixon. And waited. "Ev had worked with Presidents Eisenhower, Kennedy, and Johnson," Ford said. "I had worked with Eisenhower and Kennedy to some extent, and a lot with Johnson. Both Ev and I were longtime personal friends of Nixon. So we thought that the combination of our friendship with Nixon and our experience in working with presidents meant that Ev and I would be treated as top level people. But Nixon just turned over domestic policy to his quartet, Mitchell, Haldeman, Ehrlichman, and Colson. The net result was a real mess from the beginning."[58]

From Ford's point of view, not one of Nixon's quartet—Attorney General John Mitchell, Chief of Staff Bob Haldeman, Domestic Policy Assistant John Ehrlichman, or Special Counsel Charles Colson—respected Congress or knew how to deal with their own Republican leaders. "Nixon was preoccupied with what he enjoyed—foreign policy," Ford said. "He reveled in foreign policy, the personalities and the problems, and was outstanding in that area. I think he was bored by domestic policy."[59]

In his first week in office, President Nixon did make an effort to establish good personal relations with the bipartisan leaders of Congress. He invited them to the White House for their first discussions, then went with them back to Capitol Hill and walked on the floor of the House. The *Washington Post* reported that members gave him "a rousing welcome in the well of the House." Speaker John McCormack recessed the House so that Nixon could personally greet each member and gave a lunch for the new president in his private dining room. Nixon responded by announcing his support for a major pay raise for members of Congress—from $30,000 a year to $42,500.[60]

The Nixon gesture was good presidential politics, but it did not reflect Nixon's inner feelings. "I had a definite agenda in mind," Nixon wrote in his memoirs, "and I was prepared to use the first year of the Presidency to knock heads together in order to get things done. . . . But it didn't take long to discover that enthusiasm and determination could not overcome the reality that I was still the first President in 120 years to begin his term with both Houses of Congress controlled by the opposition party."[61]

Nixon's pessimism was also fueled by his long experience in politics: He believed that the Washington press corps was dominated by liberal Democrats who would collaborate with congressional Democrats to oppose him and his programs. With this set of mind, Nixon decided that he would deal with Congress through his White House staff and talk personally with members only when it was necessary.

Ford had never had a problem in dealing with White House staff. He had worked well with Walt Rostow, Johnson's expert on national security. Ford knew he would like working with Henry Kissinger, Nixon's national security director. He and Kissinger were longtime friends; Ford had been trading his political knowledge for Kissinger's foreign policy expertise for a decade. Ford, moreover, had the greatest respect for Bryce Harlow and Bill Timmons, two of Nixon's emissaries to Capitol Hill. Both knew Congress; as staff assistants, they had learned the process and were familiar with members' constituencies, predilections, and egos.

Ford could get along with almost everyone, but he found it impossible to work with Ehrlichman. The first time Ford asked Ehrlichman to his office to meet with other Senate and House leaders on a domestic issue, he observed that Ehrlichman was visibly bored and may have fallen asleep.[62] Nor was Ehrlichman impressed with Ford. In his memoirs, Ehrlichman wrote: "I came away from his office with the impression that Jerry Ford might have become a pretty good Grand Rapids insurance agent." With a measure of sarcasm, Ehrlichman did hand Ford a compliment: "He instinctively knew the mood and tempo of the House, because he was just like most of them."[63]

Despite his difficulties with White House aides, Ford did manage to win a series of early victories for Nixon. Ford's strength as a leader rested on knowing which Republicans—and which Democrats—shared his views on issues and programs and in knowing how to accommodate their views to mobilize a margin of victory when the bill came to a vote. No minority leader of this century was better at putting together winning bipartisan coalitions to pass or defeat legislation.

Ford's practice was to develop a series of "rolling coalitions," to use his term—combinations of the Republican minority and enough Democrats willing to switch over on a particular issue. For example, a group of economically conservative Democrats joined Republicans to pass a comprehensive reform of the federal income tax laws. Ford organized another coalition of Republicans and Democrats to pass Nixon's defense plan and still another to support the National Environmental Policy Act, a milestone in federal responsibility to protect the environment.

There were also significant legislative losses in Nixon's first year. Congress cut the president's foreign aid money, voted down his proposal to preserve the 27.5 percent oil depletion allowance, and rejected most of Nixon's proposals to trim his predecessor's commitments for Great Society spending.[64]

In September 1969, Senate Minority Leader Everett Dirksen died. With his death Ford lost a close friend who had been his most astute political mentor and strongest ally on Capitol Hill.

The second session of the Ninety-first Congress was contentious and long. Members convened in January 1970, and adjourned in January 1971, only one day before the Ninety-third Congress began. Although the press generally dismissed its accomplishments at the time, in retrospect that session produced a wide range of significant law. Working together,

Nixon aides and Republicans in Congress imposed standards on air pollution that would fundamentally change the U.S. automobile; initiated
regulations to clean up water pollution throughout the country; set limits
on farm subsidies that would affect the character of farming in the United
States; passed a federal law to give eighteen-year-olds the vote in federal
elections; provided an airport-airway trust fund that would make flying
safer and more convenient for passengers; created a new agency, the Occupational Safety and Health Administration, to protect workers on the
job; and moved to take politics out of post office operations by creating a
separate, government-owned corporation to operate the mail system.

One major Nixon disappointment was the defeat by the Senate of his
Family Assistance Plan (FAP). This comprehensive proposal would have
provided all poor people, whether unemployed or working, a minimum
federal benefit of sixteen hundred dollars yearly, if the recipient would either accept a job or enter training for a job. It was the Republicans' first
step toward broad reform of the welfare system. Nixon knew it was a risk
to add 13 million more people to the already overburdened welfare system, but he believed that a basic income for the working poor would mo-
tivate the unemployed to get a job that would in time bring their incomes
up to the point at which they would go off the welfare rolls for good.

"We fought hard," Nixon wrote. "Thanks in large part to the leadership
of Jerry Ford with help from [Ways and Means Committee chairman]
Wilbur Mills, FAP passed the House." But Senate Democrats blocked FAP
in committee. "The liberals turned on the plan and practically pummeled
it to death," Nixon said. "Liberal senators . . . could not tolerate the notion
that a conservative Republican President had done what his liberal Democratic predecessors had not been bold enough to do."[65]

Ford, as a member or as leader in the House, rarely displayed any public animosity toward anyone. But in 1970 he stepped out of character and
paid a high price for it. In a speech on the House floor, he raised questions
about the integrity of Supreme Court Justice William O. Douglas and
asked the House to create a committee to explore whether Douglas
should be impeached. On the merits Ford had a good case: Justice Douglas had accepted fees for outside legal work in clear violation of a federal
law barring federal judges from the private practice of law. It was on performance that Ford erred. He delivered a personal attack on Justice Douglas, saying—among other charges—that Douglas was showing "the first
sign of senility."

The ranks of Washington liberals who revered Douglas launched a
counterattack. Forty House Democrats accused Ford of attacking the "integrity and independence" of the Supreme Court. Ford did have strong
support: Forty-nine Republicans and fifty-two Democrats cosponsored

his resolution to investigate grounds for impeaching Douglas. But the liberals who dominated the House Judiciary Committee buried the proposal. Ford later acknowledged his mistakes: He had strayed from crucial evidence into a personal attack, and he had miscalculated the liberals' effectiveness in defending their judicial hero.[66]

In 1970, as he had every year since he became leader, Ford campaigned for fellow Republicans across the breadth of the land. He was rewarded by losing only twelve seats, far less than the typical losses for the party in the White House in off-year elections. The results were enough to encourage Ford to believe that President Nixon could be reelected by a landslide that would bring in a Republican House.

The best way to win in 1972, Ford believed, was to build a Republican record in the House that would be sound in principle and attractive to the public. On this approach, he and President Nixon were in strong agreement. At the opening of the Ninety-second Congress, Nixon announced "six great goals for the American nation and the American people: welfare reform; full prosperity in peacetime; restoring and enhancing the natural environment; improving health care and making it available more fairly to more people; strengthening and renewing state and local government; and a complete reform of the federal government."[67]

But Congress, the national press, and the people of the United States were preoccupied with the war in Vietnam. Vietnam had become Nixon's war; the longer it continued, the more it cost in lives and money, the more it damaged the President—as it had his predecessor. Twice the Senate passed Majority Leader Mike Mansfield's resolution to set a date for the withdrawal of U.S. troops from Vietnam.

Ford, again working with coalitions of Republicans and Democrats, put together a presentable record: Congress approved Nixon's tax cut; saved Lockheed, the biggest U.S. defense contractor, from bankruptcy; expanded the federal commitment for cancer research; and passed a constitutional amendment to give eighteen-year-olds the right to vote. But of the six great goals Nixon had set forth at the beginning of the Ninety-second Congress, only one was met: a federal revenue sharing program to assist state and local government, the pillar of Nixon's New Federalism.[68]

Revenue sharing was central to Republican philosophy: Each level of the federal system—national, state, and local government—should concentrate on what it does best. Mel Laird first introduced a revenue sharing bill in the House, in 1964.[69] Howard Baker's 1966 election to the Senate from Tennessee was due in great part to the revenue sharing issue.

When Nixon was preparing his message to Congress in 1971, a powerful combination of Republican leaders—Ford, Senate majority leader Hugh Scott, Laird, Baker, Governor Nelson Rockefeller of New York, and

Vice President Spiro Agnew—persuaded Nixon to include revenue sharing. Nixon agreed and committed $5 billion yearly in his budget for the program.

Ford, as Republican leader in the House, took on the toughest assignment—to get revenue sharing through the House. Most Democrats and some House Republicans were opposed at first. On the day that Nixon's bill arrived in the House and was referred to the Ways and Means Committee, Chairman Wilbur Mills and the ranking Republican, John Burns, announced they would hold public hearings with the full intention to kill the bill.

To mobilize popular support for revenue sharing, Ford organized and held together an extraordinary coalition of House members, mayors, county executives, and governors. Over time the coalition changed Mills's position; Democrats on the Ways and Means Committee even persuaded Mills to sponsor revenue sharing. In the summer of 1972 the bipartisan coalition in the House passed the bill 223 to 185. In the Senate, Baker and Senate Minority Leader Hugh Scott mobilized Republicans and joined with Democrats to pass the final version of the bill on October 13, 1972, the last day the Ninety-second Congress was in session. It was a singular victory for Ford and typical of his leadership. Once again, as captain of a bipartisan team, he had overcome all the obstacles to win a victory for party principle and his party's president. Nixon took full advantage of the political bonanza and signed the bill in a ceremony at Philadelphia's Independence Hall. Checks from the U.S. Treasury went out to every county, city, town, and village two weeks before Election Day.[70]

Ford did not attend the Philadelphia ceremony. That week he was campaigning in eleven states for Republican candidates for the House. With the polls predicting a Nixon landslide and with an array of attractive new candidates, Ford hoped to win thirty-eight additional seats in the House, enough for a majority—enough for Ford to be elected Speaker.[71]

The Tragedy of Richard Nixon

On June 17, 1972, five burglars broke into Democratic National Headquarters in the Watergate office building in Washington. The *Washington Post* broke the story the next day.

Ford, speaking in Michigan that weekend, heard about the Watergate break-in on his car radio. His first thoughts were: How can anyone be so dumb? What would they expect to find in a party headquarters? Ford's next concern was that some minor campaign functionary might provoke a scandal that would affect Republican prospects in the House elections.

Two days later Ford confronted John Mitchell, Nixon's campaign manager. Mitchell assured Ford that none of Nixon's campaign workers were involved in the break-in.[72] Later, Nixon also assured Ford that neither he nor the White House staff was involved. Ford took Nixon at his word. He had no reason to doubt his old friend. In fact, most people in the United States believed Nixon was much too smart a politician to get mixed up in anything so ridiculous as burglary of a party headquarters.

At that point, Nixon was running one of the most effective presidential reelection campaigns of modern times. His visit to China, the successful summits with Soviet general secretary Leonid Brezhnev, the progress on strategic arms limitations, the reduced casualties in Vietnam and the withdrawal of some U.S. troops, and a strong economy all combined to put Nixon well ahead of the hapless Democratic nominee, Senator George McGovern.

As expected, Nixon won by a landslide on November 7, 1972. But the Republicans gained only 12 seats in the House, far short of the 218 seats needed for control. Ford, watching the returns at his home that night, was so disappointed that he told his wife he would retire from politics.[73]

Two months later, in January 1973, two separate U.S. tragedies began to change history, First, during the trial of the Watergate burglars, one of the men who took part in the break-in wrote from his prison cell to federal judge John Sirica to reveal that the Nixon White House staff was not only involved in the Watergate crime but was paying off the other burglars, also in jail, to keep quiet about it. In a parallel tragedy, the U.S. attorney in Baltimore learned that Vice President Agnew had been taking bribes, including at least one he accepted in the White House itself. In October, Agnew was forced to resign. Under the new Twenty-fifth Amendment, Nixon would nominate a new vice president, subject to confirmation by the House and Senate. Nixon's first choice was former Texas governor John Connally, but Nixon was advised by congressional leaders that Connally could not be confirmed in either the House or Senate. Connally had just turned Republican; as a result, Democrats called him a turncoat and Republicans considered him an opportunist.

With Watergate threatening his presidency, Nixon could not risk another confrontation with Congress. The testimony of the Watergate defendants on trial in a federal court and the testimony of White House senior staff members before the Senate Watergate Committee revealed more and more evidence indicating that Nixon himself had been involved in the cover-up of the Watergate crime. Nixon knew, better than anyone else, that if he could not continue to contain the evidence of his part in the Watergate cover-up, he could be impeached by the House and convicted by the Senate.

With Connally rejected, Nixon turned to consider other candidates—Ford, his friend of a quarter century and his most loyal supporter in Congress; Governor Ronald Reagan of California; and Governor Nelson Rockefeller of New York. On the afternoon that Agnew resigned, Nixon invited House Speaker Carl Albert and Senate Majority Leader Mike Mansfield to the White House to get their suggestions about the best candidates for vice president.

Speaker Albert suggested Jerry Ford. He would be easily and quickly confirmed, Albert said. Nixon turned to Mansfield. He agreed that Ford would be a good choice.[74] Neither Nixon, Albert, nor Mansfield planned it that way, but it turned out that the two most powerful Democrats in Congress imposed the choice of Ford on the president. Once Nixon asked their advice, and they responded with the one man who could win confirmation easily in the House and Senate, the issue was settled. Albert said later: "We gave Nixon no choice but Ford. Congress made Jerry Ford President."[75]

In choosing Ford, both Albert and Mansfield believed they were selecting the next president. And so, in fact, did Nixon. When he nominated Ford, he later wrote, he had already concluded he would probably be impeached or forced to resign.[76]

The New Challenge

In preparing for his confirmation for vice president, Ford bared all the records of his private affairs and political career. "Hold nothing back," he told his staff. "I want the people to see that I am as clean as a whistle."[77]

For this first use of the Twenty-fifth Amendment, Congress ordered the most extensive investigation of a presidential nominee in history, during which 350 agents probed Ford's life, going back to his childhood, his bank accounts, his campaign expenses, his associates. The Library of Congress compiled a record and summary of every vote and speech in his twenty-five years in the House. For days the Senate Rules Committee and then the House Judiciary Committee questioned Ford about his character and his qualifications to be president.[78]

Congress and the U.S. public learned more about Jerry Ford—his beliefs, character, experience, philosophy of government, political record—than they had ever known about any presidential candidate or have known about any since then. And with that knowledge the two Houses of Congress confirmed Ford with an electoral landslide. The combined vote: 479 to 38.

When Ford was sworn in, in his beloved House of Representatives on December 6, 1973, he fully expected to serve out the balance of Agnew's term and retire from public life.[79] Events intervened. By the early summer of 1974 Nixon was fighting on three fronts to save his presidency. The Watergate special prosecutor was collecting criminal evidence against him. The House Judiciary Committee opened hearings on impeaching Nixon. The Supreme Court ruled, on July 24, 1974, that President Nixon must turn over to Judge Sirica's court the White House tapes of his discussions of Watergate.

Those transcripts, made public two weeks later, proved that Nixon had obstructed justice by attempting to have the CIA stop the FBI investigation of Watergate. With the disclosure of that evidence, Nixon lost all but nine of his last supporters in the Senate. With impeachment certain in the House, and conviction certain in the Senate, President Nixon decided to resign.[80]

Into the White House

Gerald Ford, the Republican leader of the House for nine years and the vice president for eight months, took the oath of office as president of the United States at 12:03 P.M., August 9, 1974.

Of all the friends Ford made in his public life, none was closer as a person or more caustic a critic than House Speaker Thomas P. O'Neill. Of Ford the House leader, O'Neill wrote: "Ford was a talented and forceful Minority Leader." Of Ford the president, O'Neill wrote:

> God has been good to America, especially during difficult times. At the time of the Civil War, he gave us Abraham Lincoln. And at the time of Watergate, he gave us Gerald Ford—the right man at the right time who was able to put our nation back together again. Nothing like Watergate had ever happened before in our history, but we came out of it strong and free, and the transition from Nixon's Administration to Ford's was a thing of awe and dignity.[81]

As all presidents must, Ford contended with Congress on issue after issue; but the friends he had made and kept on Capitol Hill provided Ford with the best working relationship with Congress of any president since Dwight Eisenhower.

Ford was president for 895 days. Like the man himself, his record is solid:

- He brought the country through the worst recession since the Great Depression of the 1930s.
- He ended the Vietnam War, which his three predecessor presidents could not end.
- Against heavy opposition, Ford negotiated and signed the Helsinki Accords that opened the path for the end of communism and the beginning of democracy in Eastern Europe.

- He was the last president to understand economics and the last to know how to make a serious effort to balance the federal budget.
- He pardoned President Nixon because he was convinced that the country should not preoccupy itself with a two-year trial of its dishonored former president but should instead address more compelling national and international problems. He knew it would be controversial and assumed it would probably cost him any chance to be elected in 1976, but he acted on his belief that the pardon would be in the best interests of the nation.
- Ford lost the 1976 election to Jimmy Carter, narrowly. But when Ford left the Oval Office, inflation was down, interest rates were down, employment was up, and not a single U.S. soldier was in armed conflict anywhere in the world.
- Most important of all, Ford restored the integrity of the presidency. He accomplished that by his own honesty and force of character.

Conclusion

Comity characterized Ford's relations with Congress when he was president, as it had during his years as a member of the House and as Republican leader.

From his first days in the House he felt strongly about Republican principles, said so in his arguments on the floor, and voted so. But when the debate ended, Ford always walked over to the opponent whose position he had just tried to demolish and shook his hand.

In his time in the House, most Republicans shared at least some part of his political philosophy, a set of convictions that Ford clearly stated and consistently followed. He was a fiscal conservative, a moderate on social issues, an internationalist in foreign policy, and an unwavering believer in building and maintaining strong U.S. defense forces. To him there was a profound difference between the two parties: "Democrats believe the Federal government is the best instrument for the solution of social problems such as education, housing, and poverty. Republicans believe these problems can best be served by state government, local government, the private sector, or a combination of the three."[82]

As leader, Ford relied on persuasion. He never twisted arms or threatened a colleague. In the party caucus, in a quiet talk with a member whose support he needed, and in House debate, Ford focused on facts, principles, issues. He never threatened a colleague. Only rarely did he make an emotional appeal or engage in a spirited or personal attack. His

House speeches, consequently, usually came across as routine, pre-dictable, and sometimes dull.

Long experience guided him on whether an idea would work. His years of listening to cabinet members ask for appropriations for their pro-grams gave him a realistic understanding of how well the federal bu-reaucracy could manage the money and carry out the intentions of the president and the Congress. More often than not, Ford knew more about a federal program than the cabinet officer administering it.

As a member and as Republican leader, Ford was not a man of initia-tive and ideas. Nor did he hunger for power or court the press. He was a solid and conscientious worker, industrious, informed, an accomplished listener. His expertise lay in finding the solid middle ground, bringing others to stand with him, and then giving credit for accomplishments to others.

In negotiations, Ford's affable nature and ready laugh often eased the tension in the clashes between egos and philosophy. In victory, he gave others the credit; in defeat, he would not blame someone else. Win or lose, he put the contest behind him and looked ahead to the next chal-lenge.

His eight years as leader—four in opposition to a Democratic presi-dent, four in support of a Republican president—were marked by civility and decency. As the minority leader when Lyndon Johnson was president and the House was initially more than two-to-one Democratic, Ford lost more than he won. When Richard Nixon was president and the House was still strongly Democratic, Ford won far more than he lost.

By his down-to-earth good nature, by his abiding love of the political life, this self-effacing representative of Michigan and Middle America made politics the happy adventure it is and was meant to be.

As an institution, the House operates on trust and goodwill. Ford gave his word and kept his word. He could be trusted. He told the truth.

Character: This was the merit of the man, the merit that prompted his friends to elect Ford a leader of the House and—in the greatest constitu-tional crisis since the Civil War—to make him president.

NOTES

1. Speaker Thomas P. O'Neill, interview by author , Washington, D.C., August 17, 1992.

2. Records of the Douglas County District Court, Omaha, Nebraska, 1913.

3. James Cannon, *Time and Chance: Gerald Ford's Appointment with History* (New York: HarperCollins, 1994), pp. 8–9.

4. Ibid., p. 17.

5. Ibid., p. 41.

6. Ibid., p. 39.

7. Ibid., p. 53.

8. Gerald R. Ford, interview by author, Rancho Mirage, California, April 25, 1990.

9. Cannon, *Time and Chance*, p. 54.

10. Ibid., p. 55.

11. Ibid., p. 58.

12. Ibid.

13. Ibid., p. 59.

14. Ibid., p. 60.

15. Ibid., p. 61.

16. Ibid., p. 62.

17. Ibid., pp. 62–63.

18. Ibid., p. 64.

19. Ibid.

20. Ibid., pp. 65–67.

21. Citation by the American Political Science Association, in St. Louis, Missouri, September 8, 1961.

22. Papers of Robert L. Peabody, Gerald R. Ford Presidential Library, University of Michigan, Ann Arbor.

23. Cannon, *Time and Chance*, p. 75.

24. *Congress and the Nation* (Washington, D.C.: Congressional Quarterly, 1969), 2: 1.

25. Theodore H. White, *The Making of the President—1964* (New York: Atheneum, 1965), p. 385.

26. Cannon, *Time and Chance*, p. 81.

27. Gerald R. Ford, interview by author, April 25–26, 1990.

28. *Fortune*, January 1965, pp. 140–141, 230–231.

29. Ibid.

30. Ford Leadership files, Gerald R. Ford Presidential Library.

31. Robert L. Peabody, *Leadership in Congress* (New York: Little, Brown, 1976), pp. 100–148.

32. Gerald R. Ford, interview by author, April 25, 1990.

33. Ibid.

34. Ibid.

35. Ibid.

36. Cannon, *Time and Chance*, p. 82.

37. Ibid., p. 83.

38. Gerald R. Ford, interview by author, April 3, 1995.

39. Cannon, *Time and Chance*, p. 83.

40. Press release of February 3, 1965, Ford Leadership documents, Gerald R. Ford Presidential Library.

41. *Public Papers of the Presidents of the United States: Lyndon B. Johnson, 1965* (Washington, D.C.: Government Printing Office, 1966), p. 5.

42. *Congress and the Nation*, vol. 2, p. 2.

43. Ibid., p. 3.

44. Gerald R. Ford, interview by author, April 3, 1995.

45. Gerald R. Ford, interview by author, April 25, 1990.

46. Cannon, *Time and Chance*, p. 90.

47. Ibid., p. 86.

48. Ibid.

49. Ibid., pp. 87–88.

50. *Congress and the Nation*, vol. 2, p. 30.

51. Cannon, *Time and Chance*, p. 93.

52. *Congress and the Nation*, vol. 2, pp. 8–12.

53. *Congressional Record*, August 8, 1967.

54. Cannon, *Time and Chance*, p. 93.

55. *America Votes 1968* (Washington, D.C.: Elections Research Center, 1969).

56. Cannon, *Time and Chance*, p. 96.

57. Gerald R. Ford, interview by author, April 25, 1990.

58. Gerald R. Ford, interview by author, April 3, 1995.

59. Ibid.

60. *Washington Post*, January 1969.

61. Richard Nixon, *RN: The Memoirs of Richard Nixon* (New York: Grosset & Dunlap, 1978), p. 414.

62. Cannon, *Time and Chance*, p. 99.

63. John Ehrlichman, *Witness to Power* (New York: Simon and Schuster, 1982), pp. 197–198.

64. *Congress and the Nation* (Washington, D.C.: Congressional Quarterly, 1973), 3: 2–4.

65. Ibid., p. 7; Nixon, *RN: The Memoirs of Richard Nixon*, pp. 426–428.

66. Cannon, *Time and Chance*, pp. 100–101.

67. *Public Papers of the Presidents: Richard Nixon 1971 (Vol. 1)*, (Washington, DC: Government Printing Office, 1972) pp. 50–58. "Annual Message to the Congress on the State of the Union, January 22, 1971." Also published in *Congressional Record*, January 22, 1971.

68. *Congress and the Nation*, vol. 3, pp. 12–20.

69. Mel Laird, interview by author, April 11, 1995.

70. Author's records.

71. Cannon, *Time and Chance*, p. 131.

72. Ibid., p. 106.

73. Ibid., "Prologue," p. xv.

74. Speaker Carl Albert, interview by author, July 24, 1990; Senator Mike Mansfield, interview by author, May 31, 1991.

75. Speaker Carl Albert, interview by author, July 24, 1990.

76. Richard Nixon, letter to James Cannon, May 24, 1991.

77. Cannon, *Time and Chance*, p. 229.

78. *Nomination of Gerald R. Ford to Be Vice President of the United States*, 93d Cong., 1st sess., 1973, H. Rept. 93–695; S. Rept. 93–26.

79. Gerald R. Ford, *A Time to Heal* (New York: Harper & Row, 1979), pp. 112–113.

80. Cannon, *Time and Chance*, pp. 320–323.

81. Speaker Thomas P. O'Neill, *Man of the House* (New York: Random House, 1987), pp. 260, 271.

82. Cannon, *Time and Chance*, p. 70.

10

Tip O'Neill and Contemporary House Leadership

Barbara Sinclair

An old pol who sponsored reform, a party loyalist who broke with a president of his own party over Vietnam, a champion of the adage "all politics is local" who became a national figure, a quintessential inside player who was transformed into a media celebrity—these seeming contradictions reflect the changing times of Tip O'Neill's House service and the adaptability of a superb politician. O'Neill's contribution—and that of his immediate successors—was to lead the House of Representatives as it adapted to severe internal and external shocks and to leave it a strong institution that can function legislatively even under extraordinarily difficult circumstances.

Thomas P. (Tip) O'Neill became Speaker in 1977 when the House had just undergone a series of major internal reforms and remained in that office through 1986 during a period of divided government and sharp conflict between the House majority and the president. It fell to him and his leadership team to adapt majority party leadership to the reformed House and to the adverse political climate of the 1980s.

As party leaders are chosen by their members, they must satisfy those members' expectations. The Democratic membership that reformed the House had enormously expanded opportunities for rank-and-file participation and expected to participate broadly in the legislative process; yet the members also expected the passage of legislation that furthered their reelection and policy goals. For the majority party leadership, the central conundrum of the postreform House was the uncertainty created by high participation that threatened the legislation members wanted and yet the reluctance of members to curb their participation even to increase the probability of legislative success. The election of Ronald Reagan and a Republican Senate in 1980 severely exacerbated the problem; passing legislation satisfactory to Democrats became much more difficult. O'Neill and his immediate successors developed and refined leadership strategies that made meeting their members' potentially conflicting and evolving expectations possible. In response to the problems the environment posed and to the demands of a more ideologically homogeneous Democratic membership, the majority party leadership by the late 1980s had become more active and more central to the legislative process but operated through a highly inclusive style.

Focusing on Tip O'Neill and his House career, before as well as during his tenure as a top party leader, in this chapter I examine the House institutional context and the changing external political environment and trace the development of party leadership strategies intended to cope with the problems those environments posed.

A "Go Along, Get Along" Politician in a "Go Along, Get Along" House

The House that Tip O'Neill entered in 1952 was a very different body from the one that he would lead a quarter century later. Influence was decentralized but highly unequally distributed.[1] Legislation was the product of a number of autonomous committees headed by powerful chairmen—aptly often referred to as barons—who derived their positions from their seniority on the committee. The chairman's great organizational and procedural powers over his committee and structural advantages such as the lack of recorded votes on floor amendments led to a system of reciprocity or mutual deference among committees that protected most legislation from serious challenge on the floor of the House.

A lack of resources—especially staff—and constraining norms restricted the participation of rank-and-file members. Junior members were expected to serve an apprenticeship: to listen, learn, and defer to their seniors—to go along to get along.

Party leaders also lacked resources and were further constrained in the exercise of influence by the party's ideological heterogeneity that made strong leadership potentially divisive. The Democratic membership was split between conservative southerners and more liberal northern members, with the latter more numerous but the former more senior and, thus, in control of many of the top committee positions.

Speaker Sam Rayburn's leadership style was permissive, informal, and highly personalized. In his relations with the powerful committee chairs, he relied upon personal persuasion and made few demands; in the shaping of legislation, he largely deferred to the committees and their chairs. In building floor coalitions, he also used a personalized, low-keyed approach. Members were seldom pressured to vote a given way; rather Rayburn, who obtained some leverage from the myriad of small favors he performed for members, relied upon personal persuasion and members' sense of obligation. To damp intraparty conflict, Rayburn avoided using party mechanisms such as the caucus that could provide the contending factions with a forum for direct confrontation.

Committee leaders and committee majorities saw little benefit in strong, active party leadership; leadership assistance was seldom a prerequisite to legislative success. "A modern Democratic Speaker," Congressman Dick Bolling wrote in the mid-1960s, "is something like a feudal king—he is first in the land; he receives elaborate homage and respect; but he is dependent on the powerful lords, usually committee chairmen, who are basically hostile to the objectives of the national Democratic party and the Speaker. . . . Rayburn was frequently at odds with the committee oligarchs, who rule their own committees with the assured arrogance of absolute monarchs."[2]

O'Neill was in many respects well suited to the "go along, get along" House where insider skills and patience were highly valued while ideological fervor and policy ambition were regarded with suspicion. A committed New Deal liberal, O'Neill was above all a practical street-level politician who loved the personal interactions of campaigning and legislative service; he saw politics as a way of helping people but was not much interested in the details of policy. Son of a first-generation Irish American who spent his life in local politics and government, young Thomas grew up in the politics of ethnic working-class Boston. He saw the devastation the Great Depression wrought, he experienced the discrimination of Republican WASP (white Anglo-Saxon Protestant) Americans against the Irish, and as he observed his father's efforts to help, he saw the difference government could make.[3]

In 1936, at the age of twenty-four, O'Neill won election to the Massachusetts House, having failed in a bid for a seat on the Cambridge City Council not long before. He capped his state legislative career by helping to engineer a Democratic electoral takeover of the lower chamber in the 1948 elections and then serving as Speaker from 1949 to 1953. In 1952 he won election to the U.S. House seat vacated by John F. Kennedy, who moved up to the Senate.

When O'Neill entered the House of Representatives, John McCormack of Boston was the second-ranked Democrat in the party hierarchy and served as whip, since Democrats were in the minority during the Eighty-third Congress (1953–1954). As a member of the Massachusetts Democratic delegation, O'Neill was welcome at a large roundtable in the House dining room where McCormack held court every morning before the House went into session. McCormack invited O'Neill—naturally gregarious as well as politically savvy and unencumbered by family obligations, as his wife and children remained in Boston—to accompany McCormack on his nightly round of receptions. Before long, O'Neill had become McCormack's protégé and was occasionally invited to Speaker Rayburn's "Board of Education"—an informal gathering of the movers and shakers of the House and sometimes beyond and of a few carefully selected up-and-coming junior members.

When Democrats took back control of the House in 1954, Rayburn and McCormack tapped O'Neill for service on the Rules Committee. Because of the committee's key role in bringing legislation to the floor, the assignment was quite a coup for a second-term member. As O'Neill told the story: "In January of 1955, when I returned to Congress for my second term [doorkeeper] Fishbait Miller came into the House dining room one morning to say that the Speaker wanted to see me. . . . When I got to the Speaker's office, Rayburn said, 'I know all about you from John McCormack. And I know you understand party loyalty. So I'd like to make you a member of the Rules Committee.' "[4]

For a member more interested in the politics than the policy details of legislation, Rules was a perfect assignment. It enabled O'Neill to get to know most members of the House and to do favors for many. As O'Neill explained:

Before long I had earned a reputation for knowing what was going on. Within a couple of years, my fellow members started calling me to ask what was coming up next week on the floor of the House. . . .

Once that got around, my phone was always ringing. "Tip, what's coming up next week? Will there be any roll calls? How will it affect my area? Is it a vote I can miss?" . . .

Every Friday, I'd hear from members who wanted to know whether I thought they had to be back on Monday, or whether they could afford to stay home until Tuesday. Back then, we didn't yet have an effective whip organization to give out this kind of information, so I became a kind of informal whip to many of my colleagues.[5]

The Roots of Reform

Many liberal Democrats found the distribution of influence in the 1950s House highly frustrating. As O'Neill himself later wrote, "Congress in those days was dominated by a handful of old, conservative committee chairmen from the South."[6] The committee chairmen wielded immense power; they, not the party leadership or the party as a whole, set the policy agenda and determined the substance of legislation. The chairmen thwarted the liberals' policy goals by blocking liberal legislation and frustrated their desire to participate meaningfully in the legislative process by the often autocratic way they ran their committees.[7] Liberals complained that the result of the seniority system and the committee assignment process was that committee chairmen and the membership of the most important committees were unrepresentatively conservative. And no procedure or forum for holding chairmen or committee majorities responsible to the party majority existed.

The Rules Committee on which O'Neill served was, in the 1950s, controlled by a bipartisan conservative coalition that frequently prevented liberal legislation from reaching the floor or exacted substantive concessions as the price for allowing House consideration. Because seniority determined committee chairmanships, and once a member received a committee assignment, he was considered entitled to retain it, the Speaker had little control over committees. Thus even though Howard Smith of Virginia was, in O'Neill's words, "an arrogant son of a bitch and an ultraconservative who was no more a Democrat than the man in the moon,"[8] as chair of Rules, Smith could with impunity refuse to have his committee consider rules setting the terms of debate on legislation the Speaker and a majority of his party wanted to consider.

During most of the 1950s the House Democratic party was fairly evenly divided between southerners, most of whom were conservative, and northerners, who were predominantly liberal but included moderates and a few conservatives; thus, activist liberals could do little but complain. However, when elections in the late 1950s and the 1960s brought into the House a large number of liberal northern Democrats, a reform movement developed.

Liberal Democrats in the late 1950s formed the Democratic Study Group (DSG).[9] The DSG's initial and ostensible purpose was to provide information and coordination for liberal policy efforts; in fact, it would also play the lead role in efforts to reform the House. O'Neill was not an early member of the group.

After the election of John Kennedy as president in 1960, the DSG prevailed upon Speaker Rayburn to do something about Rules. Unchecked, the committee might well prevent the Democratic-controlled House from even voting on the major elements of the Democratic president's program. Rayburn decided to pack the committee and, after an intense battle, prevailed on the floor by a narrow margin.[10]

The mass of highly significant liberal legislation passed during the mid-1960s lessened liberal dissatisfaction with the system for a time. However, in the late 1960s, in the aftermath of the loss of the overwhelming numbers they had commanded in the mid-1960s and the replacement of a skillful progressive ally with the often hostile Nixon as president, liberals again intensified their efforts to reform the chamber. O'Neill played an important role in passage of the Legislative Reorganization Act of 1970, a major fruit of the effort. Although not a leader in the reform campaign, he agreed to sponsor and led the floor fight on the key provision allowing recorded teller votes in the Committee of the Whole where bills are amended.[11]

Ascending the Leadership Ladder

In 1971 O'Neill was chosen whip by the newly elected leadership team of Speaker Carl Albert and Majority Leader Hale Boggs, both of whom had moved up a slot on the leadership ladder when John McCormack retired.[12] Fortuitous circumstances played a role in O'Neill's being tapped after Albert vetoed Boggs's first choice. O'Neill had positioned himself well. He had been a loyal leadership man on Rules. He was widely known and widely popular in the House; in addition to all the favors his Rules Committee position had enabled him to do for members, in 1970 O'Neill took over as chair of the Democratic Congressional Campaign Committee (DCCC) and in that capacity traveled extensively to help Democratic candidates—incumbents and challengers—raise money and garner votes. His early opposition to the Vietnam War and his support for reform during the struggle over the 1970 Reorganization Act made him acceptable to the liberal reform activists in the party; at the same time his long service and conformity to the norms of the pre-reform House made him acceptable to the old guard.

O'Neill began the process of reshaping a small and only sporadically active whip system into an activist organization that could function as a major leadership instrument. During the 1960s the Democratic White House had done much of the vote counting and persuasion. With the presidency in Republican hands, a more vigorous whip system was needed. O'Neill began by persuading the Speaker and the majority leader to attend the weekly whip meetings, which consequently attracted much greater attendance from whips and from committee leaders asked to report on their legislation. He increased and began to systematize the office's dissemination of information to the membership. "As I saw it, the whip office was a kind of service organization for the members," O'Neill later wrote. "And the service we provided to our constituents was information."[13]

O'Neill had been whip for less than two years when Majority Leader Hale Boggs's plane disappeared over Alaska. Boggs was campaigning for a junior colleague, as leaders were increasingly expected to do. When a massive search failed to find a trace of the plane, O'Neill, with support from Boggs's wife and staff, began to line up commitments. In January 1973, he was elected majority leader without opposition.

O'Neill's performance as majority leader during the Watergate scandal showed, as had his opposition to the Vietnam War, that he was more of a risk taker than his predecessors. By 1967, O'Neill had decided the war was wrong, and even though he knew it placed him in conflict with President Johnson, Speaker McCormack, and the views of his core constituency, O'Neill came out publicly against the war.[14] In his capacity as chair of the DCCC, a position he had retained when he became majority whip, O'Neill heard enough about the 1972 Nixon campaign's fundraising methods to suspect that a strong case for impeachment might exist. O'Neill pushed a reluctant Speaker Albert and a hypercautious Judiciary Committee Chairman Peter Rodino to start and keep the impeachment process moving.[15]

When Carl Albert retired at the end of 1976, Democrats chose O'Neill as Speaker, again without opposition. The second position in the party hierarchy was not as easily decided. After a hard-fought four-way contest, Jim Wright, a Texan with a moderate voting record who had served as a deputy whip, was elected majority leader.

Leading the Reformed House: Problems, Styles, and Strategies

The House that newly elected Speaker O'Neill was charged with leading had just undergone a major transformation.[16] The Legislative Reorganization Act of 1970 had been followed by a spate of reforms, mostly carried out in the Democratic caucus. Using their strength in that forum, the reformers—most of whom were northern liberals—made a series of changes intended to increase opportunities for rank-and-file participation in the legislative process and to enhance the responsiveness of the House legislative process to the policy preferences of party majorities. Among other things, they made the party leadership more capable of facilitating the advancement of the party majority's legislative goals.

The requirement that committee chairmen and the chairmen of Appropriations subcommittees win majority approval in the Democratic caucus was intended to make them responsive to the party majority, which was now clearly a liberal majority. A provision for regular meetings of the Democratic caucus provided a forum in which rank-and-file members could inform Democratic committee contingents of their views, and a few instances in which the caucus-instructed committees put committees on notice that they had better listen to strongly held caucus sentiments.

Policy and responsiveness motives also underlay the shifting of the committee assignment function from the Ways and Means Democrats to the new Steering and Policy Committee, chaired by the Speaker. The Speaker appoints a number of that committee's members. Ways and Means Democrats were seen as too conservative and not accountable to the party. The Steering and Policy Committee was designed to be both representative and responsive, its membership a combination of members elected from regional groups, elected party leaders, and leadership appointees.

Granting the Speaker the right to nominate all Democratic members and the chairman of the Rules Committee subject only to ratification by the caucus was a move clearly intended to give the leadership true control over the scheduling of legislation for the floor. By making Rules Democrats dependent upon the Speaker for their position on the committee, reformers made the committee an arm of the leadership.

A series of rules changes, some principally aimed at expanding participation opportunities, others also motivated by policy concerns, had the effect of increasing opportunities and incentives for participation in committee and on the floor. In an effort to spread positions of influence, members were limited to chairing no more than one subcommittee each. The subcommittee bill of rights removed from committee chairs the power to appoint subcommittee chairs and gave it to the Democratic caucus of the committee; it guaranteed subcommittees automatic referral of legislation and adequate budget and staff. The supply of resources, especially staff, available to Congress and its members was expanded and distributed much more broadly among members. The institution of the recorded teller vote in the Committee of the Whole changed the dynamics of the floor stage, increasing the incentives for offering amendments and often for opposing the committee's position. Sunshine reforms opened up most committee markups and conference committee meetings to the media and the public, encouraging members to use those forums for grand-standing as well as for policy entrepreneurship.

By the mid-1970s, increased participation by rank-and-file members at both the committee and the floor stage, the growing attractiveness of the freelance entrepreneurial style, and large numbers of inexperienced sub-committee chairmen multiplied the number of significant actors and rad-ically increased uncertainty.[17] Democratic committee contingents, Demo-cratic committee leaders, and the Democratic membership needed help passing their legislation and looked to the party leadership for assistance. The problem the party leadership faced was providing that help without constricting the participation opportunities members prized and within the context of continuing ideological heterogeneity. Although the number of House Democrats was large in both the Ninety-fifth and Ninety-sixth Congresses (292 and 277, respectively), the salient issues of the time split the party, especially but not exclusively along regional lines.[18]

The first reformed Congress, the heavily Democratic Ninety-fourth (1975–1976), failed to meet members' expectations of high legislative pro-ductivity. Unable to reconcile members' conflicting expectations, Speaker Carl Albert was criticized for being weak and ineffective and for not be-ing sufficiently accessible to members.

O'Neill was better suited than Albert to leading the new House. Natu-rally gregarious, O'Neill had maintained an open door policy since he be-came whip; members did not need an appointment to see him. Not only did he continue that policy as Speaker, he also continued to spend signif-icant amounts of time on the floor of the House where he would be even more accessible. As an O'Neill aide said, "If he's in the office too much, the Speaker gets itchy. He'll say, 'I should be on the floor or in the cloak room finding out what's going on.'"

Speaker O'Neill called his frequent one-on-one contact with members "listening to confession." According to an aide, "He plays the role of con-fessor or whipping boy for members. If they are unhappy about almost anything, not just with the House but with what the Senate or the Ad-ministration has done, they come and complain to him. It serves as a ve-hicle for the expression of their frustrations or as a catharsis." Playing the "father confessor" served to defuse tensions within the party and the House. "He listens to their problems. It's not necessary and often not pos-sible to do anything about their problems," a senior aide in another lead-ership office explained. "Listening is what's crucial. This should not be thought of as wasting time"—which, he added, is how Albert regarded it.

For all his amiability, O'Neill could when necessary be tough. He had made passage of a stringent congressional ethics code a priority, but be-

cause it included a limit on outside earned income that would significantly reduce their income, a number of Democrats on the Rules Committee balked at granting the rule the Speaker wanted. On February 24,
1977, O'Neill invited the Rules Committee Democrats to breakfast and, as
he later described it, told them, "Lookit. I've committed myself as the
leader of the party to the strongest ethics bill in the history of the country.
And I'm asking you, the Rules Committee, as the one hand-picked committee that's appointed by the Speaker. You're my handpicked people.
Now, I've been able to get this through the Obey Commission without
any difficulty and I would expect that I would be able to get it through
here."[19] A participant said that O'Neill then "went around the room and
got them to pledge support. There was a lot of screaming and moaning,
but they did." All eleven committee Democrats voted for the rule O'Neill
wanted.

The leadership team of Speaker Tip O'Neill and Majority Leader Jim
Wright developed over time a set of strategies for coping with the new
House. In addition to being heavily engaged in doing favors for individual members, as all leaderships in the post-1910 period have been, the
party leadership put great emphasis upon developing its service role. As
a senior O'Neill aide said in 1977, "This [leadership office] is a service organization."[20] The leaders strove in their scheduling decisions to be sensitive to members' needs for predictability and for time in their districts.
Through the whip system, they provided a plethora of timely and important information to the Democratic membership.

A second strategy involved including as many members as possible in
the coalition-building process. This strategy of inclusion entailed expanding and using formal leadership structures, such as the whip system, and
bringing other Democrats into the coalition-building process on an ad hoc
basis. The whip system that O'Neill had begun to invigorate in the early
1970s expanded in size and activity during the 1970s as the leaders appointed increasing numbers of deputy and at-large whips and more frequently called on the system to conduct whip counts. In 1977, O'Neill began to use bill-specific task forces on particularly important and difficult
legislation. He would pick a group of members, often including junior
members and others especially interested in the legislation at issue
though not on the committee of origin, and charge the group with mounting the campaign to pass the legislation.

The strategy of inclusion was designed to deal with several characteristics of the reformed House that made successful leadership difficult. In
the new House environment the core leadership was too small to undertake the task of successful coalition building alone; including other members provided needed assistance. The strategy of inclusion was also a way
for leaders to satisfy members' expectations that they play a significant

part in the legislative process but to do so in a manner beneficial to the party and the leadership.

Third, the leadership greatly refined the quintessential legislative strategy of using its control over procedure to structure the choices members confront on the House floor. By giving the Speaker control of the Rules Committee, the reforms had greatly enhanced the leadership's tools for structuring floor choices. In the mid-1970s, members' desires for maximum participation opportunities constrained the leadership's use of this resource. By the late 1970s, however, many Democrats were having second thoughts. The unrestricted amending process was resulting in frequent lengthy and late sessions; Republicans were becoming increasingly adept at drafting amendments that put Democrats on the record on politically difficult issues; and legislative compromises, carefully crafted in committee, were being picked apart on the floor.[21] In August 1979, over forty Democrats signed a letter to Speaker O'Neill complaining about the length of floor sessions and calling for more frequent use of restrictive rules. The Rules Committee, in response to a variety of new floor problems, had made increasing use of complex rules; now, in concert with the party leadership, it increasingly reported rules that restricted amending activity to some extent.[22] During the 1980s such rules were to become a key element of leadership strategy.

Triumphs and Tribulations: Working with Carter

"I'm a partisan Democrat," Tip O'Neill said during Carter's first year as president. "The President of the United States is the leader of my party."[23] O'Neill and his leadership team, like all majority party leaderships since Franklin Roosevelt's time, considered passing the program of a president of their own party to be among their central responsibilities; they worked loyally and hard to enact Carter's legislative priorities, even though the administration's mistakes sometimes made their task doubly difficult.

Relations between the House and President Carter got off to a rocky start because of Carter's failure to consult. Five days after the inauguration, O'Neill told Carter, "You, Mr. President, should keep us posted on what the White House is doing on legislation, so that if we have responsibility for moving it, we know what is going on."[24] Yet Carter decided to recommend cutting funds for nineteen water projects and to withdraw his fifty-dollar tax rebate without prior congressional consultation.

Carter's determination to cut water projects he considered pork barrels led to one of the very few instances of the House majority party leadership leading the fight against the president's position. Although the House leaders believed strongly in supporting a president of their own party, their first responsibility is to their party colleagues in the House and to the

House as an institution. Thus their support of a president is not uncondi-
tional, and it can vary in intensity. When Carter vetoed a public works bill
because he disapproved of some of the water projects included, the leadership opposed him and attempted to override the veto. Several years after the water projects fight the memory still rankled. "Carter wanted a
fight with the Congress and with the leadership that had saved his hide on
a lot of close votes," a participant said. "That was demagoguing."

Much more often the leaders were working to pass the president's program, and they found Carter's initial reluctance to do for members of
Congress the numerous small favors his office enabled him to do a problem. The Carter administration was recalcitrant on everything from
schedule C jobs in the regional offices, which historically have been filled
at the prerogative of members of Congress, to sending birthday greetings
to prominent constituents. Some of Carter's top staff developed a reputation for being both arrogant and ignorant; of Carter's chief of staff,
O'Neill said, "As far as Jordan was concerned, a House Speaker was
something you bought on sale at Radio Shack."[25] Carter's congressional
liaison office became notorious for not even answering members' phone
calls. Carter seemed unaware that if he wanted members of Congress to
help him, he had to help them in return, that his own success depended
on his using the resources of the presidency to help members attain their
individual goals. The president, as one House leader said, "was terribly
naive about some very basic realities."

Over time the Carter administration became somewhat more adept at
dealing with Congress. The early troubles, however, had a lasting impact.
Too many Democrats never developed any personal sense of loyalty to
the president. As a result, although the White House did get involved in
persuasion efforts, the leadership bore the brunt of the in-House effort. As
a House participant said, "There's always something [the White House
people] need help on. Sometimes it's the other way around. But they
come to us for help much more than vice versa because the Speaker has a
lot of credits, a lot of loyalty, and Carter doesn't."

Early in the Carter presidency, Speaker O'Neill engineered House passage of Carter's massive energy program, thereby giving the new administration a much needed success and winning for himself a reputation as
a strong leader. When the White House unveiled its energy package,
knowledgeable observers considered its prospects bleak. As O'Neill explained the problem:

> The energy package that was sent over by the Carter White House was so
> enormous and complex that I took one look at it and groaned. What the pres-
> ident and his staff failed to understand was that their legislation would be
> taken up by as many as seventeen different committees and subcommittees

of the House, and that each of these committees included members who opposed certain parts of the package. I shuddered to think what would be left
of the bill when it was all over—assuming we managed to get any of it
through . . . .
 [T]his one looked hopeless to me. And under the existing structure of congressional committees, there really was no way. Unless, of course, we
changed the existing structure.[26]

To overcome this problem, O'Neill decided to set up an ad hoc energy
committee. It would consider and could amend the energy bill after the
various standing committees had considered the sections within their jurisdiction. By giving the substantive committees the first opportunity to
shape the legislation, O'Neill avoided alienating their members; nevertheless, the ad hoc committee—the members of which O'Neill chose with
great care—would assure the package made sense and would allow
O'Neill to set strict reporting deadlines on the substantive committees.

The process worked as O'Neill had hoped. On August 5, 1977, only six
months after Carter's energy speech to the nation, the House passed the
legislation by a vote of 244 to 177. O'Neill had set up four task forces—
one on each of the three major amendments and one on passage—to educate and persuade members to support the party position. This was the
first use of the task force device, and all four successfully accomplished
their mission.[27]

By the end of his first year as Speaker, with victories on the energy
package and on the ethics code, O'Neill was being hailed as the strongest
Speaker since Rayburn. In that early period O'Neill showed himself to be
willing and able to innovate; the development of new leadership strategies and of a new leadership role in the legislative process was under
way. There were a number of subsequent important successes during the
Carter administration—for example, bills aiding New York City, raising
the minimum wage, and reforming Social Security during the Ninety-
fifth Congress (1977–1978) and legislation providing for Chrysler loan
guarantees, a windfall profits tax, and the implementation of the Panama
Canal treaty during the Ninety-sixth Congress (1979–1980). Overall, on
major bills that the president or a core party constituency declared top
priority, the House majority party leadership was at least reasonably successful in those two Congresses. The leadership won approximately 65
percent of its legislative battles on such big bills and suffered defeats on
20 percent; in the remaining cases, the results were mixed. There were
also some bad defeats for the House leadership and for Carter. The energy bill was severely watered down in the Senate, and O'Neill had to
pull out the stops to pass the conference report in the House. He had to
pressure Rules Committee Democrats to report out a rule that would prevent a separate vote on an unpopular provision, thus increasing the like-

lihood of floor success; he again set up a task force to mobilize the vote. O'Neill and his team were unsuccessful in getting through the House common situs picketing legislation, which was very important to labor, and hospital cost control, a major Carter priority.[28]

Although the administration's amateurishness was a factor, the mixed record of the Carter Congresses was much more the result of a heterogeneous Democratic party and of an issue agenda that accentuated the splits within the party. In the domestic policy realm, environmental, consumer protection, and energy legislation split Democrats, particularly but not exclusively along regional lines. In foreign and defense policy, a variety of issues that had come out of the debate over the Vietnam War continued to divide the Democratic party, and with a Democrat in the White House, House Republicans repeatedly offered floor amendments intended to exacerbate the split.[29]

Hard Times: The Early Reagan Years

"Jimmy Carter was a victim of bad luck and bad timing," wrote Tip O'Neill in his autobiography. "It wasn't his fault that oil prices tripled and wrecked our economy, or that a band of Iranians seized our hostages and held them for over a year."[30] Whether Carter's fault or not, he and his party paid a heavy price in the 1980 elections. Ronald Reagan won the presidency, Democrats lost thirty-three seats in the House, and to everyone's surprise, Republicans took control of the Senate. Although House Democrats still held 243 seats to 192 for Republicans, relatively conservative southern Democrats more than accounted for the margin. Given how well Reagan had fared in their districts, they were particularly inclined to interpret the election as a mandate for Reagan's program.

When Ronald Reagan was elected president, O'Neill and Wright knew, of course, that their relationship with the White House would change, that both partisan and ideological differences would introduce an element of antagonism into the relationship. Given the policies Reagan had espoused during the campaign, the Democratic leaders realized that they and the administration would often take opposite sides on domestic legislative issues. Yet the leaders still hoped for a relationship similar to that between President Eisenhower and congressional leaders Rayburn and Johnson. In announcing an agreement on the scheduling of the president's economic program, the majority leader said, "This agreement is a convincing demonstration of the capacity of responsible bipartisanship to help this institution to function at its best. It is reminiscent of the spirit of understanding and mutual trust which prevailed during the Eisenhower administration."[31]

The relationship that soon developed, however, was the antithesis of a mutually trusting one. The Democratic leaders knew that many of their members read the 1980 election returns as a mandate for a more conservative economic policy, and they realized their majority was shaky; consequently, they were willing to make what they believed to be major concessions. The same factors seem to have convinced the administration that dealing with the House Democratic leadership was unnecessary. The leaders found the president unwilling to compromise with them. One of them said, "I set out with the expectation of trying to be a bridge between the Congress and the president. I wanted to make a demonstration of our ability to work with the president, to give him cooperation and to show that we could be constructive as members of his loyal opposition. That, unfortunately, has not been possible. Each time we have sought to meet him halfway, or in some cases more than halfway, he has publicly denounced our effort, claiming that it was obstructionism."

During the first year of the Reagan administration, Speaker O'Neill and the House Democrats suffered a succession of disastrous losses. Because they did not want House Democrats to be labeled obstructionist and because the Senate, now under Republican control, could force their hand in any case, the leadership agreed to an expedited schedule for bringing the president's economic program to the floor. The administration decided to use the budget process as the primary vehicle for their economic program because doing so would allow them to make large numbers of policy changes through a small number of bills. It also made it possible for them to frame the choice members faced as voting for or against President Reagan's economic program, for or against curbing wasteful and inflation-producing federal spending in general. Public attention was deflected away from whether specific social programs, many of which were still very popular, should be cut.

The first step in implementing the administration's strategy entailed passing a budget resolution that committed the Congress to making the domestic spending cuts, defense spending increases, and tax reductions that constituted the Reagan program. Although the House Budget Committee reported a budget resolution that Democrats who controlled the committee saw as a compromise giving Reagan much of what he wanted, the administration decided to fight. On the crucial floor vote, the administration substitute defeated the Democratic budget resolution on a vote of 253 to 176; 63 Democrats defected and joined a united Republican membership on the vote.

Disappointed and embittered, many House Democrats criticized their leadership. They blamed O'Neill for taking a long-planned trip to Australia during the recess before the vote rather than staying and countering the well-orchestrated administration campaign. Wright was criticized for having supported Phil Gramm for a Budget Committee position, after Gramm then worked with the administration and Republicans to defeat the Democratic plan. Yet few members believed that the vote could have been won, even if the leadership had acted differently. By and large the defectors had responded to what they perceived as strong, clear signals from their constituencies to support Reagan. "Members were scared to death about their election," a Democrat explained. If a member has received five hundred calls from his district, "there's no way 'Tip' can go into a member's district and promise he'll make it OK."

House Democrats also lost, although on a much closer vote, on the reconciliation bill that actually legislated the Reagan spending cuts and on the tax bill. In both cases, administration substitutes won over legislation drafted by the Democratic-controlled committees after very effective administration campaigns.

O'Neill's reputation plummeted; the media now labeled him weak and ineffectual, over the hill and out of touch. House Democrats were quoted—sometimes by name—making disparaging remarks about the Speaker, and there were even calls for him to resign.[32]

The leadership responded to their membership's demoralization and dissatisfaction by intensifying the strategy of inclusion. The whip system was expanded further, the Steering and Policy Committee met more frequently, more members were invited into leadership meetings, and the Democratic caucus, relatively inactive during the Carter administration, became an important forum for the discussion of strategy as well as a safety valve. One participant commented, "There has been a lot of acrimony within the party. This is a forum for letting off steam." Because the top leadership attended all caucus meetings, members could voice their criticisms and, as another participant said, "know their message is received." Of course, the debate over how to respond to the Reagan administration raged in all the forums where House Democrats gathered, but because it was a debate in which all Democrats wanted to participate, the caucus was a frequent venue.

Although these debates often contained at least implicit criticisms of the leadership, they were in fact helpful to it. "The Speaker has mentioned to me that to give everybody an opportunity to get up and say, 'I think this is the strategy we ought to follow' broadens the leadership's ability to discern a consensus of which direction most of them are willing to go," a member explained. In addition, as other Democrats pointed out, when members believe they have had "input" into strategy decisions they are more likely to be willing to adhere to them.

By the fall of 1981, the political climate had improved for Democrats, and they began to win an occasional victory. With the 1982 elections, in which Democrats picked up twenty-six seats, Democrats won back effective control of the House. No longer did conservative southern "Boll Weevil" Democrats hold the balance of power. Furthermore, as a result of the party's electoral success, many Democrats, particularly moderate southerners, lost much of their fear of a Reagan Revolution that would sweep them out of office unless they supported the administration. House Democrats' voting cohesion jumped significantly.

Relations between the House Democratic leadership and the administration remained distant and basically hostile, but now the balance of power was more nearly equal. There were no regularly scheduled meetings between the House Democratic leadership and the president as there had been during the Ford administration and, of course, the Carter administration. Meetings were infrequent. "The Speaker gets invited down to the White House not more than once a month for anything serious," a Speaker's aide reported; the rest of the leadership team met with the president even less frequently. "They don't consult with us at all," an aide concluded.

President Reagan's inability or unwillingness to discuss policy in any detail also frustrated the leadership. "He doesn't get into discussions as Carter and Johnson and other presidents whom I've known have wanted to do," a Democratic leader reported. An aide was blunt: "To sum up what many members, Jim Wright, Tip O'Neill, and Rostenkowski among them, have concluded in their meetings with the president, he is a nonsubstance man—he doesn't know that much."

Refining Leadership Strategies

The shift in the political environment offered Democrats legislative opportunities; yet, with the presidency and the Senate still in Republican hands and a growing budget deficit that constrained policy choices, passing legislation satisfactory to Democrats presented a formidable challenge. House Democrats needed help.

The voting cohesion of House Democrats, which had jumped after the 1982 elections, continued to increase and in the late 1980s and early 1990s reached levels unprecedented in the post–World War II era. For the period 1951 through 1970, House Democrats' average party unity score was 78 percent; this fell to 74 percent for the 1971–1982 period. The scores began rising in the Ninety-eighth Congress and averaged 86 percent for the 1983–1992 period. During this same period, the proportion of roll calls on which a majority of Democrats voted against a majority of Republicans also increased, averaging 56 percent compared with 37 percent during the 1971–1982 period.[33] As policy differences among Democrats declined, so did fears that the exercise of stronger leadership would pose a threat to individual members' policy or reelection goals.

In attempting to satisfy their members' legislative expectations, the House Democratic leadership became increasingly involved in the pre-floor legislative process, working to assure that legislation got to the floor in a form acceptable to most Democrats and passable on the House floor. Early in his tenure as Speaker, O'Neill, through staff, had monitored the work of committees and occasionally intervened, through staff or person-ally, to reconcile intraparty differences that threatened floor success. The multiple referral rule, instituted in 1975, also drew the leadership into the prefloor legislative process as mediators and referees among the multiple committees considering a single bill. In the more difficult political climate of the 1980s, the demands on the leadership for active involvement grew. More of the major legislation was multiply referred, sometimes to a large number of committees; for a variety of reasons, including especially con-flict with the White House, the use of omnibus measures increased; and, again because of conflict with a conservative, confrontational president, legislative battles frequently involved high political and policy stakes. Putting together and passing such legislation often required negotiation and coordination activities beyond the capacity of committee leaders. Furthermore, on high-stakes measures, committee leaders lacked the le-gitimacy to speak for the membership as a whole. Those tasks increas-ingly fell on the party leaders.

When agreement must be reached with political actors outside the House on highly salient, high-stakes matters, members may be leery of relying solely upon the judgment of committee leaders whose perspec-tives and interest may differ from their own, thus requiring that the party leaders represent their members. Divided control, the sharp differences in policy preferences between Republican presidents and congressional Democrats, and the tough decisions that had to be made often stalemated normal processes and made a resort to extraordinary processes necessary during the 1980s and early 1990s. In the early 1980s, it became evident that the Social Security trust fund was headed toward financial difficul-ties and needed to be shored up. The issue, however, became so centrally enmeshed in partisan politics that normal processes in the administration and the Congress were completely incapable of producing and enacting a solution. In late 1981, President Reagan by executive order established a commission on Social Security, his aim being to distance himself from the political problem. The commission—a large if distinguished group that met in public—was not able to agree on a solution. In late December 1982, however, a much smaller subset of commission members began serious negotiations in informal, secret sessions. Crucial to the ultimate success of the process was the inclusion of negotiators who could act as agents of the principals whose agreement was essential—President Reagan and Speaker O'Neill. George Ball, a former commissioner of Social Security, acted as lead negotiator for the Democrats; Dick Darmen and Jim Baker negotiated for the White House. Both kept in close touch with their principals. Thus, when they reached an agreement in early 1983, it was one the president and the Speaker could accept. Only a few months later, the package was enacted into law.[34]

During the 1980s and early 1990s, normal processes frequently proved incapable of producing agreements in areas where the costs of failing to reach an accord would have been very high. "Summits," relatively formal negotiations between congressional leaders and high-ranking administration officials representing the president directly, were the recourse. Most often employed on budget matters, but foreign policy—specifically Central American policy—also occasioned such high-level cross-branch negotiations. Invariably, the party leadership has represented its membership in these negotiations.

To facilitate the passage of legislation Democrats wanted and needed, the leadership during the 1980s developed special rules into powerful devices that can be used to focus attention and debate on the critical choices, to save time and prevent obstruction and delay, and sometimes to structure the choices members confront on the floor so as to give some outcomes an advantage over others. In the mid- and late 1970s, most ordinary legislation was still considered under an open rule allowing all germane amendments; in the Ninety-fifth Congress (1977–1978), 85 percent was considered under an open rule. Many Democrats began to have doubts about the political and policy consequences of an unrestricted amending process in the late 1970s, and within the much more adverse political climate of the 1980s, most Democrats became convinced that the costs were too high. The preponderance of open rules began to decline in the late 1970s and early 1980s and then dropped sharply from the mid-1980s through the early 1990s; in the Ninety-ninth Congress (1985–1986) 57 percent of rules were simple open ones and in the 102d (1991–1992), 34 percent were. By the late 1980s most major legislation was brought to the floor under a complex and usually restrictive rule, that is, a rule that placed some restrictions on the amendments that could be offered.[35]

Although, on its face, the strategy of structuring choices via restrictive rules seems coercive, the leadership generally used it in such a way that it contributed to reconciling members' expectation of aggressive action to pass legislation the membership wanted with their potentially conflicting expectation of sensitivity to members' individual needs. Since approval of a rule required a majority of the House membership and thus usually a much larger proportion of Democrats, members had to acquiesce in having their choices constrained. They usually did so because the leadership had skillfully crafted the rule so that, on balance, approval furthered most members' goals. Frequently, the leadership attempted to provide "cover" or protection for members to enable them to vote their policy preferences without paying too big a reelection price. Sometimes the rule made possible the passage of a bill that all members knew had to be enacted but that was unpalatable on both policy and reelection grounds. And if a significant group of Democrats needed a vote on an amendment for constituency reasons, the leadership would provide the opportunity, though it would structure the choice so as to minimize the policy damage.

The vote mobilization process was also refined during the 1980s. The task force device became routine, even an institution. The regionally elected zone whips carried out the initial count of Democrats' voting intentions, as they traditionally had. The bulk of the vote mobilization work was performed by a bill-specific whip's task force now constituted by sending out a broad-based invitation to all whips and to other potentially interested Democrats. The members of the task force refined the count by checking personally on the voting intentions of members not contacted or undecided on the initial count; by one-on-one contacts, they attempted to persuade members not committed to the party position to support it. They "worked the doors," standing at the chamber doors to assure that members knew what the party position was on the vote and to answer questions if necessary; they "worked the floor," attempting some last-minute persuasion if necessary. During the late 1980s and early 1990s, about seventy task forces functioned per Congress.

Task forces provided party leaders with badly needed assistance; they enabled leaders to spend more of their time on strategy planning and to reserve their own persuasive efforts for the hard cases. Task forces provided members the opportunity to become significantly involved in legislation they cared about, even if they were junior or not on the committee of origin—an opportunity that restrictive rules made less available on the House floor.

The Public Speakership

In the early 1980s Ronald Reagan taught House Democrats a lesson about the uses of the media that altered their expectations of their own leaders. Reagan's media skills and the favorable political climate allowed him to dominate public debate and thereby dictate the policy agenda and propagate a highly negative image of the Democratic party. Unable as individuals to counter this threat to their policy and reelection goals, Democrats expected their leaders to take on the task, to participate effectively in national political discourse and thereby promote the membership's policy agenda and protect and enhance the party's image. Unlike rank-and-file

House members, the party leaders did have considerable access to the national media.

In the aftermath of the Republican takeover of the Senate in the 1980 elections, the press anointed Speaker O'Neill—now clearly the highest-ranked Democrat in Washington—as chief Democratic spokesman and thus enhanced his media access. As part of their 1982 election campaign, Republicans tried to make the Speaker, a heavy, rumpled man with a cartoonist's dream of an old pol face, into a symbol of big, out-of-control government; generic ads with an O'Neill look-alike were run nationwide. As a result, O'Neill became much better known to the public at large than any Speaker before him. (Presumably much to the Republicans' surprise, by the mid-1980s O'Neill not only became a nationally known figure but a highly popular one.) "Sam Rayburn could have walked down the streets of Spokane, Wash. without anybody noticing him," then majority whip Tom Foley said in 1986. "Tip O'Neill couldn't do that. And it's very unlikely that any future Speaker will be anonymous to the country," remarked the man who would himself become a highly visible Speaker.[36] The majority party leaders increased their contacts with the press during the 1980s. The short press conference the Speaker holds every day when the House is in session attracted increasing numbers of reporters. Although O'Neill never felt comfortable on television, the lower-ranked leaders and then Speakers Wright and Foley appeared frequently on Sunday talk shows and on such programs as the *MacNeil-Lehrer News Hour.*

Over time the leadership developed more sophisticated media strategies to get their message out. Efforts to systematize the dissemination of the Democratic party's perspective led, by the late 1980s, to the institution of the Message Group. This was a group of about eighteen members ("midlevel activists who understand the media") who met in the majority leader's office every morning that the House was in session. Their aim was to link the major item on the week's legislative schedule—"the anchor"—to one of the general themes the House Democrats were attempting to develop. The unified theme was then conveyed to other members—with the aim of "getting everyone to sing from the same hymn book"—and to the media through a variety of means, including the Message Board, a large group of Democrats responsible for organized theme-related one-minute speeches on the House floor.

The leadership also learned from more experienced media players a variety of special techniques for getting coverage. The press conference with participants especially appealing to the media—celebrities or those with human interest stories illustrating the need for a particular bill—became a part of the leadership repertoire. So too did the media event; the "Grate American Sleep Out" in which members of Congress slept on the streets of Washington for a night to call attention to the plight of the homeless received substantial media attention. "Counterprogramming" to take advantage of media routines was a not infrequent strategy during the Reagan and Bush administrations. On any day the president was known to be addressing a major issue, some event that highlighted the congressional Democrats' opposed views was planned. Media norms of fairness dictated coverage of the event.

Despite some successes, the congressional leadership's ability to influence the terms of the debate when competing with the president was severely limited. The president's standing as head of state and government and his greater media access as well as the impossibility of getting all the members to "sing from the same hymn book" contributed to the congressional party's problem in conveying a clear message to the public. Consequently, party leaders were seldom able to fully satisfy their members with how they carried out the spokesman role.

Democrats also increasingly came to expect their party leaders to take an active role in setting the congressional agenda. Congressional Democrats were dissatisfied with Reagan's and Bush's agendas. Yet even when the president's party is a minority in Congress, he has great advantages in the struggle to define the national and the congressional agenda; to get their preferred issues on the agenda, House Democrats needed their leadership's aid.

House Democrats made some attempt to counter Reagan with their own agenda even during the first Congress of his presidency, when he was politically strongest. Although O'Neill in his speech accepting election as Speaker in 1981 simply pledged cooperation, in April he announced a Democratic economic program that had been drafted by a task force chaired by Dick Gephardt. During the first half of 1981, the political tides were running too strongly in Reagan's favor, and this agenda-setting attempt sank without a trace; it produced neither legislation nor good publicity. In 1982, however, House Democrats, helped by the developing recession, were a little more successful. A leadership-appointed task force chaired by Majority Leader Jim Wright drafted an economic program, consisting mostly of various sorts of jobs programs, that did become an important part of the congressional agenda.

In December 1986, immediately after being chosen the Democrats' nominee for Speaker, Jim Wright outlined a policy agenda for the majority party and the House that included deficit reduction achieved in part through a tax increase, clean water legislation, a highway bill, trade legislation, welfare reform, and a farm bill. In his acceptance speech after being elected Speaker on January 6, 1987, and in his televised reply to Reagan's State of the Union address on January 31, Wright further specified and publicized the agenda, adding aid to education, aid to the homeless, and insurance against catastrophic illness. Special political conditions facilitated the Speaker's aggressive agenda setting. President Reagan had been weakened by the Iran-Contra scandal, the loss of a Senate majority, and his lame-duck status. House Democrats believed that they finally had the opportunity to pass legislation stymied during six years of the Reagan administration—if they were disciplined enough to exploit the opportunity. House Democrats wanted policy leadership.

The member expectations to which Speaker Wright responded, although intensified by these special circumstances, were not created by them nor were they satiated by Wright's endeavors. During the Bush administration, Speaker Tom Foley was substantially more involved in agenda setting than Albert or O'Neill ever had been; yet to the extent that he pursued that course less aggressively than Wright, Foley was subject to considerable member criticism.

The O'Neill-Wright-Foley Legacy

In the 1980s, a highly active, broadly involved, and yet inclusive House Democratic party leadership emerged, one that was frequently involved in all stages of the legislative process, that engaged in a broad range of legislative and political activities, and that included as many Democrats as possible in its efforts. The change got under way during the speakership of Tip O'Neill and continued during the Wright and Foley speakerships. These leaders' attempts to satisfy their members' demands for policy and for the opportunity to participate within the uncertain environment created by the 1970s reforms and then in the hostile 1980s political climate shaped that leadership. To be sure, these men's different personalities affected how they exercised leadership. Tip O'Neill was never a detail man and so relied heavily on others, including Majority Leader Wright, Rules Committee chair Richard Bolling, and staff, when strategy required detailed knowledge of legislation. O'Neill's unparalleled political instincts and feel for the House and its members contributed enormously to holding the party together during trying times and to the leadership's finding more often than not that delicate balance between what members considered as too permissive and too directive leadership. Wright was the most aggressive of the three in agenda setting and the quickest to intervene in committee and pressure committee chairmen. Tom Foley was more inclined to let the agenda evolve from a highly inclusive process and, as a former committee chairman, deferred to chairmen more and tended to wait longer before he intervened. These were, however, differences at the margin. House Democrats expected their leaders to produce legislative results, and to do so required an active leadership willing to use its tools assertively.

Tip O'Neill's contribution and that of his successors was to reshape majority party leadership into an instrument that made it possible for the reformed House to function legislatively, even in a period of severe legislative constraint. The 1970s reforms destroyed the old distribution of power; with the demise of powerful, autonomous committees and deferential and low-participating junior members, the House faced serious problems in legislating. In the 1980s and 1990s, the political context of huge deficits and, until 1993, divided control exacerbated the difficulties of legislating enormously. Deficits make all the choices difficult ones; divided control makes it necessary to somehow overcome deep policy differences between the president and congressional majorities in making the tough choices. Yet, despite this context, the House continued to perform its legislative functions and, during the most difficult of these times, managed to protect and even enhance its role in the U.S. political system. The activist, inclusive leadership and the more flexible and varied legislative process that was a component of such leadership made this possible.

What none of these Democratic leaders could do successfully was convey to the public their institution's considerable accomplishments. Never popular and subject to unrelenting criticism from Republicans and the media, Congress sank to new lows in public esteem. In 1994, House Democrats paid the price for a Democratic president's unpopularity, the Senate's antimajoritarian rules, and their own leaders' inability effectively to counter anti-Democrat and anti-Congress sentiments; they lost majority control of the House for the first time in forty years.

Republican Leadership in the 1980s and 1990s: From Cooperation to Bomb Throwing to Governing

Greater Democratic cohesion and stronger majority party leadership made House Republicans increasingly peripheral to the legislative process in House during the 1980s. The "action" on major legislation increasingly took place within the majority party. The Republican membership's substantial move to the right, which made bipartisanship less feasible, also increased Republicans' dissatisfaction with their minority lot.[37]

Bob Michel of Illinois, who was elected Republican leader in 1981 after six years as minority whip, had begun his House service in 1957, a time when party lines were less sharply drawn and cross-party cooperation more frequent. He served for many years on the Appropriations Committee, known for its bipartisan mode of operation. Although capable of displaying fierce partisanship, he saw the minority's role as one of constructive participation in the legislative process; negotiation and compromise, he believed, defined such participation. He and O'Neill were good friends and frequent golfing buddies; they trusted each other and could work together.

As Republicans' frustrations with their minority status grew, Michel's conciliatory leadership was called into question. In 1983 an obscure junior member named Newt Gingrich and a number of like-minded firebrands formed the Conservative Opportunity Society (COS) and began to use the televised special orders at the end of each House session to attack Democrats and the Congress in highly charged language. COS advocated a strategy based on high-visibility confrontation and polarization, a strategy that put attempting to win a majority above participation in governing.

COS members as well as Republicans more generally began complaining bitterly about majority party tyranny; specifically, they excoriated restrictive rules as devices for stifling debate and preventing the majority from working its will. Although the very nature of politics in the 1980s and early 1990s served to drive the House parties into hostile opposing camps, several events became particularly important symbols for Republicans. In 1985, House Democrats seated the Democratic candidate in a contested House election, provoking screams of theft from Republicans. In late 1987, after an unbroken string of major victories for Democrats, Republicans thought they had defeated the Democratic reconciliation bill, but Speaker Wright held open the roll call long enough to turn the results around; again Republicans charged theft.

Over the years, Gingrich and his allies maintained and intensified their campaign against the Democrats and the Congress, branding them as corrupt, out of touch, and essentially illegitimate—a message that resonated with the media's own cynical view. Democrats and initially even many Republicans considered Gingrich and his followers irresponsible "bomb throwers," but when Speaker Wright was forced to resign because of ethics charges that Newt Gingrich had brought, Gingrich's confrontational, scorched-earth strategy was validated in the eyes of many Republicans. In 1989, Gingrich defeated Bob Michel's candidate in the race for Republican whip, the number-two slot in the party hierarchy.

The 1994 elections, in which Republicans picked up fifty-two seats in the House and took control, made Newt Gingrich Speaker. Bob Michel had retired at the end of the previous Congress; although his leadership style had become more partisan and hard-edged in response to his members' demands, Michel almost certainly would have been challenged by Gingrich had he chosen to remain. Gingrich was, in fact, the de facto leader of House Republicans in the 103d Congress and was credited with engineering the extraordinary 1994 victory.

To legislate successfully, especially when control is divided, the contemporary House needs an activist, engaged majority party leadership.

Certainly in 1995, Gingrich provided such leadership. For Gingrich and his leadership team, the prerequisites for the exercise of strong leadership were there—the tools and, most critically, a membership that wanted them to lead aggressively. Strong leadership depends on both, but it is the latter that is essential.

During the 1980s and early 1990s, Republicans had imitated Democrats in adopting various party rules changes that strengthened their party leadership. The leader was given the power to make Republican appointments to the Rules Committee and a bigger voice in the making of other committee assignments, a rather elaborate whip system was developed, and committee leaders were made more accountable to the Republican membership.[38]

Relying on his enormous prestige with House Republicans, in the days after the 1994 elections Gingrich exercised power well beyond that specified in Republican conference rules. He designated Republicans to serve as committee chairs, bypassing seniority in several instances. According to the rules, the party Committee on Committees nominates chairs and the conference approves them; Gingrich preempted that process, assuming correctly that his stature would prevent anyone from challenging his choices. He also engineered a rules change to increase further the party leadership's voice on the Committee on Committees and used that new influence to reward junior Republicans who were his strongest supporters with choice assignments. A three-term limit on committee chairs, already a conference rule, was written into House rules. The change makes committee chairs less formidable competitors for power in the chamber.

The members of the new Republican majority were ideologically quite homogeneous and believed themselves to be mandated to bring about major policy change. Before the elections, House Republicans under Gingrich's lead developed and pledged themselves to a legislative agenda—the Contract with America. Thus, even as leader of the minority, Gingrich had engaged in the sort of agenda setting that Democrats were increasingly demanding of their leadership during periods of divided control, and it paid off handsomely in 1995. Even though the contract had little impact on voters' decisions—most had not even heard of it—it served an invaluable function for Republicans in the early part of the 104th Congress: It provided them with an agreed-upon agenda and thus prevented intraparty conflict over priorities, it gave a focus to their activities that paid dividends in media coverage, and it provided their leadership with immense leverage with committee chairs who were not always supportive of specific agenda items in their jurisdiction and, in any case, might otherwise have taken more time to process the legislation.

Although the conditions for the exercise of strong leadership were optimal in 1995, Gingrich faced the same balancing act the Democratic leadership confronted. Republicans wanted and needed policy results, but after forty years out of power, Republican House members also had high expectations of participating fully in the legislative process. And these expectations had to be satisfied within a climate of even greater hostility between the parties. By late 1995, the political context had begun to change. Democratic attacks and the government shutdowns branded House Republicans as extremists, and the party's (and Gingrich's) approval ratings plummeted. Opposition from the Senate and the White House blocked much of the major legislation House Republicans had passed. The 1996 elections with their murky message sapped the last of the sense of mandate that had animated the House Republican membership in the 104th Congress. Under these much more adverse conditions, the balancing act confronting the leadership becomes more difficult, and it is more essential to get it right.

The strategies the new majority party leadership team uses in its attempt to reconcile these potentially conflicting member demands are similar to those developed by their Democratic predecessors. Despite their scathing criticism of the Democratic leadership for its frequent use of restrictive rules and their own promise to bring up the legislative proposals in the contract under open rules, Republicans regularly use complex and restrictive rules to structure floor choices; in the 104th Congress, 77 percent of the rules for major measures were restrictive.[39] The narrow Republican majority and a Democratic minority willing and able to make good use of the opportunities provided by open rules made that percentage necessary if Republicans were to deliver on their campaign promises. During the 104th Congress, the Republican leadership was even more active than its Democratic predecessors in intervening at the prefloor stage to shape legislation. And Republican leaders clearly pursued the strategy of inclusion, seeking to involve their members, especially junior ones, in the legislative process under leadership auspices. Junior members were given good committee assignments, and in a few cases freshmen even got subcommittee chairmanships; a multitude of task forces was set up; the whip system was significantly expanded; and several junior members are now included in leadership meetings.

Gingrich was most innovative in his media strategy. His adept use of the media was largely responsible for his climb up the leadership ladder. The Contract with America proved to be a brilliant stroke. He learned the value of a clearly defined, high-saliency agenda from Jim Wright, but getting most Republican candidates to pledge themselves to its enactment was his own innovation. As Speaker he opened up the Speaker's daily press conferences to television and invited radio talk show hosts to broadcast from a room in the basement of the Capitol. A number of organized efforts were made to sell the contract to the people of the United

States, and at the end of the first one hundred days, Republicans ran television ads touting their accomplishments.

However, Gingrich found that the extraordinary media coverage he received in 1995 was a mixed blessing and that selling a positive message is much harder than disseminating the Congress-bashing message with which he had been so successful. He canceled his daily press conferences when reporters proved to be more interested in his ethics problems than in the Republican party's ideas and accomplishments. On key issues such as Medicare, the leadership's message strategies were unsuccessful in blunting Democratic attacks. House Republicans complained repeatedly about the ineffectiveness of their leadership's communications operation.

To function well legislatively, the contemporary House requires an activist, engaged majority party leadership. To regain its legitimacy in the eyes of U.S. citizens, the Congress needs to be perceived as legislating effectively and in the people's interest. The Republican leaders have been no more successful than their Democratic predecessors at thus shaping the image of their party and the Congress; successfully selling a positive message is much harder than propagating the negative themes that resonate so well with the news media's worldview.

NOTES

My primary data sources consist of interviews conducted between 1978 and 1994 with House members, including leaders, staff aides, and informed observers, and of observations made during periods of participant observation in the House majority leader's office during 1978 and 1979 and in the Speaker's office in 1987 and 1988. My sincere thanks to the Hon. Jim Wright and his staff for making that possible. All unattributed quotations are from interviews I conducted with a promise of anonymity.

For a fuller statement of many of the arguments in this chapter, see Barbara Sinclair, *Legislators, Leaders and Lawmaking: The House of Representatives in the Post Reform Era* (1995).

This research was supported in part by intramural grant funds from the Academic Senate, University of California, Riverside; by Presidential Chair funds from the University of California; and by grants from the Dirksen Congressional Leadership Research Center.

1. See Richard Bolling, *House out of Order* (New York: E. P. Dutton, 1965); Richard F. Fenno, "The Internal Distribution of Influence: The House," in David B. Truman, ed., *The Congress and America's Future* (Englewood Cliffs, N.J.: Prentice-Hall, 1965); Randall B. Ripley, *Party Leaders in the House of Representatives* (Washington, D.C.: Brookings, 1967).

2. Bolling, *House Out of Order*, p. 70.

3. For biographical data on O'Neill, see Tip O'Neill with William Novak, *Man of the House: The Life and Political Memoirs of Speaker Tip O'Neill* (New York: Ran-

dom House, 1987), and Paul Clancy and Shirley Elder, *Tip: A Biography of Thomas P. O'Neill, Speaker of the House* (New York: Macmillan, 1980).

4. O'Neill with Novak, *Man of the House*, p. 135.

5. Ibid., p. 137.

6. Ibid., p. 138.

7. See Bolling, *House Out of Order*.

8. O'Neill with Novak, *Man of the House*, p. 138.

9. Mark Ferber, "The Democratic Study Group: A Study of Intra-Party Organization in the House of Representatives" (Ph.D. diss., University of California, Los Angeles, 1964); Kenneth Kofmehl, "The Institutionalization of a Voting Bloc," *Western Political Quarterly* 17 (June 1994): 256–272.

10. Milton C. Cummings and Robert L. Peabody, "The Decision to Enlarge the Committee on Rules: An Analysis of the 1961 Vote," in Robert L. Peabody and Nelson Polsby, eds., *New Perspectives on the House of Representatives*, 2d ed. (Chicago: Rand McNally, 1969).

11. Roger Davidson, "Congressional Leaders as Agents of Change," in Frank H. Mackaman, ed., *Understanding Congressional Leadership* (Washington, D.C.: Congressional Quarterly Press, 1981).

12. See O'Neill with Novak, *Man of the House*, pp. 216–220.

13. Ibid., p. 221.

14. Ibid., pp. 192–199.

15. Ibid., ch. 11. Also see Jimmy Breslin, *How the Good Guys Finally Won* (New York: Ballantine Books, 1975).

16. On the reforms, see Lawrence C. Dodd and Bruce I. Oppenheimer, *Congress Reconsidered* (New York: Praeger, 1977).

17. Barbara Sinclair, *Majority Leadership in the U.S. House* (Baltimore: Johns Hopkins University Press, 1983); Burdette Loomis, "The 'Me' Decade and the Changing Context of House Leadership," in Frank Mackaman, ed., *Understanding Congressional Leadership* (Washington, D.C.: Congressional Quarterly Press, 1981).

18. Barbara Sinclair, *Congressional Realignment* (Austin: University of Texas Press, 1982), chs. 7–8.

19. Michael J. Malbin, "House Democrats Are Playing with a Strong Leadership Lineup," *National Journal* 9 (June 18, 1977): 940–946.

20. Ibid., 941.

21. Steven Smith, *Call to Order: Floor Politics in the House and Senate* (Washington, D.C.: Brookings, 1989); Sinclair, *Majority Leadership in the U.S. House.*

22. See Sinclair, *Majority Leadership in the U.S. House*; Stanley Bach and Steven S. Smith, *Managing Uncertainty in the House of Representatives* (Washington, D.C.: The Brookings Institution, 1988).

23. Malbin, "House Democrats Are Playing with a Strong Leadership Lineup," p. 942.

24. Haynes Johnson, *In the Absence of Power* (New York: Viking Press, 1980), p. 155.

25. O'Neill with Novak, *Man of the House*, p. 331.

26. Ibid., pp. 320–321.

27. Sinclair, *Majority Leadership in the U.S. House*, pp. 138–139.

28. Ibid., pp. 244–246.

29. Sinclair, *Congressional Realignment*, chs. 7 and 8.

30. O'Neill with Novak, *Man of the House*, p. 298.

31. *Congressional Record*, 97th Cong., 1st sess., March 11, 1981, vol. 127, p. 867.

32. See O'Neill with Novak, *Man of the House*, p. 350.

33. Data are from David Rohde, *Parties and Leaders in the Postreform House* (Chicago: University of Chicago Press, 1991), and *Congressional Quarterly Almanac*, various volumes.

34. John B. Gilmour, *Reconcilable Differences?* (Berkeley: University of California Press, 1990).

35. Don Wolfensberger, "Comparative Data on the U.S. House of Representatives," compiled by the Republican staff of the House Rules Committee, November 10, 1992.

36. Alan Ehrenhalt, "Media, Power Shifts Dominate O'Neill's House," *Congressional Quarterly Weekly Report*, September 13, 1986, pp. 2131–2138.

37. The best source on House Republicans in the 1980s and early 1990s is William Connelly and John Pitney, *Congress' Permanent Minority?: Republicans in the U.S. House* (Lanham, Md.: Rowman & Littlefield, 1994).

38. Ibid., pp. 26, 50.

39. Restrictive includes modified open, modified closed, and closed. Barbara Sinclair, "Transformational Leader or Faithful Agent? Innovation and Continuity in House Majority Party Leadership: The 104th and 105th Congresses" (paper prepared for delivery at the 1997 annual meeting of the American Political Science Association, Washington, D.C., August 28–31, 1997), p. 18.

Epilogue:
Leaders Talk About
House Leadership

Gerald R. Ford, Richard A. Gephardt,
and Newt Gingrich

The chapters in this volume are based on essays prepared for a conference of House leadership sponsored by the Dirksen Congressional Center and held in May 1995 on Capitol Hill. The conference was chaired by former Republican leader Robert H. Michel (R-Ill.), whose remarks appear as the Foreword of this book. Other current and recent House leaders addressed the meeting: former president Gerald R. Ford (R-Mich.), Republican leader, 1965–1973; Speaker Newt Gingrich (R-Ga.), Republican whip, 1989–1995, and since then Speaker of the House; and House Democratic leader Richard Gephardt (D-Mo.), majority leader, 1989–1995; minority leader since 1995. Their observations cover the role and responsibility of the House and of House leaders, coalition building, and policy outcomes. Their remarks are excerpted below.

President Gerald R. Ford,
Former House Republican Leader

. . . I was asked to make a few comments this morning on the House leadership and the post–World War II era based on my observations as a former House member and after, when I went to the White House. I was very fortunate to have served in the House with four post–World War II Speakers: Sam Rayburn, Joe Martin, John McCormack, and Carl Albert. They had many similarities. Many of those similarities fall under those guidelines Bob Michel indicated in his opening remarks. But like all of the personalities in the House, the 435, they have many differences. . . .

. . . [A]ll of the four that I had the honor and privilege of serving with as Speakers had their own personality, their own style, their own background. Geographically, their districts were different. But on one point they were unanimous. Each of those four, and I think all that succeeded, felt that once they became the Speaker of the House, their role changed from just being a partisan political leader, that they represented the House of Representatives. Their responsibilities, their demeanor had to change, consequently. I think that's an important point that must be made not only for the present but for the future.

Each of the four that I knew personally, and served with, had a very deep conviction about the role and the responsibility of the House. They knew, as most of us knew who came to the House, that the Constitution in Article I lays out first the House and Senate, the legislative branch. Article I of our Constitution designates the legislative branch first, followed by the executive, followed by the judicial in Articles II and III. In Article I, the House of Representatives comes first with our two-year term and the designated responsibility of the first control over the tax issue and appropriations. All of those Speakers that I served with knew of the history and tradition and the constitutionality of the House of Representatives. They were unique, I think, in that they had differences personality-wise, background-wise, and otherwise. But on the role of representing the House, they were one and the same.

One interesting thing, to me at least: Each of these four that I knew served their party as Speaker when the White House was occupied by a president of another political party. Martin was speaker when Truman was President. Joe Martin was one of the leaders, one of the forceful persons in trying to get the legislative authorization and appropriation through the House for the Marshall Plan and for the Greek-Turkish aid. Here was a Republican Speaker in the Eightieth Congress giving that kind of strong leadership to a Democratic president, Harry Truman.

Then Sam Rayburn when President Eisenhower was in the White House. Eisenhower was the primary person that put together NATO, the North Atlantic Treaty Organization. He submitted it for authorization and appropriation to a Democratic Congress under Sam Rayburn. And Sam Rayburn in conjunction with Lyndon Johnson, the Democratic leader in the Senate, primarily was responsible for that legislation being approved in the Congress.

John McCormack was Speaker when President Nixon was in the White House. Even though there were deep divisions within the Democratic party over the issue of Vietnam, John McCormack strongly supported President Nixon in a strong national defense program as it related to the Kremlin, the Soviet Union, and the Cold War.

When I was president, I was the beneficiary of the help and assistance of my long-time, dear friend Carl Albert in those very difficult days when we were trying to draw down and get our military commitment terminated in Vietnam.

The point I want to make is that on foreign and military policies, at least these four Speakers, regardless of political identification, partisan background, when it came to an issue affecting our national security, they were nonpartisan, bipartisan in how they tried to help the chief executive, the commander-in-chief.

Now let me turn, if I might, to my reaction when I went from Capitol Hill to the White House. Did I have a different appraisal of the Congress, the speakership, when I went to the White House? Yes, I must admit that when I was in Congress I used to think about those dictators up in the White House at the other end of Pennsylvania Avenue and how irresponsible and how difficult and how demanding they were. They didn't understand how the Congress operated, all those arguments. Then when I left and went down to the White House, surprisingly enough, my views changed somewhat significantly. I used to think of my dear friends and how they could be so bad. But, nevertheless, I did learn a lot in the House that paid off big dividends when I went to the White House.

After the 1974 election, we in the Republican party took a terrific shellacking. The Democrats increased their majority significantly—well over two-to-one in the House and well over two-to-one in the Senate—so I was in the White House with a very adverse number situation in the Senate as well as in the House. So we had our share of difficulties in appropriations, in authorizations, etc. I made this decision that I was going to use the veto extensively. So I did. I vetoed sixty-seven pieces of legislation in a two-and-a-half-year period. It was not the most that anybody in the White House did because I was only there two and a half years, but percentage-wise I was well ahead of anybody else, and I'm proud to say that my good Democratic friends only overrode me ten times despite the fact that they had the majority better than two-to-one.

What we developed is obvious, what we called a floating coalition. We had a minimum number of Republicans but if it was a matter involving agriculture, we would fit our little handful of Republicans with as much support as we could possibly get from our big-city Democrats. If it was a matter concerning industry or big city politics, we would have another kind of coalition—Republicans with whatever rural or agricultural Democrats we could put together. It worked well. We won fifty-seven out of sixty-seven vetoes. But it gave me the opportunity to exploit, if that's the right term, my understanding of the Congress.

I happen to believe that a presidential veto is not a negative action. The Constitution gives that authority to the president. It's written in the Constitution that the president represents all the people, not a local group here, not a limited constituency there. The president represents all fifty states, 260 million people, and he has an obligation to use the veto if the action in the House and Senate violates the broad interests of the people. The press, unfortunately, writes the veto as a negative action. They are 180-degrees wrong, as they [often] are on a lot of things. So I used the veto, and I think historically that ended up as a very effective way for a president, faced with an overwhelming opposition in the legislative branch, to at least write a record and get his point of view across to the public and to the country.

Let me just conclude by saying that I felt very fortunate to have had the opportunity of twenty-five-plus years to serve in the House with four outstanding individuals who were Speakers of the House. [They were] individuals who represented their party. But above that, [they] represented the House as a whole. They carried on the tradition of the speakership in the most appropriate fashion. Each of them I considered dear, personal friends. They were adversaries but not enemies. As a result, our friendships continued after I left the House and after I left government. I will be forever grateful for their many kindnesses and their guidance and their assistance. Thank you very, very much.

Richard A. Gephardt, House Minority Leader

I think that what President Ford said about the need to disagree without being disagreeable was at the heart of what has made our system of government work. We have always tried to separate our disagreement over issues from personal animus which would make it impossible to get the work of the people done.

When I handed the Speaker [Newt Gingrich] the gavel on the first day, I wanted to remind people of the great achievement of our country, of being able to pass power with respect and civility and decency after forty years, a long time, not long enough in my view, but to be able to pass the gavel and have the power pass with complete respect and civility and decency is a great achievement. It is the greatest achievement of our country. It is part of the reason our country has such a bright future. That stability, that understanding [is] accepted by our people.

I also have a strong feeling that the secret to our democracy is that the losers in any argument are willing to accept the loss. I often use NAFTA [the North American Free Trade Agreement] as an example, an emotional debate we had in our country. Yet, when it was over, the losers in the debate were sometimes grudgingly, sometimes not so willingly but willing to go forward with the program and try to help make it work and that is a sign of a mature democracy that works.

. . . Two things I would say that are probably different in today's leadership requirements. One is probably more than ever it's important to try to build your agreement and your policy within the party from the bottom up. It is not the easiest way to go all the time, but it is very important that you build from the bottom up. Our leadership on the Democratic side now numbers about twenty-six people. I know that the Speaker has widened the leadership group on the Republican side. . . . [I]t takes longer, it's more frustrating and it's very difficult. [But] I find [that, as in] most places in the country, inclusion and empowerment of the people on the line have to be done to get the best performance.

The second thing that I would hope that you would look at is the effect of modern communication on the House and on the legislative process. I'm not sure we're ready even yet for prime time but I can tell you that we're on more than we used to be in the living rooms of the American people to a much greater degree. It's an impact on the legislative process, probably beyond what any of us really understand. We need to search for ways to better involve the population, the voters, in the legislative process. Up to now it has been pretty much a one-way communication—turning the camera on in the Chamber and allowing them to see what is happening. We need to search for and are finding ways to involve them in a two-way communication so they can express their feelings, express their reaction to things that are happening in the House of Representatives.

Let me end by saying we're blessed to live in the greatest country that ever existed in the history of the world. It is that in part because it is democracy: Citizens have been willing to take their role as citizens in this democracy, and we've had this venerable institution, the House of Representatives, 435 ordinary human beings who come here and try to represent all of those people. Thank you very much.

Speaker Newt Gingrich

I think it [the conference topic] is a very, very important topic. One of the weaknesses of the modern American system is that we don't know how to teach conflict. A lot of government classes are extraordinarily misleading because they walk people through a sense of orderly procedure which has nothing to do with how the House and Senate operate. In fact these are arenas for conflict. This is the place people bring their hopes and their dreams, their differing ambitions, their differing desires, and we sublimate civil war by bringing people together. That's literally the purpose: to enable us to gradually alleviate the tension.

One of the characteristics of the House which you may have noticed from your previous speakers is that it is in the end a personable place. When he was in the House, he was Jerry Ford. He became President Ford, which is a much more solemn title. . . . I find that being Speaker you have a friend when people call you Speaker, but that it's much better to get them to call you Newt. In private they'll tell Newt when he's being a fool a lot faster than the Speaker. Bob Michel was always Bob. Dick Gephardt is Dick. In a sense there is a familiarity which is important.

Part of the cheerfulness and the easy-to-satirize style of a public politician is the deliberate process of applying friendship to minimize friction. When we watch a Bosnia or a Chechnya or a Rwanda, we tend to forget that all these various social conventions have grown up starting with an Anglo-Saxon tradition around 1400 or 1500 where people have learned to sublimate warfare into political processes. It's a political campaign. Mao Tse Tung wrote, "War is politics with blood. Politics is war without blood." There's a lot to that.

I think we do a very inadequate job of explaining, first of all, the process of conflict management, which is at the heart of holding together a free people and avoiding warfare and avoiding the tragedies we see around the planet.

Second, for most of American history, the House and Senate were equal to, and sometimes slightly more important than, the White House. The modern White House is largely the outgrowth, I think, of a couple of things. One is the rise of the national economy. The second is Woodrow Wilson's personality. The third is two world wars and a cold war.

[At t]he *National Review* conference the weekend after President Clinton's inauguration, George Will was the keynote speaker, and he said that this would be the least consequential presidency of the last sixty years. He said that the reason has nothing to do with President Clinton. The reason is the cold war is over and in the absence of the organizing unity of foreign policy, the presidency becomes relatively less powerful and that it's institutionally unavoidable.

I think there's a lot to that. . . . When faced with a foreign competitor, Nazi Germany or the Soviet empire, Americans pull together. Right now we're in a trade skirmish with Japan. I can tell you that whatever my feelings might be about how to have done it better, we're not going to split with the president of the United States in the middle of negotiation. President Ford will tell you that there's been a long Republican tradition on a bipartisan basis going back to [Senator Arthur] Vandenburg, from his home state, that politics stops at the water's edge, and so the president has an enormous advantage if he is unifying the nation to face outward.

When the president turns inward to get something done—any president, not just this one—if he or she doesn't have the backdrop of a foreign crisis, they then simply become the loudest voice among 540 elected federal politicians. And suddenly the whole game changes. . . .

We have now been for over 200 years a remarkably successful system at bringing together people from across the entire planet and somehow assimilating them into being American and giving them vehicles by which they can pursue happiness and they could argue over their dreams.

In a sense what Dick Gephardt and I are carrying on is a dream that President Ford, back when he was Jerry Ford in the House, and that Bob Michel also have carried on in their lifetime: a tradition of being able to like each other personally, of being able to argue about your disagreements in terms of your profession, being able to work together whenever possible, and having a bias, interestingly enough, in favor of working together. The fact is that over time all the long-run pressures are to find a way to get something done.

That's one thing that I think makes the House different from the Senate. The Senate has a bias in favor of not getting something done. I don't mean that as a joke. They are very different institutions, and they can't be seen as the same. . . . The House is the direct descendant of the House of Commons. The House of Commons was, in fact, the first modern staple of the right of common people, although common people meant owning property and paying taxes when it first started. But the whole notion [was] that you can't raise money for the government without the approval of those from whom the money comes. The . . . government can't wander off to war. . . . [A]ny morning the Congress wants to cut off funding, it is permanent and final if they can override a president's veto; and any year they refuse to continue funding, the president can't veto [that]. So there is enormous latent power in the House and Senate. And since the House originates spending and originates taxing bills, the House is, in fact, quite adequate as an institution—any time it wants to [be].

And I think, in that sense, as we leave the Cold War era, you're going to see a reassertion of Congressional initiative not because of partisanship but because of the natural pattern that the *Federalist Papers* [sub]scribes to. Four hundred and thirty-five elected officials will be closer to the people than one hundred elected officials. The 535 will be closer to the people than the president is. And therefore, in the *Federalist Papers,* they say quite clearly you will normally in peacetime see the bias toward the legislative branch, the very dispersion of the power in the legislative branch will protect freedom and, therefore, over time, we have greater freedom because of the legislative branch than we would by putting our faith in an elected temporary kingship.

And I think frankly that that is the correct model and I think in peacetime that the bias ought to be in favor of the legislative branch. [A]ll I can assure you is that I think it is well worth spending far more time studying than we do today, and that most political science and most government class books need to be rewritten, preferably with somebody who's done it at the shoulder of the person doing the writing, because it is a far more complicated and far more subtle business than is normally reported and involves a far more tense and dynamic environment than is normally written about.

About the Editors and Contributors

Roger H. Davidson is professor of government and politics at the University of Maryland at College Park. A former senior specialist at the Congressional Research Service, he has also served on House and Senate committee staffs and continues to advise members and outside groups on congressional organization. He is coeditor of *The Encylopedia of the United States Congress* (4 volumes, 1995) and coauthor of *Congress and Its Members* (6th edition, 1998), the leading text on the subject. He has served as a member of the board of directors of the Dirksen Congressional Center.

Susan Webb Hammond is professor of government at American University and editor of *Congress & the Presidency: A Journal of Capital Studies*. She has worked on congressional committee and personal staffs and continues to serve as a consultant to committees. Her publications include *Congressional Staff: The Invisible Force in American Lawmaking* (1977), *Congressional Caucuses in National Policymaking* (1998), and articles on congressional organization and reform.

Raymond W. Smock was named historian of the U.S. House of Representatives in 1983. He was appointed by the Speaker of the House upon recommendation of a bipartisan committee of House members that conducted a national search for the first historian in the chamber's history. During his twelve-year tenure, he supervised numerous publications and helped plan national commemorations of the bicentennials of the U.S. Constitution and the Congress. A graduate of Chicago's Roosevelt University and holder of a Ph.D. in history from the University of Maryland, he coedited the fourteen-volume documentary series, *The Booker T. Washington Papers*, among many other projects. His career as a professional historian has encompassed academic posts, private business, and government service. Now a freelance writer, consultant, and public speaker on topics in U.S. political and social history, he is currently completing a book, *Landmark Documents on Congress*.

Donald C. Bacon is a Washington-based writer specializing in Congress and the presidency. A former journalist and Congressional Fellow, he is coeditor of *Encyclopedia of the United States Congress* (1996), coauthor of *Rayburn: A Biography* (1987), and author of *Congress and You: A Primer on the Legislative Process* (1969).

James M. Cannon is a writer and politician. Following twenty years as a journalist, he served in lead staff positions for Nelson Rockefeller, Gerald R. Ford, and

Howard H. Baker, Jr. Cannon is the author of *Time and Chance: Gerald Ford's Appointment with History* (1994).

Anthony Champagne is professor of government and politics at The University of Texas at Dallas. He has a long-standing interest in Texas politics and in the Texas Speakers of the U.S. House of Representatives.

James S. Fleming is professor of political science at the Rochester Institute of Technology. He has published articles on the U.S. Congress and comparative politics, and he is currently working on a biography of former congressman and World Bank president Barber B. Conable, Jr.

Lewis L. Gould is the Eugene C. Barker Centennial Professor in American History at The University of Texas at Austin. His interest in Sam Rayburn grows out of his research into the history of the Democratic Party during the years of Lyndon Johnson.

Patrick J. Maney teaches American history at Tulane University in New Orleans. He is the author of *"Young Bob" La Follette: A Biography of Robert M. La Follette, Jr., 1895–1953* (1978) and *The Roosevelt Presence: A Biography of Franklin Delano Roosevelt* (1993).

Scott William Rager, who received his Ph.D. from the University of Illinois at Urbana-Champaign in 1991, has taught at several midwestern colleges and universities, including Iowa State University and Illinois State University. He is a specialist in the politics of the Progressive Era.

Barbara Sinclair is Marvin Hoffenberg Professor of American Politics at UCLA. Her publications on the U.S. Congress include *Majority Leadership in the U.S. House* (1983), *Transformation of the U.S. Senate* (1989), *Legislators, Leaders and Lawmaking* (1995), and *Unorthodox Lawmaking* (1997).

Randall Strahan is associate professor of political science at Emory University. He is the author of *New Ways and Means: Reform and Change in a Congressional Committee* (1990) and is currently working on a book on leadership and institutional change in the U.S. House of Representatives.

Elaine K. Swift is associate professor of government at Eastern Washington University and the author of *The Making of an American Senate: Reconstitutive Change in Congress, 1787–1841* (1996). Currently, she is directing a multiuniversity research project on congressional history funded by the National Science Foundation.

Nancy Beck Young received her Ph.D. from the University of Texas at Austin in 1995 and is now an assistant professor at McKendree College. In 1996–1997 she held a research fellowship at Southern Methodist University. Her book, *Texas, Her*

Texas: The Life and Times of Frances Goff (coauthored with Lewis L. Gould), appeared in 1997. She is completing a biography of Wright Patman, about whom she has published several articles. Professor Young is a historian of twentieth-century politics and women.

Index